Technological Change and Societal Growth:

Analyzing the Future

Elayne Coakes
University of Westminster, UK

Managing Director:	Lindsay Johnston
Senior Editorial Director:	Heather Probst
Book Production Manager:	Sean Woznicki
Development Manager:	Joel Gamon
Development Editor:	Hannah Abelbeck
Acquisitions Editor:	Erika Gallagher
Typesetter:	Adrienne Freeland
Cover Design:	Nick Newcomer, Greg Snader

Published in the United States of America by
Information Science Reference (an imprint of IGI Global)
701 E. Chocolate Avenue
Hershey PA 17033
Tel: 717-533-8845
Fax: 717-533-8661
E-mail: cust@igi-global.com
Web site: http://www.igi-global.com

Copyright © 2012 by IGI Global. All rights reserved. No part of this publication may be reproduced, stored or distributed in any form or by any means, electronic or mechanical, including photocopying, without written permission from the publisher. Product or company names used in this set are for identification purposes only. Inclusion of the names of the products or companies does not indicate a claim of ownership by IGI Global of the trademark or registered trademark.

Library of Congress Cataloging-in-Publication Data

Technological change and societal growth : analyzing the future / Elayne Coakes, editor.
     p. cm.
  Includes bibliographical references and index.
  Summary: "This book provides a practical and comprehensive forum for exchanging research ideas and down-to-earth practices which bridge the social and technical gap within organizations and society at large"--Provided by publisher.
  ISBN 978-1-4666-0200-7 (hardcover) -- ISBN 978-1-4666-0201-4 (ebook) -- ISBN 978-1-4666-0202-1 (print & perpetual access) 1. Technological innovations. 2. Organizational change. I. Coakes, Elayne, 1950-
  HD45.T393 2012
  338'.0640112--dc23
                    2011050233

British Cataloguing in Publication Data
A Cataloguing in Publication record for this book is available from the British Library.

All work contributed to this book is new, previously-unpublished material. The views expressed in this book are those of the authors, but not necessarily of the publisher.

Associate Editors

Steve Clarke, *The University of Hull, UK*
Gordon Hunter, *University of Lethbridge, Canada*
Alex Ramirez, *Carleton University, Canada*

Associate Editors Practitioner

Alan Henney, *Organisational Psychologist, UK*
Peter Smith, *The Leadership Alliance, Canada*
Doug Orendorff, *Sierra Systems, Canada*

Editorial Advisory Board

Guy Fitzgerald, *Brunel University, UK*
Frank Land, *London School of Economics, UK*

Special Editions Editor

Jose Abdelnour-Nocera, *Thames Valley University, UK*

List of Reviewers

Wafi Al-Karaghouli, *Brunel University, UK*
Gil Ariely, *Interdisciplinary Center Herzliya, Israel*
Sue Balint, *University of Westminster, UK*
Barbara Cargill, *Trinity College - The University of Melbourne, Australia*
Antonio Cartelli, *University of Cassino, Italy*
Jim Coakes, *University of Westminster, UK*
Ricardo Colomo-Palacios, *Universidad Carlos III de Madrid, Spain*
Fefie Dotsika, *University of Westminster, UK*
Barbara Farbey, *University of London, UK*

Galal Galal-Edeen, *Cairo University, Egypt*

Fei Gao, *East China University of Science and Technology, China*

Matthew Guah, *University Rotterdam, The Netherlands*

Thomas Harrmann, *University of Bochum, Germany*

Isa Jahnke, *University of Technology, Germany*

Roger James, *University of Westminster, UK*

Abdul Samad Sami Kazi, *VTT Technical Research Centre of Finland, Finland*

Micky Kerr, *Leeds University, UK*

Terry T. Kidd, *University of Texas Health Science Center, USA*

Brian Lehaney, *Coventry University, UK*

Jay Liebowitz, *Johns Hopkins University, USA*

Henry Linger, *Monash University, Australia*

Joe McDonagh, *Trinity College, Ireland*

Souad Mohamed, *University of Westminster, UK*

Eric Mollerman, *University of Groningen, The Netherlands*

Miles Nicholls, *RMIT University, Australia*

John O'Neill, *Australian Defence Organization, Australia*

Bruno Palvarini, *Caixa Economica Federal, Brazil*

Keith Patrick, *University of Westminster, UK*

Colston Sanger, *London South Bank University, UK*

Susanne Sondergaard, *Rolls Royce, UK*

Frank Ulbrich, *Stockholm School of Economics, Sweden*

Leoni Warne, *Australian Defense Organization, Australia*

Brian Whitworth, *Massey University, New Zealand*

Table of Contents

Section 2

Section 3

Section 4

Detailed Table of Contents

Section 1

Chapter 1

Elayne Coakes, University of Westminster, UK
Jim Coakes, University of Westminster, UK

In this paper, the authors explore the hyphenated spelling variant on papers taken from the Business Source Complete (BSC) repository. This paper finds that the hyphenated spelling variant is popular with more recent authors and that in total, socio-technical article publishing has recently recovered from the relative decline of the 1980s and 1990s. Within the socio-technical area, the topics of Work and Technology are receiving increased attention and studies of Behaviour, Change and major Stakeholder Groups are waning. The authors have critiqued the articles that indicated in their BSC Subject terms that their contents are related to Methodology but have found that few actually consider the socio-technical methodologies. Systems and socio-technical theory papers are critiqued, including papers by Enid Mumford and her work. Also discussed are lessons learned when using online repositories, such as the need to save search results to manage the surprising level of volatility of such academic databases. Finally, opportunities for future analysis are discussed, including trends; changes of emphasis within topics; researching into other academic search engines; and US based analysis.

Chapter 2

Martin Johnson, The Thalidomide Trust, UK

Nigel Sykes' 3E's concept is examined against established theory and recent work in Organizational Behaviour. The possibility that this concept offers a way of developing social synergy in work groups is explored, and considered in the context of socio-technical systems. 3E's is based on the categorisation of people in the workplace into roles labelled "Envisioners" "Enablers" or "Enactors". Role theory is explored, and its relevance to organizational success. The importance of the affective component in motivation and decision-making is identified. A research study is reported testing the 3E's concept which shows that it corresponds with measurable differences of motivational need, personality factors, and decision-making between individuals. The characteristics of successful group decision-making are linked with the 3E's differentiation. The 3E's model offers the possibility of improving person-role fit, and thus organisational performance. It proposes an integrated design for the selection and operation of teams, offering a person-role fit, optimal decision-making behaviour, and consequent social synergy.

Chapter 3

Peter Duschinsky, Imaginist Company, UK

In this article, the author investigates the nature of complexity and its role in project failure. Also, the paper proposes a model to assess complexity. It draws some conclusions about the implications for change management interventions. The author finds that projects fail when the complexity exceeds the capability of the organisation to cope. The overall aim of the article is to offer an approach to reducing this number of failed change projects.

Chapter 4

Elayne Coakes, University of Westminster, UK
Peter A.C. Smith, The Leadership Alliance Inc., Canada
Dee Alwis, University of Middlesex, UK

The concept of using future innovation to achieve "right to market" (R2M) (Koudal & Coleman, 2005) is the focus of this paper. This paper discusses the relationship between entrepreneurship and innovation and posits that they form a system where innovation is optimised when these capabilities are closely linked. The authors contend that innovation activities are best 'managed' by an organization's entrepreneur(s) and that part of this role is to identify Innovation Champions and facilitate their innovation-related activities. The authors also explore the social and community interaction necessary for innovation to flourish and explain the role of entrepreneurs in forming Communities of Innovation (CoInv) based on innovation champions and their networks. This paper argues that CoInv are essential to ensure that each separate innovation has commercial potential and is operationally accepted with support diffused throughout the organisation. The authors demonstrate these assertions through a case discussion and conclude with some final comments on the future of this research.

Chapter 5

Peter A.C. Smith, The Leadership Alliance Inc., Canada

The article proposes that any effort to successfully manage knowledge must be concerned not only with relevant technology, but also with the plethora of affective factors present in the workforce. The aim of this article is to heighten awareness of the impact of these affective factors on KM implementation, and to offer practical approaches that it is contended will assist in "getting the affective factors right".

Chapter 6

Ricardo Colomo-Palacios, Universidad Carlos III de Madrid, Spain
Marcos Ruano-Mayoral, EgeoIT, Spain
Pedro Soto-Acosta, Universidad de Murcia, Spain
Ángel García-Crespo, Universidad Carlos III de Madrid, Spain

In current organizations, the importance of knowledge and competence is unquestionable. In Information Technology (IT) companies, which are, by definition, knowledge intensive, this importance is critical. In such organizations, the models of knowledge exploitation include specific processes and elements that drive the production of knowledge aimed at satisfying organizational objectives. However, competence evidence recollection is a highly intensive and time consuming task, which is the key point for this system. SeCEC-IT is a tool based on software artifacts that extracts relevant information using natural language processing techniques. It enables competence evidence detection by deducing competence facts from documents in an automated way. SeCEC-IT includes within its technological components such items as semantic technologies, natural language processing, and human resource communication standards (HR-XML).

Section 2

Chapter 7
Sylvie Albert, Laurentian University, Canada
Don Flournoy, Ohio University, USA

Being able to connect high-speed computing and other information technologies into broadband communication networks presents local communities with some of their best chances for renewal. Such technologies are now widely perceived to be not just a nice amenity among corporations and such non-profit organizations as universities but a social and economic necessity for communities struggling to find their place in a rapidly changing world. Today, citizens want and expect their local communities to be "wired" for broadband digital transactions, whether for family, business, education or leisure. Such networks have become a necessity for attracting and retaining the new "knowledge workforce" that will be key to transforming communities into digital societies where people will want to live and work. Since the Internet is a global phenomenon, some of the challenges of globalization for local communities and regions are introduced in this article and suggestions for turning those challenges into opportunities are offered. To attain maximum benefit from the new wired and wireless networks, local strategies must be developed for its implementation and applications must be chosen with some sensitivity to local needs. New Growth theory is used to show why communities must plan their development agenda, and case studies of the Intelligent Community Forum are included to show how strategically used ICTs are allowing local communities to be contributors in global markets.

Chapter 8
Bwalya Kelvin Joseph, University of Botswana, Botswana

Botswana is keen to position itself as a knowledge-based economy as early as 2016 due to the realisation that to compete on a global scale, efficient knowledge value chains must be put in place, which includes indigenous knowledge management systems. This realisation is primarily caused by falling demand in the price of diamonds (due to the world's recession), which is the country's current economic mainstay. Today, Botswana is pushing for further economic liberalisation and diversification by employing and encouraging novel frontiers of knowledge with emphasis placed on research and efficient knowledge management as a vital resource for national development. In Botswana, the role of scientific and technical knowledge is being emphasized as the main driver of sustainable development, but not forgetting the potential contribution of indigenous and mythological knowledge to this aim. Several initiatives have been devised or implemented by both the government and the public sector to position Botswana as a knowledge-based economy. This paper surveys the fundamental concepts on which this paradigm shift is based and brings out the different initiatives that have been undertaken while emphasizing the role of research and efficient knowledge management paradigms in shaping Botswana as a knowledge-based economy.

Section 3

This paper examines online communities and describes how they can be differentiated from other Internet supported group interactions. A definition of an online community is given and three generic types are identified. These types are defined by the community models based on the value proposition for the sponsors and members. The value proposition for members is strongly influenced by the model, as facilities and opportunities for interaction are structured by the site sponsors. Where online communities offer fulfillment of specific needs, people participate and become members. Additional benefits enhance the value of membership and encourage retention and greater interactivity. Significant benefits are gained from online communities for businesses, NGOs, other community organizations and individuals. Identifying the different types of communities and their characteristics is an important stage in developing greater understanding of how virtual communities can contribute to businesses, healthcare, community needs and a myriad of other contexts. Examples of the three generic types of online communities are included for further edification.

This paper addresses the continuing convergence and integration of digital electronic media, and in particular, virtual reality as an exemplar phenomenal media. The author explores and further develops the theme that each of such media entails a specific lexicon or language of use that continually evolves. For this media to be effective, however, it must be widely understood within its community of practice. In this paper, virtual reality is discussed as an exemplar new-media application as a means of virtual representation or reflection of events or behaviours in the real world from a socio-technical perspective.

In contrast to course delivery, help seeking has not advanced with the technological capabilities and preferences of today's students. Help seeking in higher education remains primarily an individual, private, face-to-face activity. Open, online, help forums have the potential to transform help seeking into a public, social endeavor. These forums connect students with volunteer helpers who have the time, knowledge, and willingness to provide assistance with specific problems from coursework. Although many such forums currently exist and are a popular source of help seeking, they have remained largely off the radar of educational research. In this paper, a calculus help forum is examined for manifestations of convenience, connection, and control, which are commonly used to describe student expectations regarding information technology use. Results indicate that students can receive efficient, accessible, and self-regulated help. Two additional themes for student experience, comfort and communication, are proposed.

Chapter 12

The emergence of community-oriented Information and Communication Technology platforms, e.g., forum software or wikis, the penetration of media in society has increased. In academia, forms of communication and cooperation to share knowledge are changing under open Web 2.0 conditions. In this regard, teaching and learning scenarios are moving towards technology-enhanced lifelong learning communities. This contribution presents the results of a longitudinal study of a Socio-Technical Community (STC) launched in 2002. The STC, which supports the study organization as well as teaching and learning in higher education, has been evaluated from its founding to its sustainable development and transformation phase in 2009. The study shows results in three specific areas: The learners' satisfaction with the STC, the type and quality of use, and if the STC is a helpful support for students to progress through their studies more efficiently than without an STC. The central conclusion is that spaces for computer-mediated communication are important for students regarding informal learning about organizing their own studies. Informal learning with a socio-technical community is more effective than without due to its individualization of learning in large groups.

An increasing number of students, professionals, and job-recruiters are using Social Network Sites (SNSs) for sharing information. There has been limited research assessing the role of individuals seeking a job and receiving information about job openings in SNSs. In this regard, do students, non-managers, and managers benefit from job offers when they are a member of SNSs such as Facebook or LinkedIn? How can differences in receiving information about job openings be explained by the strength-of-weak-ties and structural holes theorems? Results of an online survey among 386 respondents indicate that users of SNSs with more contacts are more likely to receive information about job openings than others. Most information about job openings was transmitted via LinkedIn to professionals. Regression analyses indicate that LinkedIn professionals with more links are more likely to receive information about a job opening. In contrast, the structural holes theory is not supported in this setting. The authors argue that Higher education should actively encourage and train students to use LinkedIn to enhance their employability. Finally, new generation graduates' use of technology for different tasks and with different people than professionals is considered.

Section 4

This article describes the use of a performed persona as a device in cross-cultural design activities. The device serves to elicit knowledge and manage expectations in the context of participatory design workshops to explore the purpose and function of a tool for tracing the supply chain of ethical goods from producer to consumer. The use of the method with the staff of a wine producer in Chile is analyzed and the benefits and challenges identified in using the form live in workshops. The authors conclude that the device offers potential but also requires some confidence and skill to invoke.

In the real world, 'optimal' solutions for many production process problems do not exist. In such circumstances, 'best practice' is the realistic outcome for which practitioners aim. The reasons for this stem from many causes, including that data associated with production processes are often corrupted and/or missing. These types of processes usually rely heavily on the subjective input of the process workers on the shop floor (tacit knowledge). This paper outlines how the use of mixed-mode modelling has been utilised to help solve these types of problems. The industry examples used in the paper incorporate the concept of Communities of Practice (CoPs) in the mixed-mode models that are developed as a means of capturing tacit knowledge and incorporating it into the solution process. Additionally, CoPs need to sit comfortably within the culture and values of the organisation and employee groups, and must be clearly owned and facilitated by the community of workers whose knowledge is to be shared. Finally, CoPs should be presented as opportunities to share, compare, and learn so that a 'craft' is not lost or diminished.

Preface

INTRODUCTION

The overall mission of the *International Journal of Sociotechnology and Knowledge Development* (IJSKD) is to provide a practical and comprehensive forum for exchanging research ideas and down-to-earth practices that bridge the social and technical gap within organizations and society at large. The chapters highlighted in this book are exemplars of some of these ideas in practice.

The journal also provides a forum for considering the ethical issues linked to organizational change and development encouraging interdisciplinary texts that discuss current practices as well as demonstrating how the advances of - and changes within - technology affect the growth of society (and vice versa).

When looking at the chapters that have been submitted to the journal and that are now entered into this book for this edition, they fall into five main categories.

The first category begins with exploring the literature to identify the themes that sociotechnical thinking looks at. This chapter sets the scene for the chapters that follow.

In *Exploring Meaning,* the authors identify the major contributors to thought and the theory base and thus providing for scholars a useful base for identifying suitable theory and the timeline of the development of this theory. The first of this series was published last year in the previous book in this series and in Edition 1 of the *International Journal of Sociotechnology and Knowledge Development*.

This section of the book then continues with considering some of the organisational impacts of change and leadership with, firstly, the chapter by Martin Johnson of the Thalidomide Trust; secondly the chapter by Peter Duschinsky considering the *Change Equation* in project management; and thirdly, the chapter by myself, Peter Smith, and Dee Alwis on how to organise communities within organisations for successful innovation. Peter follows this with a discussion on the factors that affect success or failure in knowledge management in an organisation.

The book then moves on to considering the issues that employing knowledgeable and talented individuals brings - the war for acquiring this talent as described by Colomo-Palacios, Ruano-Mayoral Soto-Acosta, and García-Crespo.

The next sections of the book consider the impact of technologies and communities both local and global, from the nation to the individual, beginning with the chapter by Albert and Flouroy and the theory of New Growth, showing how strategically used ICTs are allowing local communities to be contributors in global markets. This is followed by the *Case of Botswana* as described by Joseph as a knowledge based economy.

Chapters Nine to Thirteen all consider the impact of social networks and online communities in various formats, and this is a topic that will be discussed again later after detailing the contents of the book in more depth.

There are two final chapters to cover in this preface, which stand alone in their topics. The first is *Performing Charlotte* by Light, Kleine, and Vivent; and finally a chapter by Nicholls and Cargill, concerning how to achieve *Best Practice in Manufacturing* by using tacit knowledge and Mixed-mode Modelling.

The preface will now describe these 15 chapters in more depth and add comments on the subject matter and why they are important to the sociotechnical community and to those utilising knowledge in organisations.

COMMENTARY ON CHAPTERS

The first chapter in **Section One** of this book is a literature review and is the second of its kind, the first that was published looked at a different set of papers and journals in the last edition in this series.

In this chapter, there is a trend that appears to show a revival of interest in the ideas of sociotechnology during the 1990s. This trend seems to coincide with the expansion of work systems and the realisation that these new systems were as prone to failures or limitations as early technical system implementations. Authors have gone back to the theory of how technology impacts on work and job design, pioneered by the Tavistock Institute in the 1950s. This was then used to explain issues surrounding such diverse topics as eBusiness, health technologies, mass customisation, call centre operations, and mobile phones. The chapter looks at the development of the theory and how the papers have applied it, exploring the difference between the early ideas and the later, in specific fields of study beginning with Human Resources in the very early years and moving into Job and Work Design and Operations Management in the middle years; with the emphasis moving towards Information Technology in the latter years, and most recently, Knowledge Management and Philosophy.

The chapter shows that in total, socio-technical article publishing has recently recovered from the relative decline of the 1980s and 1990s. Within the socio-technical area, the topics of Work and Technology are receiving increased attention in the more recent sample explored. At the same time, the study of Personal and Group Behaviour, and of Change, as well as the study of major Stakeholder Groups, is waning.

The success of the journal *International Journal of Sociotechnology and Knowledge Development* and its related LinkedIn site, is an indication of the reviving interest in sociotechnical thinking, moving into a world ever more externally controlled by technology.

Of course, one of the more interesting aspects of this journal is that it has a wide range of coverage of topic areas, which permits it to explore subjects that do not neatly fall into fields of study, such as Human Computer Interface or eBusiness, and there is appeal to a wide audience, bringing unusual subject matter to their attention. And indeed, authors are able to encourage practitioners to contribute their experience as well. That said, the next chapter in Section One is not unusual, but looks at how to create visionary leadership teams; however, it is written by a practitioner. Dr. Martin W. Johnson, BD, PhD, MSc, FRSA, is the Director of the Thalidomide Trust UK, which was established on the 10th of August 1973, with the object of providing support to those people who had disabilities caused because their mothers had taken the drug thalidomide during pregnancy. In this chapter, Dr. Johnson looks at the affective factors in Organizational Behaviour.

The chapter explores the possibility that this concept offers a way of developing social synergy in work groups, and considers this in the context of socio-technical systems.

The chapter reports on a 3E's research study, which tested the 3E's concept - this concept is based on the categorisation of people in the workplace into roles labelled "Envisioners," "Enablers," or "Enactors." The importance of the affective component in motivation and decision-making is identified, which shows that it corresponds with measurable differences of motivational need, personality factors, and decision-making between individuals. The study also shows that the characteristics of successful group decision-making are also linked with the 3E's differentiation. Therefore use of the 3E's model offers the possibility of improving person-role fit, and thus organisational performance, as it proposes an integrated design for the selection and operation of teams, offering a person-role fit, optimal decision-making behaviour, and consequent social synergy.

This is especially important as while leadership teams traditionally develop over a period of time, the range of current working practices precludes the direct personal contact and relationship-building that normally precedes and informs appointments into organisational roles. This includes such things as online collaborative work groups or geographically-separated teams working on short-term projects for multi-national organisations through, for example, using Enterprise Information Systems and other social-technical systems. It is clear that current working practices impact on the training and development of managerial staff due to their lack of exposure to f2f contact as opportunities to meet counterparts across the world in real-life as opposed to through a technical intermediary.

Following this chapter is a discussion relating the issues of project management and complexity and how better to predict success. The Change Equation, according to Peter Duschinsky, relates to *the social/culture and technical/process management capability* of Bostrom and Heinen's (1977) work system model and good interaction between the social and technical systems. Paying attention to either system on its own will, he argues, create problems and barriers to success.

Considering social and technical systems and their interactions within organisations is again the focus of the next chapter which the editor co-wrote with Peter Smith of the Leadership Alliance, a consultancy organisation with which the editor has a close relationship, and Dr. Dee Alwis. The chapter looks at the social and community interaction necessary for innovation to flourish and explains the role of entrepreneurs in forming Communities of Innovation (CoInv) based on innovation champions and their networks. It is argued that right to market is provided for organisations by future innovation and that this can only be provided when system capabilities are closely linked. This chapter is part of the argument, which can be followed further in the paper Coakes, Smith, and Alwis, (2011).

The fifth chapter in this book is another paper written by Peter Smith, looking at the affective factors for successful knowledge management. It looks further at the issues surrounding organisational cultural systems and the impact on these systems of personal factors that may often be unconscious. These beliefs, emotions, attitudes, and instincts are often unrecognised when considering how knowledge management can be implemented, and yet, they have a very strong effect as to how or why and even who may take part in such implementations and as to its success.

The final chapter in this section of organisational discussions looks at the importance of retaining the knowledge of, and the knowledge workers themselves in particular in high-tech organisations. Competence evidence and a software program that can detect such competence and record it are the focus of this discussion, as the authors say *competence evidence recollection is a highly intensive and time consuming task,* they describe a tool they have devised called *SeCEC-IT* that extracts relevant information using natural language processing techniques. It enables competence evidence detection by deducing competence facts from documents in an automated way. SeCEC-IT includes within its technological components such items as semantic technologies, natural language processing, and human resource communication standards (HR-XML).

Section Two of this book considers a wider perspective than merely organisations and looks at the global implications of the knowledge society and technology and its link into systems and society.

The first chapter in this section, written by a Canadian and an American, looks at the necessity for local communities to be wired into broadband connectivity for digital transactions for family, education, and leisure and not just business - whether for-profit or not-for-profit. Albert and Flournot argue that *being able to connect high-speed computing and other Information Technologies into broadband communication networks presents local communities with some of their best chances for renewal.* They also argue that these technologies are no longer niceties for communities but indeed necessities and that communities expect to be 'wired' into the broader digital world *for family, business, education or leisure.* Knowledge workers and the newer workforce, many of whom expect to be able to work from home as well as leisure places- see the phenomenon of coffee shop working that we see so much of - require this capability from the place they intend to live, and thus, in order to attract such members of the community, the locality needs to devise suitable strategies for their own individual circumstances. These applications will need to be sensitive to local needs and particularities and cannot be a generalised application. This chapter demonstrates through the use of case studies of the Intelligent Community Forum how suitable technologies for the locality are enabling such communities to participate in global as well as local markets.

The second chapter in this section looks further at the issue of how communities are developing a knowledge base by considering a larger locality - that of Botswana. The government of Botswana has recognised the need for the country to develop towards a more global economy that is based clearly and recognizably on technical and scientific knowledge rather than its previous dependence on diamonds. This is a radical shift in thinking for all concerned as it means that present economic systems are no longer viable and new systems based around knowledge contributions are needed to be developed. As Joseph puts it, *indigenous knowledge management systems* need to be put in place whilst *not forgetting the potential contribution of indigenous and mythological knowledge.* Scientific and technical knowledge are now being positioned as the vital resources and the main drivers of sustainable development. This chapter surveys the various initiatives that have been undertaken whilst recognizing that future research needs to be undertaken to ensure that harsh challenges, such as a requirement to reduce HIV-AIDS infection rates, a massive unemployment level, and a current overdependence on diamonds, need to be incorporated into the knowledge based economic transformation policies so that this may not steal away the country's dream. Particularly interesting here is the concept that knowledge management is a key sustainable competitive advantage for a developing country as opposed to the common statement for an organisation.

Next is **Section Three** of this book. This is the section which will be discussed more fully to add additional comments as to the necessity of research into this area. Social technology - or the use of technology in the social setting- affects and develops new social networks. Technology as a social technology must incorporate the classic concepts of sociotechnology in that it must develop through use and user desires, and must operate for the processes they wish it to. Sociotechnical thinking has always said that the technology (within the organisation) must be chosen by the users for the task at hand and that they must have the option to refuse to use any technology or must be able to mould the technology to perform the tasks in the way that they wish them to be performed. Social technology seemingly answers all these criteria. It has developed through users' desires - take Facebook as an example. Its rivals have fallen by the wayside as they did not provide the functionality in the way that the users wanted them to. Within organisations - as the papers chosen below argue - users cannot be forced into using social technology in the same that they can be forced into using, say, ERP systems. It must always be optional and thus always within the control of the users as what they do, how they do it, and when even though organisations such as IBM have some rules to tell people what to do with these systems and mandate certain activities, the actual content is always personal and as detailed as the user wishes.

The editor started to develop a discussion on this topic by going to a favourite journal database, Business Source Direct, which covers over 10,000 journals, and looked for recent articles on social technology, limiting the search to those within peer reviewed journals, published from 2009-2011 and with full text available, in order to read them. I got 8 articles in response. It would seem therefore that this is an under-researched area. Indeed, the first article, by Burke and Warner, claimed that the field of Organisational Development had not added anything to the discussion of social technology for many years. The second was a very short article aimed at Chief Finance Officers in which Scott Klosky (2011) argued that all organisations need to utilise social technologies in four very specific ways:

1.   To build what he calls 'rivers of information'. Social technologies permit the aggregation of information and the filtration of information, such that the information presented to employees is useful and valid.

2.   Use these technologies to build the Web-facing organisational voice and presence. Use, for instance, Facebook or Twitter, blogs, and podcasts to present the corporate image.

3.   Realise that this corporate image is very visible and ensure that the social network formed by these technologies is monitored and mined. Ensure that the corporate image and reputation is that which the organisation wishes to present.

4.   Use technology to 'crowdsource'. This is by permitting a role traditionally performed by an outsourcer (or employee) to be performed by the 'crowd' - in much the same way, I would imagine, as Google and other technology companies permit their users to de-bug programs and devise new applications for Android phones.

The third article in the list, by Zuk (2011), continues with this message of using social technology to present the 'right' face to the world. Public relations, it was argued, in this - again very short - article must use the technology of the social world such as Twitter and Facebook to its advantage to build a loyal following through these media.

In many ways, the fourth article was perhaps the most interesting, even if again, it was not technically an academic article as it identified the top 'trending topics' for 2011 in Public Relations. The Editorial by the journal *Public Relations Tactics* mentioned social media and technology in two respects - firstly in terms of crisis communication, as social media can both be a help to communicate in crises, but also that social media can create these crises, and awareness of both trends is required.

Additionally it was argued that social technology is very important for organisational and personal branding but that *average participants experience social media schizophrenia — as social media adoption and usage continues to climb in 2011, even the average user will struggle to keep up with the increased loading* (p. 12).

Steve Radick (2011), in the same journal, compares the organisational intranet to Facebook and Twitter and looks at the frustration that the intranet gives so many users. It should now also be about connecting people to people rather than people to information. Intranets should now deploy social connectivity tools to enable a new way of working within an organisation. Encourage internal blogging for instance through the intranet and focus less on the technology and more on user needs.

Article 5 (Hess, Fuller, and Campbell, 2009) looked at the instance of Recommendation Agents - a hint of the performed persona or avatar here (see discussion below on 'Performing Charlotte') as it found that personality (extraversion), vividness (text, voice, and animation), and computer playfulness were found to influence social presence, with social presence serving in a mediating role and increasing user trust in the agent. The use of social technology and its media capabilities affected trust and social presence in these agents and the degree of extrovertness displayed by these persona affected the trust in these /agents. They were seen as more convincing and appealing to the audience. Social presence, and thus trustworthiness, was also impacted by the use of social media and technology.

Article 6 in the search considered digital museums (Srinivasan, et al, 2009); article 7 was Rosga and Satterthwaite, (2009); and article 8 was Jae-Hyung (2009). This last article echoes some of the aspects of economic growth discussed in Chapter 8 of this book in that new technology, and here it is social technology that is specifically considered and the concomitant knowledge management required to develop it, is seen as basis for economic growth.

Expanding the search to those articles without full text I identified a small number of further articles. The first paper, by James Kohnen, was in fact just a book review of what looks to be not only a book about social technology but one which considers leadership and thus links to Chapter 2 of this book. A further review of the book in Professional Management by David Stephens who says that working with social networking is like any management challenge - first decide objectives and then develop the infrastructure. The author of the book under review - Li (2010) - argues that in practice it is often not the case and that frequently the major stumbling block is the management and its difficulty in understanding the technology of social networking and its power to alter public perceptions. The chapter by Raban, Ronen, and Guy (2011) looks at an individual's use of social technology in respect to people tagging within an enterprise application; Kreiner et al (2011) consider what happens when social technology facilitates interaction amongst competitors for an architectural prize and this idea is echoed in the paper by Toledano (2010) which also looks at competition and cooperation between professions and professionals as social technology develops; Chataway et al (2010) use a social technology framework in respect of global health developments.

All of these are very diverse applications of the phrase 'social technology' and yet none really seem to consider its links to sociotechnology which is perhaps surprising. The editor thus issues a challenge to readers to this preface to look at social technology and considers its relationship to sociotechnology and produce theory and concepts that link the two.

Coming back to this book's contents, the chapters in **Section Three** begin with a discussion by Gordon Hunter on how online communities are different from other Internet supported group interactions. In this chapter, Hunter argues *Significant benefits are gained from online communities for businesses, NGOs, other community organizations and individuals* and so being able to identify *the different types of communities and their characteristics is an important stage in developing greater understanding of how virtual communities can contribute to businesses, healthcare, community needs and a myriad of other contexts.*

Allan McLay continues with the identification of benefits theme with his discussion of virtual realities. New media, he argues has the capacity to add value to information *in a form capable of translation, transformation, and distribution wherever and whenever digital processes and electronic network communication is accessible. Today, this implies virtually any time, anywhere on the globe (Lister et al., 2009).*

New media enables a continuing growth in connectivity especially for communities of practice and those communities that utilise these new media may well develop new languages and practices and utilise these media in new and creative ways.

The following three chapters formed a Special Edition within the journal looking at the Net Generation. In the words of the Special Edition Editors, *Members of the Net Generation use the Web differently, they network differently, and they learn differently.*

The Net Generation, they would argue, are natural networkers using the Web extensively and simultaneously with other tasks - they multi-task and work collaboratively.

This Special Issue focused on how the Net Generation acquired and exchanged knowledge. The first chapter, by Carla van de Sande, elaborated on help seeking in the Net Generation, in particular in relation to an educational calculus help forum. She found that open forums can provide efficient, accessible, and collaborative help that allow students to acquire the knowledge they need to resolve problems from assignments. The forums investigated here connect students with volunteer helpers who have the time, knowledge, and willingness to provide assistance with specific problems from the coursework. Carla mentions that although many such forums exist in universities and are a popular source of help for students, they have remained largely off the radar of educational research and thus perhaps also of educationalists. The results of her study indicate that students can receive efficient, accessible, and self-regulated help using these forums and thus make good progress with coursework and assessments in due course can perhaps be improved. It would be interesting to repeat this research on other forms of forums to see whether more, or less, progress is made with non-mathematical forums.

The second chapter of this Special Issue, by Isa Jahnke, presented her findings from a longitudinal study evaluating the use of a university Web platform for students. This was longitudinal study of a Socio-Technical Community (STC) launched in 2002 computer-mediated communication. She found that spaces for computer-mediated communication are important for students regarding informal learning about organizing their own studies. Her chapter concludes that informal learning with a socio-technical community is more effective than without because it supports the individualization of learning in huge groups. Spaces for computer-mediated communication are important for students in relation to their informal learning about how to organise their own studies.

The final chapter that came from this Special Edition is that of Bart Rienties, Dirk Tempelaar, Miriam Pinckaers, Bas Giesbers, and Linda Lichel. These authors offer some insights on knowledge sharing for job recruitment in relation to the use of Social Network sites. They ask the very important question '*do students, non-managers, and managers benefit from job offers when they are a member of SNSs such as Facebook or LinkedIn?'*

The study of 386 Social Network Site users showed that users of social network sites with more contacts are more likely to receive information about job openings than others and indeed more information about job openings was transmitted via LinkedIn to professionals than other sites. The authors thus would encourage and train students to use LinkedIn to enhance their employability.

Now to **Section Four** - the last part of this book.

In this section, there are two chapters of a different character from some of the other chapters, and indeed neither are specifically sociotechnical, but rather, they look at the knowledge development aspect of the journal. In the first chapter, by Light, Kleine, and Vivent, readers hear about Charlotte - who is a performed persona. Performed personae are a very interesting idea and can be likened to an avatar seen on websites.

A performed persona is the concept of a constructed personality with idiosyncrasies and language usage to suggest a social identity (that may be different or an exaggeration of that which is normal). A performed persona is a character creation - perhaps related to Stanislavsky's method actor acting style (Krasner, 2000) - a stylised recreation of that personality for a purpose, in the case of this chapter, the persona was used to act as a consumer *to elicit knowledge and manage expectations.* Here the use of the persona in discussions with the staff of a wine producer in Chile was analyzed and the benefits and challenges identified. The authors concluded that the device offers potential but also requires some confidence and skill to invoke, as might only to be expected, as the actor must not only take on the language and its style of the persona in question but also their mannerisms and actions. It is interesting to contrast this with the use of an avatar on a technology site where it represents, in many cases, an alter-ego or again a constructed personality with the traits and behaviours of that personality being developed as the avatar progresses through their technical world. An artificial sharing of presumed tacit knowledge in other words.

The final chapter in this book looks at tacit knowledge in the context of best practice manufacturing. As the authors argue there is no real optimal solution only best practice and practitioners use their knowledge to create this best practice saying that *these types of processes usually rely heavily on the subjective input of the process workers on the shop floor (tacit knowledge).* In order to capture this best practice, Communities of Practice are frequently used in manufacturing, providing that they fit they the cultures and values or the organisation and employee groups and that they are *clearly owned and facilitated by the community of workers whose knowledge is to be shared.* CoPs should be presented to the workforce as opportunities to share, compare, and to learn so that a 'craft' is not lost or diminished.

Elayne Coakes
University of Westminster, UK

REFERENCES

Bostrom, R. P., & Heinen, S. J. (1977). MIS problems and failures: A sociotechnical perspective Part I: The causes. *Management Information Systems Quarterly, 1*(3), 17–32. doi:10.2307/248710

Burke, W. W. (2011). A perspective on the field of organization development and change: The Zeigarnik effect. *The Journal of Applied Behavioral Science, 47*(2), 143–167. doi:10.1177/0021886310388161

Coakes, E. W., Smith, P. A. C., & Alwis, D. (2011). Sustainable innovation and right to market. *Information Systems Management, 28*(1), 30–42. doi:10.1080/10580530.2011.536110

Editorial. (2011). *Public Relations Tactics, 18*(1), 12-13.

Hess, T., Fuller, M., & Campbell, D. (2009). Designing interfaces with social presence: Using vividness and extraversion to create social recommendation agents. *Journal of the Association for Information Systems, 10*(12), 889–919.

Klososky, S. (2011)... *Financial Executive, 27*(4), 10–11.

Kohnen, J. (2011). Open leadership: How social technology can transform the way you lead. *Quality Management Journal, 18*(2), 61–62.

Krasner, D. (2000). *Method acting reconsidered: Theory, practice, future.* Palgrave Macmillan.

Lee, J.-H. (2009). A comparative study of the effects of social and physical technologies on economic growth: The Korean perspective. *Proceedings of the Northeast Business & Economics Association,* (pp. 98-102).

Li, C. (2010). *Open leadership: How social technology can transform the way you lead.* Jossey-Bass.

Lister, M., Dovey, J., Giddings, S., Grant, I., & Kelly, K. (2009). *New media: A critical introduction* (2nd ed.). Abingdon, UK: Routledge.

Raban, D. R., Ronen, I., & Guy, I. (2011). Acting or reacting? Preferential attachment in a people-tagging system. *Journal of the American Society for Information Science and Technology, 62*(4), 738–747. doi:10.1002/asi.21490

Rosga, A. J., & Satterthwaite, M. L. (2009). The trust in indicators: Measuring human rights. *Berkeley Journal of International Law, 27*(2), 253–315.

Srinivasan, R., Boast, R., Furner, J., & Becvar, K. M. (2009). Digital museums and diverse cultural knowledges: Moving past the traditional catalog. *The Information Society, 25*(4), 265–278. doi:10.1080/01972240903028714

Stephens, D. (2010). Opening up to new media. *Professional Manager, 19*(6), 46.

Zuk, R. (2011). Tactics. *Public Relations, 18*(3), 7.

Section 1

Chapter 1

Exploring Meaning:
The Implications of a Hyphen for Socio-Technical Theory and Practice

Elayne Coakes
University of Westminster, UK

Jim Coakes
University of Westminster, UK

ABSTRACT

In this paper, the authors explore the hyphenated spelling variant on papers taken from the Business Source Complete (BSC) repository. This paper finds that the hyphenated spelling variant is popular with more recent authors and that in total, socio-technical article publishing has recently recovered from the relative decline of the 1980s and 1990s. Within the socio-technical area, the topics of Work and Technology are receiving increased attention and studies of Behaviour, Change and major Stakeholder Groups are waning. The authors have critiqued the articles that indicated in their BSC Subject terms that their contents are related to Methodology but have found that few actually consider the socio-technical methodologies. Systems and socio-technical theory papers are critiqued, including papers by Enid Mumford and her work. Also discussed are lessons learned when using online repositories, such as the need to save search results to manage the surprising level of volatility of such academic databases. Finally, opportunities for future analysis are discussed, including trends; changes of emphasis within topics; researching into other academic search engines; and US based analysis.

INTRODUCTION

This paper is the second of a series looking at trends in socio-technical publishing. Our overall aim as discussed in Paper 1 (referred to here as P1 - see Volume 1, Edition 1 of this journal) is to provide a meta-analysis of academic ideas related to the socio-technical field, as demonstrated by their output in journals, books and published book reviews. In this paper we discuss the search conducted on Business Source Complete for the hyphenated variants of the spellings. We draw on published work from 1959 to June

DOI: 10.4018/978-1-4666-0200-7.ch001

Copyright © 2012, IGI Global. Copying or distributing in print or electronic forms without written permission of IGI Global is prohibited.

2009 to highlight the major areas of concern; the research domains; the theories and frameworks utilised in research; the social and technological emphasis; the underpinning understanding of socio-technology; the journals most favoured for publication; and the most prolific authors within selected fields of expertise.

We draw conclusions on our searches of Business Source Complete (BSC), the largest international database of academic publications (10,000 journals) available within the UK, looking at the spelling variants socio-technology and socio-technical. As explained in Paper 1, the reason for splitting the search is the large numbers of papers under consideration. Additionally, we have drawn on the analysis of our first paper to assist in developing the analysis of the further papers and to enable comparisons.

In this paper we start by discussing the search methodology and our results for the top publications and then consider what our results mean in terms of publishing trends. This is followed by a term analysis and a discussion of papers that look at the Subject topic Methodology. We then discuss the papers using the hyphenated spelling that consider Systems and related theory as we did in P1 and compare our results. Finally we draw our conclusions, discuss our future planned papers in this series and indicate future research requirements.

HOW THE RESEARCH WAS UNDERTAKEN: METHODS AND SOURCES

In this current paper we consider the results of a meta analysis of the BSC repository for the second of the most commonly used spelling variants: socio-technology and socio-technical.

The meta search was carried out on the complete repository with no filters engaged. This repository contains academic journals, trade publications, magazines, books/monographs, and book reviews (usually published in journals). The search was conducted in two phases but here we report on the second search. Search number one looked in all abstracts for the term socio-technology and socio-technical – see P1 - and in Search number two we replicated the search using the hyphenated forms socio-technology, socio-technical. The abstract was chosen as the search field as it is here that authors, in particular in academic journals, state the field of study that the article uses for theory input. The searches were undertaken during late 2008 up to June 2009. Note that access to the journals and abstracts may have been limited by the terms of the chosen (University of Westminster) repository link to Business Source Complete.

During our late 2008 search of the hyphenated terms we found that BSC now offered both Subject classification of the academic papers and a Thesaurus classification. Very few papers were now given a Subject listing but most were now given a Thesaurus listing. Thesaurus terms, as used by the BSC Repository do not match the Subject terms. Keywords for some articles are also available but only when so identified by an author. Thus a typical Repository entry will include the publication details; the authors and their abstract – although this is not always complete if it is considered too long; Thesaurus terms; Subject terms; and keywords if provided. There can be multiple terms of course. We thus can find several articles classified under multiple Thesaurus terms. Additionally, it should be noted that the Thesaurus terms are volatile and change with great regularity – thus we make no claims for the validity of these findings on publication only on the research dates when we searched the repository – in fact some changed during the process of research e.g., Industrial Management and Business Enterprise were Thesaurus terms in October 2008 but not in June 2009 and Human Engineering and Information Science had been added. Subject terms had also changed. While the validity of the conclusions is not affected, the total numbers within Tables 1 and 2 therefore do not quite agree, because of BSC's changes over time.

Overall in late 2009 we find 396 papers classified with the hyphenated spelling in the repository.

Regardless of classifications, the repository searches have, however, continued to emphasise that use of socio-technical thinking whether the term used is hyphenated or not, has increased rapidly in recent publications. Figure 1 does demonstrate the greater popularity of the use of the hyphenated spelling variant as against the non-hyphenated and also the increased trend in interest in the topic since 1999. Paper 1 [P1] being our first paper published in Volume 1, Edition 1 of this journal. Paper 2 being this current paper.

SEARCH RESULTS AND DATA MANIPULATION

In Tables 3-7, we consider the retrieved results in terms of the 'top ten' for each.

The BSC repository classified journals, trade publications, and professional magazines each with top authors and subject fields as well as the top publications in that category - see Tables 4, 5, 6 and 7 for these details.

Full Harvard style details of all the papers were retrieved into a very large spreadsheet. A total list was created and then BSC's subject terms were used to sub-classify the papers. This sub-classification was then imported into a Word document, accepting any key terms added by the author; and the BSC subject terms for each paper. This document was utilised for the key word analysis.

Trends in Publishing Using a Hyphenated Spelling

In Paper 1 we began to analyse the trends in publication of papers using socio-technical theory to explain their area of study. Now we continue

Table 1. Academic thesaurus classifications

Academic Thesaurus Classification term	Number of papers classified overall (inc. those not in Journals).	Number of papers classified in Journals
Technology	47	47
Information Technology	41	39
Management	41	38
Information Resource Management	27	27
Research	28	26
Information Science	9	9
Human Engineering	13	13
Knowledge Management	18	18
Decision Making	13	13
Industrial Management	35	34

Table 2. Academic subject classification

Academic Subject Classification Term	Number of papers classified overall	Number of papers classified in Journals
Social Sciences	13	11
Social Aspects	14	14
Social Systems	10	10
Sociological Aspects	8	8
Communication and Technology	7	6
Social Informatics	6	6
Evaluation	0	7
Human – Machine Relationships	3	0
Accidents	4	4
Methodology	15	15
Medical Informatics	3	3

Figure 1. Numbers of published papers analysed in the two (IJSKD) papers

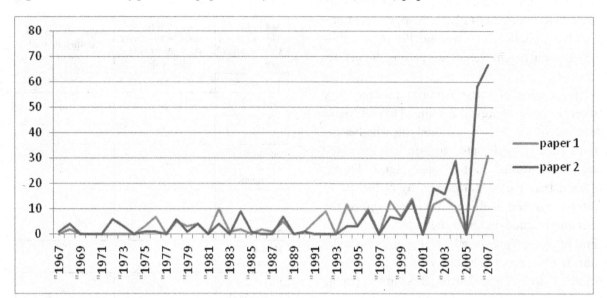

Table 3. Overall top 10 results in alphabetical order

Top authors	Top publications	Top Subject Terms	Top Thesaurus terms
Aanestad, Margunn	Energy Policy	ACCIDENTS	Business enterprises
Bana e Costa, Carlos A.	Engineering Construction & Architectural Management	COMMUNICATION & technology	Decision making
Berkhout, Frans	Ergonomics	EVALUATION	Industrial management
Chengtao Wang	European Journal of Information Systems	METHODOLOGY	Information resources management
Grobler, Francois	Journal of Cleaner Production	PERSONALITY	Information technology
Holst, Marita	Journal of Manufacturing Technology Management	SOCIAL aspects	Knowledge management
Mirijamdotter, Anita	Journal of the Association for Information Systems	SOCIAL informatics	Management
Porra, Jaana	Social Studies of Science (Sage)	SOCIAL sciences	Organizational behavior
Rappert, Brian	Systems Research & Behavioral Science	SOCIAL structure	Research
Smith, Adrian	o Technology Analysis & Strategic Management	SOCIOLOGICAL aspects	Technology

this analysis within the BSC repository using the socio-technical spelling variant.

In Paper 1 the top subject areas for papers were: GREAT BRITAIN; INDUSTRIAL MANAGEMENT; INFORMATION TECHNOLOGY; ORGANISATIONAL CHANGE; TEAMS IN THE WORKPLACE; TECHNOLOGICAL INNOVATION; TECHNOLOGY; UNITED STATES; and WORK DESIGN. Here we see a difference. In Table 1 above we indicate the top subject areas, journals, and authors. Whilst we would expect to see no duplications within authors (as people will choose their spelling variant and keep using it unless forced

Table 4. The top 10 within academic journals (alphabetical)

Top authors	Top Journals	Top Subject Terms
Aanestad, Margunn	Energy Policy	BUSINESS enterprises
Bana e Costa, Carlos A.	Ergonomics	INDUSTRIAL management
Berkhout, Frans	European Journal of Information Systems	INFORMATION resources management
Chengtao Wang	Journal of Cleaner Production	INFORMATION technology
Grobler, Francois	Journal of Manufacturing Technology Management	KNOWLEDGE management
Holst, Marita	Journal of the Association for Information Systems	MANAGEMENT
Jieying Zhang	Research Policy	ORGANIZATIONAL change
Porra, Jaana	Social Studies of Science (Sage)	RESEARCH
Rappert, Brian	Systems Research & Behavioral Science	TECHNOLOGICAL innovations
Vergragt, Philip J.	Technology Analysis & Strategic Management	TECHNOLOGY

Table 5. The top 10 within trade publications

Top authors	Top Trade Publications	Top Subject Terms
Comfort, Louise A.	BRW	ASSOCIATIONS, institutions, etc.
James, David	Computer Weekly	DEAD
Overell, Stephen	Hotel & Motel Management	EMERY, Fred
Terlaga, Ray	Information Strategy: The Executive's Journal	HOSPITALITY industry
Withiam, Glenn	PA Times	HOTELS -- Rates
	Personnel Today	INDUSTRIAL engineering
		INTERPERSONAL relations
		PROJECT management
		PSYCHOANALYSIS
		PUBLIC administration

Table 6. The top 10 within professional magazines

Top authors	Top Professional Magazines	Top Subject Terms
Barnes, J. A.	Academy of Management Review	BOOKS -- Reviews
Butteriss, Margaret	Administrative Science Quarterly	COMMUNICATION & technology
Cross, D. T.	Bulletin of the American Society for Information Science & Technology	COMPUTER-aided design
Deane, P.	Economic Journal	CORPORATIONS -- Growth
King, M. A.	Fortune	HERBST, P. G.
Lonsdale, J. M.	Industrial & Commercial Training	INDUSTRIAL management
Mitchell, B. R.	Journal of Occupational Psychology	MANAGEMENT
Norris, K.	Organization Studies	MANUFACTURING processes
Shull, Fremont	People Management	NONFICTION
Whittington, G.	Training & Development Journal	SOCIO-Technical Design: Strategies in Multidisciplinary Research

Table 7. The top 10 within books

Top authors	Subject
Beckford, John	BEST practice
Guston, David H.	CREATIVE ability in business
Herzberg, Frederick	DECISION making
Mausner, Bernard	EMPLOYEES -- Attitudes
Snyderman, Barbara B.	EXPERTISE
	FEIGENBAUM, Armand
	MOTIVATION (Psychology)
	POLICY sciences
	QUALITY
	TOTAL quality control

by publishers to do otherwise), we might expect the subject areas to have some congruence and similarity, but we see none. This might be the result of a spelling variant becoming the norm for use within a specific academic field, or could also be the result of the changes identified elsewhere in this article, in the repository.

Looking at the top journals and publications we see only two journals that are in both spelling variant lists – Social Studies of Science and Technology Analysis and Strategic Management. We do however, see some similarities in the academic fields in which the journals operate, for instance in P1 we have the journal Theoretical Issues in Ergonomics Science and here we see the journal Ergonomics. We also see that the majority of journals are operating the Information Systems / Technology field, as might be expected. Unexpectedly, in this current list we also have the addition of the journal Energy Power and the Journal of Cleaner Production.

Looking now at Table 5 which lists those papers published in Trade Publications again we a different set from P1 apart from the PA Times. In P1 there were only three such publications identified: Computer Weekly; PA Times and Travel Weekly. Looking at Trade Publications we now see 5 in the list: PA Times now joined by a fellow publication

in this field – Personnel Today; Hotel and Motel Management replacing Travel Weekly; and two business related publications – Business Review Weekly and Information Strategy.

Now looking at the Professional Magazines (Table 4), of the 14 retrieved items only 10 were actually articles, the remaining being discarded as adverts etc. In Table 6 we see a few articles that are appearing in similar fields of application as in P1- for instance, in P1 we found 2 training magazines, here we have the different but still training oriented magazine: Industrial and Commercial Training; in P1 we saw Personnel Psychology and here People Management. The one repeated magazine is the Academy of Management Review and we see also two other business related magazines: Fortune and Business History. The remaining magazines are the Economic Journal; the Bulletin of the American Society for Information Science and Technology; Organizational Studies; and Administrative Science Quarterly.

Looking now at the subject areas covered in these magazines and comparing them to the subject areas of P1, we see book reviews taking prime place as might be expected. However, we also see that prominent theoreticians are also discussed – William Pasmore in P1 and P.G. Herbst and C. Orper in this current list. The remainder of subject areas are not related. In P1 they were Organisational Change and the Learning Organisation; here they are Educational Technology; Schools; Communication and Technology; and the Industrial Organisation.

Looking at the books published (Table 7) we see three books with multiple authors being published using the hyphenated spelling variant against two in P1. in P1 also, these 2 were actually subsets of the Bloomsbury Business Library reference set, whereas here they are three different reference sets – *Motivation to Work*; *The Quality Gurus*; and the *Policy Studies Review Annual* some with multiple authors. The subject matters in the Bloomsbury sets were very limited and related closely to the Trist and Bamforth history of the movement and theory

Figure 2. Overall total of hyphenated spelling publications

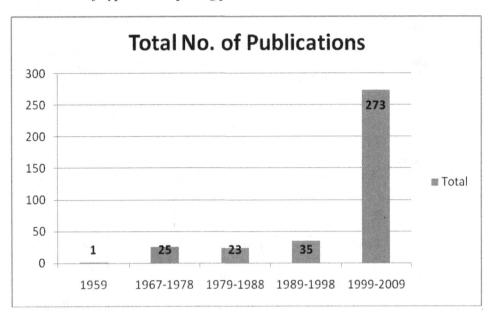

development being about IT: MINERAL INDUSTRIES; COAL MINES; EDUCATORS; and SOCIAL PSYCHOLOGISTS for example. In our current hyphenated set we see a more wide ranging subject area that is related to internal organisational capabilities such as EMPLOYEE ATTITUDES; JOB SATISFACTION; CREATIVE ABILITY; THE QUALITY OF WORKING LIFE; EXPERTISE; and BEST PRACTICE.

We can now turn to publication trends in terms of years bearing in mind the previous warnings noted both in this paper and P1 about such trends and the volatility of the BSC repository.

As with the socio-technology spelling variant we see a substantial increase in papers being published from 1999 onwards, even greater than before (despite duplications within the BSC list that needed to be removed before such calculations could be made). Since 1999 we have seen 273 (Figure 2) publications, and looking in more depth at this period (Figure 6) we see a strong rise in numbers of papers published in 2006 and 2007, with a small drop in 2008 but numbers for this year alone still exceeding the total numbers of papers published between 1989-98. It is too soon

to tell whether this is a start of a trend towards an increasing use of socio-technical theory to underpin discussions or whether it has peaked and we will now see a drop of interest. Note however, that this trend of increasing interest in the topic was duplicated in Chart 1, P1. Indeed by August 2009 there were already over 30 papers published with a hyphenated spelling.

All these trends need to be set against the background of increasing volumes of articles published over the years (shown below in Figure 3). We do not comment further on this very large increase other than to say the total numbers of journals has risen; the total number of academics in an increasing number of universities has also risen; but also, perhaps more importantly, the pressure to publish has also risen.

Looking at Figure 3 we can see that the total number of articles published per decade has increased more than 8 fold, while the number of socio-technical (hyphenated) publications has increased 11 fold. But in terms of all socio-technical spellings, the volume of publication has increased by 7 fold.

Figure 3. Business source complete all journal articles

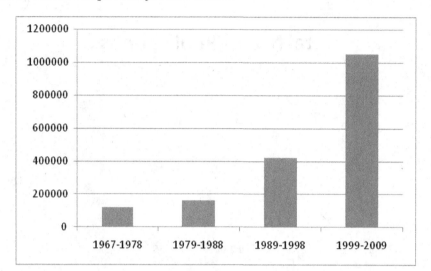

Figure 4. Socio-technical articles: rate per 100,000 of all articles (hyphenated spelling)

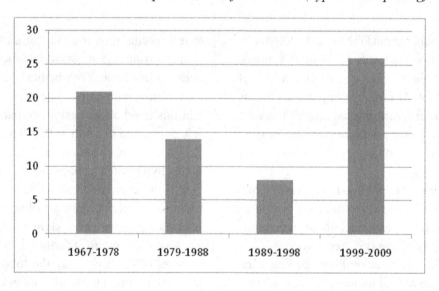

In Figure 4 we now show the number of occurrences of hyphenated socio-technical occurrences of Figure 2, to show how many socio-technical articles there are per 100,000 published per decade.

Thus Figure 5 shows that socio-technical work was a popular topic in the decade starting 1967, declining in the subsequent 2 decades, before recovering in the current decade.

Looking at Figure 6, we see that the numbers of papers published in each academic field by decade and Figure 7 shows these as a percentage of the papers published in that academic field. We therefore can see that 100% of the papers in the subject fields of LEARNING; HUMAN-MACHINE RELATIONSHIPS; COMMUNICATIONS AND TECHNOLOGY; SOCIAL INSTITUTIONS; and ACCIDENTS were published during the 1999-2009 decade. Figure 8 shows the subject area publications as a percentage of the total publications in that decade where we can see that papers identified as related to social sys-

Figure 5. Socio-technical articles: rate per 100,000 of all articles (all spellings)

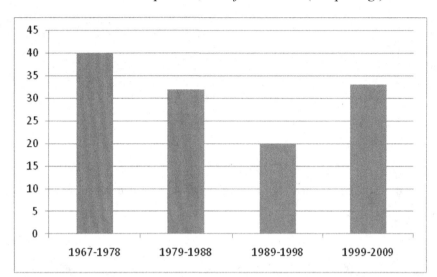

Figure 6. Publication totals 1999-2009

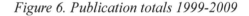

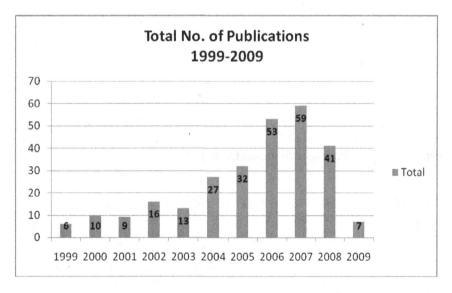

tems for instance were 50% of the publications in 1989-98. The most popular subject areas in 1999-2009 were METHODOLOGY; SOCIAL SYSTEMS; SOCIOLOGICAL ASPECTS; and COMMUNICATION AND TECHNOLOGY, followed by SOCIAL SYSTEMS, and SOCIOLOGICAL ASPECTS. The least popular topic in this decade was SOCIAL INSTITUTIONS. SOCIAL IN-FORMATICS was not published as a subject area until 1989-98 and both social sciences and

EVALUATION were subject terms in 1979-88 but not in 1989-98 (see Figure 9).

Figures 10, 11 and 12 show the publication trends by BSC Thesaurus terms. Note that a 'thesaurus' was not available when Paper 1 [P1] was complied and so we show these terms as new items of identification.

The top ten thesaurus terms for academic journals are identified in Figure 10: Technology;

Figure 7. Publications within academic field

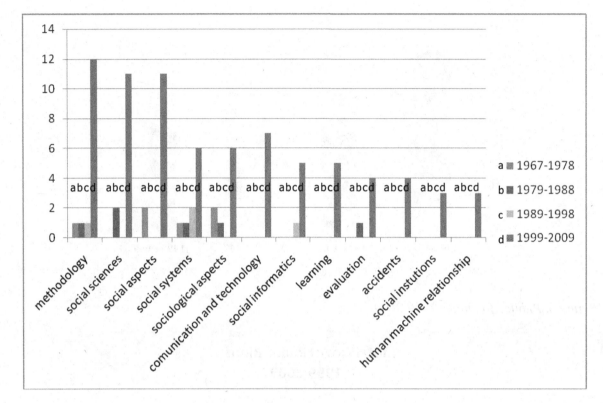

Figure 8. Percentages of publications within academic fields

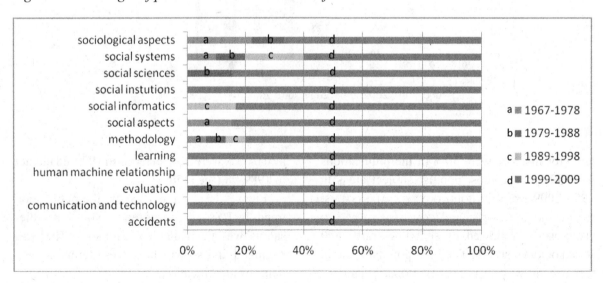

Figure 9. Subject area percentages of total publications by decade

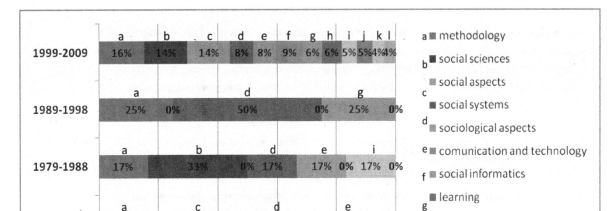

Figure 10. Academic journal thesaurus term as used by decade of publication

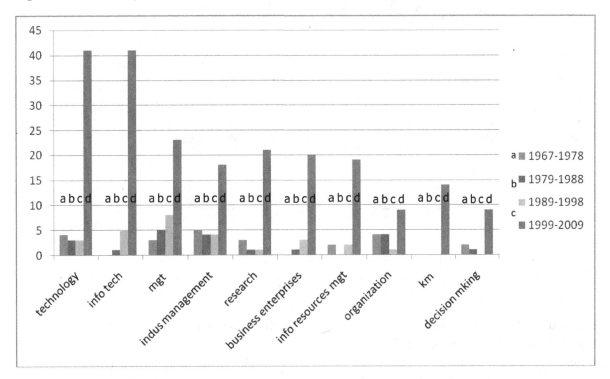

Figure 11. Trends in use of thesaurus term in journal publications

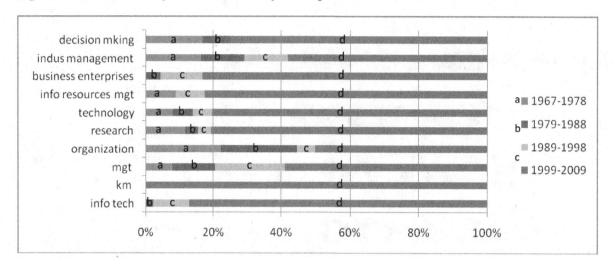

Figure 12. Academic journal thesaurus term as a percentage of publications by decade

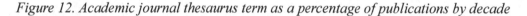

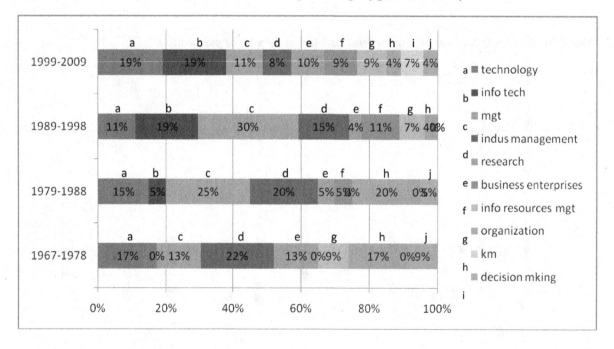

Information Technology; Management; Industrial Management; Research; Business Enterprises; Information Resource Management; Organisations; Knowledge Management; and Decision Making. Figure 11 shows these terms by decade of publication and Figure 12 shows by

each decade the percentage of publications under each term.

In Thesaurus terminology, only Knowledge Management is a 'newcomer' – not having been published before 1999 when it was identified within 7% of the total publications. The most popular Thesaurus identifications in 1999-2009

Figure 13. Non-academic publications per decade

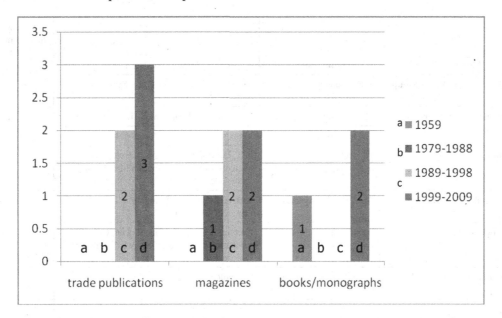

were Technology and Information Technology at 19% each of the total publications, followed by Management at 11% and Research at 10%, Decision Making at 4% being the least identified thesaurus term – see Figure 12.

Figure 13 shows the non-academic publications by decade – there was 1 book published in 1959 and 2 between 1999 and 2009; 1 magazine article (noting of course that all references to training courses, announcements of lectures etc have been removed) in 1979-88, and 2 1989-98, and a further 2 between 1999 and 2009; in trade publications 2 articles were published between 1989 and 1998, and 3 between 1999 and 2009; thus following slightly the upward trend of publications of related articles in the last decade.

ANALYSING THE PAPERS

Having now established a pattern of publication, considering both the journal outlet and numbers of papers published, we now turn to what the papers contained.

Term Analysis

As in P1 we analysed the Keywords and Subject terms allocated to each publication to see trends in topics' popularity.

In this second paper, analysing results this time for socio-technical and socio-technology (with the hyphen), the same higher level categories and sub categories of keyword and subject terms have been used as in P1's (non-hyphenated) analysis.

In order to undertake this analysis we again identified the contents of the papers which we undertook through Content Analysis techniques.

Recap of Methodology Used to Develop the Themes

As in P1, the "author keywords" and "subject terms" supplied by BSC were all extracted but not the newly added BSC Thesaurus terms. These were then tabulated and duplications were counted and noted. The raw list of keywords we compiled this way eventually reached a length of 2370 words or phrases (P1's analysis gave 1750). Grouping

Table 8. Top level categories, theme boundaries and major sub-themes

Category	Validating statement	Main sub categories	% change of themes in current analysis: upwards or downwards
1. Domain, macro industry group	Socio-technical context is	Organisation; Manufacturing; Services; The State.	+5
2. Stakeholders / major groups	Major group of players is	Employees; Labour; Union; Team; Managers.	-29
3. Work	The activity is	Management Process; Process; Work.	+19
4. Technology and ICT	The technical / information context is	ICT; Information Systems (development); Systems Theory; Information Management; Knowledge Management.	+28
5. Analysis (macro); not behaviour	Analytical approaches are	Analysis; Planning; Simulation; Design; Engineer; Model; Legal.	+8
6. Group behaviour	Group and cultural issues are	Culture; Communications; Social; Organisational Behaviour; Knowledge; Power; Philosophy.	-25
7. Personal behaviour	Individual perspectives are	Psychology; Ethics.	-23
8. Change	Change involves	Change; Learning.	-26
9. Medical	(creates own boundary without need for further refinement)		-6

of these phrases was performed using the same groups as were developed in P1.

This gave the key terms as shown in Table 8. A tenth category of 'bin' was used for keywords that were not useful. Each concept was identified by a key phrase to establish the boundaries of that data set. From these set boundaries we looked for the linkages that emerged from the initial taxonomy and then grouped the subject and keyword terms into term trees and hierarchies of concepts and identified a number of main sub-categories for each theme. The categorisation, for the earlier and the current analysis, is shown in Table 8: in this coding we used an emergent taxonomy that was checked and rechecked for validity as the themes and terms emerged during the searches.

The changes indicated in the final column indicates roughly a change in the concerns of the authors writing. We see an increase in the concerns relating to the technical or information context of the writing and the activity under discussion, but a decrease in concerns about what the change

might involve or what individual perspectives might be; or who the major group of players are, and what group and cultural issues might be related to the topic under discussion in these papers. We leave it to our readers to speculate on the causes or reasons for these changes.

As stated in P1, deriving the authors' concerns through a thematic taxonomic analysis of their abstracts, we would argue, (see Busha & Harter, 1980; Palmquist, accessed 2005, 2006) allows for both a qualitative as well as a quantitative analysis. It also provides a statistical analysis of text whilst using the same data set for categorisation and concept analysis; it provides insight into the researchers' ideas and pre-occupations; and additionally, a relatively exact analysis that is evidentially based.

Within these 9 key domains we developed 76 second level concepts and Figure 1 shows that 75% of our analysed articles were published in the period 1999 to 2008. This demonstrates different levels of importance of keywords and subject terms

Table 9. Tree for domain 1

Domain	Second level concepts	Numbers of third level concept occurrences within the 2nd level concept	
		Paper 1	P2 (modified pro rata to match grand total of P1 sample size)
Macro Industry Group	Agriculture	15	1
	Environment	18	57
	Industrial	21	29
	Manufacturing	18	8
	Market	9	11
	Mining	7	0
	Organisation	55	51
	Services	16	10
	State	12	7
	Transport	11	28
	Urban/Rural	4	0
	Utilities	15	9
	Total	*201*	*210*

Table 10. Tree for domain 2

Domain	Second level concepts	Numbers of third level concept occurrences	
		P1	P2
Stakeholders	Employees	21	22
	Managers	6	8
	Owners	5	1
	Sub group	19	11
	Teams	28	18
	Unions	4	0
	Total	*83*	*59*

from that used in our previous analysis where Chart 1 [P1 p. 16] shows that 41% of articles were from that same time period.

In Table 9 we show the term tree and hierarchy for the first and most macro of our Domain areas, which is Macro Industry group; the second level of this domain gives the actual industry that was used/written about in the paper; and the third level of the hierarchy lists the number of further, more detailed concepts that fall within each industry group. Thus we see that within Environment there were originally 9 sub-concepts which include (for example) Climatic Changes; Ecology; Energy; Conservation; Sustainability. Tables 10-18 repeat this analysis for the remaining domains. Each Table shows the results for the analysis from P1 and a comparator for the current – P2 – analysis of the hyphenated spelling variant. Each comparator Figure has been modified pro-rata down to match the grand total of the P1 sample size. Thus, for

Table 11. Tree for domain 3

Domain	Second level concepts	Numbers of third level concept occurrences	
		P1	**P2**
Work	Processes	14	18
	Product Management	4	3
	The management process	79	95
	Total	*97*	*116*

example, the P2 Figures for Environment without this modification would have been 78 rather than 57 shown in the table below.

In terms of general research domains, we see in Table 9 a dramatic increase in Environment by 217% and Transport by 153%, offset by a decline in keywords for Manufacturing by -55%, Services by -36%, Utilities by -41% and State domains by -36%.

In terms of keywords for major groups of players we see that the main changes were a reduction in keywords for special interest Sub Groups (-42%) and fewer Teams keyword uses (-37%).

In Table 11 we see that for the Activities and Work domains there was more interest in Processes in general (+25%) and the Management Process (+20%).

In Table 12 we see that the entire Technical/ Information domain has increased by 28%. Major increases were in Information Management (149%); Information Systems (social) (152%); Information Systems Development (135%); Architecture (99%); and Telecommunications (59%). Interestingly, there were 40% fewer mentions of Information Systems Design, and, based on a relatively small sample of 16, Library mentions were down by 73%.

Table 13, which considers the domain of Analytical Approaches, shows that the domain only grew a little (up by 8%). However, within the domain the second level concept of Economics grew significantly (up by 125%). Planning also grew (by 107%), as did general Analysis - 105%, with Finance also increasing by more than

two thirds. The concept of Analysis and Design of Work, which was previously the biggest category in this domain, dropped sharply by 48% and, based on a smaller sample, Manufacturing Systems mentions almost disappeared entirely.

In terms of keywords for Group Issues, Individual Perspectives and (general) Change, in each of the domains (6, 7 and 8) there was a drop of approximately 25%. Communication and Group Behaviour however, rose sharply, by 77% and 58% respectively. Power was divided into 3 categories, all of which dropped by 20% to 60%. There was also less interest seen in Participation (down 56%); Culture (down 22%); Knowledge (down 40%); and Organisational Behaviour (down 68%); although all these categories in our original paper had only modest sample sizes of between 15 and 30 keywords.

Looking at Table 15 we see that there were 23% fewer uses of keywords for Individual Perspectives. Psychology was down 30% and Motivation was down by a similar amount (31%).

In Table 16 we can see that all keyword uses for Change were down; Learning is down by 20%; and Organisational Change by 48%.

Table 17 demonstrates that Medical keywords have retained much the same importance in both analyses.

Note here that the grand totals, for P1 and for P2 (adjusted as per Table 1 and including the 'bin' category of less useful terms) both come to 1735 terms.

Table 12. Tree for domain 4

Domain	Second level concepts	Numbers of third level concept occurrences	
		P1	P2
Technology and Information Communication Technology (ICT)	Architecture	7	14
	ICT	12	18
	Information Management	20	50
	Information Systems	28	26
	Information Systems Design	11	7
	Information Systems Development	19	45
	Information Systems (Social)	9	23
	Information Technology	30	37
	Internet	29	28
	Knowledge Management	15	15
	Library	16	4
	Mobile Information Technology	4	5
	Software	8	5
	Systems Theory	14	12
	Systems, Manufacturing	21	20
	Technology	35	44
	Telecommunication	17	27
	Total	*295*	*377*

Discussing the Papers

The authors then examined the second level terms.

Again, we identified as key those papers that discussed the theoretical aspects of the field and/or looked at the theory as compared to other theories such as System Theory.

In the context of both articles P1 and this P2, it was decided that the search papers' approaches to "Theory", "Systems", "Systems Theory" and those that included "Socio-technical theory" or "Socio-technical Systems Theory" should be the basis for the analysis. The justifications and definitions for these terms remain the same for both papers and were explained in P1.

However, before looking at Systems Theory as in P1, we will first consider another category of papers – those relating to METHODOLOGY.

If we now look in more detail at the papers published using the hyphenated form of spelling that are duplicated across the Subject and Thesaurus terms we also see that a number explore the Theory and Methodology related to socio-technology. These papers are worth exploring further here (before we go onto the discussion of the papers related to Systems Theory and its variants as in P1). BSC identifies 15 papers between 1977 and 2009 that fit this criteria (see Table 19)- note here that the Journal of the Association for Information Systems published a Special Edition in 2007 on the life and work of Enid Mumford who died in 2006 and thus many of the papers discussed are

Table 13. Tree for domain 5

Domain	Second level concepts	Numbers of third level concept occurrences	
		P1	P2
Analysis (Macro)	Academic Discipline	36	26
	Analysis	36	74
	Analysis – Decision	30	26
	Analysis – Organisation	22	28
	Analysis – Processes	13	15
	Analysis – Social	50	59
	Analysis – Socio-technical	20	24
	Design	15	12
	Design – Engineering	10	13
	Economics	15	34
	Finance	15	25
	Legal	10	12
	Planning	18	37
	Quality	11	12
	Research Approach	87	94
	Simulation	6	5
	Systems – Manufacturing	14	1
	Theory	27	27
	Work Analysis and Design	102	53
	Total	*537*	*579*

Table 14. Tree for domain 6

Domain	Second level concepts	Numbers of third level concept occurrences	
		P1	P2
Group Behaviour	Behaviour – Group	19	30
	Behaviour – Organisational	16	5
	Communication	17	30
	Culture	31	24
	Knowledge	23	14
	Language	8	0
	Participation	20	9
	Philosophy	18	18
	Power	74	38
	Total	*226*	*169*

Table 15. Tree for domain 7

Domain	Second level concepts	Numbers of third level concept occurrences	
		P1	P 2
Personal Behaviour	Ethics	5	8
	Motivation	34	23
	Psychology	42	29
	Psychology - cognition	7	7
	Total	*88*	*68*

Table 16. Tree for domain 8

Domain	Second level concepts	Numbers of third level concept occurrences	
		P1	P2
Change	Change	31	21
	Innovation	33	30
	Learning	44	35
	Organisational change	31	16
	Total	*139*	*102*

Table 17. Tree for domain 9

Domain	Second level concepts	Numbers of third level concept occurrences	
		P1	P2
Medical	Medical	31	29

to be found in this Special Edition. Note also here that a repeated search without the hyphen returns 11 papers between 1975 and 2007 but that the Olphert and Damodaran (2007) paper is to be found in both searches. We start our discussion below in date order from newest to oldest.

The Gray and Hovav (2008) paper concerns itself with thinking about the future and looks at three methodologies – that can assist in understanding this future – the Delphi method, cross-impact analysis and scenarios. The authors say Although much IS research deals with evaluating and improving existing information systems, researchers are also called upon to think about the future of our field, of hardware, software, and specific applications and their implication on

organizational strategy or society (p212). In their abstract they consider these future items to be socio-technical phenomena and events or variables. Socio-technical thinking is not used as a way of considering these events so this paper does not concern itself with its use within the methodology field.

The second paper in date order is by Hermann and Kuehnle (2007). According to the author (p. 1022) the paper intends to contribute to interpretations of present and future developments in manufacturing and manufacturing research. It designs hypothetical expert consolidated projections for the future of manufacturing with the focus on social impacts from information and communications technologies (ICT)..... The paper

Table 18. Methodology papers

Author	Year	Title	Journal
Gray, Paul Hovav, Anat	2008	From Hindsight To Foresight: Applying Futures Research Techniques In Information Systems.	Communications of AIS
Hermann Kuehnle	2007	Post mass production paradigm (PMPP) trajectories	Journal of Manufacturing Technology Management
Gilbert, Claude Amalberti, Rene Laroche, Herve Paries, Jean	2007	Errors and Failures: Towards a New Safety Paradigm.	Journal of Risk Research
Porra, Jaana Hirschheim, Rudy	2007	A Lifetime of Theory and Action on the Ethical Use of Computers: A Dialogue with Enid Mumford.	Journal of the Association for Information Systems
Stahl, Bernd Carsten	2007	ETHICS, Morality and Critique: An Essay on Enid Mumford's Socio-Technical Approach	Journal of the Association for Information Systems
Olphert, Wendy Damodaran, Leela	2007	Citizen Participation and engagement in the Design of e-Government Services: The Missing Link in Effective ICT Design and Delivery.	Journal of the Association for Information Systems
Cook, Stephen C. Ferris, Timothy L. J	2007	Re-evaluating systems engineering as a framework for tackling systems issues.	Systems Research & Behavioral Science
Mirijamdotter, Anita Somerville, Mary M. Holst, Marita	2006	An Interactive and Iterative Evaluation Approach for Creating Collaborative Learning Environments.	Electronic Journal of Information Systems Evaluation
Berkhout, Frans	2006	Normative expectations in systems innovation	Technology Analysis & Strategic Management
van Merkerk, Rutger Robinson, Douglas	2006	Characterizing the emergence of a technological field: Expectations, agendas and networks in Lab-on-a-chip technologies.	Technology Analysis & Strategic Management
Kansal, Vineet	2006	Enterprise Resource Planning Implementation: A Case Study.	Journal of American Academy of Business, Cambridge
Kuipers, Ben De Witte, Marco C	2005	Teamwork: a case study on development and performance.	International Journal of Human Resource Management;
Herrmann, Thomas Hoffmann, Marcel Kunau, Gabriele Kai-Uwe Loser, Gabriele	2004	A modelling method for the development of groupware applications as socio-technical systems.	Behaviour & Information Technology
Globerson, Shlomo Salvendy, Gavriel	1984	A Socio-Technical Accounting Approach to the Evaluation of Job Performance.	International Journal of Operations & Production Management
Bostrom, Robert P. Heinen, J. Stephen	1977	MIS Problems and Failures: A Socio-Technical Perspective Part I: The Causes.	MIS Quarterly

assumes a specific driver/impact constellation, which emphasises socio-technical relations and focuses on organisation and ICT use in manufacturing environments as decisive and limiting influences. However, that is the final mention of socio-technical ideas in the paper – the methodology referred to in the Subject description is the 4F methodology for developing strategy formulation of Klopp and Hartmann (1999).

The next paper is that by Gilbert, Amalberti, Laroche, and Paries (2007). This is an unusual paper in that its subject terms are mainly relating

Table 19. The remaining 15 papers

Author	Year	Title	Journal
Marples D L	1968	Roles in a Manufacturing Organization.	Journal of Management Studies
Cummings, Thomas G.	1978	Self-Regulating Work Groups: A Socio-Technical Synthesis.	Academy of Management Review
Manz, Charles C.; Stewart, Greg L.	1997	Attaining Flexible Stability by Integrating Total Quality Management and Socio-technical Systems Theory.	Organization Science
Majchrzak Ann; Borys Bryan	2001	Generating testable socio-technical systems theory.	Journal of Engineering & Technology Management
Mumford, Enid.	2006	The story of socio-technical design: reflections on its successes, failures and potential.	Information Systems Journal
Kroes, Peter; Franssen, Maarten; Poel, Ibo van de; Ottens, Maarten.	2006	Treating socio-technical systems as engineering systems: some conceptual problems.	Systems Research & Behavioral Science
Gregoriades, A.; Sutcliffe, A. G.	2006	Automated assistance for human factors analysis in complex systems.	Ergonomics
Hanseth, Ole; Jacucci, Edoardo Grisot, Miria; Aanestad, Margunn.	2006	Reflexive Standardization: Side Effects and Complexity in Standard Making.	MIS Quarterly
Schwaninger, Markus.	2006	Theories of viability: a comparison.	Systems Research & Behavioral Science
Preda Alex.	2006	Socio-Technical Agency in Financial Markets; The Case of the Stock Ticker.	Social Studies of Science (Sage)
van Merkerk, Rutger; Robinson, Douglas.	2006,	Characterizing the emergence of a technological field: Expectations, agendas and networks in Lab-on-a-chip technologies.	Technology Analysis & Strategic Management
Verbong, Geert; Geels, Frank	2007	The ongoing energy transition: Lessons from a socio-technical, multi-level analysis of the Dutch electricity system (1960–2004)	Energy Policy
Thomas Herrmann; Kai-Uwe Loser; Isa Jahnke.	2007	Sociotechnical walkthrough: a means for knowledge integration.	Learning Organization
Lyytinen, Kalle Newman, Mike	2008	Explaining information systems change: a punctuated socio-technical change model.	European Journal of Information Systems
Cassano-Piche, Vicente, K. J. Jamieson, G. A.	2009	A test of Rasmussen's risk management framework in the food safety domain: BSE in the UK.	Theoretical Issues in Ergonomics Science

to risk and safety, e.g. risk assessment; process safety management; industrial safety; health risk assessment; accidents; and natural disasters. The authors discuss the studies in French literature relating to major accidents resulting from the increasing complexity of socio-technical systems especially chemical and nuclear energy activities. These systems are naturally unstable, they argue, and thus a recognition of errors and failures is called for and a systematic critique of the underpinning existing paradigm for safety and security models. They also argue that a) no world is perfect; and b) errors and failures are natural - Errors (and all failures) can neither be reduced to departures from the rules, nor considered as abnormalities or exceptions. They are an integral part of habitual, normal functioning, irrespective of the level on which they are situated. As such, they have an ambivalent status from the safety point of view (p. 968). They conclude that an interdisciplinary reflection is required to consider such socio-technical systems and their failure, but that political considerations may stifle this debate, especially in France.

Looking now at the paper by Porra (2007) entitled 'A lifetime of theory and action on the ethical use of computers: a dialogue with Enid Mumford'. This paper is to be found catalogued under the Thesaurus terms of Methodology and the subject terms of System Theory with the author's key word of Action Research. The paper was the result of an interview with Enid Mumford (2003) and includes a discussion of the four theoretical foundations of her work in the information systems research field: ethics; socio-technical theory; general systems theory; and action research. Four examples of Enid Mumford's work are offered as cases for study: Turners Asbestos Cement and Rolls Royce Aerospace undertaken in the 1970s; Digital Equipment Corporation in the 1980s and SKIL undertaken in the 1990s. Mumford's projects in the nineties were almost all concerned with using a socio-technical approach to assist managers to select and shape information systems to meet their particular needs (p. 470). The paper then details an interview with Enid Mumford (2003) giving a full transcript.

A second paper about the work and legacy of Enid Mumford's research by Carsten (2007). Carsten's paper has a significant number of Subject terms attached to it: Research; Management; Technology; Information Technology; Information Resource Management; Information And Communication Technology; Ethics; Methodology; Communication And Technology; Humanistic Ethics. In Keyword terms Carsten offered: Critical Theory; Enid Mumford; Participation; and ETHICS. ETHICS here stands for Effective Technical and Human Implementation of Computer-based Systems which was the system development methodology developed by Enid Mumford. Carsten when describing his paper in his abstract says that its overall aim was to suggest a way that (the community and theorists involved in) socio-technical design can further (develop and advance) Enid Mumford's humanistic aim to

improve life using information and communication technology (p. 479). He also suggests that the critical research in information systems approach and the field of computer and information ethics share Mumford's aim of finding a way to design and use technology that is ethically acceptable.

A final paper from this Special Edition that is also catalogued under methodology is by Olphert and Damadoran and looks at eGovernment as an example of a participatory approach to ICT design. The Subject terms for this paper are: Associations; Institutions; Research; Citizenship; Internet In Public Administration; Moral Development; Information Society; Critical Thinking; Methodology; Social Responsibility; and Sociological Associations. The Keywords as offered by the authors are: Capacity Building; eGovernment; Citizen Engagement; Participatory Design; and Socio-technical System Theory.

The authors, Olphert and Damadoran, say that in their paper they provide An extension of Enid Mumford's ideas about the benefits and process of participation based on an analysis of recent citizen engagement initiatives (p. 91) and that they endorse her strongly held belief that computers should be used to enhance the quality of (human) life in this case in relation to Governmental initiatives to enhance the democratic process and to deliver public services. They say that There is now wide acknowledgement in academic and research communities that IS project outcomes are a product of the complex and inevitable interdependencies between the technical and social (i.e., human and organisational) components of systems – whether these are work organisations or entire societies (p. 492). The paper discusses the ETHICS methodology and considers some developments in the field of STS such as the work by Pava (1986); Clegg (2000) and Klein (2005). Participatory IS design is now considered a known benefit such that there are ISO standards (13407, 1999) to promote user involvement at key stages of design and development. Olphert and Damadoran reviewed 20 cases of citizen engagement (participation) that demonstrate the benefits of this engagement in both the output and outcome arenas. In particular they look in depth at the delivery of eGovernment in the UK which is now at a mature stage of delivery. eGovernment is clearly a social and technical system situated in the wider economic and political environment and as such has a multiplicity of factors influencing its design, delivery and development. The disappointing outcome of this study showed that technical factors were being developed without explicit attention to the human and organisational aspects, i.e., to the social system (p. 499)... Evidence from the exploratory research ... suggests that the participation and engagement of citizens in eGovernment developments has been superficial and limited to peripheral aspects of the lives of most people involved (p. 500). Evidence also shows that such services are falling short of their targets for performance and adoption by their intended users, which many analysts agree is a result of the failure to include end-users in their development and design.

We now look at the papers that were not in the Special Edition but also discuss Methodology starting with Cook and Ferris (2007). This paper considers the topic of systems engineering as a Framework. The systems issues it is looking at include the development of large socio-technical systems – they argue that systems engineering is an appropriate methodology for any problem situation where the solution can be expected to involve a substantial technical component (p. 169). In its origin it had been characterised as being a hard systems approach appropriate for solving mechanical-unitary problems where it is relatively easy to meet agreed objectives. The authors discuss a number of more recent papers which assert that the role of a systems engineer is far more complex and diverse than the simple unitary space assigned by theorists such as Flood and Jackson (1991a), and contend that systems engineering can be considered a metamethodology which would include the philosophy of engineering, the

philosophy of systems engineering and systems thinking (again referring back to general systems theory and von Bertalanffy). It is analogous to Total Systems Intervention (Flood and Jackson, 1991b), and yet also should be recognized within the Total Systems Intervention framework as the appropriate methodology to address issues in any category sector of the matrix, where it is anticipated that the solution is likely to involve design of something involving a substantial amount of technology (p. 180).

Mirijamdotter, Somerville, and Holst (2006), in contrast, discuss collaborative learning environments. Their subject terms include: Computer Software; Learning; Computer-assisted Instruction; and the Internet in Education. They discuss the results of an international project relating to interactive design for a technology enabled learning environment. They claim this to be a new approach whereby students were involved substantively in the design and evaluation teams. The systems thinking methodology was utilised to collaboratively evaluate the development.

Berkhout (2006) has an interesting and contrasting list of Subject terms: Technological Forecasting; Technology Assessment; Social Action; Social Policy; Methodology; and Social Problems. He tells us that his paper is concerned with the way technological expectations are generated, articulated and deployed in processes of large-scale socio-technical change (p. 299). He also says (p. 300) We argue that because expectations are intrinsic to social action, visions of the future are ubiquitous, but individual and specific. Agents will act in relation to their private version of what the future may hold. The paper looks specifically characteristic features and forms of these visions of the future as they relates specifically to socio-technical regimes. He additionally considers visions and their deployment in the context of actor networks in systems innovation processes and how these visions may be articulated and adopted and modified through diffusion.

The paper by van Merkerk and Robinson (2006) concerns itself with 'Lab-on-a-chip technologies'. The subject terms include: COMPUTER NETWORKS; LABORATORIES; STRATEGIC PLANNING; TECHNOLOGY ASSESSMENT; DYNAMICS; DRUGS; AND TECHNICAL INSTITUTES. The paper investigates emerging technological fields through studying the dynamics of expectations, agenda building and early networks ... where there is a major challenge in unveiling the socio-technical dynamics leading to path emergence (p. 411). Expectations within the early stages of technology developments (by the actors) play a crucial role in defining roles, building interest and obligation constructing within the set of networks involved - these network interactions shape the activities and growth rate of the technology development. The dynamics of path building within these networks are socio-technical.

Vineet Kansal (2006) considers enterprise resource planning; best practice; organizational effectiveness; competitive advantage; and paradigms (in the social sciences). Here he looks at ENTERPRISE RESOURCE PLANNING (ERP) as a socio-technical challenge that requires a fundamentally different outlook from technologically driven innovation, and will depend on a balanced perspective where the organization as a total system is considered (p. 165). He concludes The comprehensive nature of ERP organizational and inter-organizational users, creates a complex socio-technical system in which a large percentage of costs and benefits are well hidden or they emerge after ERP implementation (p. 169).

Kuipers and De Wittes' (2005) paper looks at TEAMWORK. This a QUALITY OF WORK LIFE paper considering INDUSTRIAL MANAGEMENT, a traditional area for the socio-technical methodology. Indeed the case described is that of Volvo in Sweden and semi-autonomous teams but not the classic case relating to their car development but that of their truck and bus division. Their study seemed to indicate that that the traditional socio-technical areas of job enlargement and job enrichment are key aspects of individual empowerment and are also important for developing individual quality of working life satisfaction and involvement.

Herrmann, Hoffman, Kunau, and Kai-Uwe's (2004) Loser discussed a modelling method for the development of groupware applications – looking at PSYCHOLOGY, ENGINEERING and DESIGN. Groupware applications are classified as socio-technical systems and require a specific modelling methodology to develop. They differentiate between social systems and technical systems saying (p. 119): Social systems are characterized by phenomena such as communication and cooperation between human individuals, emergence of meaning systems, self-referential development of structures and learning processes, self-consciousness, and autonomy. In contrast, technical systems are characterized by artifacts, control, anticipation, state-transitions, preprogrammed adaptability, learning in respect to purposes which are determined from outside the system etc. they state that socio-technical design approaches, because they adhere to the early concepts of systems theory, cannot handle the lack of anticipation of the system's evolution or the problems with contingency. Newer systems theory can, however, help but have deficits to support the design of socio-technical systems such as groupware. They suggest that the closed-system perspective of living systems suggested by Maturana and Varela (1987), the neo-constructivists view on reality (von Glasersfeld, 1996) and the dimension of self-reference (von Forster, 1981, p. 121) are the most relevant. They also choose the modelling method SeeMe (see Herrmann & Loser (1999) as being most relevant for the design of STS as it could easily represent incompleteness, contingency and multiple views on reality.

Looking now at Globerson and Salvendy (1984) we find a discussion of ACCOUNTING METHODS, PERSONNEL MANAGEMENT and HUMAN CAPITAL as measures of productivity and their limitations. In order to overcome these identified limitations a socio-technical accounting system which evaluates personnel, jobs and the value of human assets is developed. Clearly this paper has been significantly superseded now by Intellectual Capital and other human Capital valuations as described in the knowledge management field of theory.

Our final paper in this section is by BOSTROM and Heinen (1977). These authors published a seminal pair of papers in this year in MIS Quarterly giving a socio-technical perspective on MIS problems and failures. However, only part I of these two discusses any issues relating to methodology when looking at ORGANIZATIONAL BEHAVIOUR; BUSINESS FAILURE; and MISMANAGEMENT. The STS approach to designing work systems was fairly new at the time of writing of this article and thus needed significant explanation to their audience. Classically they cite (p. 18) Lucas (1975) as saying that the major reason most information systems have failed is that we have ignored organizational behaviour problems in the design and operation of computer-based information systems (40, p. 6). The article describes 7 conditions which are the cause of inadequate design and unsuccessful change strategies. These are:

1. The system designer's implicit theories. Their assumptions that they make about people and users impact their decisions on their design and also are rarely challenged being rather implicit acceptances.
2. The concept of responsibility held by systems designers.
3. Limited conceptualisations of frameworks for organisational work systems or user systems as used by the system designers.
4. Limited view of the goal of an MIS system as held by the system designers.
5. The failure of system designers to include relevant groups (i.e., users and stakeholders) in the design referent group.
6. The rational and /or static view of the systems development process as held by system designers.

7. The limited set of change technologies available to systems designers who attempt to 'improve' organisations. (pp. 19-20)

One important point to note from the discussions above of the papers that indicated from their Subject area classifications that they were discussing METHODOLOGY. In almost all cases it was not a socio-technical methodology that was under discussion. The Subject term seemed merely to indicate that the papers had a distinct methodology discussion or section. This is another point to note when retrieving papers from a repository such as BSC – the Subject classifications can often be misleading. It is wise to be as creative and lateral thinking as possible, in order to retrieve your required research.

"Systems" Paper Analysis

In P1 the authors examined the second level terms and it was decided that the papers' approaches to Theory, Systems, Systems Theory and those that included Socio-technical Theory or Socio-technical Systems Theory should be the basis for the socio-technical field analysis.

In P1 we found 42 papers to assess but in this search we found only 18 such papers, although three have already been discussed above as methodology papers.

Table 19 gives the authors, years, paper titles and journals of the remaining 15 papers, in date order.

In the sections below we now discuss the content and arguments of these 15 papers, apart from those already discussed above.

The Early Papers

We only consider two papers to be within the "Early Years": Marples (1968) and Cummings (1978). Both papers consider the working environment of people – Marples' case in a factory but in Cummings' article he considers theory relating to the self-regulated or autonomous work group, specifically drawing on the work of the Tavistock Institute; his work is not limited to the factory environment.

According to Marples' abstract The article reports on a management study at Hoffmann Manufacturing Co. in Great Britain. The purpose was to collect information about the factory's operation, educate employees by engaging them in the research, and identify training needs at the company. The results focus on: the socio-technical system where the inspection manager needs to be a good communicator and responsible to a chief inspector; system control where the foreman is a service channel with varying loads of breakdowns; and problem-portfolios (p. 183). The socio-technical and organizational issues discovered echoed many of the findings of the Tavistock Institute and the contradiction inherent in the factory method of working, Marples' saying (p. 202): On the face of it, the production system is one which would call for a 'mechanistic' method of management with dearly defined roles and vertical communication. In respect of ongoing production it has. But for the new developments and changes an 'organismic' system is required and tends to obtain, with a wider range of communications and less clearly defined roles. The author further comments that routine tended to drive out innovation and those managers with the longest experience were those least likely to initiate change.

Cummings explains that self-regulating groups are a direct outcome from socio-technical systems theory and socio-technical design of work. He states (p. 626) that socio-technical designers attempt to structure work systems so that they can meet environmental demands while remaining relatively resilient to external disruptions. They will use the work group rather than the individual job as the basic building block of work design. The article provides an extensive analysis of how this design is carried out but also explores the theory surrounding motivation referring to Hackman and Oldham (1976). Self-regulating groups will

provide three psychological conditions that lead to both work effectiveness and personal satisfaction: (a) personally meaningful work; (b) responsibility for work conditions; and (c) knowledge of results (p. 629). Cummings links socio-technical systems design with that of the work of Hackman and Oldham (1976) and for job design (a common discussion in the early years' authors within P1). He concludes (p. 633) Self-regulating groups are more effectively implemented to the extent that: (a) attention is given to the social processes by which members develop their own ways of working together and of adjusting their activities to task and environmental conditions; (b) their organizational context is organic; and (c) their organizational climate fosters experimentation, trust, and collaboration among workers and managers.

The Later Years

The remainder of the papers are 'later' years of publication as there was a gap between 1978 and 1997. However, this set of papers shows the repeated pattern of a significant number being published from 1999 onwards – with only the one paper in 1997 and the next being 2001 and then we see another gap until 2006 and later. The paper in 2006 being by Enid Mumford herself.

The interesting difference between this current set of hyphenated papers and that of the set in P1, is that we see no real pattern emerging of the topics and indeed these current papers concern an extremely wide range of subject matters from Food Safety to Engineering to Finance. This being so, we will just consider each paper in date order.

Manz and Stewart (1997) discuss in their paper a conjunction of Total Quality Management (TQM) and Socio-technical Systems Theory. This again was a topic visited in P1 by a number of authors who suggested that there was a strong link in the two concepts. Here the authors attempt to combine the two approaches to simultaneously achieve organizational stability and flexibility through work design. They explain the socio-technical systems theory (STS) is explicitly grounded in general systems theory as expounded by von Bertalanffy (1950). This linked social and technical systems that operate independently of each other, joint optimization of both being the most desirable outcome – and here they refer back to the Cummings (1978) papers discussed above. The difference between STS and TQM is the consideration of the social forces and the emphasis on team work that is empowered and autonomous. Additionally, a major difference between the two theories is the type of production or service setting that is established. TQM requires management to establish defined control systems whilst STS permits teams to establish their own control systems. Integrating the two methods of work provides a number of potential benefits such as stability for long-term success; flexible systems that will adapt to environmental change; the continuation of change towards to autonomous ways of working when short-term performance is 'harmed' as problems encountered in developing these ways of working are discovered. It is argued that integration and alignment through combining these two theories will permit not only quality of work-life improvement but also improve productivity and quality for the overall organisation.

Majchrzak and Borys (2001) concern themselves with STS theory in an engineering environment. They repeat the discussion relating to general systems theory and von Bertalanffy adding that Gerwin and Kolodny, (1992) refer to STS as a "paradigm" consisting of a conceptual scheme, a methodology, a design process, a set of values about work, contextual conditions such as interdependence with the environment, and an historical tradition built on psychology, sociology and workplace research (p. 220). This framework is very general they argue and thus there are many alternative views of STS. They mention the classical approach of the Tavistock Institute (described in Trist and Murray, 1993), the participative design approach of Emery in Australia (Emery, 1993b),

the democratic dialogue approach in Sweden, and the Dutch integral organizational renewal (IOR) approach (Ulbo de Sitter et al., 1997). In addition.... there are other perspectives, including the job design perspective of Davis (Davis & Taylor, 1972), the Swiss KOMPASS model, the deliberation model (Pava, 1983) and Hewlett-Packard's Bulls Eye STS model. The commonality between these views are the design practices and their underlying set of principles about how organisations and the people within them will function in an effective manner. Majchrzak and Borys (2001) argue that these varying views and perspectives offer contradictory explanations such that STS researchers and organisational scientists will ignore each others' literature. Indeed organisational researchers will often marginalise the work of STS and do not test these principles against their own design principles and thus the quality of work (as discussed by Manz and Stewart above) is frequently not considered. One outcome is that the proponents of the differing STS views will argue about the contents and components of the other contradictory views, rather than testing principles and models that can bridge the various possibilities of theory and produce a practice that is viable and acceptable to more theorists. This middle ground theory is explored, developed and researched in the paper through a longitudinal research study. The new theory is not only rooted in existing STS perspectives but

- It is comprehensive, addressing all the elements in an organization.
- It incorporates Cherns's design principles as representative of classic STS.
- It considers both social and technical elements of the organization.
- It incorporates quality of work life as an important element of the organizational design.
- It offers the capability to handle variation through variance control strategies. (p. 232)

It of course differs from previous theory in a number of ways which are explicated in the paper which noted that numerous new theoretical propositions were needed, including:

- Distinguishing between a theory of ideal organizational features versus a theory of constrained designs.
- Distinguishing between strategy-specific and generic ideal design features.
- Need for alignment in business strategies (p. 234)

In 2006 Enid Mumford wrote what will become a seminal paper on her work and socio-technical design. In her paper she traced the history of socio-technical design, emphasizing the set of values it embraces, the people espousing its theory and the organizations that practise (d) it (p. 317). As previous papers above and in P1 discussed the relationships of STS with TQM, here Mumford looked at its relationship with Action Research. She states that whilst in the 1960s and 1970s organisations improved working practices using STS, the economic conditions of the 1980s and 1990s led to downsizing and cost cutting. This economic situation may be reflected in the paucity of papers we are exploring here in this paper. Mumford's paper again gives a history of the movement and discusses the principles, this time considering some examples from Scandinavia and Western Europe as well as the USA. She specifically mentions the work of Eijnatten in the Netherlands as a counter-indicator (Eijnatten & Zwaan, 1998), where he considers that most production systems are over complex and need to be simplified and a variant of STS can assist in this. However the concept of STS as a design principle has not been widely established despite the requirement of flatter hierarchies for more skilled workforces. Interestingly she also comments about the work of Soros (1998) and his prediction that capitalism was unstable and was taking little or no account of social and political factors. Soros, she says, believes that there may well be a cascading decline of the stock markets. But also Mumford says that many commentators do not see technology as a driving force for change rather a facilitator. What can socio-technical design offer for the future? Mumford suggests that the value systems are key - although technology and organizational structures may change, the rights and needs of the employee must be given as high a priority as those of the non-human parts of the system (p. 338). The world of socio-technical design is democratic, humanistic and provides both freedom and knowledge to those who are part of it. (p. 339)

Also in 2006 we find a further six papers looking at socio-technical theory. We begin our discussion of these in alphabetical order, starting with the paper by Kroes, Franssen, Poel and Ottens (2006). This paper is particularly concerned with systems engineering. As with STS, systems engineering originates from general systems theory but suffers from a conceptual problem of how to draw up the boundaries of an engineering system: For engineering systems this problem manifests itself conspicuously with regard to the status of non-technical elements, such as social, political, economic and institutional ones (p. 803). According to this view every engineering system is located in a three-dimensional space spanned by Technology, Management and Society (p. 804). Kroes et al suggest that engineering systems must therefore by right be called socio-technical systems as there must needs be both a technical infrastructure and a social infrastructure to these systems without which they cannot operate. Indeed the system is in continual flux and is being changed by the actors within – they are re-designing the system as per the classic socio-technical principle of control of variation being best done by those undertaking the work.

Next we discuss the paper by Gregoriades and Sutcliffe (2006) which looks at the command control rooms of military vessels - in the case discussed a naval offshore patrol vessel – a somewhat different setting from previous discussions of STS here. The authors look at a complex socio-technical system where there are periods of both high and low intensity work loading. There is an in-depth discussion of the psychological issues relating to both high and low work loading including boredom when the workload is low and degradation of concentration due to stress when it is high. A model of the system design is constructed using the i* agent-oriented modelling framework (Yu, 1994, Liu et al., 2003). The i* framework models socio-technical systems as networks of agents (human or machine), goals, system qualities called soft goals, tasks, and resources. Agents, goals, and tasks are connected by dependency relationships, i.e. a goal depends on an agent to achieve it. Other relationships are means – ends (tasks are the means to achieve goals) (p. 1267). The paper demonstrates a tool that can be combined with the i* analysis method and scenario modelling – it concludes that the value of the tool lies in in exploratory 'what if' assessment of different socio-technical designs rather than in absolute performance predictions per se. (p. 1285).

Hanseth, Jacucci, Grisot, and Aanestad (2006) look at ICT standards and complexity in the context of developing a Norwegian electronic patient record system. As with so many of these systems, the attempt failed and produced a more fragmented record than the previous paper version. The paper, they claim, makes three key contributions. First, it demonstrates the socio-technical complexity of IS standards and standardization efforts. Second, it provides an empirical case showing how this complexity may generate reflexive processes that undermine the initial aims of standardization. Third, the paper suggests a theoretical interpretation of this phenomenon by means of complexity theory and the theory of reflexive modernization (p. 564). IS standards have a socio-technical complexity and can be studied from a number of perspectives – firstly the role of network externalities especially those that make standards increasingly difficult to change; complexity also is considered relevant as there is a variety of work practices and organisational structures that need to be considered; additionally we need to consider the speed of technical change and its impact on standards. Also there is the increased heterogeneity of the potential actors to be considered. Complexity meant that the attempt to achieve order actually resulted in disorder as multiplicities, inconsistencies, ambivalences and ambiguities emerged. It is clear that the close intertwining of technical standards with local and highly professional work practices (in terms of professional disciplines and geography) provided an intense socio-technical complexity. The author's further comment that to some extent our case represents a general class of problems associated with the interactions between the complexity of information infrastructures, information processing, and local work practices (p. 577). Thus socio-technical complexity is a major issue within the search for IS standards and it is only possible to mitigate this by attempting to simplify.

Schwaninger (2006), in contrast, considers theories of viability as an orientator to help actors in the socio-technical domain to cope with complexity. Here he looks at both variants of the viability theory to consider their potential in respect of social systems and finds that the systems are in fact complementors rather than competitors. System viability has been made familiar by the work of Stafford Beer (1979) through his Viable System Model (VSM) whereby social systems cope with complexity by means of adaptation- and learning-processes in which control and communication play a decisive role (p. 338). Autonomy is crucial and basic within the system as it has the freedom and responsibility to regulate itself which implies adaptation and learning, this autonomy being limited by the interdependence of hierarchies and functions. Autonomy, of course, is a key component within socio-technical theory itself.

We see yet another theme emerging with Preda (2006) and the case of the Stock Ticker in financial markets. The Stock Ticker was invented in 1867 as a printing telegraph powered by a battery that printed onto a paper tape the name of the security being traded and the stock price. In 1960 it was upgraded to become electronic. The theory presented is again not specifically socio-technical theory, but rather theory related to financial and economic technicalities; in addition the concept that technology contributes to developing new paths of social action is discussed.

Verbong and Geels (2007) look at the Dutch electricity system from 1960-2004. In particular they consider the change to renewable options and the barriers to making a transition to sustainability, looking at socio-technical dynamics, problems and windows of opportunity. There are three interlinked parts to the socio-technical regime: the network of actors and social groups; the formative and normative rules that guide the actors; and the material and technical elements in the electricity generating activities. These existing regimes are inter-linked and locked (we have seen this as a theme within VSM, as discussed above in Schwaninger) in dependency due to vested interests and sunk capital as well as organisational capital and norms. There is also a socio-technical macro landscape which forms the external environment within which regimes may change, but new technologies find it hard to break through without intervention. In the example given there was Government intervention and a subsequent change in the rules and social networks. Technical adjustments were required and the transition continues to shift through co-evolution and is heavily influenced by external realities.

We now come to the paper by Herrmann, Loser, and Jahnke of 2007. This was in a Special Edition of the Learning Organisations (edited by Coakes and Ramirez) on knowledge sharing within socio-technical contexts. Here they discuss what they call the Socio-technical Walkthrough which combines a communication process within a set of workshops to provide the specifications of a socio-technical system under development. Knowledge

would be shared through these workshops and a more successful system, it is claimed, would be developed. Systems theory is used as the basis for the underpinning discussions, in particular that of Maturana and Varela (1980). They approach the socio-technical paradigm as "the study of the relationships and interrelationships between the social and technical parts of any systems" (Coakes, 2002, p. 5) (p. 452)...whereby using the socio-technical model of Coakes (2002, p. 11) these components are people, tasks, structure and technology as seen in relation to their environment. The systems they describe evolved with contributions from the users and stakeholders, and participants valued the discussions conducted in the workshops.

Lyytinen and Newman (2008) contribute to the theory discussion with a paper about a Punctuated Socio-Technical Information System Change model. They claim that The model recognizes both incremental and punctuated socio-technical change in the context of information systems at multiple levels – the work system level, the building system level, and the organizational environment. It uses socio-technical event sequences and their properties to explain how a change outcome emerged (p. 589). Change is often, they say, seen as process and planned outcomes frequently go awry due to unexpected occurrences. Linear concepts of change also fail to realise the complexity inherent in the change process. Change is episodic, and attempts to explain these complex features are made by the new model which can cope with punctuated change at many levels. This model accepts that such change for IS can be extremely difficult due to routinisation, cognitive inertia and motivational gaps; along with other issues including emergence and unpredictability.

Our final paper for discussion and critique is that by Cassano-Piche and Jamieson (2009). Again this explores a different field of application from previous papers; here looking at food safety and BSE. As with so many of these areas the context under consideration was that of a complex socio-technical system, but here a risk framework by Rasmussen (1997) was tested to try and explain the accidents and failures in food production. The outcome was that the predictions made by the framework were found to be true in their exploration; from this they contend that we should consider why complex socio-technical systems often fail to be safe and to that accidents continue to happen.

CONCLUSION

This article, as the second in a series, has continued the task of a meta-analysis of (mainly) business journal articles that use socio-technical theory or socio-technology methods as a dominant theme in their writing. We have shown through the charts and Tables the trends in authors and publishing, and subject areas that these papers address. Through content analysis we have identified the constant themes and addressed the development of theory from 1968 – the earliest publication date found through our BSC search for the two terms – socio-technical and socio-technology - to current dates. We can see a trend that appears to show a revival of interest in the ideas of socio-technology during the 1990s. This trend seems to coincide with the expansion of work systems and the realisation that these new systems were as prone to failures or limitations as early technical system implementations. Authors have gone back to the theory of how technology impacts on work and job design that was pioneered by the Tavistock Institute in the 1950s. Authors used this to explain issues surrounding such diverse topics as eBusiness, health technologies, mass customisation, call centre operations, and mobile phones. We have looked at the development of the theory and how the papers have applied it. We have explored the difference between the early ideas and the later, in specific fields of study beginning with Human Resources in the very early years and moving into Job and Work Design and Operations Management in the middle years;

with the emphasis moving towards Information Technology in the latter years and most recently Knowledge Management and Philosophy.

Through this exercise we have learnt a significant amount about the issues surrounding the use of the BSC repository and the associated search engine. For example, we have seen results, their categorisation and their presentation change significantly within a short time period. Therefore we recommend that future researchers save each full set of results and texts after performing a search, in order to stabilise the data that they will be using. For instance some repositories will export the results to EndNote or another referencing system, for storage.

While further analysis is required (see below), we have shown that in total socio-technical article publishing has recently recovered from the relative decline of the 1980s and 1990s. Within the socio-technical area, the topics of Work and Technology are receiving increased attention in the more recent sample we have explored. At the same time, the study of Personal and Group Behaviour, and of Change, as well as the study of major Stakeholder Groups, is waning.

Clearly this is not a finished task, as we still need to consider these trends against those of the other searches. This will be carried out in our further papers, using the understanding we have derived from this paper and comparing our current themes with those found in these different spelling variants. In paper 3 we will consider both of the spelling variants in the alternative UK repository known as the World of Knowledge/ Science which also subscribes to 10,000 journals mostly in the engineering, computing, social science, and arts and humanities fields of study. A current search (August 2009) of this repository looking for both spelling variants, shows some 1600 papers published – of course, some of these will be duplicates of those already studied in P1 and P2, but most will be new as they are drawn from different academic fields. In paper four we will consider US publishing as a separate topic.

Additionally a future paper will further analyse trends over time in the popularity of topics.

Given the recent recovery in socio-technical publishing, we await with interest the evolution of such thought and publishing, which we will continue to assess.

REFERENCES

Beer, S. (1979). *The Heart of Enterprise*. Chichester, UK: Wiley.

Berkhout, F. (2006). Normative expectations in systems innovation. *Technology Analysis and Strategic Management*, *18*(3/4), 299–311. doi:10.1080/09537320600777010

Bostrom, R. P., & Heinen, S. J. (1977). MIS Problems and Failures: A Socio-Technical Perspective Part I: The Causes. *Management Information Systems Quarterly*, *1*(3), 17–32. doi:10.2307/248710

Busha, C. H., & Harter, S. P. (1980). *Research Methods in Librarianship – Techniques and Interpretation*. New York: Academic Press.

Cassano-Piche, Vicente, K. J., & Jamieson, G. A. (2009). A test of Rasmussen's risk management framework in the food safety domain: BSE in the UK. *Theoretical Issues in Ergonomics Science*, *10*, 283–304. doi:10.1080/14639220802059232

Clegg, C. W. (2000). Socio-technical Principles for System Design. *Applied Ergonomics*, *31*, 463–477. doi:10.1016/S0003-6870(00)00009-0

Coakes, E., & Ramirez, A. (2007). Solving Problems in Knowledge Sharing with Sociotechnical Approaches. *The Learning Organization*, *14*(5).

Cook, S. C., & Ferris, L. J. T. (2007). Re-evaluating systems engineering as a framework for tackling systems issues. *Systems Research and Behavioral Science*, *24*(2), 169–181. doi:10.1002/sres.822

Cummings, T. G. (1978). Self-Regulating Work Groups: A Socio-Technical Synthesis. *Academy of Management Review*, *3*(3), 625–634. doi:10.2307/257551

Davis, L. E., & Taylor, J. C. (1972). *Design of Jobs*. London: Penguin.

Eijnatten, F. M. V., & Zwaan, A. V. D. (1998). The Dutch approach to organizational design: an alternative approach to business process reengineering. *Human Relations*, *51*, 289–318. doi:10.1177/001872679805100305

Emery, M. (Ed.). (1993). *Participative Design for Participative Democracy*. Canberra, Australia: Australian National University.

Flood, R. L., & Jackson, M. C. (1991a). *Creative Problem Solving*. Chichester, UK: Wiley.

Flood, R. L., & Jackson, M. C. (1991b). Total systems intervention: a practical face to critical systems thinking. *Systems Practice*, *4*, 197–213. doi:10.1007/BF01059565

Gerwin, D., & Kolodny, H. (1992). *Management of Advanced Manufacturing Technology*. New York: Wiley.

Gilbert, C., Amalberti, R., Laroche, H., & Paries, J. (2007). Errors and Failures: Towards a New Safety Paradigm. *Journal of Risk Research*, *10*(7), 959–975. doi:10.1080/13669870701504764

Globerson, S., & Salvendy, G. (1984). A Socio-Technical Accounting Approach to the Evaluation of Job Performance. *International Journal of Operations & Production Management*, *4*(3), 36–42. doi:10.1108/eb054718

Gray, P., & Hovav, A. (2008). From Hindsight to Foresight: Applying Futures Research Techniques in Information Systems. *Communications of AIS*, (22), 211-234.

Gregoriades, A., & Sutcliffe, A. G. (2006). Automated assistance for human factors analysis in complex systems. *Ergonomics, 49*(12/13), 1265–1287. doi:10.1080/00140130600612721

Hackman, R., & Oldham, G. R. (1976). Motivation Through the Design of Work: Test of a Theory. *Organizational Behavior and Human Performance, 16*, 250–279. doi:10.1016/0030-5073(76)90016-7

Hanseth, O., Jacucci, E., Grisot, M., & Aanestad, M. (2006). Reflexive Standardization: Side Effects and Complexity in Standard Making. *Management Information Systems Quarterly, 30*, 563–581.

Hermann, K. (2007). Post mass production paradigm (PMPP) trajectories. *Journal of Manufacturing Technology Management, 18*(8), 1022–1037. doi:10.1108/17410380710828316

Herrmann, T., Hoffmann, M., Loser, K.-U., & Kunau, G. (2004). A modelling method for the development of groupware applications as socio-technical systems. *Behaviour & Information Technology, 23*(2), 119–135. doi:10.1080/01449 290310001644840

Herrmann, T., & Loser, K.-U. (1999). Vagueness in models of socio-technical systems. *Behaviour & Information Technology, 18*(5), 313–323. doi:10.1080/014492999118904

Herrmann, T., Loser, K.-U., & Jahnke, I. (2007). Sociotechnical walkthrough: a means for knowledge integration. *The Learning Organization, 14*(5), 450–464. doi:10.1108/09696470710762664

ISO. (1999). *International Standard 113407, Human Centred Design*. International Standards Organisation.

Kansal, V. (2006). Enterprise Resource Planning Implementation: A Case Study. *Journal of American Academy of Business, 9*(1), 165–170.

Klein, L. (2005). *Working Across the Gap: The Practice of Social Science in Organisations*. London: H. Karnac.

Klopp, M., & Hartmann, M. (1999). *Das Fledermausprinzip – Strategische Früherkennung für Unternehmen*. Stuttgart, Germany: Logis.

Kroes, P., Franssen, M., Poel, I., & van de, & Ottens, M. (2006). Treating socio-technical systems as engineering systems: some conceptual problems. *Systems Research and Behavioral Science, 23*(6), 803–814. doi:10.1002/sres.703

Kuipers, B. S., & De Witte, M. C. (2005). Teamwork: a case study on development and performance. *International Journal of Human Resource Management, 16*(2), 185–201. doi:10.1080/0958519042000311390

Liu, L., Yu, E., & Mylopoulos, J. (2003). Security and privacy requirements analysis within a social setting. In *Proceedings of the IEEE Joint International Conference on Requirements Engineering*, Los Alamitos, CA (pp. 151-161). Washington, DC: IEEE Computer Society Press.

Lucas, H. C. (1975). *Toward Creative Systems Design*. New York: Columbia University Press.

Lyytinen, K., & Newman, M. (2008). Explaining information systems change: a punctuated socio-technical change model. *European Journal of Information Systems, 17*(6), 589–613. doi:10.1057/ejis.2008.50

Majchrzak, A., & Borys, B. (2001). Generating testable socio-technical systems theory. *Journal of Engineering and Technology Management, 18*(3/4), 219–241. doi:10.1016/S0923-4748(01)00035-2

Manz, C. C., & Stewart, G. L. (1997). Attaining Flexible Stability by Integrating Total Quality Management and Socio-technical Systems Theory. *Organization Science, 8*(1), 59–70. doi:10.1287/orsc.8.1.59

Marples, D. L. (1968). Roles in a Manufacturing Organization. *Journal of Management Studies*, *5*(2), 183–204. doi:10.1111/j.1467-6486.1968.tb00828.x

Maturana, H., & Varela, F. (1987). *The tree of knowledge: Biological roots of human understanding*. Boston: New Science Library.

Mirijamdotter, A., Somerville, M. M., & Holst, M. (2006). An Interactive and Iterative Evaluation Approach for Creating Collaborative Learning Environments. *Electronic Journal of Information Systems Evaluation*, *9*(2), 83–92.

Mumford, E. (2006). The story of socio-technical design: reflections on its successes, failures and potential. *Information Systems Journal*, *16*(4), 317–342. doi:10.1111/j.1365-2575.2006.00221.x

Olphert, W., & Damodaran, L. (2007). Citizen Participation and engagement in the Design of e-Government Services: The Missing Link in Effective ICT Design and Delivery. *Journal of the Association for Information Systems*, *8*(9), 491–507.

Palmquist, M. (2005). Retrieved from http://www.colo-state.edu/Depts/WritingCenter/references/research/content/page2.htm

Pava, C. (1983). *Managing New Office Technology: An Organizational Strategy*. New York: Free Press.

Pava, C. (1986). Redesigning Socio-technical Systems Design: Concepts and Methods for the 1990s. *The Journal of Applied Behavioral Science*, *22*(2), 201–222. doi:10.1177/002188638602200303

Porra, J., & Hirschheim, R. (2007). A Lifetime of Theory and Action on the Ethical Use of Computers: A Dialogue with Enid Mumford. *Journal of the Association for Information Systems*, *8*(9), 467–478.

Preda, A. (2006). Socio-Technical Agency in Financial Markets: The Case of the Stock Ticker. *Social Studies of Science*, *35*(5), 753–782. doi:10.1177/0306312706059543

Rasmussen, J. (1997). Risk Management in a Dynamic Society: A Modelling Problem. *Safety Science*, *27*, 183–213. doi:10.1016/S0925-7535(97)00052-0

Schwaninger, M. (2006). Theories of viability: a comparison. *Systems Research and Behavioral Science*, *23*(3), 337–347. doi:10.1002/sres.731

Soros, G. (1998). *The Crisis of Global Capitalism*. London: Little, Brown and Company.

Stahl, B. C. (2007). ETHICS, Morality and Critique: An Essay on Enid Mumford's Socio-Technical Approach. *Journal of the Association for Information Systems*, *8*(9), 479–490.

Trist, E., & Murray, H. (1993). *The Social Engagement of Social Sciences* (*Vol. 2*). Philadelphia: University of Pennsylvania.

Ulbo de Sitter, L., Friso den Hertog, J., & Dankbaar, D. (1997). From complex organizations with simple jobs to simple organizations with complex jobs. *Human Relations*, *50*(5), 497–534. doi:10.1177/001872679705000503

Ulich, E., Schupbach, H., Schilling, A., & Kuark, J. (1990). Concepts and procedures of work psychology for the analysis, evaluation and design of advanced manufacturing systems: a case study. *International Journal of Industrial Ergonomics*, (5): 47–57. doi:10.1016/0169-8141(90)90027-Y

van Merkerk, R., & Robinson, D. (2006). Characterizing the emergence of a technological field: Expectations, agendas and networks in Lab-on-a-chip technologies. *Technology Analysis and Strategic Management*, *18*(3/4), 411–428. doi:10.1080/09537320600777184

Verbong, G., & Geels, F. (2007). The ongoing energy transition: Lessons from a socio-technical, multi-level analysis of the Dutch electricity system (1960–2004). *Energy Policy, 35*(2), 1025–1037. doi:10.1016/j.enpol.2006.02.010

Von Bertalanffy, L. (1950). The Theory of Open Systems in Physics and Biology. *Science*, (3): 23–29. doi:10.1126/science.111.2872.23

Von Förster, H. (1981). *Observing Systems: Selected Papers of Heinz von Förster*. Seaside, CA: Intersystems Publications.

Von Glasersfeld, E. (1996). *Radikaler Konstruktivismus*. Frankfurt, Germany: Suhrkamp.

Yu, E. (1994). *Modelling strategic relationships for process reengineering* (Tech. Rep. No. DKBS-TR-94-6). Toronto, Canada: University of Toronto.

This work was previously published in The International Journal of Sociotechnology and Knowledge Development, Volume 2, Issue 2, edited by Elayne Coakes, pp. 1-34, copyright 2010 by IGI Publishing (an imprint of IGI Global).

Chapter 2
Designing Visionary Leadership Teams

Martin Johnson
The Thalidomide Trust, UK

ABSTRACT

Nigel Sykes' 3E's concept is examined against established theory and recent work in Organizational Behaviour. The possibility that this concept offers a way of developing social synergy in work groups is explored, and considered in the context of socio-technical systems. 3E's is based on the categorisation of people in the workplace into roles labelled "Envisioners" "Enablers" or "Enactors". Role theory is explored, and its relevance to organizational success. The importance of the affective component in motivation and decision-making is identified. A research study is reported testing the 3E's concept which shows that it corresponds with measurable differences of motivational need, personality factors, and decision-making between individuals. The characteristics of successful group decision-making are linked with the 3E's differentiation. The 3E's model offers the possibility of improving person-role fit, and thus organisational performance. It proposes an integrated design for the selection and operation of teams, offering a person-role fit, optimal decision-making behaviour, and consequent social synergy.

INTRODUCTION

Leadership teams have been explored extensively, and a number of different schemas have been proposed – including that of Belbin (1982), but also Holland (1985). The main finding of these

researchers has been that leadership teams need to contain a diversity of members, with different skills. Collins (2001) reports that successful organizations have balanced leadership teams whose members possess different capabilities, while Miller (1990) shows that unbalanced leadership teams are connected with organisational failures. The inference is that enduring organisational suc-

DOI: 10.4018/978-1-4666-0200-7.ch002

Copyright © 2012, IGI Global. Copying or distributing in print or electronic forms without written permission of IGI Global is prohibited.

cess depends on the ability of leaders to identify and maintain a diversity of capabilities within their teams, thus creating social synergy (Whitworth, 2009).

While leadership teams traditionally develop over a period of time, a range of current working practices preclude the direct personal contact and relationship-building that normally precedes and informs appointments into organisational roles. This includes such things as online collaborative work groups or geographically-separated teams working on short-term projects for multi-national organisations (e.g. using enterprise information systems). The technical aspects of this kind of work arrangement are usually designed to ensure speed and security of information, together with customised databases ensuring efficient system or project control.

This leaves open how one can assess people's fitness for roles. Neglect of the social aspect (role expectation, person-role fit) of work groups using information systems and technology is a potential cause of problems. The fact that modern work teams are almost inevitably socio-technical systems is not widely appreciated, but 3E's offers the possibility of social contextualisation leading to the "higher level system" proposed by Whitworth (2009). There is an obvious problem in attempting to achieve the social synergy arising from a credible person-role fit where technology serves to obstruct traditional human contact. There is nowadays extensive use of psychometric systems as an adjunct to team-building (e.g. the Myers-Briggs test) in the hope that this type of analysis and feedback can help determine the person-role fit within teams, and accelerate the acceptance of personality differences between team members.

Various psychometric tools have been devised to try and produce measures of difference between people, mainly with ambiguous results. As far as personality factor research goes, the most confident finding is that the "Conscientiousness" factor is the only one that consistently correlates

with individual performance (McCrae & Costa 2006). The reader might be forgiven for thinking this was (a) a statement of the obvious, and (b) a good example of circular reasoning!

This present study is based on the work of Nigel Sykes[1] (Warwick Business School, Centre for Small and Medium-sized Enterprises (SMEs)). He has proposed a team structure for developing organisations which he argues could represent a critical success factor. This proposal implies that it is possible to establish a "human psychological process of meaning exchange" (Whitworth 2009) as a result of acknowledging the differing psychologies of people occupying different organisational roles. (And therefore differences in their styles of behaviour and communication).

There is little obvious difference between the team sizes involved in developing SMEs, and work groups with operational autonomy formed within larger organisations for various purposes. All such groups or teams are, in effect, attempts to create autonomous workgroups (a term for groups combining a socio-technical systems perspective with group based job enrichment design – Furnham, 2005). This concept is therefore being explored because of its potential relevance to all such work groups. If valid, this offers an approach particularly helpful for the social synergy of (geographically) remote work groups reliant on information systems for coordinating joint working.

Sykes proposes the categorisation of people in the workplace into roles labelled "Envisioners" "Enablers" or "Enactors" (3E's) corresponding with intrinsic differences between individuals. His taxonomy is based on the Biblical roles of Prophet, Priest, and King,[2] which he argues reflects the fundamental diversity of the optimal work group.

3E's prescribes the basis for building an integrated leadership team and its critical internal relationships. These roles are balanced around a shared "idea" (Figure 1). It will be shown that the emotional component of decision-making is very significant, and that the 3E's model could

Figure 1. 3E's concept showing principal "zones"

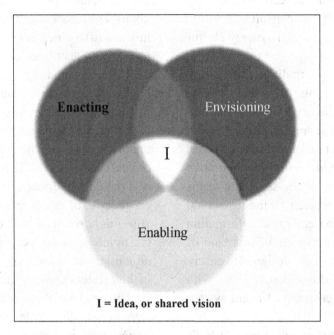

I = Idea, or shared vision

operate effectively as a result of prescribing an optimal structure for group decision-making. If this concept is valid (i.e. relates both to genuine patterns of work roles and to measurable differences between individuals) then it should be possible to design an on-line measurement tool which could help identify a broad optimal role fit for each work group member.

The 3E's roles correspond with descriptions of individual behaviours:

- **Envisioner.** Given to Expansive thinking, inventive, innovative, and creative. Characterised by creative imagination, and the desire to communicate this. A broad-focussed perception, which could appear to be a behaviour pattern of "flitting about" between ideas, appreciating novelty, and difficulty concentrating on a single task. Some emotional volatility likely.
- **Enabler.** A good organizer, an interpreter of vision, good at processing ideas and happy with detail. Friendly and likeable, but also good at managing and organising people, a "people-person". Someone who can be readily motivated and enthused by the output of the Envisioner.
- **Enactor.** Takes tasks to implementation, concerned with progress, and has focussed attention. Entrepreneurial, very goal-oriented, and with the ability to gather and lead teams in executing the task. May well have the ability to stand back and see "the big picture" strategically, but only with the aim of focussing tightly on the necessary sequence of tasks.

LITERATURE SURVEY

3E's resembles the analyses of Belbin (1982) and Holland (1985). Belbin identified nine management roles (Implementer, Shaper, Completer/Finisher, Plant, Monitor/Evaluator, Specialist, Coordinator, Team Worker, Resource Investigator) within management roles grouped into three sets similar to the 3E's classifications:

- The "Doing/Acting" group includes tasks of the Enactor.
- The "Problem solving" group includes tasks of the Envisioner.
- The "People/Feelings" group includes tasks of the Enabler.

Holland (1985) identified six categories of people types and roles in his RIASEC model (Realistic, Investigative, Artistic, Social, Enterprising, and Conventional). He says work environments take on the characteristics of those who populate them because they reflect their preferences. Holland's work relates to organisations with large numbers of employees, but is concerned with differentiation between all employees, not just those in the management teams. Both Belbin and Holland are describing the diversity of people occupying workplace roles.

Many researchers have explored the ways in which people approach the decision to accept potential roles in organisations (role expectations). Factors include the personal qualities of role occupants as well as the behaviour expected of them (Lennard and Bernstein 1966; Sarbin and Williams 1953; Hargeaves 1967; Kahn *et al* 1964). Role clarity has been shown to be a very important factor in determining how people behave in their roles (Lyons, 1971). People feel a need for role clarity, and it enhances job satisfaction while reducing employee turnover. Organizational roles develop over time, and individuals play an important part in "making" roles that they have (Haga et al., 1974, March & March, 1977; 1978).

Kahn et al. (1964) showed that men suffering from role ambiguity experienced lower job satisfaction, higher job-related tension, greater futility and lower self-confidence. Occupying a clear and appropriate workplace role seems closely related to individual wellbeing. Dearborn & Simon (1958) and Bagby (1957) showed how

roles are capable of radically affecting the perceptions of individuals confronted with the same set of information. These findings indicate that it is important to ensure that people are employed in well-defined roles, and that occupying a clear role may improve the performance of individuals.

Hackman and Oldham (1980) theorised that there are three critical psychological states relevant to the world of work, namely *"Experienced meaningfulness, Experienced responsibility, and Knowledge of Results"*. "Experienced Meaningfulness" was the combination of "Skill variety, Task identity, and Task significance". The first of these depends on the capability of the individual, the second on their correct positioning and resourcing in the workplace, while the third depends on relationships with the wider team (social context).

Clear definition of roles, person-role fit, and an arrangement of team members into an appropriate social context are therefore critical for:

- Individual well-being;
- Quality of working life;
- Individual and team performance in the workplace.

Collins (2001) and Miller (1990) report studies of the success and failure of large corporations. Collins identified companies which outperformed their peers over periods of decades, and studied the range of factors that could be related to such performance. Analysis of the management teams showed that successful organizations have balanced leadership teams whose members possess different capabilities yet share a common purpose and set of values. Miller's studies were of major corporate failures, which he linked to a taxonomy of four leadership types and a culture which was dominated by only one of these types at any one time.

Augoustinos and Walker (1995) note that *"the development of consensual knowledge demonstrates the inherently social nature of cognition – the societal context within which cognitive and affective processes take place interacts with and determines individual processes"*. Work groups are innately involved in *"the development of contextual knowledge"*, so one implication of the findings of Collins (2001) and Miller (1990) is that societal context is a critical factor for effective teamwork, which 3E's proposes to overcome. 3E's is thus a socio-technical proposal, prescribing a societal context which facilitates *"cognitive and affective processes"*.

MEASURING INDIVIDUAL DIFFERENCES

Furnham (2005) identifies five basic factors for exploring the variables involved in personality and work-related behaviour. These are:

- **Ability** – carrying out multiple processes to achieve a specific goal.
- **Demographic factors** – e.g. sex, age, class, education.
- **Intelligence** –abstract and critical thinking.
- **Motivation** – a concept that refers to the tendency to attend to some stimuli rather than others, with accompanying emotion, and the drive to cause some actions rather than others.
- **Personality** – all those fundamental traits or characteristics of the person that endure over time and that account for consistent patterns of behaviour.

In this analysis, 3E's appears to be considering individuals on the basis of their role preferences and relationship to the shared "Idea". It assumes that an "affective" (i.e. emotional) reaction to the corporate vision is the trigger for subsequent motivated behaviour. There is no discussion about the differences in skills or competences between individuals, or the impact of age and experience on individuals and the organisation. From Furnham's analysis, therefore, the only measures we

can consider are the variables of motivation and personality. And, since 3E's proposes that motivation arises when the corporate vision is communicated, then the appropriate field of motivation is intrinsic motivation.

MOTIVATIONAL DIFFERENCES

3E's implies that the intrinsic needs of the individual require an appropriate extrinsic setting before motivated behaviour occurs. This is strongly supported by the work on Goal-setting (Locke & Latham, 1990, Latham & Kinne, 1974), which shows that individuals will perform as an effective team when an appropriate goal-setting methodology is implemented. The relevant findings about goal-setting were that higher performance would be more likely if:

- Goals were challenging and specific;
- Task feedback is provided;
- Team members are involved in setting the goals.

3E's offers a framework based around a shared goal, so if the differentiation into the three roles is related to differences in individual intrinsic motivation, then higher team performance should follow.

SUCCESSFUL SHARED VISION

The 3E's concept centres on a shared goal (corporate vision - the "I" in Figure 1). Johnson (1999) demonstrated that successful corporate vision:

1. Shows a future achievement aim that can readily be visualised;
2. Receives contributions from a variety of sources;
3. Attracts the involvement of individuals with the specialist skills needed;

4.   Can be communicated easily;

5.   Is powerfully motivational;

6.   Intends to serve an important need for other people;

7.   Accords with the values of prospective supporters.

Characteristics 1, 2 and 3 relate directly to the goal setting methodology outlined by Locke and Latham (1990). 3E's proposes that the Envisioner "attracts the involvement" of the people who come "around the shared vision". The communication of the vision (the transition from the Envisioner zone to the Enabler zone) is when motivated behaviour becomes evident, so this aspect corresponds to characteristics 4 and 5 above. The words "needs" and "values" relate to emotional engagement with the task, so comes (on the 3E's model) prior to the other characteristics in the proposed sequence of events. This also reflects the findings of Collins (2001) on the importance of "common purpose" and "shared values" in creating a high-performing organisation. Therefore, the Envisioning task produces an effective response (emotional engagement) with the shared vision manifesting in motivated behaviour.

These factors indicate a link between goal-setting, individual motivation, internal group relationships, and an emotional component involved in group decisions. However, unless there is differentiation in motivated behaviour related to differences between the intrinsic needs of the individual, then the idea that the three 3E's roles relate to intrinsic differences could not be upheld.

MOTIVATIONAL NEEDS

McClelland (1987) cited several motivational needs studies on Need for Achievement (nAch), Need for Power (nPow), and Need for Affiliation (nAffil). He reports that characteristic behaviours of people with strong **nAch** include:

- Taking moderate calculated risks;
- Being persistent pursuing goals;
- Trying to "do things better";
- Being restless in work, wanting to move on to new tasks;
- Seeking higher status.

People with strong **nAffil** tend to:

- Have extensive interpersonal networks.
- Be more concerned with how the group is getting along than with completion of the task.
- Act to avoid conflict.
- Be less likely to get promoted to high-level management.

nPow measures a need for influence and/or impact. It relates to

- Persuading and influencing skills,
- Seeking management jobs,
- Attempting to establish control over their environment.

Cormack and New (1997) say these three needs underlie the majority of individual behaviour in the workplace, and explain why people prefer some work settings to others. Behaviour associated with strong nAch is similar to that attributed to the Enactor, and also resembles descriptions of characteristic entrepreneurial behaviour. Behaviour associated with strong nAffil is descriptive of the Enabler.

PERSONALITY FACTORS

Personality factor analysis is based on extrinsic aspects of individual behaviour. The analysis began with studies of words used to describe individual behaviour, and these were then grouped into sets of related words. There is now a broad acceptance of the "Big Five" personality factors (Goldberg, 1990): Neuroticism, Extraversion, Openness, Agreeableness, and Conscientiousness. Each of these five factors incorporates a wide range of behavioural descriptions. McCrae & Costa (2006) note that these factors remain stable across time, and list up to six facets for each dimension. Again, if the 3E's roles are based on intrinsic aspects of individual behaviour, then this should be identifiable by the external (extrinsic) aspects of their behaviour as measured by a "Big 5" psychometric.

Burch *et al* (2006) show that the Psychoticism scale of the Eysenck Personality Questionnaire (EPQ) is related to divergent thinking and creativity. Psychoticism is a compound variable on the "Big 5" dimensions, correlating with low Agreeableness, low Conscientiousness, and high Neuroticism (Costa & McCrae, 1992). The Envisioner is described as someone who is creative and inventive so the Psychoticism profile should be evident.

Conscientiousness facets such as order, dutifulness, self-discipline, and deliberation contra-indicate the popular image of the creative individual, though they are descriptive of the Enabler. In addition, the Extraversion facets of activity, and excitement seeking would identify the Envisioner, though McCrae & Costa (2006) note that assertiveness, another facet of extraversion, is an attribute of people who are natural leaders (a trait of the Enactor).

Openness to experience includes the areas of fantasy, ideas, and aesthetics, all of which are linked to creativity and inventiveness, and should indicate the Envisioner, while openness to actions is indicative of the Enactor. Agreeableness (because of the relationship and interpersonal skills ascribed to the type) appears indicative of the Enabler, particularly with facets such as trust, compliance, and tender-mindedness.

DECISION-MAKING DIFFERENCES, FLAWED JUDGMENT AND INTUITION

Tversky and Kahneman (1974) discovered a number of systematic biases in individual decision-making and judgment which they titled "heuristics", similar in cognitive terms to optical illusions. One of these heuristics is "Anchoring and Adjustment". They found that if people are shown a number (e.g. on a wheel of fortune) and then asked to estimate a completely unrelated quantity they do not already know (e.g. the number of nations in Africa, or the population of Turkey) their answers will be influenced by the number they were first shown. Piattelli-Palmarini (1994) demonstrated that these heuristics appear to be common across countries and cultures, suggesting they are intrinsic features of human brain function.

The brain is capable of recognising and reacting to situations before the individual consciously realises what is happening. Gladwell (2005) shows that people can develop positive heuristics; mental shortcuts which help us make correct decisions "in the blink of an eye". He describes several people with "intuitive expertise", and explains how these capabilities can be improved with training. Many successful leaders describe using intuition, or "gut decision-making" as key to their success (Buchanan & O'Connell, 2006).

Neuropsychology

Morse (2006) reports developments in the neuropsychology of decision making illuminating the relationship between "reason" and "emotion". The early assumptions of normative theory held that the more emotionally detached we could be, then the more accurate our decisions would be. When a person has brain damage affecting the prefrontal cortex, the area that processes emotions, they often struggle with making even routine decisions, even though they are able to comprehend all the factors relevant to the decision. Patients with injuries to parts of the limbic system, a group of brain structures important in generating emotions, are similarly affected. Morse (2006) asserts that the prefrontal cortex is the "seat of will power", by which he means the ability to take the long-term perspective in evaluating risks and rewards.

- Decision-making therefore involves a linkage between the emotional and rational aspects of individual behaviour.

Morse (2006) goes on to say *"people's decision-making and management styles probably arise from common motivational impulses in the brain...if management is hardwired to be more risk-seeking, or risk avoiding, or more driven to pursue a goal than to achieve it, that's going to affect how he manages and makes decisions".*

- The decision-making behaviour of individuals is therefore likely to demonstrate personality and motivational variations between individuals.

Group Decisions

Surowiecki (2006) defines three principal types of group decision-making problems (cognition, coordination, and cooperation). He shows how the diversity of groups tends to produce better decisions and more quickly than individuals acting alone, and also that effective group decision-making depends on a relationship based on equality and trust. People *"can coordinate themselves to achieve complex, mutually beneficial ends even if they're not really sure, at the start, what those ends are or what it will take to accomplish them".* Sykes, therefore, is possibly identifying the minimum range of behaviours and relationships in an ideal small group reflecting the range of diversity needed for effective group decision-making. The distribution could be:

- **Cognition:** problem solver (Envisioner),
- **Coordination:** directing team members for the execution of the task (Enactor),
- **Cooperation:** ensuring team members are properly supported and equipped, and understand the shared vision (Enabler).

Surowiecki uses the examples of the Apollo 13 mission of 1970, and the Columbia Space Shuttle disaster of 2003 to illustrate how the change in organisational culture of NASA in the intervening 30 years resulted in a radical change to NASA's decision-making processes. He argues that the capacity to deliver innovative solutions of the type that saved Apollo 13 had been lost through the progressive institutionalisation of the organisation. Had this not happened, it is likely that Columbia could have been saved. The ability of the organisation to generate solutions to unexpected emergencies had certainly been severely impaired. Following the 3E's model, it may be argued that NASA had diminished the role of the Envisioner at the critical level of decision-making.

These illustrations indicate a role appropriate to the Envisioner in decision making (innovative problem solving) which modern information systems arguably should facilitate rather than inhibit, especially if the need is to involve this capability at short notice (i.e. when there's an emergency taking place) and at some physical distance from the situation itself. The Envisioner could thus be a good candidate for developing a "role-technology fit" when the role is linked to appropriate information and communication systems.

SUMMARY

3E's appears to incorporate long-established findings and principles concerning management teams and workplace roles (Belbin, 1982; Holland, 1985).

- The benefits of matching people to roles and offering greater role clarity are substantiated by the work of Kahn et al (1964) and several other researchers.
- It is a prescriptive design for the social aspect of a socio-technical system.
- Furnham's (2005) five basic factors for exploring the variables involved in personality and work-related behaviour were considered. It was shown that only two of these, motivation and personality differences were relevant to 3E's.
- Motivational needs analysis (McClelland, 1987) and Big 5 personality factor analysis were found to offer measures potentially capable of discriminating between the 3E's types.
- A review of decision-making studies showed that this is related to the neuropsychology of the individual and is therefore another possible way of differentiating between individuals.
- The emotional component of decision-making was seen to be a critical factor.
- Surowiecki's (2006) typology of group decision-making problems resembles the 3E's typology.

As an organisational management/leadership model, 3E's appears to differ from earlier models in:

- Identifying a minimum of three key roles important in building successful organisations;
- Describing the relationship between these roles;
- Assuming that the different behaviours relate to intrinsic differences between people.

The idea of segregating organisational leadership roles has a long history, but does not appear to have been linked to a personality typology as simplified and distinct as proposed in 3E's. As this idea is based on the concept of three roles, the Envisioner, Enabler, and Enactor, it was considered feasible to test the concept by comparing role preferences with measures of motivation, personality, and decision-making.

RESEARCH QUESTIONS

This study aimed to establish if there was validity in the core proposition that Envisioning, Enabling, and Enacting correspond to three leadership roles and to differences between individuals. If these role preferences do not correspond to intrinsic differences, then the 3E's concept as a whole would effectively be invalidated. The specific question researched was:

- Is the self-identification of people with the roles of 'Envisioner', 'Enabler' and 'Enactor' measurable against the motivational needs, personality factors, and relevant dimensions of descriptive decision-making of those individuals?

Candidates were supplied with the 3E's role descriptions and were asked which role was "most like them". They were tested on Big 5 personality factors using an on-line test. Motivational needs were tested using the Cormack questionnaire (Cormack & New, 1997), and the Decision Making test was the (developmental) DNA test (Dewberry & Narendran on-line test 2006 version (Dewberry & Narendran, 2007; Soane, Dewberry, & Narendran, 2009)). They were then asked to specify their "ideal job". Candidates were aged from 20-65, 32 were women and 36 men. A number of ethnic minority and disabled candidates took part. All were recruited using personal networks, and approximately half the group had participated in seminars where 3E's had been explained, while half had not.

Of 68 respondents, 25 chose "Envisioner", 26 "Enabler", and 17 "Enactor" as the role "most like" themselves. No-one said that none of the roles resembled them. Given the small size of the group, this showed a remarkably even distribution between the three roles.

STATISTICAL VALIDATION OF RESULTS

The overall results for the Cormack and Big 5 tests were analysed, and these were compared with the self-selected sub-group results. 68 respondents completed both the Cormack questionnaire and the Big 5 questionnaire. The analysis studied the relationship of the overall and sub-group results to normative distribution and the standardised effect sizes (Hedges test) between the sub-groups and the overall results (used as a control). Negative figures for Skewness on every dimension showed a small variation from normal distribution, but these ranged from -.08 (Extraversion) to a maximum of -.48 (Conscientiousness). The majority of kurtosis scores were slightly negative, from -.73 (emotional stability) to .014 (nAffil), though agreeableness was positive at 0.78. The overall effect of the skew and kurtosis is small, and the skew probably results from the design and scoring systems of the tests themselves. The majority of findings are based on significant differences between the scores, reported simply in terms of "low" or "high".

RELATIONSHIP TO NORMATIVE DISTRIBUTION

The Hedges test showed several effect size scores greater than ± 0.3, although the full range of all scores only lay between −0.57 and +0.55. More significantly, two of the dimensional scores in each sub-group were greater than ± 0.5. These results show that despite the relatively small

sample size, the group as a whole was a reasonable representation of the normal population, and the sub-groups did not exhibit major deviations from the normal population.

EFFECT SIZE SCORES

The key effect size scores listed for the sub-groups show also that the variations in the scores on certain dimensions where the groups differed were statistically significant. For the Envisioners, the Conscientiousness score was −0.5 and the Openness score was 0.52. For the Enablers, the nPow score was −0.54 and the Openness score −0.57. The Enactors score for nAch was 0.55 and for Conscientiousness was 0.53. These highlight the dimensions where these sub-groups diverge from the overall group most markedly, and indicate that significant correlations with these dimensions in the respective groups should be expected.

MOTIVATIONAL NEEDS

The motivational needs test showed a significant difference between the relative average scores of "Enabler" group and the other two groups. Chart 1 (Figure 2) illustrates the pattern of an average nAffil score for Enablers higher than either the nAch and nPow scores.

GROUP MOTIVATIONAL CHARACTERISTICS:

- **Enactors:** the high score for nAch reflects descriptions of entrepreneurs and generalised leadership behaviour;
- **Enablers:** the high score for nAffil shows the relational focus expected of this group;
- **Envisioners:** At first sight, this group resembles the Enactors. Statistical analysis produced significant differences.

Figure 2. Chart 1: Motivational need scores averaged by grouped types

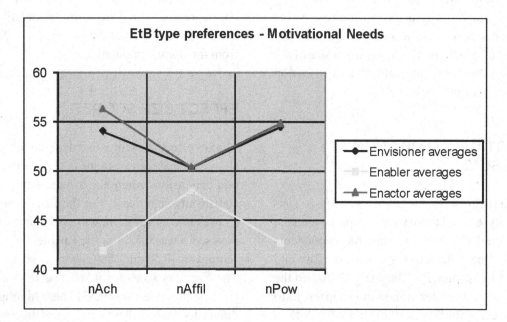

MOTIVATIONAL NEEDS STATISTICAL ANALYSIS

Chart 2 (Figure 3) shows the nAch: nAffil correlation discriminating between all three groups. For the Enablers, nAch covarys very closely with nAffil (by a factor of +0.79). This means that the profile of low nAch and high nAffil can be regarded as a "signature" of the Enabler (the two dimensions covarying consistently in this relationship). For the Enactors, a factor of 0.01 shows an almost complete lack of covariation, while for the Envisioners a correlation of +0.27 is significant.

BIG 5 PERSONALITY DIMENSIONS

The group average scores are shown in Chart 3(Figure 4). Characteristics are:

• **Extraversion.** Envisioners and Enactors high, and significantly higher than Enablers;

• **Conscientiousness.** Enablers and Enactors very high, significantly higher than Envisioners;

• **Emotional Stability.** Enablers and Enactors high, significantly higher than Envisioners;

• **Agreeableness.** Enablers high, higher than Envisioners and Enactors;

• **Openness to Experience.** Envisioners and Enactors high, significantly higher than Enablers.

• **Envisioners** show high Extraversion (E), lower Conscientiousness (C) and Agreeableness (A), low Emotional Stability (ES), and high Openness (O): the EPQ psychoticism pattern of low Agreeableness, low Conscientiousness, and high Neuroticism is evident, but it is important to note that here this is coupled with high Extraversion and high Openness.

• **Enablers** show low Extraversion, very high Conscientiousness, a mid-range score for Emotional Stability, high Agreeableness, and very low Openness. In the workplace,

Figure 3. Chart 2: Motivational needs correlations

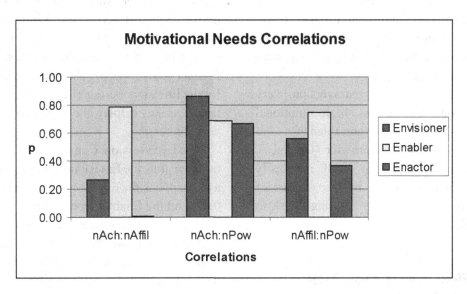

Figure 4. Chart 3: Big 5 personality factor scores averaged by grouped types

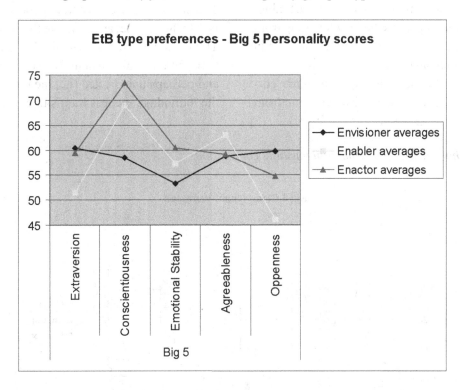

this would describe someone who is very companionable, thorough in their work, not very inquisitive or outgoing, and quite sensitive to others' feelings. An ideal team member, in fact.

- **Enactors** show high Extraversion, very high Conscientiousness, high Emotional Stability, medium Agreeableness, and a slightly lower score for Openness. Outgoing, very hot on detail, not easily deflected (particularly by the worries of others), and very likely to bring a task to completion.

BIG 5 PERSONALITY FACTORS: STATISTICAL ANALYSIS

In Chart 4 (Figure 5) the Extraversion: Agreeableness correlation separates the Enabler group from the other two, replicating the distinctions seen in the motivational analysis.

The Conscientiousness: Agreeableness correlation distinguishes the Envisioner group from the other two very sharply (from –0.21 to +0.73 marks an almost perfect distinction of 0.94 between the Envisioner and the Enactor, while a separation 0.75 between the Envisioner and the Enabler is also sharp). The negative covariation for the Envisioner group (i.e. the more Conscientiousness they display, the less Agreeableness) is very interesting.

The Extraversion: Conscientiousness correlations separate the Envisioner from the Enabler by a factor of 0.3, the Envisioner from the Enactor by 0.81, and the Enabler from the Enactor by 0.49. All of these are significant degrees of difference. The negative covariation between these dimensions for the Envisioner looks like a stereotypical description of the "Creative" type.

The Extraversion: Openness correlations resemble those for Extraversion: Conscientiousness. The Envisioners were separated from the Enablers by a factor of 0.22, and from the Enactors by 0.53. This negative covariation for the Envisioner group between these dimensions is also quite striking, and perhaps unexpected (i.e. the more Extravert the individual, the less Inquisitive etc.).

Figure 5. Chart 4: Big 5 discriminant variable correlations

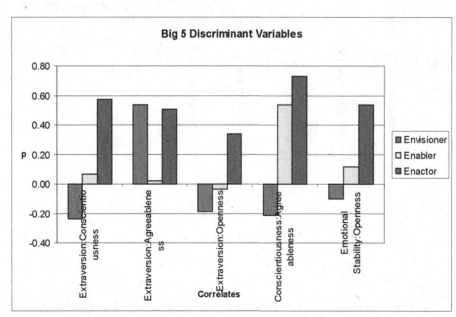

Table 1. Ideal job analysis categories

Envisioner	Enabler	Enactor
Creative Advertising	Accountant	Project Manager
TV/radio presenter	HR management	Chief Executive Officer
Graphic design	General Manager	Barrister
Creative Writing	Farmer	Medical Specialist
Scientific Research	Solicitor	Sales Representative
Communicator	Nurse	Military Officer
Artist	General Practitioner	Adventurous sports
Film Director	Pastor	Engineer
Inventor	Teacher	Explorer

Emotional Stability: Openness correlation also distinguishes the three groups in the same way as the Extraversion: Conscientiousness and Extraversion: Openness correlations. The separation here between the Envisioners and the Enactors is by a factor of 0.21, and between Envisioners and Enactors it is 0.64. Enablers and Enactors are separated by a factor of 0.43.

It is probable that the individual facets which result in a high score (for example) for Extraversion and Openness for Envisioners are different from those which produce an apparently similar result for Enactors, and this is underlined by the very distinct differences between the correlations. If we just consider correlations between the Big 5 dimension scores for the individuals in the different groups giving factors in excess of $\pm$ 0.5, we can see several. Those separating the Envisioner group from the Enactors by this amount include Extraversion: Openness, Conscientiousness: Agreeableness, and Emotional Stability: Openness.

IDEAL JOB ANALYSIS

A job category list was developed linking the 3E's role descriptions with a range of easily recognisable jobs (see Table 1). This was informed by Belbin (1982), Holland (1985) and Cormack and New (1997). It was used as a template to analyse the job preferences given by the candidates.

Of 22 "Envisioners" 12 (55%) conformed to the list, 3 preferring Enabler-type jobs, and 7 preferring Enactor-type jobs. Of 24 "Enablers" 22 (92%) conformed to the list, 2 preferring Envisioner-type jobs. Of 16 "Enactors" 13 (81%) conformed to the list, 2 preferring Enabler-type jobs, and one preferring an Envisioner-type job. Overall, 47/62 (76%) expressed job preferences consistent with the types of jobs predicted for their preferred roles.

The simple question: "what would your ideal job be?" proved to be a very challenging projective test, and for Enactors and Enablers produced an accuracy of response in excess of 80% and 90% respectively. Some candidates reported that it had taken them several days to reach a conclusion, because they felt forced to review their life aims very thoroughly. While developing the category list could improve the accuracy of scoring, it is plain that it is not immediately helpful for identifying "Envisioners".

DECISION ANALYSIS

Only 31 useable sets of DNA Decision tests were received, 5 Envisioners, 18 Enablers and 8 Enactors. Some respondents reported that they found this test very difficult. The different response rate for the different groups may itself be a reflection of the personality factor variation between the groups! While the sample was too small for reliable analysis, the differences shown in Chart 5 (Figure 6) are generally supportive of the expectations.

- Envisioners
  - showed greatest post-decision flexibility,
  - were most likely to procrastinate, and
  - least likely to make complex decisions slowly.
- Enablers were:
  - most likely to use conscious thought rather than intuition;
  - most likely to be self-disciplined;
  - most likely to actively seek information in making their decisions.
  - They were least likely to sequence their actions.

- Enactors
  - showed least post-decision flexibility, and
  - were least likely to postpone decisions or to procrastinate;
  - were most likely to be intuitive rather than conscious; and
  - make complex decisions slowly.

DISCUSSION

The 3E's model proposes an optimal structure of relationship between the three roles, and assigns characteristic behaviours to each of these roles. A study of the literature showed that this analysis of workplace roles resembles a number of others (e.g. Belbin, 1982; Holland, 1985), except that 3E's proposes a simpler initial set of distinctions between key roles. The description of the optimal behaviour of leadership teams was derived from

Figure 6. Chart 5: DNA decision test result

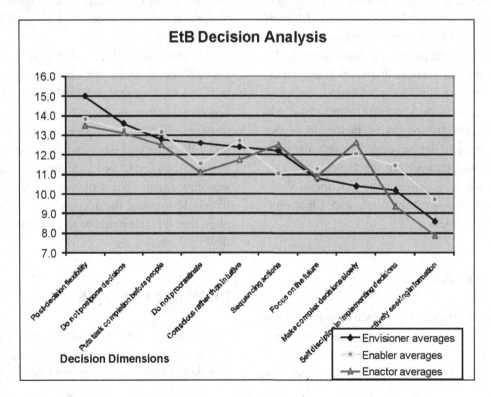

Miller (1990), but was also supported by Collins (2001). Sykes' attempt to synthesise these aspects seems original, as is his argument for a defined pattern of relationships between the three key members of the leadership team.

Surowiecki (2006) has proposed characteristics for group decision-making which resemble the relational proposals of 3E's, and has also described a diversity of three types of decisions possibly related to the 3E's type behaviours. The obvious starting point for an examination of the whole concept was evaluating the concept of three roles and corresponding people types.

The study explored possible ways of measuring the differences between people consistent with the different behaviours described for the three types labelled "Envisioner" "Enabler" and "Enactor". The summarised findings are:

1. All candidates accepted one of the three role descriptions as "most like me".
2. Motivational need analysis identified Enablers, with:
   a. higher scores for nAffil than for nAch or nPow; and
   b. nAch: nAffil correlation of low nAch to high nAffil.
3. Average Personality Factor scores also demonstrated differences between the groups:
   a. Envisioners tended to have
      i. high Extraversion and high Openness;
      ii. lower scores for Conscientiousness and Agreeableness; and
      iii. low Emotional Stability.
      iv. The pattern for Conscientiousness, Agreeableness, and Emotional Stability resembled the EPQ psychoticism pattern (Burch et al., 2006).
      v. Distinctive "signatures" for Envisioners are strong negative correlations for:

   1. Extraversion: Conscientiousness;
   2. Conscientiousness: Agreeableness;
   3. Emotional Stability: Openness.
   b. Enablers tended to have
      i. low Extraversion, high Conscientiousness,
      ii. average Emotional Stability,
      iii. above average Agreeableness,
      iv. low Openness.
      v. Distinctive "signatures" for Enablers are very low correlations for:
         1. Extraversion: Agreeableness
         2. Extraversion: Openness.
   c. Enactors tended to have:
      i. high Extraversion;
      ii. high Conscientiousness;
      iii. high Emotional Stability;
      iv. average Agreeableness;
      v. above-average Openness.
      vi. Distinctive "signatures" for Enactors are very high correlations for:
         1. Emotional Stability: Conscientiousness;
         2. Emotional Stability Agreeableness;
         3. Emotional Stability Openness.
4. Descriptive Decision Analysis showed variations between the groups consistent with the general themes, though the analysis was limited by the small samples. The difference between the Enactors (very effective at reaching decisions, very unlikely to change their minds) and the Envisioners (difficulty making up their minds, very prone to change a decision once made) was very distinctive.
5. 76% of candidates identified "ideal jobs" consistent with the preferred roles.

While the types and roles labelled Enabler and Enactor are widely recognised and easily identified, this study highlights the role of the Envisioner. It was noted that the capabilities of the Envisioner related not only to "positive" creative input to the decision making process of the leadership team, but also the capability of creative problem solving in times of crisis. This was exemplified by the story of the change in the organisation of NASA and its relationship to the Apollo 13 problem and the Columbia space shuttle disaster.

The possibility that information systems may offer create a "role-technology" fit facilitating the involvement of the Envisioner was noted.

An important aspect of the Envisioner is the characteristically low level of Emotional Stability. Another way of interpreting these findings is to see the Emotional Stability score as describing a "bandwidth" of emotional experience, where the Envisioner has a much wider bandwidth than the others. This may be linked to the ability to stimulate emotional responses in other members of the group, which then affects the overall decision making process. This also manifests in personal motivation, which was shown to be linked to intrinsic (and therefore emotionally-linked) needs. The study of corporate vision (Johnson, 1999) showed those characteristics of successful vision which were linked to emotional responses (values, motivation, needs of others etc.). The Enactors, on the other hand, were likely to be very careful working out the required task, take a careful decision, and then be hard to deflect. This can be seen to be linked to the typical high level of Emotional Stability (suggesting a "narrow bandwidth" of emotional experience compared to the other groups). The essential problem is that many work groups have a tendency to "screen out" people with different personality types (Miller, 1990), and therefore develop failure-prone organisations. This could be the basis for the change in NASA remarked on by Surowiecki (2006), where the Envisioner role/type appears to have been lost. In losing the range of emotional

experience brought by the Envisioners, the team will looses the additional creative and problem-solving capabilities they bring.

CONCLUSION

1. The study shows that people express a preference for one of the three roles titled 'Envisioner' 'Enabler' and 'Enactor' in roughly similar numbers. These roles relate to more complex role structures described by other writers and are characteristic of successful teams. This points towards a method of creating social synergy in work groups.

2. The results of the Motivational Needs, Personality Factor, and Decision-making tests show that the individual role preferences are related to intrinsic differences. Any socio-technical system should be designed so as to incorporate and accommodate such differences.

3. The range of characteristic behaviours measured spanned a very broad spectrum of motivational and personality differentiation, and the 3E's role breakdown appears to define the minimum number and range of people types likely to contain the full range of basic personality factors reflected by the Big 5 and motivational analysis.

4. The capabilities described for the 3E's resembled the differentiation of group problems described by Surowiecki (2006). This was supported by the more limited results of the descriptive decision-making analysis.

5. This strongly suggests that the 3E's role differentiation of Envisioner, Enabler, and Enactor prescribes the minimum composition of a work group or leadership team, while the principle of equality of status of the 3E's roles within the work group could be critical for effective group decision-making.

COMMENT

The use of on-line tests (Personality Factors Decision-making) showed a resistance to the more complex and demanding DNA test. The Personality Factor analysis showed that it should be possible to construct a simple on-line Personality Factor test to differentiate people on the 3E's typology. An "ideal job" test may provide an even more exact separation. If this were tied to an analysis of work group roles into 3E's typology, then the possibility of creating work groups with social synergy would be high even if they had never met face-to-face. 3E's therefore offers a possibility of integrating both the social factors of role-person fit with the demands of remote work groups and teams using information systems as their working environment.

REFERENCES

Augoustinos, M., & Walker, I. (1995). *Social Cognition; an integrated introduction* (p.177). London: Sage.

Bagby, J. W. (1957, May). A cross-cultural study of perceptual predominance in binocular rivalry. *J Abnorm Psychol.*, *54*(3), 331–334. doi:10.1037/h0046310

Belbin, R. M. (1982). *Management Teams: Why They Succeed or Fail.* New York: Halsted Press.

Buchanan, L., & O'Connell, A. (2006, January). A Brief History of Decision making. *Harvard Business Review*, 32–41.

Burch, G. St. J., Pavelis, C., Hemsley, D. R., & Corr, P. J. (2006). Schizotypy and creativity in visual artists. *The British Journal of Psychology*, *97*, 177–190. doi:10.1348/000712605X60030

Collins, J. (2001). *Good to Great.* London: Random House.

Cormack, D., & New, G. (1997). *Why did I do that? Understanding and mastering your motives.* London: Hodder & Stoughton.

Costa, P. T., & McCrae, R. R. (1992). *Revised NEO Personality Inventory (NEO PI-R) and NEO Five-Factor Inventory (NEO-FFI) professional manual.* Odessa, FL: Psychological Assessment Resources.

Dearborn, D. C., & Simon, H. A. (1958). Selective Perception: a Note on the Departmental Identifications of Executives. *Sociometry*, *21*, 140–144. doi:10.2307/2785898

Dewberry, C., & Narendran, S. (2007, August). *The Development of the DASA: a Comprehensive Self-Report Measure of Decision-Making Ability and Style.* Presented at Twenty-first Research Conference on Subjective Probability, Utility and Decision-making, Warsaw, Poland.

Furnham, A. (2005). *The psychology of behaviour at work: the individual in the organization.* Hove & New York: Psychology Press.

Gladwell, M. (2005) *Blink; the power of thinking without thinking.* London: Allen Lane.

Goldberg, L. R. (1990). The structure of phenotypic personality traits. *The American Psychologist*, *48*(1), 26–34. doi:10.1037/0003-066X.48.1.26

Hackman, J., & Oldham, G. (1980). *Work redesign.* Reading: M. A: Addison-Wesley.

Haga, W. J., Graen, G., & Dansereau, F. Jr. (1974). Professionalism and role making in a service organisation: a longitudinal investigation. *American Sociological Review*, *39*, 122–133. doi:10.2307/2094281

Hargreaves, D. H. (1967). *Social Relations in a Secondary School.* London: Routledge and Kegan Paul.

Holland, J. L. (1985). *Making Vocational Choices: A Theory of Vocational Choices and Work Environments* (2nd ed.). Englewood Cliffs, NJ: Prentice Hall.

Johnson, M. W. (1999, September/October). A feasibility test for corporate vision. *Strategic Change, 8*(6), 335–348. doi:10.1002/(SICI)1099-1697(199909/10)8:6<335::AID-JSC442>3.0.CO;2-7

Kahn, R. L., Wolfe, D. M., Quinn, R. P., Snoek, D. J., & Rosenthal, R. A. (1964). *Organizational Stress: Studies in Role Conflict and Ambiguity.* Chichester: Wiley.

Latham, G. P., & Kinne, S. B. (1974). Improving job performance through training in goal setting. *The Journal of Applied Psychology, 59,* 187–191. doi:10.1037/h0036530

Lennard, H. L., & Bernstein, A. (1966). Expectations and behaviour in therapy. In B.J. Biddle & E. J. Thomas (Eds.), *Role Theory* (pp. 179-185). New York: Wiley.

Locke, E. A., & Latham, G. P. (1990). Work motivation: The high performance cycle. In U. Kleinbeck, H_H. Quast, H. Thierry, & H. Hacker (Eds.), *Work Motivation.* Hillsdale, NJ: Lawrence Erlbaum.

Lyons, T. F. (1971). Role Clarity, need for clarity, satisfaction, tension, and withdrawal. *Organizational Behavior and Human Performance, 6,* 99–110. doi:10.1016/0030-5073(71)90007-9

March, J. C., & March, J. G. (1977). Almost random careers: the Wisconsin School Superintendency 1940-1972. *Administrative Science Quarterly, 22,* 377–409. doi:10.2307/2392180

March, J. C., & March, J. G. (1978). Performing sampling in social matches. *Administrative Science Quarterly, 23,* 434–453. doi:10.2307/2392419

McClelland, D. C. (1987). *Human Motivation.* New York: Cambridge University Press.

McCrae, R. R., & Costa, P. T. (2006). *Personality in Adulthood.* New York: Guildford.

Miller, D. (1990). *The Icarus Paradox: how exceptional companies bring about their downfall.* New York: Harper Business.

Morse, G. (2006). Frontiers: Decisions and Desire. *Harvard Business Review,* 42–51.

Piattelli, P. (1994). *Inevitable Illusions: how mistakes of reason rule our minds.* New York: Wiley.

Sarbin, T. R., & Williams, J. D. (1953). *Contributions to Role Taking Theory.* Working Paper. University of California. Berkeley.

Soane, E., Dewberry, C., & Narendran, S. (2009). The role of perceived costs and perceived benefits in the relationship between personality and risk related choices. *The Journal of Risk.*

Surowiecki, J. (2006). *The Wisdom of Crowds: Why the Many are Smarter Than the Few.* London: Abacus.

Tversky, A., & Kahneman, D. (1974). Judgements under uncertainty: heuristics and biases. *Science, 185,* 1124–1131. doi:10.1126/science.185.4157.1124

Whitworth, B. (2009). The Social Requirements of Technical Systems. In B. Whitworth (Ed.), *Handbook of Research on Socio-Technical Design and Social Networking Systems.* Information Science reference.http://www.igi-global.com/reference/details.asp?ID=33019.

ENDNOTES

[1]   Nigel Sykes' "Egg to Butterfly" Theory is set out in University of Warwick Centre for Small and Medium Sized Enterprises' work-

ing papers, series ISSN 0964-9328 no 71 (2000), *Envisioning Enabling, and Enacting: Metamorphosing the Enterprise*; and no. 92 (2002) (same title). An abridged version of this paper titled 'Envisioning, Enabling and Enacting: Individual and Organisational Development as Metamorphosis was published in *Organisations & People; special edition Applying Positive Psychology* Volume15, number2 May 2008 (Quarterly Journal of AMED).

[2] "The core basis of the theory came from Prophet, Priest and King and Prophet, Pastor and Apostle. ... The harmoniser of these extremes or bandwidth of positions being the pastor (priest). It was only later ... that I realised the individual type, left to dominate becomes a dominion or stronghold, hence pride, flying too near the sun and death *(ref: The Icarus Paradox, Miller 1990)*." From an Email, N Sykes, 15 December 2008

This work was previously published in The International Journal of Sociotechnology and Knowledge Development, Volume 2, Issue 1, edited by Elayne Coakes, pp. 12-35, copyright 2010 by IGI Publishing (an imprint of IGI Global).

Chapter 3
The Change Equation

Peter Duschinsky
Imaginist Company, UK

ABSTRACT

In this article, the author investigates the nature of complexity and its role in project failure. Also, the paper proposes a model to assess complexity. It draws some conclusions about the implications for change management interventions. The author finds that projects fail when the complexity exceeds the capability of the organisation to cope. The overall aim of the article is to offer an approach to reducing this number of failed change projects.

INTRODUCTION

In November my book 'The Change Equation' was published (Duschinsky, 2009). Its contention is that projects fail when the complexity of the project exceeds the capability of the organisation to cope with the changes needed and that it should be possible to predict the success or failure of a project by understanding the complexity of that project in the context of the capability of their organisation.

By 'capability' I mean both the social/culture and technical/process management capability – the two domains of Bostrom and Heinen's (1977)

work system model. In fact I argue in the book that it is only by achieving a balance between these two aspects of an organisation's capability that projects can succeed. Successful organizational performance depends on good interaction between the social and technical systems. Paying attention to either system on its own will create problems and barriers to success.

In the course of researching and developing the book, I became very interested in project complexity and its role in keeping the proportion of successful projects at a scandalously low level of around 30%, year in, year out. (In fact it's getting worse… but more of that in a minute.) When Dr. Elayne Coakes asked me to give a workshop to the Westminster Business School faculty on

DOI: 10.4018/978-1-4666-0200-7.ch003

Copyright © 2012, IGI Global. Copying or distributing in print or electronic forms without written permission of IGI Global is prohibited.

'Issues of Complexity in Project Management and its implications for Change Management', I jumped at the chance. This article is an account of the arguments and conclusions I presented at that workshop.

DEFINITION OF TERMS

First let's define what we mean by project success - and failure.

"A successful project is one which achieves its outcome(s) on time, within budget and to the required level of quality, realising the benefits identified in the Business Case." (Dept of Finance and Personnel, 2009)

"Failure is usually defined by the host organisation in terms of projects that are late or over budget, an inability to fully realize the expected benefits or gain the acceptance and enthusiastic support of users and management" (Cannon, 1994)

The definitive source for our understanding of the rate of project failure is the Standish Group's annual survey. The latest survey (Figure 1) found that only 32% of projects succeeded. 44% were 'Challenged' and 24% failed outright.

In fact the definition used by the Standish Group is quite generous. Successful projects include those that come in more or less to time and budget and deliver most of the planned benefits. 'Challenged' projects have overrun their planned timescales and budgets (some by a substantial degree) but have delivered at least some of the expected benefits. So a failed project is one that simply has not delivered. This includes those that have been abandoned before they get to completion.

So if 32% of the projects were classed as successful in the 2009 survey, that means only 32% came in *more or less* to time and budget and delivered *most* of the planned benefits. If I was a surgeon, solicitor or construction engineer with this performance history, you wouldn't be giving me your business, so why do we put up with it

Figure 1. Standish Group report 2009 (as cited in Wieberneit, 2009)

in the project management domain? And note that it was 35% in 2006! So things are actually getting WORSE.

Other surveys confirm the high failure rate: Harvard Business School also found that only 30% of change efforts among the Fortune 100 produced a positive bottom-line improvement (1997). PricewaterhouseCoopers reported that only 25% of IT projects succeed. According to them, 25% fail completely and 50% are late, over budget and deliver less than the expected benefits.

This trend seems to apply to all kinds of change projects: a survey by Martin Smith (2003) gave the picture of success and failure as presented in Figure 2.

So why do projects fail? Here are some of the reasons we all know about:

- A focus on the technology instead of the business benefits;
- Poor specification of the system and lack of due diligence on supplier capability;
- Failure to gain senior management championship;
- Inadequate resources;
- Poor project management;
- Lack of user involvement.

But if we all know about the reasons, why are change projects still going wrong so often? Let's look at some examples to see whether they reveal what's going on, and why so many projects fail. Some of these project failures are truly spectacular:

C-Nomis was an HM Prison Service system that was supposed to give prison and probation officers real-time access to offenders' records. In June 2005, the project was given the go-ahead at a cost of £234m. In March 2007 the Home Secretary, John Reid is quoted as saying: *"the main C-NOMIS base release, encompassing full prison and probation functionality, will be available no later than July 2008"*. (Collins, 2009). But just 4 months later C-NOMIS was abandoned. It was two years behind schedule and its estimated costs had tripled to £690m. Hadn't anyone thought to tell John Reid?

The problems that beset C-Nomis originated in a project board that was out of touch with the project's progress, a specification that underestimated the complexity of the project and a failure to limit changing stakeholder requirements: "no cumulative view of the impact of change requests on costs and timescales". The Commons Public Accounts Committee report verdict: "a spectacular failure – in a class of its own"! (Ford, 2009)

Figure 2. Success rates for five types of organisational change

Type of organizational change	Literature search (1990-2001)			Our sample	
	Number of studies	Sum of sample sizes	Median success rate (%)	No. of projects	Success rate (%)
Re-structuring and downsizing	9	4,830[a]	46	49	10
Technology change	5	1,406[a]	40	32	28
Mergers and acquisitions	9	395[a]	33	37	14
Re-engineering and process design	7	3,442[a]	30	75	23
Culture change	3	225[a]	19	59	19

Note: [a] One or more reports did not state the sample size

Martin E. Smith
Changing an organisation's culture: correlates of success and failure

Leadership & Organization Development Journal
24/5 [2003] 249-261

Remember the Terminal 5 fiasco? The Daily Mail called it "a national disgrace" (Daily Mail, 2008). It resulted in over 28,000 lost bags, 700 cancelled planes and more than 150,000 passengers missing flights and getting very irate! The cause? A series of small glitches in the baggage handling system which came together to create such a backlog that the system broke down. None of these problems was thought to be serious enough to postpone the opening of the terminal.

Perhaps the starkest example of the impact a project failure can have was the collapse of the London Ambulance Service Computer-Aided Despatch (CAD) System in October 2002. Reputedly, 46 people didn't get an ambulance in time and died!

What went wrong? Again it was a coincidence of a number of relatively small problems. The National Audit Office report (2009) said: "Though the small software error was the straw that broke the camel's back, the responsibility for the LAS's CAD system failure does not lie solely on the single developer who made the error or even the developing organization to which he belonged. Rather, the attitudes of key LAS members toward the project and the unreasonable restraints they placed on the project allowed the failure to occur. This was is a collision of social, human & technical systems."

Of course, it's not just in the public sector that projects fail. Here's Gilles Bouchard, CIO of HP's global operations in 2004 talking about an ERP centralisation project that went awry: "We had a series of small problems, none of which individually would have been too much to handle. But together they created the perfect storm." (quoted in Wailgum, 2009) The project eventually cost HP $160 million in order backlogs and lost revenue—more than five times the project's estimated cost.

And I could go on, but the point is made. It didn't seem to matter how well a project is planned – if a sufficient number of apparently insignificant problems come together at the same time and the project becomes too complex for the organisation to cope with, it will fail. What is particularly interesting about all these examples is the pattern that emerges: things always seemed to be going along fine…until suddenly they weren't! The speed with which these projects failed was often breathtaking. What's going on?

I believe that's to do with the nature of complexity.

THE DIMENSIONS OF COMPLEXITY

There are a number of discussions in the literature about complexity, each of which focuses on a different dimension.

The importance of complexity to the *project management process* is widely acknowledged - for example:

"Project complexity:

- Helps determine planning, coordination and control requirements;
- Hinders the clear identification of goals and objectives of major projects;
- Is an important criteria in the selection of an appropriate project organizational form;
- Influences the selection of project inputs, e.g. the expertise and experience requirements of management personnel;
- Is frequently used as a criteria in the selection of a suitable project procurement arrangement;
- Affects the project objectives of time, cost and quality. Broadly, the higher the project complexity the greater the time and cost" (Baccarini, 1996, p. 201)

Complexity is discussed specifically in relation to *software and IT projects*, for example:

"Complexity is the enemy in software, inherent complexity software rises exponentially" (Brooks, 1987)

"IS projects are intrinsically uncertain (Elvin, cited in Bronte-Stewart, 2005). The management complexity arises from the necessity to deal simultaneously with several tensions:

- Innovation versus risk;
- Learning versus control;
- The need for organisational change to deliver business benefit versus stakeholder resistance to change;
- Multiple stakeholder perceptions of the purpose of the project;
- The need to deliver value to the organisation versus managing effectively to satisfy time, quality and cost objectives;
- Managing detail and the big picture."

And finally, complexity is a recurrent theme in *organisational development and change management* literature, where it is associated with:

- The intricate inter-relationships of individuals;
- Of individuals with artefacts (such as IT) and with ideas;
- The effects of inter-actions within the organisation, as well as between institutions within a social eco-system." (Mitleton-Kelly,1998)

The sheer scale of interconnectivity expressed in this description and the fact that each of these relationships is constantly changing and evolving, means that Organisational Complexity is the most interesting dimension to consider, when looking for the underlying causes of project failure.

Thomas Docker (2009) makes a useful distinction here:

"Technically complex projects are complex because of the human aspects and not the technical intricacies, which are just complicated".

Docker suggests that:

Complicated = not simple, but ultimately knowable

Complex = not simple and never fully knowable

'Never fully knowable' sounds a bit like Chaos Theory. In fact there is a strong resemblance between the state in Chaos Theory known as 'edge of chaos' and Organisational Complexity. 'Edge of chaos' is where instability is first created – the 'tipping point' - then resolved, through the repeated iteration of tiny patterns – an adaptive feedback loop. In Organisational Complexity, the participants are constantly changing and evolving through time (Eva Mitleton-Kelly calls this the 'Evolving Adaptive System'), so the rules of interaction are in flux, making the final outcome unknowable, as Docker understood.

But the Chaos Theory works quite well as a metaphor. As we've seen, change projects are vulnerable to the runaway effect, the sudden accumulation of small interconnected problems leading to the 'tipping point' and disaster.

Thomas Frey, Senior Futurist at the DaVinci Institute, and Google's top rated futurist speaker, identified this:

"As complexity increases, the cost of managing the complexity increases at an exponential rate until the system finally collapses." (Frey, 2009)

The key word here is EXPONENTIAL.

COMPLEXITY IS EXPONENTIAL

We are surrounded by exponentiality, but we do not act as if we understand it!

For example, compound interest:

"Scientists have developed a powerful new weapon that destroys people but leaves buildings stand-

ing – it's called the 17% interest rate." (Johnny Carson, the Tonight Show, 1980)

"All that we had borrowed up to 1985 was around $5 billion, and we have paid about $16 billion; yet we are still being told that we owe about $28 billion. If you ask me what is the worst thing in the world, I will say it is compound interest." (President Obasanjo of Nigeria, 2000)

Or population growth (see Figure 3).

Consumption of resources is following close behind population growth, so our energy usage is depleting the world's natural resources exponentially and climate change is also following an exponential runaway profile.

We live in a world that can change exponentially, so why don't we understand exponentiality? According to Richard Stoyeck, an American financial advisor (2009), its because we have brains that are hardwired to plot things out linearly:

"The software in our brains compels us to think about progressions as being simple arithmetic ones".

So as a species, and a society, we deal poorly with uncertainty in non-linear domains.

"The greatest shortcoming of the human race is our inability to understand the exponential function." That's what Professor Albert Bartlett thinks. He is emeritus Professor of Physics at the University of Colorado, so he probably knows! (Bartlett, 1969, page 201)

As a consequence of this weakness in our mental capability, the complexity of a project is typically underestimated. And that has serious consequences. The time and skilled resources that are allocated to a project will be broadly in line with our understanding of its complexity, so a project that is more complex than we thought will suffer from being under-resourced, is likely to overrun its planned time and budget and, ultimately, is doomed to fail (to some degree).

So to manage this better and bring more projects to successful fruition, we need to be able to assess the exponential complexity of a project - and in terms that senior budget-holders who are responsible for allocation of resources will understand. Exponential complexity is really a short-hand for

Figure 3. Population growth (Wikipedia 2009)

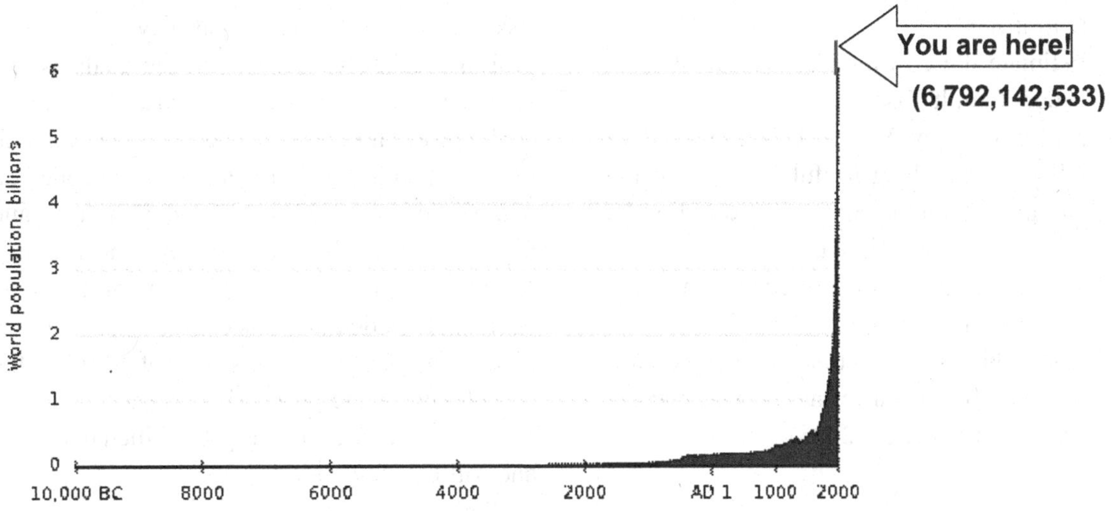

Figure 4. Population and carbon emissions (Nowpublic, 2009)

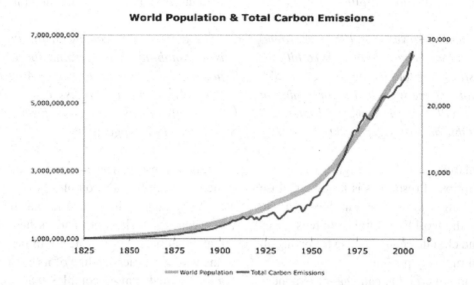

'exponential risk' so we should be able to apply conventional risk management techniques to do the job. Why does that not work?

According to David Christiansen, author of 'Information Technology Dark Side, a Corporate IT Survival Guide', most risk management approaches work something like this:

- "Make a list of risks;
- Estimate the likelihood the risk will occur (call it X);
- Estimate the cost the risk will create if it occurs (call it Y);
- Multiply X by Y - that is supposed to tell you something useful it might be the amount of contingency you need for the risk, or something like that;
- When the risks you anticipated happen, they become issues.
- When the risks you didn't anticipate happen, you become a former project manager..." (Christiansen, 2008)

In his typically amusing fashion, David is saying something quite fundamental. Although powerful in mitigating technical complexity – i.e., Docker's 'complicated' element, conventional risk management methodologies do not really allow for the coincidence of apparently low-risk problems coming together to cause the 'runaway' effect that, we have seen, is a characteristic of Organisational Complexity and exponentially complex projects. The other problem with conventional risk management tools is that they need skilled project managers to carry out the analysis and are not easily read and understood at Board level.

Wouldn't it be great if there was an indicator of project complexity that takes this exponential complexity into account – and is simple and high-level enough to be conveyed in a single 'dashboard' picture? It clearly wouldn't obviate the need for a detailed risk analysis, but it would give us a snapshot assessment of whether the complexity of the project had been judged correctly when allocating budgets, skilled resources and roll-out timescales.

Well, we can...

THE EXPONENTIAL COMPLEXITY MODEL

If complexity is exponential, we only actually need 3 factors to build an exponential scale:

X * Y * Z

That won't represent all the risks, but if we select the right 3 factors, it should give us a good indicator. So what are our 3 factors? They must be:

- Common to all projects;
- Quantifiable (at least to a good approximation) by stakeholders;
- Sufficiently powerful in combination to lead to an accurate assessment of the complexity of a project.

After some experimentation, I found 3 factors that satisfied these conditions:

S: the number of stakeholders involved (an approximation might be everyone represented on steering and project groups)

P: the number of business activities and processes that will be affected (for example the number of manual processes an automation project will 'touch' and change)

T: Expected implementation timescale in months (from issue of spec/ITT to planned completion of roll-out)

Why these?

1. **The number of people or Stakeholders involved:** The more people (roles) are involved in the decision-making and implementation of the project e.g., IT manager, user groups, product suppliers, consultants and sub-contractors, the more difficult it is to make sure you have consulted and trained all who need to be involved.

2. **The number of business activities or Processes affected:** The more far-reaching the solution, in terms of the business activities affected, the harder it is to make sure you have covered all the links and interfaces with other activities. Implementation is also more complicated and you cannot afford for the business to come to a stop because the new system doesn't work properly.

3. **Elapsed Time (in months) to implement:** The longer it takes from your initial definition of what you want to achieve, to the time you can actually get the system to deliver these benefits, the more likely it is your project will fail. This is because the world does not stand still. Your needs will change and you will be tempted to add new requirements and that adds complexity.

Multiply these 3 factors together: Stakeholders x Processes x Time and you have the Exponential Complexity Factor.

When I get to this point in the workshops I run, I ask delegates to first tell me where they thought their project sits on a 4-point scale:

Simple / Not simple / Complex / Too complex

Then they do the calculation and we position the project on the Exponential Complexity Model (see Figure 5).

Try it for yourself. Where do you think your project lies on this scale?

Now do the numbers... Don't worry about getting all the numbers absolutely right – an approximation will do for the purpose of the exercise.

What did you find?

Any gap between your initial perception of complexity and the Exponential Complexity Factor you calculated represents a potential cause of failure. Here's a quick guide to what it means:

Simple project – if the total scores around 300 or less, yours is a relatively simple project. Follow a structured project plan and get help if you have not tackled this type of project before.

Not simple – if the number is between 300 and 3,000, make sure you have planned the project properly and brought in an experienced project manager – it isn't as simple as you thought. And don't let it grow like Topsy!

Complex project – a figure between 3,000 and 7,000 shows that yours is actually a complex project. Appoint a sponsor who will champion the project, select a project team with sufficient experience and identify a business manager who will keep the project focused on getting the business benefits you first defined. Whichever project management method you use, stick to it! Make sure senior management is being kept in the picture and that there is an option to stop the project if it isn't going to plan. If you don't have the experience to do this yourselves, scale down the project or seek help – before you start.

Too complex - a figure between 7,000 and 30,000 is definitely getting too complex to be dealt with as a single project and beyond 30,000 you definitely need to break it down into separate projects and employ a skilled programme management team. Highly complex projects like this require full-time, very experienced programme managers and dedicated implementation resources.

Failure to allocate sufficient skills and resources will result in the new systems not being taken up within the planned timescale – leading, at best, to lower than planned efficiency benefits, and too frequently, to total disaster.

COMPLEXITY AND THE IMPLICATIONS FOR CHANGE MANAGEMENT

Now that we have a mechanism to assess the complexity of the project, albeit crudely and at a high level, I want to turn to the question posed by the title of this article: what are the implications for change management?

Let's go back to the discussion about the difference between 'complicated' and 'complex'. If a project is complex, involving people, the outcomes are said to be unknowable. But this flies in the face of conventional change management approaches. The way change is managed in an organisation is

Figure 5. The Exponential Complexity Model

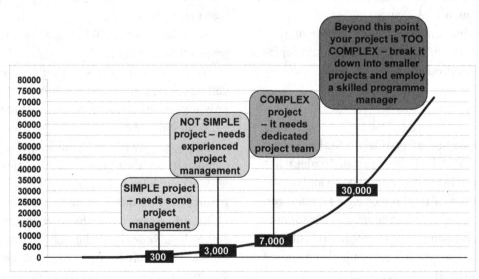

Stakeholders x Processes x Time (in months)

usually associated with a particular change project or programme, such as the introduction of new systems, reorganisation or restructuring to improve efficiency and reduce cost, a merger or acquisition – in short anything that changes "the way we do things here". So change management is usually about managing specific process changes into the organisation to achieve a planned outcome and typically involves communication, training and support activities which run alongside the other technical and logistics activities in the project or programme.

When an organisation moves away from equilibrium or from established patterns of work and behaviour, as in a change project, new ways of working are created. These need to be recognised, supported and embedded for the project to succeed. Conventional change management attempts to control the outcomes by imposing changes in behaviour and over-riding the individual's need to 'invent their own route to the future' … so people give up, fall back on 'what's in it for me' and the change project fails.

So the nature of complexity and the unknowability of outcomes have important implications for Change Management.

Eva Mitleton-Kelly again:

"Although the intention of change management interventions is to create new ways of working, they may block or constrain emergent patterns of behaviour if they attempt to design and control the outcome. However, if re-design were to concentrate on the provision of enabling infrastructures while allowing the new patterns of relationships and ways of working to emerge, new forms of organisation will arise which would be more attuned with the culture of the organisation. The emergent organisation will thus be unique and not susceptible to copying. It will furthermore be more robust and sustainable." (Mitleton-Kelly, 1998)

The Socio-technical approach has something to offer here:

"The goal of socio-technical design is to produce a system capable of self-modification, of adapting to change, and of making the most of creative capacities of the individual for the benefit of the organisation" (Coakes, 2001, p. 6).

What are the conditions you need in order to tap into an individual's creativity? I would argue that they include:

- An environment of trust, created by the leader/s of the organisation;
- Confidence in one's identity and role in the organisation;
- An infrastructure that encourages and rewards sharing and innovation.

Only in such a climate of trust and confidence will people be motivated to look over the parapet to find out about others' needs and priorities, to see the end-to-end processes and recognise the need for change, even if (as often happens) it only makes their own job more difficult. This doesn't happen overnight – it needs good leadership and communication, a nurturing not a blaming culture and the right infrastructure to support this emergent behaviour. Putting this culture and enabling infrastructure in place, then embedding the emergent behaviour, cannot be achieved within the implementation lifecycle of a project. It has to start beforehand – and continue long after the project team have gone on to the next project.

But most change management interventions occur within the timescales of a change project. If 'consulting the staff' is an item on the project's Change Management plan, your project will probably end up with the other 70% in the Standish Group's 'failed' or 'challenged' categories. Take note!

SUMMARY

In summary:

- Projects fail when the complexity of the project exceeds the capability of the organisation to cope;
- Complexity is exponential and is typically underestimated;
- Conventional change management interventions which attempt to design and control the outcomes can cause a change project to fail;
- A complexity 'gap analysis' will help to predict whether a project is likely to succeed or fail;
- Putting the culture and enabling infrastructure in place for a project to succeed cannot be achieved within the implementation lifecycle of a project – you have to start earlier and continue after the completion of the project.

REFERENCES

Baccarini, D. (1996). The concept of project complexity - a review. *International Journal of Project Management, 14*(4), 201–204. doi:10.1016/0263-7863(95)00093-3

Bartlett, A. (1969). Sustainability 101: Arithmetic, Population, and Energy. In *Proceedings of the Energy Efficiency Policy Symposium*, Honolulu, Hawaii.

Bostrom, R. P., & Heinen, J. S. (1977). MIS Problems and Failures: A Socio-Technical Perspective. *Management Information Systems Quarterly*, 11–28. doi:10.2307/249019

Brooks, F. P. (1987, April). No Silver Bullet: Essence and Accidents of Software Engineering. *Computer Magazine*.

Cannon, J. (1994). Why IT Applications Succeed or Fail: The Interaction of Technical and Organizational Factors. *Industrial and Commercial Training Journal, 26*(1), 10–15. doi:10.1108/00197859410051226

Christiansen, D. (2008, February 25). Estimating Project Risk. *Information Technology Dark Side, a Corporate IT Survival Guide*. Retrieved from www.techdarkside.com

Coakes, E. (2001). *Knowledge Management in the Socio Technical World: The Graffiti Continues*. London: Springer Verlag.

Collins, T. (2009). *What went wrong*. Retrieved from http://www.computerweekly.com/blogs/tony_collins/2009/05/what-went-wrong-with-234m-c-no.html

Daily Mail. (2008, April 15). *Two BA executives quit terminal 5 fiasco insurers refuse cover future luggage losses*. Retrieved from http://www.dailymail.co.uk/news/article-1015373/Two-BA-executives-quit-Terminal-5-fiasco-insurers-refuse-cover-future-luggage-losses.html

Dept of Finance and Personnel. Northern Ireland. (2009). *Successful Projects in Government*. Retrieved from http://spring.dfpni.gov.uk/annexa/project-management-sec1.htm

Docker, T. (2008). *CITI*. Retrieved from www.citi.co.uk

Duschinsky, P. (2009). *The Change Equation*. Cirencester, UK: Management Books 2000.

Elvin, R. (2005). *Developing a risk estimation model from IT project failure (Tech. Rep.)* (Bronte-Stewart, M., Ed.). Paisley, UK: Paisley University.

Ford, R. (2009, March 12). *The Times*. Retrieved from http://www.timesonline.co.uk/tol/news/politics/article5891179.ece

Frey, T. (2006). *Watching the Income Tax System Implode*. Retrieved from www.futuristspeaker.com/2009/03/watching-the-income-tax-system-implode

Frey, T. (2009, March 27). The exponential nature of complexity - why the income tax system will collapse. *Impactlab*. Retrieved from www.impactlab.com/2009/03/27/watching-the-income-tax-system-implode

King, L. (2009). ERP and e-commerce systems creating £600,000 bill. *CIO Magazine*. Retrieved from http://www.cio.co.uk/news/3202489/erp-and-e-commerce-systems-creating-600000-bill/?otc=44

Mitleton-Kelly, E. (1998, April 12). *Organisations as complex evolving systems*. Paper presented at the OACES Conference, Warwick.

Musick, E. (2006). *The 1992 London Ambulance Service Computer Aided Dispatch System Failure*. Retrieved from http://erichmusick.com/writings/06/las_failure.html

National Audit Office report. (2009, March 12). *The National Offender Management Information System*. London: The Stationery Office. Retrieved from http://www.nowpublic.com/environment/correlation-between-population-growth-and-emissions-growth-chart

Pascale, R., Millemann, M., & Gioja, L. (1997). Changing the way we change (Harvard Business School survey). *Harvard Business Review*, 75(6), 127–139.

PricewaterhouseCoopers Survey. (2007, March 8). Leadership flaws add to IT project failures. *Computing magazine*. Retrieved from http://www.computing.co.uk/computing/news/2184964/leadership-flaws-add-project

PublicService.com. (2009, March 12). *Offender IT is a 'spectacular failure*. Retrieved from http://www.publicservice.co.uk/news_story.asp?id=8869

Shah, A. (2005, July 2). The Scale of the Debt Crisis. *Global Issues*. Retrieved from http://www.globalissues.org/article/30/the-scale-of-the-debt-crisis

Smith, M. E. (2003). Changing an organisation's culture: correlates of success and failure. *Leadership and Organization Development Journal*, 24(5), 249–261. doi:10.1108/01437730310485752

Standish Group International, Inc. (2009, June 11). *Extreme Chaos, 2004-2009* (T. Wieberneit quote). http://blog.ciber.com/article.cfm?articleid=2009111592458

Stoyeck, R. (2009). *The Magic of Compounding*. Retrieved from www.stocksatbottom.com

Wailgum, T. (2009). *Famous ERP Disasters Dustups and Disappointments*. Retrieved from http://www.cio.com/article/486284/10_Famous_ERP_Disasters_Dustups_and_Disappointments

Wikipedia. (2009a) *Population Growth*. Retrieved from http://en.wikipedia.org/wiki/File:Population_curve.svg

This work was previously published in The International Journal of Sociotechnology and Knowledge Development, Volume 2, Issue 2, edited by Elayne Coakes, pp. 63-74, copyright 2010 by IGI Publishing (an imprint of IGI Global)

Chapter 4
Leveraging Communities for Sustainable Innovation:
A Commentary

Elayne Coakes
University of Westminster, UK

Peter A.C. Smith
The Leadership Alliance Inc., Canada

Dee Alwis
University of Middlesex, UK

ABSTRACT

The concept of using future innovation to achieve "right to market" (R2M) (Koudal & Coleman, 2005) is the focus of this paper. This paper discusses the relationship between entrepreneurship and innovation and posits that they form a system where innovation is optimised when these capabilities are closely linked. The authors contend that innovation activities are best 'managed' by an organization's entrepreneur(s) and that part of this role is to identify Innovation Champions and facilitate their innovation-related activities. The authors also explore the social and community interaction necessary for innovation to flourish and explain the role of entrepreneurs in forming Communities of Innovation (CoInv) based on innovation champions and their networks. This paper argues that CoInv are essential to ensure that each separate innovation has commercial potential and is operationally accepted with support diffused throughout the organisation. The authors demonstrate these assertions through a case discussion and conclude with some final comments on the future of this research.

INTRODUCTION

The concept of using future innovation to achieve "right to market" (R2M) (Koudal & Coleman, 2005) is the main focus of this paper. R2M is defined as introducing the right products at the right time in the right markets with the right supply chain, and then continually updating, optimising, and retiring them as necessary. This paper fills a gap in the innovation literature by contributing broad-based critical theoretical and practical insights for an organization attempting to successfully solve the challenging problems

DOI: 10.4018/978-1-4666-0200-7.ch004

Copyright © 2012, IGI Global. Copying or distributing in print or electronic forms without written permission of IGI Global is prohibited.

associated with implementing successful R2M initiatives in newly emerging global contexts (Friedman, 2000).

Current literature has largely overlooked that entrepreneurship and innovation form a system such that maximum business benefit is derived by optimising interaction between these drivers, especially when market opportunities are extremely transitory and fraught with risk. Previous papers have concentrated almost exclusively on entrepreneurial networking with extra- rather than intra-organizational partners; on isolated innovative processes; and on broad cultural contexts. This paper highlights the essential function that corporate entrepreneurs and innovators must play together to ensure that each separate innovation not only has commercial potential but is operationally accepted with support diffused throughout the organisation.

We assert that in the entrepreneur-innovation system it is the corporate entrepreneur's role to promote and manage innovation processes based not only on the entrepreneur's acute commercial understandings and intuitive market sensitivities, but also on an appreciation of the social learning and knowledge sharing that is a feature of a vibrant innovation environment. We therefore posit that two critical features of the proposed entrepreneur's role are the identification of 'innovation champions' (Glynn, 1996; Howell, 2005) and their influence networks, and the facilitation of all manner of innovative capability through the guidance, the support, and the development of a type of CoP that we term Communities of Innovation (CoInv).

Based on the literature innovation champions we show are unique people with singular innovation-related potential who need not only procedural and resource support to ensure their idiosyncratic experience-based social learning and knowledge sharing, but also the social and cognitive support that is provided through the social activity and Human Capital exploration that takes place via CoInv. Providing the guid-

ance, the support, and the development of these CoInv must all be situated within the mandate of an organization's entrepreneur(s) - these activities will be even more critical to successful R2M in today's increasingly dynamic and complex globalised markets (Friedman, 2000).

The insights provided in this paper will enable an organization to plan and adopt a systemic broad-based R2M strategy and implementation, robust with respect to emerging globalisation complexities, and strongly grounded in sound theoretical ideas that ensure its innovations now and in the future are focused, agile, timely, and R2M significant.

The paper is structured as follows: firstly we discuss Entrepreneurship and Innovation followed by a discussion of Innovation Champions; we then look at the role of Innovation and communities especially Communities of Innovation; we then consider how to identify Innovation Champions and demonstrate this method through a Case discussion, concluding with some final comments on the future of this research.

Entrepreneurship and Innovation

Koudal and Coleman (2005) have studied the growth strategies and supporting operations of nearly 650 companies around the world. They conclude that although innovation may be difficult, without it companies will eventually languish and fail. *Although in every* industry, the leading companies are innovators, the lauded exemplars keep changing (Muller, Valikangas, & Merlyn, 2005; Peters & Waterman, 1982) and such high turnover suggests that the underlying problem isn't so much one of innovation as one of *sustained* innovation. Indeed a number of authors (Thornbery, 2001; Zahra, 1995; Pinchot, 1985) have noted that without the presence of some form of entrepreneurial activity to exploit opportunities as they arise, innovation remains little more than a short-term aspiration, rather than a sustainable tangible one.

It is important that innovation operates with regard for commercial realities and some authors insist that innovation is the process of bringing new problem-solving ideas *into use* (Amabile, 1988; Muller et al., 2005; Moss Kanter, 1983). Tidd (2001) argues that just the invention of new knowledge is insufficient, and Sullivan (1998) and Teece (1998) argue that innovation has only occurred if the new knowledge has been implemented or commercialised in some way. Consistent with these views, we follow McFadzean et al. (2005) in defining entrepreneurship as the *promotion* of innovation in an uncertain environment, and innovation as the process that through its products, services, and processes adds value and novelty to the organization, its suppliers; and customers.

The 5th Generation of Innovation theory (Rothwell, 1994) argues that current innovation requires systems integration and networking (of suppliers, customers, and competitors or complementors - see Porter's Five Forces (as renewed by Brandenburger and Nalebuff, 1996, and by Porter, 2008). This is not a physical network but rather a social and R&D system of networks, and a synthesis of individual behaviours as well as structural organisational variables (Bernstein & Singh, 2006). Bessant et al. (2005) assert that these behaviours include agility, flexibility, the ability to learn fast, and the lack of preconceptions of the way that things might progress or evolve. Kline and Rosenberg (1986) and Kogut (1988) argue that levels of innovativeness will depend on the firm's (or its actors') access to the external skills and knowledge that entrepreneurs can introduce to an organization. Becker and Dietz (2004) confirm this by arguing that the addition of external capabilities will have a positive effect on innovation activities and success.

McFadzean et al. (2005) quote Amit et al. (1993; p. 816) saying that the two concepts of entrepreneurship and innovation should be linked together, and McFadzean et al. (2005) and Shaw et al. (2005) make a strong case for considering these concepts as two elements of a system. It is argued here that the future of innovation will indeed be founded on entrepreneurship and innovation being treated as a system where both add value and that high synergy will be formed when their interaction is optimised. In this regard it is further argued that the corporate entrepreneur's role includes promotion and 'management' of the organization's innovation processes e.g. as explored in this paper, such that it will lead to sustained competitive advantage and organisational viability; in other words successful R2M capability.

Champions of Innovation

Howell (2005) states that 90% of raw ideas never get beyond the idea-generator's desk and only 3% of the remaining 10% obtain sufficient backing to become projects with less than 1% being commercially launched. She argues that one reason for the high failure rate of new ideas is their failure to attract a champion. Glynn (1996) points to the existence of 'innovation champions' who have the social, political or interpersonal knowledge to influence the acceptance of innovative change. Van de Ven (1986) says that one of the key issues for organisations is gaining appreciation of ideas, needs and opportunities for innovations. According to Archilladelis et al. (1971; p. 14) the presence of innovation champions makes a "decisive contribution to the innovation by actively and enthusiastically promoting its progress." Smith (2005a) describes the personal characteristics of these "opinion leaders" and their relevance to innovation.

The role of innovation champions in promoting innovation is embodied in the framework for innovation diffusion developed by Rogers (1995). Rogers defines innovation diffusion as the process by which an innovation is communicated through certain communication channels over time among the members of a social system. Rogers emphasizes *innovativeness* as an aspect of his process - this is the extent to which an individual is relatively quicker in adopting an innovation than others. Rogers proposes five categories of innovativeness:

1. *Entrepreneurs/Innovators* are gate keepers in the flow of new ideas into a social system.
2. *Early adopters* decrease uncertainty about a new idea by adopting it and by then conveying a subjective evaluation to near-peers.
3. The *early majority* that follow in adopting an innovation and who through their position between the early and the late adopters are important links for further diffusion
4. The *late majority* for whom almost all of the uncertainty about a new idea must be removed before they adopt.
5. *Laggards* that are extremely cautions and may never adopt the innovation.

In any organisation, such champions will be a small percentage of the entire community. Innovation champions are active in supporting innovation and seeking out opportunities, but they need to be encouraged and motivated by management. Howell and Higgins (1990) say that "without champions organisations may have a lot of ideas but few tangible innovations. The challenge facing management is to identify and effectively manage existing champions and to nurture potential champions" (p. 55). Champions naturally have a range of networks in which they participate and may be characterised as renaissance people (Howell, 2005) with a large variety of interests and a diversity of activities. They tend to have had a long tenure in the organisation (Howell & Higgins, 1990) with experience in many divisions and locations, and an in-depth knowledge of the industry.

Innovation and Communities

Leonard-Barton and Sensiper (1998) argue that innovation depends upon the individual and collective expertise of employees, and innovation

is characterised by an iterative process of people working together building on the creative ideas of one another. Rosenfeld and Servo (1991) emphasize that whilst creativity is individual, innovation is inclusive and a social process involving many people (West & Farr, 1990). Numerous examples are provided by Hargadon (2003), based on ten years of research, demonstrating that revolutionary innovations result from the creative combining of ideas, people and objects rather than flashes of brilliance by lone inventors. Stacey (2001) places self-organising human interaction, with its ability for emergent creativity, at the centre of the knowledge creating process, and suggests that organisational knowledge depends on the qualities of the relationships between people.

Moss Kanter (1998) argues that the generation of new ideas that activates innovation is facilitated by diversity and breadth of experience, including experts who have a great deal of contact with other experts in their fields; links to users; and links to 'outsiders'. Communities, we therefore argue, are one of the supporting organisational forms for innovation. Creativity often springs up at the boundaries of disciplines and specialties, so innovative communities will work through collaboration with other communities, organizations, and also communities in other organisations. In the study by Kontoghiorghes et al. (2005) it was found that the factors that most strongly predicted rapid change adaptation, and innovation introduction, were related to participative and open organisational systems permitting joint problem solving without boundary interference. These factors also included the safety of a place where they had the freedom to take risks and develop new ideas, be creative, and challenge existing organisational norms. Innovators today (Menzel, Aaltio, & Ulijn, 2007) ask for social knowledge alongside the technological knowledge to make innovations meaningful. In particular we can see that tacit knowledge will best be shared and made explicit via spaces ("Ba") intended for such knowledge sharing and creation (Nonaka & Reinmoller, 2000; pp. 98-111).

Authors such as Adaman and Devine (2002) suggest that entrepreneurship is founded in social interaction occurring within and outside the organisation, and in this paper we propose that a critical aspect of the entrepreneurial role is the development of innovatory capabilities through knowledge creation. These are communities where innovation may be incubated and entrepreneurship facilitated. McFadzean et al. (2005; p. 352) define this aspect of corporate entrepreneurship as "The effort of promoting innovation from an internal organisational perspective, through the assessment of potential new opportunities, alignment of resources, exploitation and commercialisation of said opportunities." Organisational learning, we argue, is an essential pre-requisite to, and an integral component of such promotion, and this learning, according to Alegre and Chiva (2008), comes from mechanisms: experimentation, risk taking, interaction with the external environment, dialogue, and participative decision-making. Therefore, following Cayer (1999) we propose that innovation is the product of organisational learning, and that successful organisational innovation must be based (1996) in co-ordination mechanisms that support the problem-solving efforts of the organisation's Human Capital, and the dynamic processes of sense making within organisations (Drazin, Glynn, & Kazanjian, 1999); we say it is through CoInv that these mechanisms may be supported and enacted.

Communities of Practice and Communities of Innovation

Given that community socialisation processes are critical to entrepreneurship and innovation, CoP (Communities of Practice) offer a promising practical vehicle for their eventuation. Wenger et al. (2002; p. 4) have provided a widely accepted definition of CoP as "Groups of people who share a concern, a set of problems, or a passion about a topic, and who deepen their knowledge and expertise in this area by interacting on an ongoing basis." Brown and Duguid's (1991) study of CoP explains how shared learning is entrenched in complex, collaborative social practices, and many current authorities propose that CoP provide an valuable framework for inter-agent context specific knowledge sharing, sense making, and knowledge creation (Coakes & Clarke, 2005). In other words, CoP are knowledge creation and sharing networks (Cross, Prusak, & Parker, 2001) and CoP are comprised naturally of members of many social networks (Shenkel, Teigland, & Borgatti, 2001). Lesser and Storck (2001) say that we must think of a CoP as an engine for the development of social capital. Social capital, in particular, they argue shortens the learning curve, increases responsiveness to customer experiences, reduces rework and prevents reinvention, and also increases innovation.

Here we argue that CoP as normally constituted are in reality mostly concerned with the development of *best practices* through the sharing, but typically the recycling (Cavaleri & Seivert, 2005), of existing 'accepted' knowledge. Innovation, as we have said above, relates to expanding an organisation's boundaries in both practice and product, and thus requires a different supporting mindset from that of sharing existing knowledge. CoInv in contrast are a form of CoP that are very specifically dedicated to the support of innovation, and their formation and sustainability must be, it is argued, the responsibility of those individuals charged with organizational entrepreneurship.

CoInv are a very important *new* concept that this paper theorises can be formed from innovation champions and their social networks, to provide safe places for the creation and support of innovatory ideas. They can be considered as epistemic communities, where experts will gather – but the expertise being that of innovation rather than of a technical or other skill or practice. Since CoInv will be comprised of those individuals that actively champion new ideas, and those who wish to be associated with them and to develop innovation, support for new ideas is automatic, and innovation champions will be inclined naturally to form CoInv when given appropriate support and leadership. Behaviour that demonstrates creativity will be valued and if supported will be reinforced. In other words, CoInv will be the place where creativity not only flourishes but is trained to flourish. The net result of an open and flexible culture and structure which develops these supportive communities must be greater opportunities for innovatory behaviours and ultimately more successful innovations. There are a number of special features to this Community: membership is not open but limited to those with an interest in or experience of, innovation; the 'practice' is non-specific; it is intended to mentor champions of innovation; it is outward facing and customer oriented; it contains all levels of staff but more senior will predominate with longer levels of organisational service; there will thus be generative learning.

As stated above, innovation champions already have extensive social networks in place and the challenge to the organisation and those charged with entrepreneurship is to transform these networks into CoInv. Howell (2005) has identified six crucial things that champions require from the workplace: to work within an innovative environment; to work with other innovators; to be challenged and to learn; to be (socially) connected within and without the organisation; to be recognised for their work; and to work for management that supports their activities. Once a CoInv is formed all the other champion requirements, as identified by Howell, naturally fall into place.

Evangelista and Sirrilli (1998) identified lack of skilled champions of change as a key factor in innovation failure but identifying them is an organizational challenge since they tend to emerge informally in an organisation (Tushman & Nadler, 1986). Below we demonstrate how to identify and amplify the influence of these champions of innovation.

Identifying Innovation Champions and Mapping Their Social Networks

Identifying particular social networks, legitimately influential individuals, and visualising the complexities of their relationship patterns and communication channels, have traditionally been difficult, time consuming, and expensive. Network Visualisation and Analysis (NVA) is an important part of this effort and its application to CoP formation by Smith (2005b). In NVA, data regarding "who relates to whom" are collected from the larger organisational community, or from other groups such as CoP. Based on these data, NVA reveals the complexities of how people communicate and interact in networks and opens them to better management and optimisation. In particular, NVA may be used to identify innovation champions (Smith, 2005a).

The example described below is derived from a consultancy intervention and demonstrates how NVA has been used to detect influential innovation champions who were then formed into communities (CoInv) that supported practices to bring about sustainable innovation.

In this example, a major retail company undertook an NVA project targeting its senior managers across the company. The objectives were to identify the most influential and entrepreneurial managers with respect to facilitating innovation, and to provide insight into the current characteristics of the organisation-wide network of communications and trust-tagged relationships that hinder or promote the introduction and implementation of new ideas. It was anticipated that when the influential innovation champions had been identified, their capabilities could be enhanced and leveraged through appropriate organization and support.

The NVA process involved email-delivering a question relating to the above innovation objective to all members (100 individuals) of the three most senior management levels across all the company's locations and departments. Members of this target community responded by picking names from a list displayed to them on the Internet. This list contained names of all the individuals targeted for the study. The study community was further amended as respondents were free to write in names of individuals not identified in the original target group, including external sources (these individuals were not asked to answer the question).

The question posed was:

• Imagine that you are on a project to develop an innovative approach to creating "a sensational place at Head Office". Who are the 'ideas' people you want on the project team with you, from your own or other areas?

The final response rate was 75% indicating that conclusions drawn could be considered well founded. KNETMAP™ (Know Inc., 2006) was the Web-based data-gathering tool that was used in the study to pose the question and collect responses. This software was also used to build the relationship maps based on data submitted in response to the question. It provided results that were both qualitative and quantitative. After completion of the network visualisation, analysis, and interpretation, results were reported to the study sponsors for further dialogue and finally for action.

NVA provided the names for a significant number of individuals demonstrating noteworthy innovation influence. Individual attributes such as location, management level, and years of service etc. were included in the target community database, and further analysis of the networks based on such personal criteria were carried out.

On completion of the NVA effort, CoInv for the development and support of innovation were set up across the company by linking the individuals drawn from the list of innovative individuals. All NVA related information was used to facilitate setting up CoInv using already existing trust-tagged networks. Inter-branch sharing was further promoted by intermittent face-to-face gatherings and by nominating individuals at each branch with responsibility for acting as "weak links" (Cross & Parker, 2004) to ensure that continuity between CoInvs were maintained. Communication and knowledge sharing was further facilitated by using action learning (Smith, 2005c). A management programme was also introduced to heighten awareness of the benefits of networking and knowledge sharing, particularly through membership in CoInvs and CoPs.

The long term benefits of these activities with respect to enhanced innovation can only be surmised; however, immediate benefits were evident in the increase in networking and knowledge sharing across the company, and the company has just celebrated 100 years of being in business in very creative style in spite of current economic conditions.

CONCLUSION

Based on the literature cited we have argued that innovation champions are special people with a particular personality type and psychological profile. In order for the necessary knowledge sharing to take place between champions, and for them to succeed in promoting innovations through the organisation from idea and concept through to marketable product, they need not only procedural and resource support, but also social and cognitive support. We say this social support can be provided by a special type of CoP - a CoInv.

We have argued that entrepreneurship and innovation must interact to provide maximum business benefit and to achieve strategic drivers. We further assert that the corporate entrepreneur should promote and manage the innovation process based on commercial understanding, through identifying innovation champions and their influence networks, and through leveraging innovative capability through the formation of CoInv.

Although further rigorous research studies are required as this paper is based on only one case, it is suggested, based on the example described, that NVA methodology can be used to identify innovation champions. We argue that these champions, with appropriate organizational support, will be naturally motivated to form CoInv.

In a papers under development we further discuss how organisational learning is critical to entrepreneurship and innovation, and how the concept of the Learning Organisation (Senge, 1990), and more particularly of the Evolutionary Organization (Smith & Saint-Onge, 1996), will foster the learning processes required for both entrepreneurship and innovation to thrive, and further facilitate the development of CoInvs; we note that Senge (2004) in relation to building learning organisations, advises organizations to find those individuals who are ready for change and then create core communities from them.

REFERENCES

Adaman, F., & Devine, P. (2002). A reconsideration of the theory of entrepreneurship: a participatory approach. *Review of Political Economy*, *14*(3), 329–355. doi:10.1080/09538250220147877

Alegre, J., & Chiva, R. (2008). Assessing the impact of organizational learning capability on product innovation performance: An empirical test. *Technovation*, *28*, 315–326. doi:10.1016/j.technovation.2007.09.003

Amabile, T. M. (1988). A model of creativity and innovation in organisations. In Straw, B. M., & Cummings, L. L. (Eds.), *Research in Organisational Behaviour* (*Vol. 10*, pp. 123–167). Greenwich, CT: JAI Press.

Amit, R., Glosten, L., & Muller, E. (1993). Challenges to theory development in entrepreneurship research. *Journal of Management Studies*, *30*(5), 815–834. doi:10.1111/j.1467-6486.1993.tb00327.x

Becker, W., & Dietz, J. (2004). R&D co-operation and innovation activities of firms-evidence for the German manufacturing industry. *Research Policy*, *33*, 209–223. doi:10.1016/j.respol.2003.07.003

Bernstein, B., & Singh, P. J. (2006). An integrated innovation process model based on practices of Australian biotechnology firms. *Technovation*, *26*(5/6), 561–572. doi:10.1016/j.technovation.2004.11.006

Bessant, J., Lamming, R., Noke, H., & Phillips, W. (2005). Managing innovation beyond the steady state. *Technovation*, *25*(12), 1366–1376. doi:10.1016/j.technovation.2005.04.007

Brandenburger, A., & Nalebuff, B. (1996). *Coopetition*. New York: Currency Doubleday.

Brown, J. S., & Duguid, P. (1991). Organisational learning and communities of practice: toward a unified view of working, learning and innovation. *Organization Science*, *2*, 40–57. doi:10.1287/orsc.2.1.40

Cavaleri, S., & Seivert, S. (2005). *Knowledge Leadership*. Burlington, MA: Elsevier.

Cayer, C. (1999). Innovation - a product of the learning organisation. In *Proceedings of the 4th International Conference on ISO 9000* (pp. 1-6).

Coakes, E., & Clarke, S. (Eds.). (2005). *Encyclopedia of Communities of Practice in Information and Knowledge Management*. Hershey, PA: Idea Group Reference.

Cross, R., & Parker, A. (2004). *The Hidden Power of Social Networks*. Boston: Harvard Business School Press.

Cross, R., Prusak, L., & Parker, A. (2001). Knowing what we know: supporting knowledge creation and sharing in social networks. *Organizational Dynamics, 30*(2), 100–120. doi:10.1016/S0090-2616(01)00046-8

Drazin, R., Glynn, M. A., & Kazanjian, K. (1999). Multilevel theorising about creativity in organisations. *Academy of Management Review, 24*(2), 286–307. doi:10.2307/259083

Evangelista, R., & Sirilli, G. (1998). Innovation in the Service Sector: Results from the Italian Statistical Survey. *Technological Forecasting and Social Change, 58*, 251–269. doi:10.1016/S0040-1625(98)00025-0

Friedman, T. (2000). *The Lexus and the olive branch*. New York: Anchor Books.

Glynn, M. A. (1996). Innovative genius: a framework for relating individual and organisational intelligences to innovation. *Academy of Management Review, 21*(4), 1081–1111. doi:10.2307/259165

Hargadon, A. (2003). *How Breakthroughs Happen*. Boston: Harvard Business School Press.

Howell, J. M. (2005). The right stuff: identifying and developing effective champions of innovation. *The Academy of Management Executive, 19*(2), 108–119.

Howell, J. M., & Higgins, C. A. (1990). Champions of Technological Innovation. *Administrative Science Quarterly, 35*, 315–341. doi:10.2307/2393393

Kline, S. J., & Rosenberg, N. (1986). An overview of innovation. In Landau, R., & Rosenberg, N. (Eds.), *The Positive Sum Strategy*. Washington, DC: National Academy Press.

Know Inc. (2006). *KnetMap*. Retrieved from http://www.knowinc.com

Kogut, B. (1988). Joint Ventures: Theoretical and Empirical Perspectives. *Strategic Management Journal, 9*, 312–332. doi:10.1002/smj.4250090403

Kontoghiorghes, C., Awbre, S. M., & Feurig, P. L. (2005). Examining the relationship between learning organization characteristics and change adaptation, innovation, and organizational performance. *Human Resource Development Quarterly, 16*(2), 183–211. doi:10.1002/hrdq.1133

Koudal, P., & Coleman, G. C. (2005). Coordinating operations to enhance innovation in the global corporation. *Strategy and Leadership, 33*(4), 20–32. doi:10.1108/10878570510608013

Leonard-Barton, D., & Sensiper, S. (1998). The role of tacit knowledge in group innovation. *California Management Review, 40*(3), 112–132.

Lesser, E. L., & Storck, J. (2001). Communities of practice and organisational performance. *Knowledge Management, 40*(4). Retrieved from http://www.research.ibm.com/journal/sj/404/lesser.html

McFadzean, E., O'Loughlin, A., & Shaw, E. (2005). Corporate entrepreneurship and innovation part 1: the missing link. *European Journal of Innovation Management, 8*(3), 350–372. doi:10.1108/14601060510610207

Menzel, H. C., Aaltio, I., & Ulijn, J. M. (2007). On the way to creativity: Engineers as intrapreneurs in organizations. *Technovation, 27*(12), 732–743. doi:10.1016/j.technovation.2007.05.004

Moss Kanter, R. M. (1983). *The Change Masters*. New York: Simon and Schuster.

Moss Kanter, R. M. (1988). When a thousand flowers bloom: structural, collective, and social conditions for innovation in organisations. *Research in Organizational Behavior, 10*, 169–211.

Muller, A., Valikangas, L., & Merlyn, P. (2005). Metrics for innovation: guidelines for developing a customized suite of innovation metrics. *Strategy and Leadership, 33*(1), 37–45. doi:10.1108/10878570510572590

Nonaka, I., & Reinmoller, P. (2000). Dynamic Business Systems for Knowledge Creation and Utilization. In Despres, C., & Chauvel, D. (Eds.), *Knowledge Horizons: The Present and the Promise of Knowledge Management* (pp. 89–112). Oxford, UK: Butterworth-Heinemann.

Peters, T. J., & Waterman, R. H., Jr. (1982). *In Search of Excellence: Lessons from Americas Best Run Companies.* New York: Warrner Books.

Pinchot, G. (1985). *Intrapreneuring: Why you Don't Have to Leave the Corporation to Become and Entrepreneur.* New York: Harper and Row.

Porter, M. E. (2008). The Five Competitive Forces that Shape Strategy. *Harvard Business Review*, 79–93.

Rogers, E. M. (1995). *Diffusion of Innovation* (4th ed.). New York: Free Press.

Rosenfeld, R., & Servo, J. C. (1991). Facilitating change in large organisations. In Henry, J., & Walker, D. (Eds.), *Managing Innovation.* London: Sage.

Rothwell, R. (1994). Towards the fifth-generation innovation process. *International Marketing Review, 11*(1), 7–31. doi:10.1108/02651339410057491

Senge, P. M. (1990). *The Fifth Discipline.* New York: Doubleday.

Senge, P. M. (2004). Learn to Innovate. *Executive Excellence, 21*(6), 3–4.

Shaw, E., O'Loughlin, A., & McFadzean, E. (2005). Corporate entrepreneurship and innovation part 2: a role- and process-based approach. *European Journal of Innovation Management, 8*(4), 393–408. doi:10.1108/14601060510627786

Shenkel, A., Teigland, R., & Borgatti, S. P. (2001). *Theorizing structural properties of communities of practice: a social network approach.* Paper presented at Academy of Management annual conference.

Smith, P. A. C. (2005a). Knowledge sharing and strategic capital: the importance and identification of opinion leaders. *The Learning Organization, 12*(6), 563–574. doi:10.1108/09696470510626766

Smith, P. A. C. (2005b). Organisational change elements of establishing, facilitating, and supporting CoPs. In Coakes, E., & Clarke, C. (Eds.), *Encyclopedia of Communities of Practice in Information and Knowledge Management* (pp. 400–406). Hershey, PA: Idea Group Reference.

Smith, P. A. C. (2005c). Collective learning within CoPs. In Coakes, E., & Clarke, C. (Eds.), *Encyclopedia of Communities of Practice in Information and Knowledge Management* (pp. 30–31). Hershey, PA: Idea Group Reference.

Smith, P. A. C., & Saint-Onge, H. (1996). The evolutionary organization: avoiding a Titanic fate. *The Learning Organization, 3*(4), 4–21. doi:10.1108/09696479610148109

Stacey, R. D. (2001). *Complex Responsive Processes in Organizations: Learning and Knowledge Creation.* London: Routledge.

Sullivan, P. (1998). *Profiting from intellectual capital: Extracting value from innovation.* New York: John Wiley and Sons.

Teece, D. J. (1998). Capturing value from knowledge assets: the new economy, markets for know-how and intangible assets. *California Management Review, 40*(3), 55–79.

Thornbery, N. (2001). Corporate entrepreneurship: antidote or oxymoron. *European Management Journal, 19*(5), 526–533. doi:10.1016/S0263-2373(01)00066-4

Tidd, J. (2001). Innovation management in context: environment, organization and performance. *International Journal of Management Reviews, 3*, 169–183. doi:10.1111/1468-2370.00062

Tushman, M. L., & Nadler, D. (1986). Organizing for innovation. *California Management Review, 28*(3), 74–92.

Van de Ven, A. H. C. (1986). Central problems in the management of innovation. *Management Science, 32*, 590–607. doi:10.1287/mnsc.32.5.590

Wenger, E., McDermott, R., & Snyder, W. M. (2002). *Cultivating Communities of Practice.* Boston: Harvard Business School Press.

West, M. A., & Farr, J. (1990). *Innovation and Creativity at Work.* Chichester, UK: Wiley.

Zahra, S. A. (1995). Corporate entrepreneurship and financial performance: the case of management leveraged buyouts. *Journal of Business Venturing, 10*(3), 225–247. doi:10.1016/0883-9026(94)00024-O

This work was previously published in The International Journal of Sociotechnology and Knowledge Development, Volume 2, Issue 3, edited by Elayne Coakes, pp. 1-10, copyright 2010 by IGI Publishing (an imprint of IGI Global).

Chapter 5
Affective Factors for Successful Knowledge Management

Peter A.C. Smith
The Leadership Alliance Inc., Canada

ABSTRACT

The article proposes that any effort to successfully manage knowledge must be concerned not only with relevant technology, but also with the plethora of affective factors present in the workforce. The aim of this article is to heighten awareness of the impact of these affective factors on KM implementation, and to offer practical approaches that it is contended will assist in "getting the affective factors right".

INTRODUCTION

For more than a decade Knowledge Management (KM) has been vigorously proposed as a means to optimize enterprise performance and sustainable competitive advantage in the face of the rapidly increasing complexity and ambiguity of our modern global business environments (Nonaka & Takeuchi, 1995; Davenport & Prusak, 1998; Choo & Bontis, 2002; Marqués et al, 2006; Karaszewski, 2008).

During the early '90s KM essentially referred only to information systems (I/S) technologies related to informational databases, artificial intelligence, and Internet/intranet applications where information is shared across I/S networks. An understanding emerged during this period that to derive actionable meaning from information it was essential that the explicit and tacit dimensions of organizational knowledge be developed in a complimentary and dynamically reciprocal manner (Nonaka & Takeuchi, 1995).

DOI: 10.4018/978-1-4666-0200-7.ch005

Copyright © 2012, IGI Global. Copying or distributing in print or electronic forms without written permission of IGI Global is prohibited.

By the late-90s there was emphasis on treating KM in a more systemic organizational sense to include the social as well as the I/S technological aspects of any attempt to manage organizational knowledge. The work of Davenport and Prusak (1998) led the way in emphasizing that any effort to manage knowledge must be concerned not only with the I/S technology, but also the associated social issues. Wiig (2000; p. 14) cited a number of authors to support his contention that "*Overall KM will become more people-centric because it is the networking of competent and collaborating people that makes successful organizations*". Since that time a broad-based acceptance of the inclusive nature of KM has developed, together with a more practical appreciation of the perils of KM (Chua & Lam, 2005; Dufour & Steane, 2007).

In parallel there has been increasing acknowledgement of the impact of organizational culture on the success or failure of KM initiatives (Guzman & Wilson, 2005; Pyöriä, 2007) including the constructive or detrimental influences of the more personal affective, sometimes unconscious, factors such as beliefs, emotions, attitudes, and instincts (Gabriel & Griffiths, 2002; Scherer & Tran, 2003; Smith & McLaughlin, 2003; Malhotra, 2004; Lucas, 2005; Figler & Hanlon, 2008).

The aim of this article is to heighten awareness of the impact of affective factors on KM implementation, and to offer practical approaches that it is contended will assist in "getting the affective factors right". First a tried-and-true model for optimizing KM performance is reviewed that has been utilised successfully with a broad range of organizations for almost two decades (Smith & Sharma, 2002a; p. 767). Next this model is used to frame descriptions of initiatives that shape various affective factors for successful KM implementation. In exploring and defining the drivers for successfully implementing KM, the concept of a Personal Knowledge Management System (PKMS) is described.

BACKGROUND

Most managers will agree that their organization's capability to act is heavily dependent on its knowledge assets and how they are managed. In this regard, information technology (I/T) may be used to create, capture, organize, access and use the intellectual assets of the organization; however as Davenport and Prusak assert (1998; p. 123) "Knowledge management is much more than technology, but 'Techknowledgy' is clearly part of knowledge management". In other words I/T is an enabler (Allee, 1997). Coakes (2006; p. 581-582) tabulates the several roles and ways that I/T may support KM, but counsels "Successful knowledge management continues to need a socio-technical approach where the social aspects of knowledge creation, storage, and sharing need to be considered alongside the technical" (Coakes, 2006; p. 591).

As understanding of KM has become more sophisticated, the traditional notion of knowledge as the assets of strictly defined "professional" groups has become untenable when compared to an organization's wide-ranging knowledge requirements (Heiskanen, 2004), and the awareness that knowledge-bytes must be shared and distributed has gained ground in the past decade (Nosek, 2004; Kafai & Resnick, 1996; Resnick et al, 1993).

At the same time there has been a growing interest in the dynamic aspects of knowledge husbandry. Nonaka and Konno (1998) model the acquisition and construction of knowledge as a cyclic process based on socialization, externalization, combination, and internalization. Socialization includes the essential social interaction needed to learn new knowledge; externalization converts tacit knowledge to explicit; combination facilitates transfer of explicit knowledge to explicit knowledge; and internalization converts the explicit knowledge back to tacit knowledge.

Nosek (2004) considers this acquisition and construction of knowledge as a collective process of sense-making, rather than an individual process. This author asserts that we must abandon the concept of knowledge sharing as transmitting data in favor of the notion of "... effecting the right 'cognition', in the right agents, at the right time" (Nosek, 2004, p. 54). Sense-making here is interpreted as "the process whereby people interpret their world to produce the sense that shared meanings exist" (Leiter in Gephart, 1993, p. 1469-70), and the collective process involves people actively engaging in interpreting the social world through textual accounts and ongoing dialog that describes and make sense of the social world (Gephart, 1993; Weick, 1979).

The emerging emphasis on the importance of socialization for effective knowledge management and on the socio-technical concerns related to I/T knowledge systems has focused attention on the prevailing organizational culture. Culture here is defined as the shared values, beliefs and practices of the people in the organization (Schein, 1992), and includes the critical impact of non-rational affective factors. Many organizations operate under a facade of rationality (Smith & Sharma, 2002b) so that affective factors typically remain un-acknowledged or un-discussable, and less than optimum KM performance is often attributed to other (often blameless) organizational undertakings (Smith & McLaughlin, 2003). In order to capture the anticipated benefits of KM, an organization must strike an appropriate balance between rationality/technical efficiency and non-rational factors during implementation. In the next section some practical approaches are offered that will assist in "getting the affective factors right".

GETTING THE PEOPLE FACTORS RIGHT

A systemic model based in Chaos theory (Fitzgerald, 2002) is recommended to frame descriptions of initiatives that shape various affective factors for successful KM performance. The model consists of three 'fields' termed Focus, Will and Capability. The generic model is presented in Figure 1, and represents here a performance system directed to satisfying the KM outcomes desired.

The three fields form a dynamic system. Focus represents a clear definition and understanding of the KM system proposed; Focus is associated with questions such as What ..?; How ..?; Who ..?; Where ..?; When ..?; Why ..? The field of Will represents strength of intent to action the performance defined in Focus; Will is very strongly associated with the affective factors noted above. Capability represents the wherewithal to transform into reality the KM system defined in Focus; Capability is associated with such diverse areas as skills, software/hardware, budgets etc. A change in any one of these fields may effect a change in the state of one or both of the other fields.

Optimal KM performance is favoured when Focus, Will and Capability form a self-reinforcing system, with all fields in balance and harmony. As Figure 1 shows, current performance potential is represented by the degree of overlap of the circles; optimal performance is represented by complete congruence of all three circles. Areas where only two fields overlap in Figure 1 are typical of real-life situations. These imbalances lead to misdirected and wasted efforts as well as loss of performance. For example, organizations often concentrate on developing a technology-based KM system (strong Capability) without regard for the fact that their employees don't understand why KM is needed (weak Focus), and

Figure 1. *KM performance system*

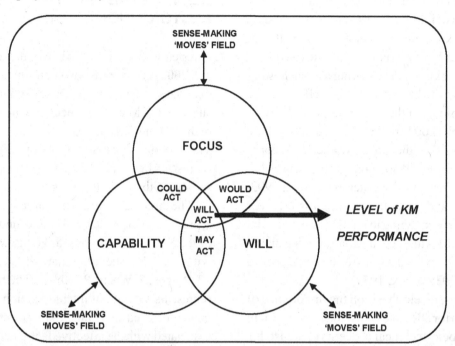

without sensitivity to an individual's feelings that their knowhow - their source of power - is being removed (absent Will).

Reasons preventing organizations from achieving well-targeted Focus, Will, and Capability are complex and illogical, as one would expect where tacit feeling-laden concerns are involved. For example, organizations typically operate with a façade of rationality although Will involves irrational issues. Will is often perceived as negative, linked to inappropriate expressive arenas of life rather than to the goal-orientation that drives organizations. Emotional maturity is equated with the control or repression of feelings, and the word "emotional" is used in a belittling sense as a deviation from intelligence (Putnam & Mumby, 1993, p. 36). In 1973 Egan wrote "Emotional repression in organizations is undoubtedly still a far greater problem than emotional overindulgence" (p. 61). Thirty-six years later this statement is as true as ever.

The three fields also constitute a strange attractor that according to Chaos theory assists individuals make meaning to produce order from chaos and help structure what is happening at the individual's level. The emergent KM system is formed as a result of all the interacting/interdependent activities that take place as individuals interpret the strange attractor's fields and take action – in other words, *KM will be pulled naturally into being rather than being pushed*.

In the following subsections initiatives are outlined that an organization may undertake to influence the three fields so that supportive affective factors may develop. Each field is treated individually; however, how activities initiated to shape one field influence one or more other fields is noted.

Focus must pull people toward a visionary core through their involvement, and the most critical element of Focus is the organization's KM "vision". Vision makes its strongest contribution to Focus when it results from a sharing of the individual yearnings of all employees, and the organizational vision must be aligned to the people, rather than the people to the vision (Mahesh, 1993; p. 230-231; Kouzes & Posner, 1995; p.129-133). Encouraging individual managers to explore with their teams development of a shared local KM vision (consistent with that of their organization) for their particular function is often sufficient. Note that when employees themselves clarify the KM Focus, the process helps them develop the appropriate Will.

Capability includes the physiological needs of individual employees, and it is important to satisfy these needs since they directly correlate with the quality of individual performance (Fortune, 1997). According to Maslow (1943) human beings have an innate requirement to satisfy a hierarchy of needs, including self-actualization (Mahesh, 1993; p. 35). Self-actualisation is critical to the development of the cultural traits that successful KM implementation demands; however, it is very important that needs at lower levels of Maslow's hierarchy be satisfied before attempting to introduce Will-related activities aimed at self-actualisation.

Will may best be shaped by pulling it into being via the initiatives discussed above for Focus and Capability; however, activities may be undertaken that shape Will more directly. For example by addressing how people in an organization meet to discuss a KM initiative. Often at meetings the last thing people want is to reveal their real underlying concerns. On the surface, all may appear well, and discussion proceeds in a calm and dignified manner; however, under the surface, a more turbulent encounter is taking place that will profoundly affect any subsequent actions.

One way to picture a meeting is to imagine people as icebergs floating together in the sea. When icebergs meet, the submerged parts of the icebergs (people's unawareness), which is much greater than the visible tips of the icebergs

(people's awareness), meet first. Gaunt (1991) provides details of the group conscious and unconscious awareness at various levels of an 'iceberg', and points out that the content is often defeated by the unarticulated process, which is largely about building trust. For example, the iceberg tip might be articulated as "How do I develop a KM system for my organization?" whereas the underlying problem that will need resolution might more realistically be defined as "How do I and the people in my team deal with feelings related to power loss and vulnerability etc?" Such KM icebergs cannot be fused into a cohesive whole by examining and responding only to their tips.

Concerns such as these may be explored through group dynamics (most notably psychoanalysis, field and systems theories, and Gestalt). Egan (2002) has proposed a system of counselling skills whereby emotions can be explored and resolved or managed. In the next section, group interventions (PKMS Workshops) that are used to build on Egan's work are described. These interventions help in the development of insight into unconscious difficulties and highlight blocks to effective working - without such interventions, no *meaningful* KM progress is likely.

Personal Knowledge Management System (PKMS) Workshops are recommended to give individuals opportunities to explore and define the strange attractor fields discussed above. Participants review barriers and anxieties related to their personal understanding and experience of KM, and develop a PKMS populated with appropriate personally-relevant cognitive, affective and resource related factors. Workshop activities are based on a form of action learning pioneered by Gaunt (1991). This approach utilises counselling and group work skills that draw on psychodynamic and Gestalt theories. It is favoured over the "project model" advocated by Revans (1982) because of its recognition that affective factors influence performance.

During a workshop, participants are familiarised with Egan's problem solving process (Egan, 2002). This process is about exploring a problem, then moving to a detailed understanding of the underlying issues, followed by action planning. People develop the skills to look below the waterline of the 'iceberg', and explore the semi- and un-conscious motivations and defences operating when KM is being introduced.

Longer-term action learning groups are formed at the end of a workshop program, and this activity is captured in an individual's PKMS, and as appropriate, in the overall organisational KM system. A large number of individuals can pass through the PKMS workshops in a few weeks, meaning that in a few months an organization can develop a very knowledgeable KM implementation community.

FUTURE TRENDS

Given the antipathy in so many organizations to acknowledging anything other than surface level affective factors as critical to performance, and in particular to KM which is so dependent on social complexities for its success, practice is not quickly going to inform theory. This is however a very fruitful area for research and promising work continues to appear; for example Byron (2008).

CLOSING REMARKS

In this article reasons why non-rational affective factors can critically help or hinder a KM initiative have been discussed. Means for acknowledging, exploring and positively influencing these affective factors have been reviewed. The intention has been to heighten awareness and understanding of these factors, and to emphasise that by addressing them proactively KM initiatives have a much greater chance of living up to their promise.

REFERENCES

Allee, V. (1997). 12 principles of knowledge management. *Training & Development, 51,* 71–75.

Byron, K. (2008). Differential effects of male and female managers' non-verbal emotional skills on employees' ratings. *Journal of Managerial Psychology, 23*(2), 118–134. doi:10.1108/02683940810850772

Choo, C. W., & Bontis, N. (Eds.). (2002). *The strategic management of intellectual capital and organizational knowledge*. New York: Oxford University Press.

Chua, A., & Lam, W. (2005). Why KM projects fail: a multi-case analysis. *Journal of Knowledge Management, 9*(3), 6–17. doi:10.1108/13673270510602737

Coakes, E. (2006). Storing and sharing knowledge: supporting the management of knowledge made explicit in transnational organizations. *The Learning Organization, 13*(6), 579–593. doi:10.1108/09696470610705460

Davenport, T. H., & Prusak, L. (1998). *Working Knowledge*. Boston, MA: Harvard Business School Press.

Dufour, Y., & Steane, P. (2007). Implementing knowledge management: a more robust model. *Journal of Knowledge Management, 11*(6), 68–80. doi:10.1108/13673270710832172

Egan, G. (1973). *Face to face*. Monterey: Brooks/Cole.

Egan, G. (2002). *The skilled helper*. Pacific Grove: Brooks/Cole.

Figler, R., & Hanlon, S. (2008). Management development and the unconscious from an analytical psychology framework. *Journal of Management Development, 27*(6), 613–630. doi:10.1108/02621710810877857

Fitzgerald, L. A. (2002). Chaos: the lens that transcends. *Journal of Organizational Change*, *15*(4), 339–358. doi:10.1108/09534810210433665

(1997)... *Fortune*, (October): 13.

Gabriel, Y., & Griffiths, D. S. (2002). Emotion, learning and organizing. *The Learning Organization*, *9*(5), 214–221. doi:10.1108/09696470210442169

Gaunt, R. (1991). *Personal and group development for managers: an integrated approach through action learning*. Harlow: Longmans.

Gephart, R. P. (1993). The textual approach: risk and blame in disaster sense-making. *Academy of Management Journal*, *36*(6), 1465–1514. doi:10.2307/256819

Guzman, G. A. C., & Wilson, J. (2005). The "soft" dimension of organizational knowledge transfer. *Journal of Knowledge Management*, *9*(2), 59–74. doi:10.1108/13673270510590227

Heiskanen, T. (2004). A knowledge-building community for public sector professionals. *Journal of Workplace Learning: Employee Counselling Today*, *16*(7), 370–384.

Kafai, Y. B., & Resnick, M. (1996). *Constructionism in practice: designing, thinking, and learning in a digital world*. Mahwah, NJ: Lawrence Erlbaum Associates.

Karaszewski, R. (2008). The influence of KM on global corporations' competitiveness. *Journal of Knowledge Management*, *12*(3), 63–70. doi:10.1108/13673270810875868

Kouzes, J. M., & Posner, B. Z. (1995). *The leadership challenge* (2nd ed.). San Francisco: Jossey-Bass.

Lucas, L. M. (2005). The impact of trust and reputation on the transfer of best practices. *Journal of Knowledge Management*, *9*(4), 87–101. doi:10.1108/13673270510610350

Mahesh, V. (1993). *Thresholds of Motivation*. New Delhi: Tata McGraw-Hill.

Malhotra, Y. (2004). Why knowledge management systems fail? Enablers and constraints of knowledge management in human enterprises. In M.E.D. Koenig & T.K. Srikantaiah (Eds), *Knowledge management lessons learned: what works and what doesn't* (pp. 87-112). Medford, NJ: Information Today.

Marqués, D. P., & Simón, F. J. G. (2006). The effect of knowledge management practices on firm performance. *Journal of Knowledge Management*, *10*(3), 143–156. doi:10.1108/13673270610670911

Maslow, A. (1943). Theory of human motivation. *Psychological Review*, *50*, 370–396. doi:10.1037/h0054346

Nonaka, I., & Konno, N. (1998). The concept of 'BA' – building a foundation for knowledge Creation. *California Management Review*, *40*(3), 40–54.

Nonaka, I., & Takeuchi, H. (1995). *The knowledge-creating company*. New York: Oxford University Press.

Nosek, J. T. (2004). Group cognition as a basis for supporting group knowledge creation and sharing. *Journal of Knowledge Management*, *8*(4), 54–64. doi:10.1108/13673270410556361

Putnam, L. L., & Mumby, D. K. (1993). Organizations, emotion and the myth of rationality. In S. Fineman (Ed.), *Emotion In Organizations* (pp. 36-57). London: Sage Publications.

Pyöriä, P. (2007). Informal organizational culture: the foundation of knowledge workers' performance. *Journal of Knowledge Management*, *11*(3), 16–30. doi:10.1108/13673270710752081

Resnick, L. B., Levine, J. M., & Teasley, S. D. (Eds.). (1993). *Perspectives on socially shared cognition*. Washington, DC: American Psychological Association.

Revans, R. W. (1982). *The origins and growth of action learning*. London: Chartwell-Bratt.

Schein, E. H. (1992). *Organizational culture and leadership* (2nd ed.). San Francisco: Jossey-Bass.

Scherer, K., & Tran, V. (2003). Effects of emotion on the process of organizational learning. In M. Dierkes, A. Antal, J. Child, & I. Nonaka (Eds.), *Handbook of Organizational Learning and Knowledge* (pp. 369-92). Oxford: Oxford University Press.

Smith, P. A. C., & McLaughlin, M. (2003). Succeeding with knowledge management: getting the people-factors right. In *Proceedings of the 6th World Congress On Intellectual Capital & Innovation*. Hamilton, Canada: McMaster University.

Smith, P. A. C., & Sharma, M. (2002a). Developing personal responsibility and leadership traits in all your employees, part 1: shaping and harmonizing the high-performance drivers. *Management Decision*, *40*(8), 764–774. doi:10.1108/00251740210441018

Smith, P. A. C., & Sharma, M. (2002b). Rationalizing the promotion of non-rational behaviors in organizations. *The Learning Organization*, *9*(5), 197–201. doi:10.1108/09696470210442132

Weick, K. E. (1979). *The social psychology of organizing*. Reading, MA: Addison-Wesley.

Wiig, K. M. (2000). Knowledge management: an emerging discipline rooted in a long history. In C. Despres & D. Chauvel (Eds.), *Knowledge horizons*. Boston, MA: Butterworth-Heinemann (pp,3-26).

KEY TERMS AND DEFINITIONS

Affective Factors: Individuals sustain consciously, semi-consciously and unconsciously an extensive variety of affective factors that vary widely and dynamically in response to their appreciation of past, present and future contexts. Affective factors are beliefs, attitudes, emotions and instincts, and may include mind-sets, trust, uncertainties, power needs, fears, impulses, anxieties, openness, anger, spirituality, love, and survival etc.

Focus, Will and Capability: In the KM performance model described in this article Focus represents a clear definition and understanding of the KM system proposed; Will represents strength of intent to action the performance defined in Focus; and Capability represents the wherewithal to transform into reality the KM system defined in Focus.

Personal Knowledge Management System: Each individual has a unique understanding of the Focus, Will and Capability that the organization has articulated for effecting a given KM system and what Focus, Will and Capability they personally possess; either or both of these perceptions are prone to error. The notion of a Personal Knowledge Management System involves an individual exploring any such misconceptions and populating their own knowledge-base with appropriate personally-relevant cognitive, affective and resource related knowledge. This activity helps equip an individual to best contribute to implementing the given KM system, and is best carried out in a social learning process such as action learning, where personal development is integrated with action.

Chaos Theory, Strange Attractors, and Fields: Chaos theory involves a fundamental way of seeing the world based on change-related theories dealing with complexity and chaos that have emerged over the last five decades from physics and the study of non-linear systems. According to Chaos theory the world is formed of complex dissipative structures in which disorder can be a source of order, and growth is found in disequilibrium. The richness of the diverse elements in a complex system allows the system as a whole to undergo spontaneous self-organization. Even the most chaotic of systems stay always within certain boundaries called "strange attractors" providing order without predictability. Control under these conditions may be created through the use of invisible forces called "fields" that structure behaviour. An organization must develop a visionary core at its "centre" to provide such fields. The organizational meaning articulated becomes a "strange attractor", and in this way individuals make meaning to produce order from chaos, giving form to work, and structure to what is happening at the level of the individual.

This work was previously published in The International Journal of Sociotechnology and Knowledge Development, Volume 2, Issue 1, edited by Elayne Coakes, pp. 1-11, copyright 2010 by IGI Publishing (an imprint of IGI Global).

Chapter 6
The War for Talent:
Identifying Competences in IT Professionals through Semantics

Ricardo Colomo-Palacios
Universidad Carlos III de Madrid, Spain

Marcos Ruano-Mayoral
EgeoIT, Spain

Pedro Soto-Acosta
Universidad de Murcia, Spain

Ángel García-Crespo
Universidad Carlos III de Madrid, Spain

ABSTRACT

In current organizations, the importance of knowledge and competence is unquestionable. In Information Technology (IT) companies, which are, by definition, knowledge intensive, this importance is critical. In such organizations, the models of knowledge exploitation include specific processes and elements that drive the production of knowledge aimed at satisfying organizational objectives. However, competence evidence recollection is a highly intensive and time consuming task, which is the key point for this system. SeCEC-IT is a tool based on software artifacts that extracts relevant information using natural language processing techniques. It enables competence evidence detection by deducing competence facts from documents in an automated way. SeCEC-IT includes within its technological components such items as semantic technologies, natural language processing, and human resource communication standards (HR-XML).

DOI: 10.4018/978-1-4666-0200-7.ch006

Copyright © 2012, IGI Global. Copying or distributing in print or electronic forms without written permission of IGI Global is prohibited.

INTRODUCTION

The use of IT solutions has become a key issue in many organizations worldwide. Organizations currently use multiple IT/IS solutions to support their activities at all management levels (Trigo, Varajao, & Barroso, 2009). Software costs as a percentage of total computer system costs continue to increase; while associated hardware costs continue to decrease (Huang & Lo, 2006). Software development is a collaborative and knowledge intensive process where success depends on the ability to create, share and integrate information (Walz et al., 1993), among other factors. Software development is an intense human capital activity, especially intense in intellectual capital (Sommerville & Rodden, 1996). Although the importance of human factors has been widely recognized as key for software engineering, researchers should put a larger focus on the humans involved in software engineering than what has been done to date (Feldt et al., 2008). However, poor management of human factors in technical projects, and software engineering projects can be considered as technical projects, can hinder the use and effectiveness of technology (Ives & Olsen, 1984).

Individual differences have been identified as one of the paradigms for the research of human factors in software development (Curtis, 2002). IT workers' professional practice must be continually revised and improved in order to adapt workers competences to technical innovations, and their soft skills to evolving markets (Casado-Lumbreras et al., 2009). In this scenario, competence at the individual level is required for the creation of core competence, which is crucial for today's organizations at the structural level (Bassellier, Reich, & Benbasat, 2001). But in spite of this importance, the world is facing an IT professionals shortage. Thus, attracting students in order to shape tomorrow's labor horizon has become a major issue of concern in educational institutions (Garcia-Crespo et al., 2009). According to the analysis by Morello,

Kyte, and Gomolsky (2007), many young people see IT as an unattractive career option: it is both hard work and "uncool". Additionally, this negative image is confirmed by the paradox that the strategic contribution of IT is recognized within enterprises, but the status of the IT department is low (Avison, Cuthbertson, & Powell, 1999). The shortage of IT professionals has been pointed out by many authors (e.g., Acharya & Mahanty, 2008; Agarwal & Ferratt, 2002; Mithas & Krishnan, 2008; Wells & Bogumil, 2001). As a consequence of this, the war for talent (Michaels, Handfield-Jones, & Axelrod, 2001) in the IT sector has its battlefield outside and inside the company and the internal recruitment of professionals must be done basing selection requirements against competence evidences. But in spite of the importance of competence evidences and knowledge sharing proficiencies pointed out by Liebowitz (2009), only a small number of companies have access to this data and develop their repository throughout the year.

Given the need of the corporations around the world to get competence evidences in a trusted and automatic way SeCEC-IT is presented in this paper. SeCEC-IT is a tool that based on the work performed by IT professionals in the context of software engineering development projects, extracts relevant information from software artifacts (programs, documents,…) using natural language processing and enables competence evidence detection by deducing competence facts in an automated and semantic way. These competence facts can be transferred to common human resource management tools that can exploit this information using competency management interchange standards so that it can be used for internal recruiting to projects, or to support knowledge management issues.

The remainder of this paper is organized as follows: the relevant literature in the collection of competence evidences is outlined and the main research efforts about semantic technologies are summarized. The architecture for the SeCEC-IT approach is presented along with the description of the implementation of the proof of the concept architecture. Finally, conclusions, implications for HRM, and future work are discussed.

COLLECTING EVIDENCES OF COMPETENCE

Competences and competence management has proved to be an extremely important area of study including fields such as pedagogy, psychology, and technology. The term "competence" has been applied in reference to many different domains of behavior (Waters & Sroufe, 1983). Anderson and Messick (1974) have catalogued 29 diverse referents ranging from specific skills (fine motor dexterity) to abstract concepts such as consolidation of identity.

According to McClelland (1973), competency is comprehended as the relation between humans and work tasks, that is, the concern is not about knowledge and skills in itself, but what knowledge and skills are required to perform a specific job or task in an efficient way (McClelland, 1973). In a subsequent analysis of the term in the scientific literature, Draganidis and Mentzas (2006) state that a competency must be defined in terms of:

- **Category.** A group to which homogeneous and/or similar competencies belong;
- **Competency.** A descriptive name for the specific competency;
- **Definition.** Statement(s) that explains the basic concept of this competency;
- **Demonstrated behavior.** Behavior indicators which an individual should demonstrate if the specified competency is possessed.

The competence approach was a major innovation in the human resource development field in the 1990s (Collin & Holden, 1997). McClelland

(1987) suggested that competence ought to become the basis for more effectively predicting individual performance in organizations. Moreover, competences can be defined as features related to effective working performance (Boyatzis, 1982). That could be the reason why competence is often used in the sense of performance, however, this is not entirely accurate (Bassellier, Horner Reich, & Benbasat, 2001). Nonetheless, competence is a factor that, coupled with motivation, effort and supporting conditions, may have a direct impact on performance (Schambach, 1994).

In the IT field there are many attempts to adopt and study the competence paradigm in various areas (e.g., Acuña & Juristo, 2004; Colomo-Palacios et al., 2010; Ruano-Mayoral et al., 2010; Trigo et al., 2010; Turley & Bieman, 1995). However, competence evidence collection, in general, and in software development teams, in particular, has received little attention in both theory and practice. In the work of Ruano-Mayoral et al. (2007) an antecedent of the system presented in this paper is presented. This system is a mobile tool to collect and store competence evidences, however, the collection of such evidences is performed manually. Taking this antecedent into account, the main purpose of this paper is to present a tool aimed to detect and classify competence evidences within software development projects through using software artifacts in an automated and semantic way.

SEMANTICS: A NEW PARADIGM ENABLED BY TECHNOLOGY

The information contained in Web pages was originally designed to be human-readable. As the Web grows in both size and complexity, there is an increasing need for automating some of the time consuming tasks related to Web content processing and management.

In this scenario, the Semantic Web can be seen as a vision for the future of the World Wide Web, where the unit of information is the data, instead of the web page as in the traditional Web. Around that vision of a web of data, the W3C consortium has promoted the development of several technologies to describe resources by means of ontologies and rules. The Semantic Web represents a revolution in many senses. The term "Semantic Web" was coined by Berners-Lee, Hendler and Lassila (2001), to describe the evolution from a document-based web towards a new paradigm that includes data and information for computers to manipulate. Ontologies (Fensel, 2002) are the technological cornerstones of the Semantic Web, because they provide structured vocabularies that describe a formal specification of a shared conceptualization. Ontologies were developed in the field of Artificial Intelligence to facilitate knowledge sharing and reuse (Fensel et al., 2001). Ontologies provide a common vocabulary for a domain and define, with different levels of formality, the meaning of the terms contained, and the relations between them. Knowledge in ontologies is mainly formalized using five kinds of components: classes, relations, functions, axioms, and instances (Gruber, 1993). The theory which supports the use of ontologies is a formal theory within which not only definitions but also a supporting framework of axioms is included (Smith, 2003).

Taking full advantage of ontologies, the Semantic Web provides a complementary vision as a knowledge management environment (Warren, 2006) that, in many cases has expanded, and replaced, previous knowledge and information management archetypes (Davies, Lytras, & Sheth, 2007). Thus, the Semantic Web has emerged to be a new and highly promising context for knowledge and data engineering (Vossen, Lytras, & Koudas, 2007). The goals of the Semantic Web initiative include the integration of data from different sources in a machine processable format in order to make them accessible to computer programs and facilitating the use of data in ways that had not been thought of when the data was entered or recorded (Battré, 2008). It is agreed that the

semantic enrichment of resources would lead to better search results (Scheir, Lindstaedt, & Ghidini, 2008). In this new scenario, the challenge for the next generation of the Social and Semantic Webs is to find the right match between what is put online, and methods for doing useful reasoning with the data (Gruber, 2008).

There are several works that reflect the importance of semantic technologies and their impact in competence systems and models. Semantic technology has been applied for project management teams construction (Gómez-Berbís et al., 2008); knowledge management for software projects (Colomo-Palacios et al., 2008); technical competence assessment (Colomo-Palacios et al., 2010); knowledge sharing and reuse (Lanzenberger, 2008); assisting the learning process (Naeve, Sicilia, & Lytras, 2008; Collazos & García, 2007); competence development efforts (Dodero et al., 2007); or assisting work assignment (Macris, Papadimitriou, & Vassilacopoulos, 2008); to cite some of the most recent initiatives.

SECEC-IT: ARCHITECTURE AND CASE STUDY

One of the key elements in the SeCEC-IT picture is capturing competence evidences and enabling internal and established Human Resource Management (HRM) solutions to use them. Due to this potential, the reliability and precision of the competence evidences and their usability will be drastically increased. On the other hand, there is a need to develop a solution that could interconnect with a set of companies. The best tool for this purpose is the HR-XML standard.

The HR-XML Consortium is an independent, nonprofit organization dedicated to the development and promotion of a standard suite of XML specifications to enable e-business and the automation of human resources-related data exchanges. SIDES, one of the recommendations published by the HR-XML Consortium can be seen as a suite of data exchange standards for staffing issues. One of the multiple parts of SIDES is a competence schema designed to fulfill the following requirements (Allen, 2003):

- The competence schema is simple and sufficiently flexible and generalized so that it is useful within a variety of business contexts;
- The schema provides structure to enable competences to be easily compared, ranked, and evaluated;
- The schema is capable of referencing competence taxonomies from which competence descriptions were taken or used;
- The competence schema is relatively simple and compact so that it does not add to the complexity of the process-specific schemas within which it is used.

For the purpose of our work, the competence schema allows integration with other Human Resources Management Systems but, to achieve the full capacity of competence analysis that this framework seeks, it is necessary to build an extension of the competence schema to store some extra information about each competence evidence. The extension was used by the authors in the past and can be found in Ruano-Mayoral et al. (2007).

In what follows an explanation of SeCEC-IT will be given showing its architecture and a use case.

ARCHITECTURE

The architecture of SeCEC-IT is based on component groups that interact among themselves, to offer an automatic solution to the problem proposed. The conjunction of these systems permits the correct operation of the whole set of components, and obtaining the necessary data to achieve the desired outcome. Since interoper-

ability is one of the most challenging problems in modern cross-organizational information systems (Mocan et al., 2009), much emphasis is put on interoperability issues, done via web services. The final architectural approach is a tailor-made value-added technological solution. Components might be related to the behavior as specified in the collaboration among those elements, turning those structural and behavioral elements into progressively larger subsystems, and the architectural style that guides this organization. Figure 1 shows how these different subsystems communicate and the flow of exchanged messages, in order to process the final system response. In the following sections the internal working of every element will be detailed.

As mentioned above, the architecture is comprised of three operating layers or subsystems. Firstly, the interface layer is composed by a number of interfaces through which end systems can interact with SeCEC-IT. Secondly, the logic layer encompasses the reasoning, inference, and business logic management functionalities. Finally, the persistence and storage layer is composed by semantic repositories, storing the competence evidence ontology. In the following, we will detail several of the core components in each layer.

- INTERFACE. This layer presents two components, namely HRM Interface and Repository crawler.
  - HRM Interface. This component allows the communication with external HRM solutions using a web service. Three different kinds of data are exchanged:
    - Competence descriptions included in HRM Solutions. These descriptions will feed the crawler that will seek relevant information relative to these descriptions in the set of software artifacts.

Figure 1. System architecture

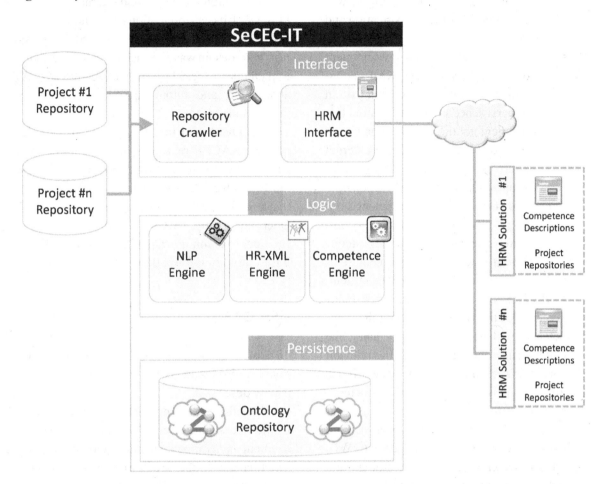

- Instructions of how to locate and reach project repositories (URL).
- HR-XML formats containing information elaborated by the system that is transmitted to HRM external systems in response to a given query.
  ○ Repository Crawler. This component, given a project repository, 'crawls' documents and sends them to the NLP engine in search of competence evidences.

- LOGIC. This layer provides cutting-edge functionalities through the following components:
  ○ NLP engine. Given a (set of) document(s) in a project repository and a set of human resources, NLP seeks for relevant competence evidences, such as participation of a programmer in a requisite extraction process. In this module several well known tools are implemented, including GATE to syntactic annotate noun phrases and JAPE to extract all phrases related to competence evidences. Once a competency evidence

is found, the Competence Engine will be responsible of its classification and storage.

- ○ HR-XML Engine. This component constructs a valid HR-XML document from a query by reading data in the persistence layer, and returns this document to the interface layer, in order to be delivered to the external system.
- ○ Competence Engine. Is responsible for dealing with the competence ontology and stores information of competency evidences in the persistence layer. It hides competence complexity to other components of the system.
- PERSISTENCE. Finally, the persistence layer stores the knowledge about the competence evidences. On the one hand, the Competence ontology defines the relevant characteristics of each competence. All this information is used to describe competences suitable for our system (technical competence). This ontology has been defined using the Ontology Web Language (OWL) (Bechhofer et al., 2004). The storage and ontology reasoning has been developed based on the Jena framework.

On the other hand, the competence evidences and their location relative to their project repositories are also stored in a database. Both the competence ontology schema and its populated instances are stored in the KAON2 ontology repository. KAON2 is an infrastructure for managing OWL-DL ontologies. In the case of SeCEC-IT, Jena is the backbone technology that relies on a MySQL database. Jena is a framework for building Semantic Web applications that provides a programmatic environment for RDF, RDFS and OWL, SPARQL and includes a rule-based inference engine.

About implementation and internals, SeCEC-IT is a Web based application build under Java EE (by using Java Enterprise Edition 5 SDK). Business logic design was done using MagicDraw. This tool enables Model Driven Architecture (MDA) architecture and automatic code generation by using AndroMDA.

The Java-based tool RACER is also implemented. RACER reasoning engine and the Jena framework are crucial for the business logic manager layer, the former for the reasoning and the latter for the RDF Management and SPARQL Querying. Lastly, JAXB is used for XML handle (in order to communicate with others) and JENA 2 for ontology information issues.

USE CASE

To explain the realization of SeCEC-IT in a functional environment, as referred before, a use case is now described.

The software development company SEMDEV would like to implement a new knowledge management and competence management program. The final aim of this program is to assign people to projects basing these decisions in resource availability and competence. Now managers perform project staffing currently just by using availability and through using informal information, but the company owners want to implement a more scientific approach that permits personnel assignation closing the gap between competence and project role.

SEMDEV sends to SeCEC-IT the information needed to start the crawling process. Firstly, the access to current software development projects repositories (giving an external granted access to a PDF and code repository), on the other hand, the set of competences and human resources aimed for SEMDEV. These competences are adapted to SeCEC-IT competence ontology and the crawling process starts. The Repository Crawler component looks for relevant information in the repository and sends relevant information to the NLP Engine. This component extracts relevant competence evidences from documents and sends this information to the Competence Engine. The Competence Engine populates the competence ontology by creating a number of instances for given competences and human resources.

For example, the analysis of a number of software artifacts may imply that the resource RCP is competent in Requirements Engineering, but his results in Software Testing are low according to several comments in their proofs. The Competence Engine will store this information in the Persistence Layer that will be stored in the KAON2 ontology repository. Once all documents are crawled, the system regularly performs an update check in order to find out if there are new versions of documents and, thus, new competence evidences.

Later on, SEMDEV implants a HRM tool (such as Meta4 PeopleNet) to support competence development and management as well as project staffing based on competences. In this new scenario, SEMDEV human resource administrators can ask SeCEC-IT for competence evidences. Let's imagine that more information about competence evidences are needed for RCP. In this case, PeopleNet could ask to SeCEC-IT for this information using the HRM Interface. Once this order is received, the HR-XML engine extracts this information from the Ontology Repository using SPARQL and forms a correct HR-XML format in order to be sent to PeopleNet using the HRM Interface.

CONCLUSION AND FUTURE WORK

The advent of the information age represents both a challenge and an opportunity for knowledge and competence management. New forms of knowledge extraction and expert location are deeply impacting companies around the world. IT companies are facing a war for talent in which, every project must be scheduled according to the availability of resources and their competences. In this new scenario, counting on with tools to seek competency in work environment can enable a better personnel management that could be a competitive advantage for the company.

SeCEC-IT, following the path of some previous works (Colomo-Palacios et al., 2008; Colomo-Palacios et al., 2010; García-Crespo et al., 2009; Ruano-Mayoral et al., 2007) brings new features to competence management in software development projects: the transformation of plain text to competence evidences in an automatic way. This competence evidences could be used, by means of the interfaces implemented, for staffing and teaming purposes or as a support to performance appraisal.

But SeCEC-IT is not only relevant for IT professionals and managers. Counting on a tool that can derive competency evidences directly from software artifacts could be a competitive advantage for the firm. Moreover, HRM personnel could also benefit from this. Having in mind that sometimes IT workers perform a highly technical work, it's very difficult for HRM departments to infer competency from their work without the assistance of an IT manager a highly IT qualified individual. But, having in mind the lack of available time, it's sometimes difficult for HRM personnel to know the competency levels of IT professionals apart from the yearly assessment. This information could be of great benefit for the corporation and its applications are multiple: improve the person-role fit, detect competency gaps, improve internal recruitment process and perk up professional development and career planning.

Taking into account the possibilities initiated by the current research effort, four separate lines of future research may be considered. In the first place, the integration of certain Web 2.0 contents as a source for competence evidences. In the second place, authors suggest to expand the possibilities of the system to deal with cultural, gender and performance differences. In the third place, integrate the tool into a wider program in which affective factors pointed out by Smith (2010) must be taken into account. Lastly, it is aimed to integrate SeCEC-IT in Computer Aided Software Engineering tools and, in particular, in effort and duration estimation tools for software development projects.

ACKNOWLEDGMENT

This work is supported by the Centre for the Development of Industrial Technology (CDTI) (Ministry of Science and Innovation) under Sem-IDI project IDI-20091150.

REFERENCES

Acharya, P., & Mahanty, B. (2008). Manpower shortage crisis in Indian information technology industry. *International Journal of Technology Management*, *38*(3), 235–247. doi:10.1504/IJTM.2007.012712

Acuña, S. T., & Juristo, N. (2004). Assigning people to roles in software projects. *Software, Practice & Experience*, *34*(7), 675–696. doi:10.1002/spe.586

Agarwal, R., & Ferratt, T. W. (2002). Enduring practices for managing IT professionals. *Communications of the ACM*, *45*(9), 73–79. doi:10.1145/567498.567502

Allen, C. (Ed.). (2003). *HR-XML recommendation. Competencies (Measurable Characteristics). Recommendation*. Retrieved March 5, 2010, from http://www.hr-xml.org/

Anderson, S., & Messick, S. (1974). Social competency in young children. *Developmental Psychology*, *10*(2), 282–293. doi:10.1037/h0035988

Avison, D. E., Cuthbertson, C. H., & Powell, P. (1999). The paradox of information systems: Strategic value and low status. *The Journal of Strategic Information Systems*, *8*(4), 419–445. doi:10.1016/S0963-8687(00)00026-3

Bassellier, G., Reich, B. H., & Benbasat, I. (2001). IT Competence of Business Managers: A Definition and Research Model. *Journal of Management Information Systems*, *17*(4), 159–182.

Battré, D. (2008). Caching of intermediate results in DHT-based RDF stores. *International Journal of Metadata. Semantics and Ontologies*, *4*(3), 183–195.

Bechhofer, S., van Harmelen, F., Hendler, J., Horrocks, I., McGuinness, D. L., Patel-Schneider, P. F., & Stein, L. A. (2004). *OWLWeb Ontology Language Reference*. Retrieved from http://www.w3.org/TR/owl-ref/

Berners-Lee, T., Hendler, J., & Lassila, O. (2001). The Semantic Web. *Scientific American*, *284*(5), 34–43. doi:10.1038/scientificamerican0501-34

Boyatzis, R. E. (1982). *The Competent Manager. A model for effective performance*. New York: John Wiley & Sons Ltd.

Casado-Lumbreras, C., Colomo-Palacios, R., Gómez-Berbís, J. M., & García-Crespo, Á. (2009). Mentoring programmes: a study of the Spanish software industry. *International Journal of Learning and Intellectual Capital*, *6*(3), 293–302. doi:10.1504/IJLIC.2009.025046

Collazos, C. A., & García, R. (2007). Semantics-supported cooperative learning for enhanced awareness. *International Journal of Knowledge and Learning*, *3*(4/5), 421–436. doi:10.1504/IJKL.2007.016703

Collin, A., & Holden, L. (1997). The nacional framework for vocational education and training. In Beardwell, I., & Holden, L. (Eds.), *Human Resource Management: A contemporany perspective* (pp. 345–377). London: Pitman.

Colomo-Palacios, R., García-Crespo, A., Gómez-Berbís, J. M., Casado-Lumbreras, C., & Soto-Acosta, P. (2010). SemCASS: technical competence assessment within software development teams enabled by semantics. *International Journal of Social and Humanistic Computing*.

Colomo-Palacios, R., Gómez-Berbís, J. M., García-Crespo, A., & Puebla Sánchez, I. (2008). Social Global Repository: using semantics and social web in software projects. *International Journal of Knowledge and Learning*, *4*(5), 452–464. doi:10.1504/IJKL.2008.022063

Colomo-Palacios, R., Tovar-Caro, E., Garcia-Crespo, A., & Gomez-Berbis, M. J. (2010). Identifying Technical Competences of IT Professionals. The Case of Software Engineers. *International Journal of Human Capital and Information Technology Professionals*, *1*(1), 31–43.

Curtis, B. (2002). Human Factors in Software Development. In Marciniak, J. J. (Ed.), *Encyclopedia of Software Engineering* (pp. 598–610). New York: Willey & Sons.

Davies, J., Lytras, M. D., & Sheth, A. P. (2007). Semantic-Web-Based Knowledge Management. *IEEE Internet Computing*, *11*(5), 14–16. doi:10.1109/MIC.2007.109

Dodero, J. M., Sánchez-Alonso, S., & Frosch-Wilke, D. (2007). Generative Instructional Engineering of Competence Development Programmes. *Journal of Universal Computer Science*, *13*(9), 1213–1233.

Draganidis, F., & Mentzas, G. (2006). Competency based management: a review of systems and approaches. *Information Management & Computer Security*, *14*(1), 51–64. doi:10.1108/09685220610648373

Feldt, R., Torkar, R., Angelis, L., & Samuelsson, M. (2008). Towards individualized software engineering: empirical studies should collect psychometrics. In *Proceedings of the 2008 international workshop on Cooperative and human aspects of software engineering (CHASE '08)* (pp. 49-52).

Fensel, D. (2002). *Ontologies: A silver bullet for knowledge management and electronic commerce*. Berlin: Springer.

Fensel, D., van Harmelen, F., Horrocks, I., McGuinness, D. L., & Patel-Schneider, P. F. (2001). OIL: An ontology infrastructure for the semantic web. *IEEE Intelligent Systems*, *16*(2), 38–45. doi:10.1109/5254.920598

García-Crespo, A., Colomo-Palacios, R., Gomez-Berbís, J. M., & Tovar-Caro, E. (2009). IT Professionals' Competences: High School Students' Views. *Journal of Information Technology Education*, *8*(1), 45–57.

Gómez-Berbís, J. M., Colomo-Palacios, R., García Crespo, A., & Ruiz-Mezcua, B. (2008). ProLink: A Semantics-based Social Network for Software Project. *International Journal of Information Technology and Management*, *7*(4), 392–404. doi:10.1504/IJITM.2008.018656

Gruber, T. R. (1993). A translation approach to portable ontology specifications. *Knowledge Acquisition*, *5*(2), 199–220. doi:10.1006/knac.1993.1008

Gruber, T. R. (2008). Collective knowledge systems: Where the social web meets the semantic web. *Web Semantics: Science. Services and Agents on the World Wide Web*, *6*(1), 4–13.

Huang, C. Y., & Lo, J. H. (2006). Optimal resource allocation for cost and reliability of modular software systems in the testing phase. *Journal of Systems and Software, 79*(5), 653–664. doi:10.1016/j.jss.2005.06.039

Ives, B., & Olsen, M. H. (1984). User involvement and MIS success: A review of research. *Management Science, 30*(5), 586–603. doi:10.1287/mnsc.30.5.586

Lanzenberger, M., Sampson, J., Rester, M., Naudet, Y., & Latour, T. (2008). Visual ontology alignment for knowledge sharing and reuse. *Journal of Knowledge Management, 12*(6), 102–120. doi:10.1108/13673270810913658

Liebowitz, J. (2009). My Top 10 Lessons on Lessons Learned Systems. *International Journal of Sociotechnology and Knowledge Development, 1*(1), 53–57.

Macris, A., Papadimitriou, E., & Vassilacopoulos, G. (2008). An ontology-based competency model for workflow activity assignment policies. *Journal of Knowledge Management, 12*(6), 72–88. doi:10.1108/13673270810913630

McClelland, D. (1987). *Human Motivation.* Cambridge, MA: Cambridge University Press.

McClelland, D. C. (1973). Testing for competence rather than for 'intelligence'. *The American Psychologist, 28*, 1–14. doi:10.1037/h0034092

Michaels, E., Handfield-Jones, H., & Axelrod, B. (2001). *The War for Talent.* Boston: Harvard Business Press.

Mithas, S., & Krishnan, M. S. (2008). Human Capital and Institutional Effects in the Compensation of Information Technology Professionals in the United States. *Management Science, 54*(3), 415–428. doi:10.1287/mnsc.1070.0778

Mocan, A., Facca, F. M., Loutas, N., Peristeras, V., Goudos, S. K., & Tarabanis, K. A. (2009). Solving Semantic Interoperability Conflicts in Cross-Border E-Government Services. *International Journal on Semantic Web and Information Systems, 5*(1), 1–47.

Morello, D., Kyte, A., & Gomolski, B. (2007). *The quest for talent: You ain't seen nothing yet.* Retrieved March 4, 2010, from http://www.gartner.com/DisplayDocument?ref=g_search&id=569115&subref=advsearch

Naeve, A., Sicilia, M. A., & Lytras, M. D. (2008). Learning processes and processing learning: from organizational needs to learning designs. *Journal of Knowledge Management, 12*(6), 5–14. doi:10.1108/13673270810913586

Ruano-Mayoral, M., Colomo-Palacios, R., García-Crespo, A., & Gómez-Berbís, J. M. (2010). Software Project Managers under the Team Software Process: A Study of Competences Based on Literature. *International Journal of Information Technology Project Management, 1*(1), 42–53.

Ruano-Mayoral, M., Colomo-Palacios, R., Gómez-Berbís, J. M., & García-Crespo, A. (2007). A Mobile Framework for Competence Evaluation: Innovation Assessment Using Mobile Information Systems. *Journal of Technology Management & Innovation, 2*(3), 49–57.

Schambach, T. (1994). *Maintaining professional competence: an evaluation of factors affecting professional obsolescence of information technology professionals.* Unpublished doctoral dissertation, University of South Florida, FL.

Scheir, P., Lindstaedt, S. N., & Ghidini, C. (2008). A Network Model Approach to Retrieval in the Semantic Web. *International Journal on Semantic Web and Information Systems, 4*(4), 56–84.

Smith, B. (2003). Ontology. An Introduction. In Floridi, L. (Ed.), *Blackwell Guide to the Philosophy of Computing and Information* (pp. 155–166). Oxford, UK: Blackwell.

Smith, P. (2010). Affective Factors for Successful Knowledge Management. *International Journal of Sociotechnology and Knowledge Development, 2*(1), 1–11.

Sommerville, I., & Rodden, T. (1996). Human social and organizational influences on the software process. In Fuggetta, A., & Wolf, A. (Eds.), *Software Process (Trends in Software 4)* (pp. 89–110). New York: John Wiley & Sons.

Trigo, A., Varajao, J., & Barroso, J. (2009). A practitioner's roadmap to learning the available tools for Information System Function management. *International Journal of Teaching and Case Studies, 2*(1), 29–40. doi:10.1504/IJTCS.2009.026297

Trigo, A., Varajão, J., Soto-Acosta, P., Barroso, J., Molina-Castillo, F. J., & Gonzalvez-Gallego, N. (2010). IT Professionals: An Iberian Snapshot. *International Journal of Human Capital and Information Technology Professionals, 1*(1), 61–75.

Turley, R. T., & Bieman, J. M. (1995). Competencies of exceptional and nonexceptional software engineers. *Journal of Systems and Software, 28*(1), 19–38. doi:10.1016/0164-1212(94)00078-2

Vossen, G., Lytras, M. D., & Koudas, N. (2007). Editorial: Revisiting the (Machine) Semantic Web: The Missing Layers for the Human Semantic Web. *IEEE Transactions on Knowledge and Data Engineering, 19*(2), 145–148. doi:10.1109/TKDE.2007.30

Walz, D. B., Elam, J. J., & Curtis, B. (1993). Inside a Software Design Team: Knowledge Acquisition, Sharing, and Integration. *Communications of the ACM, 36*(10), 63–77. doi:10.1145/163430.163447

Warren, P. (2006). Knowledge Management and the Semantic Web: From Scenario to Technology. *IEEE Intelligent Systems, 21*(1), 53–59. doi:10.1109/MIS.2006.12

Waters, E., & Sroufe, L. (1983). Social Competence as a Developmental Construct. *Developmental Review, 3*, 79–97. doi:10.1016/0273-2297(83)90010-2

Wells, L. A., & Bogumil, W. A. (2001). Immigration and the global IT work force. *Communications of the ACM, 44*(7), 34–38. doi:10.1145/379300.379307

This work was previously published in The International Journal of Sociotechnology and Knowledge Development, Volume 2, Issue 3, edited by Elayne Coakes, pp. 26-36, copyright 2010 by IGI Publishing (an imprint of IGI Global).

Section 2

Chapter 7
Think Global, Act Local:
How ICTs are Changing the Landscape in Community Development

Sylvie Albert
Laurentian University, Canada

Don Flournoy
Ohio University, USA

ABSTRACT

Being able to connect high-speed computing and other information technologies into broadband communication networks presents local communities with some of their best chances for renewal. Such technologies are now widely perceived to be not just a nice amenity among corporations and such non-profit organizations as universities but a social and economic necessity for communities struggling to find their place in a rapidly changing world. Today, citizens want and expect their local communities to be "wired" for broadband digital transactions, whether for family, business, education or leisure. Such networks have become a necessity for attracting and retaining the new "knowledge workforce" that will be key to transforming communities into digital societies where people will want to live and work. Since the Internet is a global phenomenon, some of the challenges of globalization for local communities and regions are introduced in this article and suggestions for turning those challenges into opportunities are offered. To attain maximum benefit from the new wired and wireless networks, local strategies must be developed for its implementation and applications must be chosen with some sensitivity to local needs. New Growth theory is used to show why communities must plan their development agenda, and case studies of the Intelligent Community Forum are included to show how strategically used ICTs are allowing local communities to be contributors in global markets.

DOI: 10.4018/978-1-4666-0200-7.ch007

Copyright © 2012, IGI Global. Copying or distributing in print or electronic forms without written permission of IGI Global is prohibited.

INTRODUCTION

Whatever economic and social changes occur globally, they are eventually felt locally. Thomas Friedman (2006), author of *The World is Flat*, Don Tapscott and Anthony Williams (2008), authors of *Wikinomics*, and numerous others have pointed to the ways global developments change for good or bad the future prospects of local communities, of local enterprises and their citizens. Many aspects of the various globalization scenarios they describe are not always hopeful, and community leaders who think about such things are understandably nervous. Change cannot be held back; but community leaders can have some control over how they plan to deal with change.

Among the driving forces in the shifting economic and social order of nations is the rapid and widespread adoption of computer processing and the ease with which information in digital form can now be exchanged over wired and wireless communication networks. Technological advancements are viewed as tools that human beings employ to better their condition. From the perspective of community, the whole point of a telecommunications solution is that the pace of human enterprise can be accelerated and the reach of human players can be extended inward and outward for the benefit of all.

"Think Global" in this article has to do with the fact that communities everywhere are being affected by the rapid, transformational changes brought by information and communication technologies (ICTs). This is a global phenomenon. Whether these changes are positive or negative will depend on strategies that communities develop to make use of them. "Act Local" has to do with the steps communities take to insure a networked infrastructure that is sound and sustainable, one that will allow citizens to innovate around those ICTs, to develop new business opportunities and to promote a better quality of life. Local strategies for preparing citizens to think more broadly will go a long way toward promoting the right kinds of growth for communities as the broadband Internet opens new doors for local development.

Near-instant access to information stored on remote web sites and much easier, more personalized communication via the Internet have changed the very definition of global reach and of what local means. Eger (2007, 1) says, *"No technology in human history is having, or is likely to have, such tremendous influence on life and work and play, and in the transforming process, on our physical space, as the Internet."* As scary as the Internet is, participation in the panoply of networks being created within the broadband Internet space seems irresistible, and may actually be a competitive necessity. Certainly, local citizens and institutions who have managed to get themselves better connected are seeing the advantages of being linked to their neighbors regionally and around the globe.

With pervasive digital networks in place, the economics of access, innovation and distribution have undergone radical transformation. Communities are choosing to use these networks to better identify and promote their assets. Local institutions and local businesses are finding ways to more efficiently connect and collaborate with one another, to cluster their businesses for maximum impact. Whether those points of collaboration stay within communities or reach beyond them, computers and telecommunications will be the basic technological infrastructure on which most of the newly formed alliances are grounded. The assumption of this article is that a deliberate and reasoned approach to ICT adoption and use can increase the prospects for community transformation that is under local control.

The Intelligent Community Forum is a New York City-based think tank that studies economic and social development of modern communities. From the mission section of its web site, the ICF says:

Whether in industrialized or developing nations, communities are challenged to create prosperity, stability and cultural meaning in a world where jobs, investment and knowledge increasingly depend on broadband communications. For the 21st Century community, connectivity is a double-edge sword: threatening established ways of life on the one hand, and offering powerful new tools to build prosperous, inclusive economies on the other. ICF seeks to share the secrets of success of the world's Intelligent Communities in adapting to the demands of the Broadband Economy, in order to help communities everywhere find renewal and growth. (www.intelligentcommunity.org)

As its goal, the ICF seeks: to identify and explain the emergence of the broadband economy and its impact at the local level; to research and share best practices by communities in adapting to their changing economic environments and positioning their citizens and businesses to prosper; and to celebrate the achievements of communities that have overcome challenges to claim a place in the economy of the 21st century. Since the authors have served as Advisors to this organization from its founding in 2004, this paper will introduce several ICF cases (and others) as a useful guide for community leaders who wish to think more rationally about using ICT tools to refocus their economic development efforts.

The authors believe that "networked communities," sometimes called intelligent or smart communities, are the advanced guard of a large scale movement toward using knowledge for the betterment of peoples' lives. In the context of communities installing high-speed telecommunication facilities with the idea of improving economic development and quality of life, there is evidence to suggest that results are being achieved and even greater opportunities can be expected from the rapid enhancement of digital processing, production, storage, retrieval and distribution globally. The next step to be taken, a step that can only be taken at the local level, is to grow public awareness and involvement.

COMMUNITY'S ROLE IN ICT DEVELOPMENT

When time, location and distance are identified as problems, communities can now think seriously about ways to address them using a combination of digital processing and telecom networks, building local capability through partnerships based on outreach. Such a change can of course be quite drastic in one-industry towns, particularly as residents begin to take seriously the idea of a more diversified economy. Creating new social compacts between non-profit organizations and private and commercial sectors permits a different kind of thinking about the larger purposes of these organizations and the way they use natural and human resources. Such upside down thinking opens up all kinds of opportunities for strengthening the economic fabric of communities.

Local societies are finding that being "networked" – both within and without - can make available entirely new genres of products and services, many of which can be produced right in the community. Local citizens can now think about what products and services they will be able to create, repurpose and redistribute as revenue-producing goods and as not-for-profit innovations and applications. These are the basic concepts advanced in Flournoy's *Broadband Millennium: Communication Technologies and Markets* (2004).

The Internet is the ultimate consumer-targeted overbuilder[1] destined to be everyone's competitor and everyone's competitive solution. It seems logical to assume that the Internet will prove to be bigger and more powerful than all the other media combined, because it will be the network that connects them all. The Internet has dropped the cost of creating, storing, retrieving, and sending information. Those citizens with the technologies, skills, and financial resources to access the Internet will be the ones deciding for themselves whether to live in town or work from the lake house, whether to spend their leisure time enjoying spectator sports or playing chess on-line.

In this new on-line world, applications will fuse computing, communications, entertainment, information, education, commercial, and community activities. Personal media will take a more prominent place alongside mass media. Anytime, anywhere media, accessible on demand, will challenge the old one-suits-all models that everyone knew were the way they were solely because of economics - mostly for the benefit of advertisers trying to aggregate a mass audience.

Today, families can start their own businesses from home running catalog stores, retail outlets, auto exchanges, and ad agencies at low cost with a minimum of equipment and expertise. These businesses can be open twenty-four24 hours a day, seven 7 days a week, and involve the kids, the grandparents, and half the local neighborhood. These businesses can be like the old hometown mom- and- pop stores, where customers seek out products tailored to their personal needs and, where attention is given to service (pp. 26-27).

The Internet – along with the applications it has spawned – is freeing local entrepreneurs of many of the constraints of time, distance and expense that here-to-fore had set barriers to innovation. In using computers and telecommunications, users can now go in search of the information they need, connect to local and distant collaborators and create markets where they did not exist before. These developments have enabled a change of mindset among community leaders as well as ordinary citizens in thinking about possible futures. Less than a decade ago, proponents of economic development were very much focused on physical assets. Communities in Canada, the USA and elsewhere were developing business parks and analyzing the cost of locating invest-

ment in localities as strategies for attracting new plants and creating new jobs. Business parks are still being developed, but some communities focus them as ICT parks so that they can cultivate a knowledge culture around ICTs.

The advent of ICTs has allowed a slight change of emphasis. Having ICT capabilities allow communities to sell other types of resources—especially knowledge resources such as information and expertise—with promotions being built around services that transcend geographical place. Now, ICT-based communities can in reality be at the very center of the universe as a node in a global network where everybody is connected to everybody else and information services hold value equal to the production of material goods.

Citizens could not have seriously thought about any of this before the user technologies and public infrastructure were in place. But once broadband is a reality and can be accessed at any time for any reason, people begin to see what it can do. We believe that when we teach people to use these tools in schools and businesses, and the capacity and software is made accessible to everyone, a culture of digital creation and use will emerge. Businesses as well as ordinary citizens will come up with innovative ways to meet the challenges they face. Some will adapt applications that have proved successful elsewhere while others will innovate; most will see the benefit of extending approaches tried out at the office or home and, finding their efforts work, will share their creations more broadly. Either way, people will be self-creators of economic and social development using the information and communication technologies at hand.

From a resource-based perspective, adding virtual organizations brings strategic advantages. Communities can use their new online networks to identify core competencies within the region and plan for the kinds of clustering that can create new development opportunities. Existing economic players will hopefully be able to grow their current operations. External attraction programs will identify potential new projects from outside that might work locally. It may be expected that such projects will attract new resources, including investors and franchises. The multiplier effect of a single cluster can be significant and an in-depth assessment of those opportunities are best achieved through a community-based strategic planning process as will be discussed later on. Northeast Ohio is a perfect example of the level of change that a well planned ICT strategy can bring to a region:

Officials of the non-profit organization OneCleveland, who installed a fiber network connecting major institutions of the northeast Ohio region beginning in 2000, argued convincingly that a shared community platform was the best way to cost-effectively improve access to education and facilitate workforce development. OneCleveland and its partners, now called OneCommunity, have connected more than 1,500 sites in 18 counties, including schools, libraries, higher education institutions, hospitals, government offices, and arts and cultural organizations (ICF - Northeast Ohio, 2008).

Even though Cleveland was a "rust belt" remnant of once-thriving steel manufacturing and automobile assembly plants along the southern edge of Lake Erie, its proponents believed that continuous infrastructure improvements and multi-sector collaboration could lead to positive synergies and be a more hopeful way forward. Information technologies were introduced and linked to almost every facet of community life in the region, including the Rock and Roll Hall of Fame, the Cleveland Clinic, the Cleveland Public Library, Cuyahoga Community College, Case Western Reserve University, the Ken State Urban Design Institute and others. As a result, OneCleveland's initiatives have not gone unnoticed and unappreciated. In 2006, it tied for ninth place among the 100 most active locations for first-time investments in start-up or early-stage

companies, according to *Entrepreneur* magazine, up from 61st place in 2005 (Vanac, 2007).

In 2008, Scot Rourke, President of OneCleveland, was selected Entrepreneur of the Year by the Intelligent Community Forum. In his acceptance speech, he said:

... before a self-sustaining digital economy takes root, the seeds of a fiber network must be sowed and fertilized with content. It means more than linking cable. It also means fostering collaboration and knowledge-sharing among institutions of culture, arts, research, and government. It means delivering the products of this sharing to others in ways that inspire and lead to definitive outcomes... Northeast Ohio is quickly becoming an exciting sandbox to play in when testing and optimizing new technologies. Thus, one of the goals in participating in wireless demonstrations is to eliminate start-up barriers and create an environment that is inviting for entrepreneurs, businesses, researchers, and others (Rourke, 2008, p.1).

Rourke explained that, as a consequence of being a regional community network, OneCleveland was asked to help implement new technology applications. It was one of three regions in the world chosen by Intel to pilot applications intended to enhance government services and promote economic growth. A second example: an application for strengthening the city's mobile workforce using wireless technologies for meter-reading (electric, gas, water) allowed the region to demonstrate gains in efficiency and effectiveness. He noted a third example, the permitting processes needed by building inspectors in the city of Cleveland that once took weeks or months was reduced to as little as a few hours (p.1). Cleveland challenged everyone in the community to look for ways to use ICT to improve efficiency and to create opportunities. The synergy created by multi-organizational collaboration continues to create measurable output that strengthens the community and prepares it to compete globally.

WHY DEVELOPMENT
MUST BE PLANNED

Paul Romer, economics professor at Stanford University, and an expert on economic growth, has made distinctions between "accidental" and "planned" strategies of development. He says: "The problem with the classical description of laissez-faire is its suggestion that the best of all possible arrangements for economic affairs has already been discovered and that it requires no collective action. The lesson from economic growth is that collective action is very important and that everything, including institutions, can always be improved" (Romer, 1993, p. 388).

Rarely are communities blessed with an abundant natural resource sufficiently sought-after that economic growth and job creation flow automatically. More often, community leaders have to take matters into their own hands to identify local assets and facilitate those partnerships that can capitalize on community strengths. Silicon Valley in California is an example of a region that was uniquely positioned to launch a new industry; yet what happened in that region was more accidental than planned. Its rapid growth and international prominence largely flowed from small entrepreneurial firms creating and manufacturing technologies and software for the age of the computer. Stanford University was the source of many of the ideas and talent, and the University itself benefited from the research and development work of Fairchild Semiconductor mass producing integrated circuits, Intel Corporation producing DRAM chips, Apple computer building microcomputers, Sun Microsystems creating servers and graphic workstations, Cisco Systems producing network gear, Netscape Communications introducing a user-friendly browser, and Yahoo and others making the contents of the Internet readily available to the general public. Education, talent, capital, environment and timing were all contributors (Metcalfe, 1998).

Although no amount of advance planning could have anticipated what actually happened in Palo Alto, a great deal of thought undoubtedly had to have been invested as Silicon Valley began to take on its mythic shape. Few communities or regions will be fortunate enough to inherit economic success by doing no planning at all. Most will require a strategy that will involve the collaborative efforts of local or regional stakeholders to manage change (Berry, 2007).

Paul Romer is joined by Joseph Cortright, an advocate of endogenous growth theory, sometimes called "new growth theory." It suggests that "technological advances come from things that people do" (Romer, 1994, p. 12). The idea is that economic growth develops from within communities, not from waiting for forces to play out abroad. In any given community, growth will more likely be driven by local players who see a need for change, share a vision and advocate for a new environment as a matter of urgency. This approach requires communities and regions to work collaboratively to build the basis for an improvement in the economy. New growth theory experts suggest that a key economic strategy is to focus on raising a greater sense of ownership and awareness throughout society, helping citizens understand that everybody is responsible – not just the mayor, the city council and the chamber of commerce – for identifying, creating and implementing the innovations that lead to economic growth. The reason that this concept is so important is that knowledge-based growth that is grounded in local assets has the potential to stimulate a self-reinforcing cycle leading to more growth (Cortright, 2001, p. 25).

The relevance of new growth theory is demonstrated by Sunderland UK, one of the demonstration cities of the Intelligent Community Forum. A former shipbuilding and mining city in the north of England, Sunderland engineered a dramatic turn-around based on "self-development" and "knowledge-based growth" after a period of hard times. In the 1980s, Sunderland's unemployment rate exceeded 22%. Today, the city is ranked as one of the top ten most competitive business locations in the UK, with new job creation approaching 5% annually. This city stands as an example of a successful strategy of transformation, in which a high-level of change was achieved through planning, public participation and concerted development activity around it. According to descriptions of Sunderland growing out of the ICF Intelligent Community of the Year award process, "this transformation was due to neither luck nor location, but to visionary leadership, good planning and unrelenting commitment" (ICF - Sunderland, 2007).

Today, as always, the most sustainable forms of development are the steps taken by locals to solve their own problems. McGuire et al (1994) used the concepts of "locality-based development" and "self-development" to frame community capacity building, where capacity is defined by the level of citizen participation, leadership, infrastructures, and development instruments. What is new in local communities are the tools and infrastructure that allow local businesses, government, non-profits and ordinary citizens to take better advantage of the opportunities showing up in the digital economy. The information and communication technologies making the biggest difference in communities are the computers and software and the telecommunications lines that link everyone to everyone else.

The critical job of connecting people to the Internet via broadband technology and planning around its use has changed the economic model of many communities. Tianjin, China, for example, illustrates what can happen when private sector development is supported with an ICT strategy. In 2004, Tianjin's electronics and information manufacturing industries saw an increase in output of 38% over the previous year, and exports increased by 52%. This increase in its high-technology industry productivity within one year followed adoption of its "informatisation" plan. In the ICF

write-up of these achievements, the ICF observed that "the pace of Tianjin's transformation is set by many factors, from the sheer scale of effort required to have an impact on its large, urban-rural population to the willingness of the central government in Beijing to embrace change. Measured by how far it has come in a short time, Tianjin is a notable success" (ICF – Tianjin, 2006). The case of Tianjin also demonstrated the benefits of public-private collaboration:

Tianjin is the biggest coastal city and largest seaport in northern China. It was a contender for the Intelligent Community of the Year award in 2006 and again in 2007. According to the ICF reports, the city is one of four Chinese municipalities under the direct jurisdiction of the central government. Northern China was late to the Internet and broadband revolution, and there was a clear sense of urgency in Tianjin's efforts to catch up. The municipal government set its sights on building powerful information technology and service industries, and eagerly embraced broadband and IT as means to make government more efficient and responsive, and business more productive (p.1).

Tianjin contains large rural areas where farming is the predominant industry. A "village to village" program has, with help from satellites, connected nearly 4,000 villages to the Internet and has helped to transform rural life. One small company, Jinmao Co. Ltd. in Wang Zhuang Village, was founded with the equivalent of US$62 in 1984 to manufacture manual agricultural tools. After setting up a Web site in 1996, the company began receiving orders from throughout China and expanded its products to include painting, cleaning, gardening and other tools. Their products are now available in five of the six biggest furniture chains in China, and the company's sales have reached US$18 million (p.2).

Some 50 percent of Tianjin total exports were from the technology sector.

The city's latest project is the Digital City industrial park, designed as a home for China's fast-growing software, electronics, biotech and new-energy industries. Now under construction on 10 km (3.8 sq. miles) of land, the new park will become home to a sector that saw a 32% increase in total revenues from 2003 to 2005 and which now produces 50% of the city's exports (p.2).

The commonly perceived instruments of economic and social development are the resources already within the community and thus, each community or region must take stock and plan for growing entrepreneurship activity, capital investment, growth of existing enterprises, a good education system, and creating an environment where individuals can thrive. This means fostering an environment where individuals can better themselves physically, spiritually, and economically. Social policy should be conceived as a key instrument that works in tandem with economic policy to ensure equitable and socially sustainable development (Mkandawire, 2001, p. 1), as will be demonstrated in the many examples of ICT projects that can be undertaken by both private and non-profit sectors.

Through data collection, planning and marketing, along with establishing an environment that is supportive of development, community leaders hope to be able to attract those firms and new investments that serve the unique needs of the place where they live and work. Even if communities are disinterested in physical growth, they will still have citizens and institutions that require access to communication networks. Thus, such ICTs as wireless phones, laptop computers, high-speed Internet, teleconferencing, geo-positioning and satellite audio systems have become highly attractive in the private lives of local residents as well as with business. The same has become true in terms of the availability of health, education, entertainment and business applications that make use of these tools.

As communities build networks of institutional and personal partnerships around an efficient infrastructure or a broadband application, they may also be developing the kind of social cohesion and cooperation that becomes the basis for community re-engineering. It is easy to see how established sectors will be, and must be, overhauled and improved as process and product innovations appear locally. For example, new medical and scientific advancements present opportunities to stimulate local enterprises related to research, testing and demonstration using wireless technologies, home-based telehealth and expert systems. There is no way of knowing what is possible until organizations and individuals come together to review what others are doing and to think about opportunities within the local context. This planning begins by researching what is possible, dreaming about new ways of doing things and setting out to make needed changes.

Since communities' most valuable assets are people, the human dimension must be considered in the planning process: how can the community leverage, attract and grow its own knowledge workers? How to ensure that citizens will have the training and skills necessary to work in those sectors where digital is spoken? How to ensure equitable access to technologies and infrastructure for all? How to minimize negative impact? And how to bring groups together to address the new opportunities and become more innovative? These were among the questions reviewed by Albert, Flournoy and LeBrasseur in their book on *Networked Communities: Strategies for Digital Collaboration* (2009). These are issues that communities must ponder if they wish to participate in the ICT economy, and to do it effectively they must think about developing strategic plans with ICT as a focus, or at least as an important leg within their strategy.

An interesting illustration of the value of properly assessing internal resources and identifying needs through strategic planning is the case of a skills inventory performed by the Eastserve

Project of Manchester, UK, where a report convincingly demonstrated that more than 40% of the region's businesses could not recruit locally. The new economic development strategy of the EastServe Project challenged local residents to attend ICT-related courses at the local Higher Education College and nine local community online centers. Understanding industry needs and providing training can go a long way toward creating new opportunities (ICF - Manchester, 2006).

Strategic planning is integral to developing a successful collaborative model for networked communities. McGuire et al (1994) researched small, non-metropolitan communities and concluded that those communities who implemented a strategic planning process possessed higher levels of development capacity than those who did not. The more successful communities had improved knowledge of internal capacities and were aware of opportunities stemming from the international environment, and were better able to put into action plans to create and sustain jobs.

There is reason to believe that communities are coming to take planning seriously. As an example, a 2007 survey of Canadian community economic development organizations[2] revealed that, of those responding, 84% of communities prepared formal strategic plans. However, few considered the impact of globalization and emerging technologies in their plans, with less than 50% including these analyses in their research. In the Canadian survey, those strategic plans that considered the impact of globalization also investigated the impact of emerging technologies. Similarly, those plans that evaluated capital assets also considered human assets. The process of community development planning is well understood, but with the advent of the Internet, the content, the context and implications of planning have been greatly expanded. The next section will explore some of the opportunities for making better use of ICTs in private and public development and thus provide a reason to consider these issues more seriously in the planning process.

OPPORTUNITIES IN PRIVATE AND PUBLIC SECTOR DEVELOPMENT

So how do we capitalize on broadband infrastructure and information and communication technologies once they are in place? Tables 1 and 2 give an overview of typical economic and community development projects involving private and public sectors, and suggest ICT activities that might support and enhance such projects. As can be surmised from these tables, ICTs may be applied to a variety of value-added and complementary services. In the first of these, the authors present and discuss here a small number of such opportunities, focused mainly around developing an entrepreneurial mindset, clustering and/or strategic alliances, and involving the private sector in job creation.

Already present in most communities are the basic skills needed to bring innovative ideas to commercial reality. The most likely people to provide support for the entrepreneurs' inventions in the marketplace can be found among those currently working in retail, warehousing, brokerages, hospital management, food services, recreation centers, and architectural and design shops performing similar activities. Local investors may get behind ideas that emerge from within the community or take an interest in those projects whose business case comes from without the community.

Generating new opportunities for entrepreneurship is a task ready-made for the Internet. Examples include online support services to those who daily use the Internet—think searching and downloading, buying and selling, formal and informal education, upgrading software and repairing web devices. For new online applications, think blogs, discussion groups, e-trading, data management, security, file sharing, and publications. These are micro-level opportunities that show up when the users, working in the new online environment, find they need help doing more, better, faster, more economically. Young

Table 1. Private sector ICT development opportunities [3]

Economic Development Activities	Typical Economic Development Strategies	Where ICT Can Fit
Private Sector Development	• Entrepreneurship development • Promoting innovation • Investor attraction • Cluster development • Investment data (land, buildings, capital, human, technology, new markets), & market intelligence, • Property improvement programs • Product development • Co-op advertising, networking & group packaging • "Shop Local" campaigns • Local business growth promotion • Immigration • Import replacement • Event organization • Tourism marketing	• Online help for entrepreneurship • Venture capital information networks • Collaborative networks for innovation • Investor attraction online • Cluster development and linkages • Investment databases (land, buildings, capital, human, technology, new markets) & market intelligence collected and marketed online • IT service development (call centres, data management) • Co-op advertising, networking & group packaging online • "Shop Local" campaigns using portal technologies • E-commerce • E-entertainment • Tele-work • New online applications and devices (i.e. blackberries, iPhones) • Immigration promotion websites • Event promotion portals • Tourism marketing

people tend to have a greater level of comfort spending time in cyberspace. Young people can perhaps be more easily trained to do these types of jobs. The adult community, on the other hand, is where business experience and capital will most likely be found. As can be predicted, all segments of the community will eventually be customers

as well as providers of online services and will have a stake in the outcome. Working together, the chances will greatly increase that new applications and new businesses will emerge and thrive under these conditions. The community has a role to play in developing an environment conducive to ICT entrepreneurial innovations (incubators,

Table 2. Public/non-profit/partnership ICT development opportunities [4]

Economic Development Activities	Typical Economic Development Strategies	Where ICT Can Fit
Public Sector, Non-Profit Development & Social Development	• New program development (government administration, health, education, social organizations) • Public-private partnerships (new project development, fund raising, purchasing) • New public infrastructure (fiber optics, wireless, cable, satellite, radio & TV) • Quality of life projects (affordable housing, telecommunication, transportation, arts & culture, sports & recreation, professional services) • Festival & event organization • Youth retention & attraction of specialized skills	• Online government including payment of taxes and fees, agents and counseling, self-help forms, registrations, live audio/video of council meetings and public hearings, polling of citizens • Virtual libraries & museums • E-health, E-learning • Portals for community initiatives, public-private partnerships • Online voting • Information exchanges, creations of meta data & search engines • Skills inventories • Public communication & citizen exchanges • Tracking of progress of development projects

venture capital, demonstrations of applications, training, etc.), and bringing stakeholders together (seminars, networking events, mentoring, etc.).

Using ICTs to promote clustering and facilitate strategic alliances are other opportunities worth considering. In numerous communities, consultants, engineers and architects have made a special effort to work together as a way to bring in more business by bidding on bigger projects. Players of common interest can be encouraged to come together in strategic alliances to sell products online to provide a better value proposition for international markets. Cooperation in advertising and packaging is an example: the City of Sudbury, Canada, encouraged tourist operators to work together to package their products into a series of "get-aways" on a community portal (Archives of the ICF - Sudbury, 2006). That approach resulted in an increase in tourist business for all participants in the cluster. Sharing marketing costs and pooling finances for advertising campaigns can sometimes pay off for the community as a whole.

Such clustering and alliances can occur at the local level or within a geographical region, and can involve diverse competencies and expertise. In brief, the idea is to utilize broadband infrastructure to take better advantage of the resources right there within the affiliated communities, to increase effective performance, to gain visibility and to extend reach. Building teams with more competitive capabilities can stimulate future activity and allow the participating organizations to increase comfort levels with information technologies and interconnecting networks that might be used for purposes not yet foreseen. Clusters tend to appeal to those firms who see greater advantage in collaboration than competition, especially in seeking markets outside the region.

Community leadership teams increasingly include corporate executives who may help identify new opportunities for business and job creation; for example, opportunities for import replacement, database development to attract private sector investment, skills inventories to identify

the knowledge base available locally. In short, it takes many different perspectives to come up with a good plan and the more players involved, the more projects are likely to ensue. To create a big impact, a continuous process of innovation and engagement is needed.

Upside down thinking is also critical (Albert, Flournoy & LeBrasseur, 2009). Communities in New Brunswick, Canada, realized more than a decade ago that they could use their remoteness as an asset, overcoming problems of location with investments in broadband. Facing a depressed economy and loss of jobs, these eastern-Canadian province communities were able to market their reasonably-priced and bilingual human resources as the basis for call centre operations. The increased skills and knowledge gained by residents enabled them to do other kinds of work, online and offline. New Brunswick was able to diversify its economy, increase ICT and other skills and give residents other reasons not to move away (Balka, 2000).

Public sector organizations are obviously also large players and often instigators of ICT visions. But it is the effective combination of non-profit organizations working collaboratively with private companies that will create sustainable ICT opportunities in community and economic development. Table 2 (below) lists some examples of public/non-profit and public-private partnership opportunities and innovative program delivery models. These application examples extend the reach and the breath of services that can be offered in any given region, improve access to information, facilitate citizen participation in decision-making, and enhance quality of life. These kinds of initiatives allow communities to retain their young professionals. A select few of these opportunities are discussed as examples below namely around technology parks, portals, shared telecommunication infrastructure, and municipal online services.

One example of public-private sector collaboration that significantly involves the participation of members of the municipal government is the creation of ICT technology parks. Taipei, Taiwan, was the 2007 Intelligent Community of the Year and much of what the ICF found exceptional about Taipei was the level of private sector commitment to community development. Three technology parks were planned. These were to be combined to form the "Taipei Technology Corridor" (their version of Silicon Valley).

Some 2,203 companies came to be located in the first two parks, employing more than 85,400 staff. The city's comparative and competitive advantage was its vision to aggregate its businesses and its knowledge workers into designated locations. At the time of the award, the third technology park was still in process. That park was expected to incorporate such socially attractive features as housing, education, entertainment, arts and culture and logistics. The entire complex was a collaborative between government and the private sector (ICF - Taipei, 2006).

Web portals are a popular topic in intelligent community demonstrations. A number of Intelligent Community award applicants have used the Internet as a way to report data as well as collect it - as with measurements of air, water and environmental quality, traffic statistics, school performance and crime - all with a view to increase public participation and awareness and to encourage stewardship. Improved online communication was seen as a key to encouraging citizens to participate in decision-making, to building community pride and stimulating volunteerism.

Electronic communication has led to public discussion and decisions about environmental issues, such as carbon sequestration and energy conservation. Access to the Internet has helped address such matters. There is also much talk of using information technologies and communication networks to allow employees to work from home, and to make government more efficient. Such an approach was observed in Gangnam-Gu, a progressive suburb of Seoul, Korea, that had

invested heavily in broadband communications. Gangnam was the ICF Community of the Year for 2008. In reporting on this award, ICF officials wrote by way of background:

The Gangnam District lies to the south of the Han River, which snakes through South Korea's capital city from east to west. This district of 557,000 people contains 2.5% of Seoul's people but produces 25% of its gross domestic product. High-rise apartments make up 80% of its residential areas, and the district is home to the corporate headquarters of such Korean firms as POSCO and Korea Telecom, as well as the IT venture companies on Teheran Road, South Korea's Silicon Valley (ICF – Gangnam-Gu, 2008, p. 1).

The ICF noted the extent to which public officials in Gangnam were doing their work from home, using residential networks and mobile devices to conduct government business. Since the government of Korea had subsidized the installation of wide-area broadband fiber optic infrastructures that reached into residential as well as business areas, staying connected from home or from other locations about the city and region was not difficult. Commuting under the crowded conditions of the capital city often took up a lot of time. So civil servants began to look to the always-on connectivity and mobility of the high-speed Internet as a way to maintain efficiency at work. There was, of course, always the problem of a lack of personal time since people were taking their offices with them wherever they were, but more and more Gangnam-Gu workers opted for time flexibility in work practices. Work efficiency and energy savings each played a role in this innovation in public sector development.

In winning the top award, the Gangnam-gu example illustrated several other important applications and innovations. The ICF's write-up explained that the community

... was quick to seize on broadband as a means to make government more transparent, increase citizen participation, and even to help citizens who remained outside the local broadband economy. About 350,000 citizens are registered users of the district's Web portal, and 210,000 are subscribers to an email system that asks for their comment on proposed laws and regulations. They seem to take their responsibilities seriously. Recently, the district proposed installation of surveillance cameras in a particular alley in a residential district. A local human rights organization opposed the move on privacy grounds. When polled by email, however, 82% of residents supported the move and installation subsequently led to a 40% reduction in crimes in the area (p. 3).

Several intelligent community presentations to the ICF have demonstrated successful examples of municipalities driving the broadband agenda, principally in terms of increased capacities, greater coverage, minority access and civic participation. In communities where public stewardship is an acknowledged value, it is logical that private and public organizations are seeing the merit in sharing the cost and management of local telecommunications infrastructures. Broadband networks are as necessary to social development as they are to economic development. In the so-called "smart" communities, access to the Internet quickly becomes thought of as just another essential utility, like electricity, water, streets, sidewalks and sewage. These are services that everybody eventually uses, and eventually nobody is willing to do without, not at the office, not at home or out and about in the community. This situation, however, must be nudged on by decisive action by public or non-profit sector organizations, as was the case for the City of Fredericton, New Brunswick, Canada:

New Brunswick is a rural province, with only 730,000 people living in an area the size of Ireland (home to 4 million). As with most rural regions,

broadband was sparsely available and only at high prices. Not even city government could obtain a simple wide area network to connect its facilities. In 2000, the City Council decided that it had to act. By aggregating the demand of city government, the University and a dozen local businesses, the Council was able to purchase bulk commercial bandwidth at a more competitive cost. The following year, Fredericton began building its own fiber network, which it has expanded every year since then to the present 22-kilometer (17-mi) fiber ring. The municipal-owned carrier, e-Novations, operates as a co-op and provides each member with guaranteed bandwidth as well as additional peak capacity based on availability.

By proving the existence of broadband demand, e-Novations spurred competition. Private carriers built out additional capacity, so that 70% of households and 85% of businesses are now connected to broadband, with monthly prices ranging from C$22 for a 256Kpbs circuit up to C$100 for 18 Mbps service (ICF – Fredericton, 2008, p. 1).

Fredericton's story is interesting for its success in building capacity that reaches such a large percentage (though not all) of its citizens. But there is more to tell in how social and economic development, taken in parallel, enabled an entirely new set of opportunities in environmental sustainability. Here is the way this added dimension was portrayed in the ICF report:

The city contains an estimated 70% of New Brunswick's knowledge-based businesses. In 2004, after an intensive effort to improve its management and administration, Fredericton became one of the few cities in North America to achieve the ISO 9001 quality certification. Four years earlier, the city joined the Partners for Climate Protection program and committed to reducing its greenhouse gas emissions to 20% below 1990 levels by the year 2010. The city has moved on multiple fronts to achieve this goal, from using water-based paint for traffic lines and reducing streetlight wattage to converting traffic lights to light-emitting diodes (p. 2).

The city explained how its advanced ICT infrastructure played a role. A Municipal Automatic Logic System controls lighting and HVAC in 16 municipal buildings in order to reduce energy use. In the process, it reduced greenhouse gas emissions by 6 percent from 1996 to 2004, and continues to generate about C$180,000 in annual savings. In order to reduce the power consumption of streetlights without endangering the public, Fredericton turned to a GIS mapping system. The city used summer students to gather data on the location and wattage of every street light in the community. Its engineering staff entered the data into the GIS system and used it to develop a comparison between the lighting requirements for each street and the actual facilities in place. This guided decision-making about wattage changes, which allowed Fredericton to reduce energy use by 228,000 kilowatt hours per year, saving C$43,000 annually. In the Fredericton case, fighting climate change and ensuring broadband access were perceived to be part of the same initiative.

These examples are but a few that demonstrate the inter-connectedness of community economic and social development concepts and show how ICTs can play a key role.

CONCLUSION

The high-speed Internet has given individuals, institutions and businesses ways to more efficiently connect and collaborate with one another, locally and globally. With pervasive digital networks in place, the economics of access, innovation and distribution have undergone radical transformation. The costs continue to drop throughout the value chain of products and services. Evidence of cost savings and increased opportunities for job creation, economic growth, and improved quality of life is a good basis for the argument that communities need to consider more carefully the ways information technologies and communication networks factor into community development.

Such initiatives as those mentioned in Tables 1 and 2 will likely require increased collaboration and a change in thinking in most communities. Public and non-profit organizations will need to have a vision for supporting private sector growth, and the opposite is also true. Identification of community development teams working in collaboration with user groups will lead to recommendations concerning policies and concrete steps for making effective use of ICTs for local development (Bertrand & Larue, 2004). Such teams will be needed to promote a bottom-up approach to sustainable development that takes into account the lifestyles, needs and gaps that may exist in the community and region (Cam, 2004).

Changes being wrought globally by new technologies filter down. Communities can chose to manage those often-disruptive changes locally, or be overrun by them. The authors have two key suggestions. First, local leaders should take the time to study the ways other communities are addressing the impact of globalization and emerging technologies, as a way to educate themselves. Secondly, the local leadership are advised to have a strategy for deciding what initiatives should be given highest priority and what are the best ways to build ownership and involvement of the whole community.

ACKNOWLEDGMENT

From Networked Communities: Strategies for Digital Collaboration, by Sylvie Albert, Don Flournoy, and Rolland LeBrasseur, 2009. Hershey, PA (USA): IGI Global. Copyright 2008 IGI Global. Adapted with permission.

REFERENCES

Albert, S., Flournoy, D., & LeBrasseur, R. (2009). *Networked Communities: Strategies for Digital Collaboration.* Hershey, PA, USA: IGI Global.

Archives of the ICF - Sudbury. (2006). Intelligent Community Applications. *Top (Madrid)*, 21.

Balka, E. (2000). *New Brunswick: the call centre capital of North America.* Simon Fraser University. Retrieved August 25, 2008 from http://www.emergence.nu/events/budapest/balka.pdf

Berry, F. (2007). Strategic planning as a tool for managing organizational change. *International Journal of Public Administration, 30,* 331–346. doi:10.1080/01900690601117812

Bertrand, F., & Larrue, C. (2004). Integration of the Sustainable Development Evaluation Process in regional planning: Promises and problems in the case of France. *Journal of Environmental Assessment Policy and Management, 6*(4), 443–463. doi:10.1142/S1464333204001821

Cam, C. N. (2004). A conceptual framework for socio-techno-centric approach to sustainable development. *International Journal of Technology, Management, and Sustainable Development, 3*(1), 59–66. doi:10.1386/ijtm.3.1.59/0

Cortright, J. (2001). New growth theory, technology and learning: A practitioner's guide. *U.S. Economic Development Administration, 4,* 35.

Dwivedi, Y. K., & Lal, B. (2007). Socio-economic determinants of broadband adoption. *Industrial Management and Data Systems Journal, 107*(5), 654–671. doi:10.1108/02635570710750417

Eger, J. M. (2007). *Smart growth and the urban future. World Foundation for Smart Communities.* Retrieved November 5, 2007 from http://www.smartcommunities.org/library_cities.htm

Flournoy, D. (2004). *The Broadband Millennium: Communication Technologies and Markets.* Chicago: International Engineering Consortium.

Friedman, T. L. (2006). *The World is Flat.* Farrar, Straus and Giroux, N.Y.

ICF – Fredericton. (2008). *Top 7 Intelligent Community Award.* Retrieved August 25, 2008 from http://www.intelligentcommunity.org/index.php?src=gendocs&ref=Top7_2008_Fredericton_NB_Canada&category=Community

ICF – Gangnam-Gu. (2008). *Top 7 Intelligent Community Award.* Retrieved August 25, 2008 from http://www.intelligentcommunity.org/index.php?src=gendocs&ref=Top7_2008_Gangnam_Korea&category=Community

ICF - Manchester. (2006). *Top 7 Intelligent Community Award.* Retrieved August 25, 2008 from http://www.intelligentcommunity.org/index.php?src=gendocs&ref=Top7_2006_Manchester_UK&category=Community

ICF - Northeast Ohio. (2008). *Top 7 Intelligent Community Award.* Retrieved August 25, 2008 from http://www.intelligentcommunity.org/index.php?src=gendocs&ref=Top7_2008_Northeast_Ohio_USA&category=Community

ICF - Sunderland. (2007). *Top 7 Intelligent Communities of the Year.* Retrieved August 25, 2008 from http://www.intelligentcommunity.org/index.php?src=gendocs&ref=Top7_2007_Sunderland_UK&category=Community

ICF - Taipei. (2006). *Top 7 Intelligent Community Award.* Retrieved August 25, 2008 from http://www.intelligentcommunity.org/index.php?src=gendocs&ref=Top7_2006_Taipei_Taiwan&category=Community

ICF - Tianjin. (2006). *Top 7 Intelligent Community Award*. Retrieved August 25, 2008 from http://www.intelligentcommunity.org/index.php?src=gendocs&ref=Top7_2006_Tianjin_China&category=Community

McGuire, M., Rubin, B., Agranoff, R., & Richards, C. (1994). Building development capacity in non-metropolitan communities. *Public Administration Review, 54*(5), 426–433. doi:10.2307/976427

Metcalfe, R. (1998, March 2). *Asian tour provides useful insight on Silicon Valley's worldwide Internet edge*. IDG.net, www.infoworld.com.

Mkandawire, T. (2001). Social policy in a development context. *United Nations Research Institute for Social Development*. Retrieved August 25, 2008 from http://www.unrisd.org/unrisd/website/document.nsf/0/C83739F8E9A9AA0980256B5E003C5225?OpenDocument

Romer, P. (1992). *Two strategies for economic development: Using ideas and producing ideas*. Retrieve reference info.

Romer, P. (1993). Implementing a national technology strategy with self-organizing industry investment boards. *Brookings Papers on Economic Activity: Microeconomics, 2*, 345. doi:10.2307/2534742

Romer, P. (1994). The origins of endogenous growth. *The Journal of Economic Perspectives, 8*(1), 3–22. doi:10.1257/jep.8.1.3

Rourke, S. (2008). *Shedding light on a sustainable future*. Intelligent Community Forum. Retrieved on August 31, 2008 at http://www.intelligentcommunity.org/.

Tapscott, D., & Willians, A. D. (2008). *Wikinomics*. New York: Penguin Group.

Vanac, M. (2007). JumpStart ranks 9th in early stage investments. *Cleveland.com*. Business Section. Retrieved October 20, 2008 from http://blog.cleveland.com/business/2007/06/jumpstart_ranks_9th_in_early_s.html

ENDNOTES

[1] As noted in the book, an "overbuilder" is a competitive cable, telephone, wireless or satellite provider that enters the market with a similar product that seeks to provide a service that is perceived by the user public to be better than that offered by the legacy player.

[2] MBA student Albert Chulak at Laurentian University sent a survey to 745 economic development organizations across Canada through EDAC, with a response rate of 11%.

[3] Adapted from Albert, S; Flournoy, D; and LeBrasseur R. (2008). Networked Communities: Strategies for Digital Collaboration, IGI Global, Hershey, PA.

[4] Adapted from Albert, S; Flournoy, D; and LeBrasseur R. (2008). Networked Communities: Strategies for Digital Collaboration, IGI Global, Hershey, PA.

This work was previously published in The International Journal of Sociotechnology and Knowledge Development, Volume 2, Issue 1, edited by Elayne Coakes, pp. 59-79, copyright 2010 by IGI Publishing (an imprint of IGI Global).

Chapter 8
Towards a Knowledge–Based Economy – the Case of Botswana:
A Discussion Article

Bwalya Kelvin Joseph
University of Botswana, Botswana

ABSTRACT

Botswana is keen to position itself as a knowledge-based economy as early as 2016 due to the realisation that to compete on a global scale, efficient knowledge value chains must be put in place, which includes indigenous knowledge management systems. This realisation is primarily caused by falling demand in the price of diamonds (due to the world's recession), which is the country's current economic mainstay. Today, Botswana is pushing for further economic liberalisation and diversification by employing and encouraging novel frontiers of knowledge with emphasis placed on research and efficient knowledge management as a vital resource for national development. In Botswana, the role of scientific and technical knowledge is being emphasized as the main driver of sustainable development, but not forgetting the potential contribution of indigenous and mythological knowledge to this aim. Several initiatives have been devised or implemented by both the government and the public sector to position Botswana as a knowledge-based economy. This paper surveys the fundamental concepts on which this paradigm shift is based and brings out the different initiatives that have been undertaken while emphasizing the role of research and efficient knowledge management paradigms in shaping Botswana as a knowledge-based economy.

DOI: 10.4018/978-1-4666-0200-7.ch008

Copyright © 2012, IGI Global. Copying or distributing in print or electronic forms without written permission of IGI Global is prohibited.

BACKGROUND AND INTRODUCTION

The recent past has seen most advanced and nominal economies undergo significant structural changes. One of the key characteristics of the changes is the growing importance of knowledge in all sectors of socio-economic activities. In the African context, most countries have either solely depended on agriculture or mining in which land is the key resource, and have later transformed into industrial economies where natural resources and labour are the main resources. These countries are now transforming themselves into knowledge-based economies (KBE) where knowledge is the key resource. This assertion is further supported by Leung (2004) who states that for countries to thrive in this knowledge age, there is a need for transformation to knowledge-based economic concepts. To bring the topic of KBE into the limelight, it is necessary to look at several other attributes that need to be incorporated in such a programme such as encouraging the culture of innovation; efficient training programmes for the development of an appropriate human resource base; putting in place efficient knowledge distribution and dissemination channels; encouraging innovation and research; and through putting in place an enabling environment by having appropriate legal, institutional and regulatory frameworks, and so on.

Innovation is an expression of the productive use of knowledge. A formal definition of innovation is "the application in any organization of ideas new to it, whether they are embodied in products, processes, services, or in the systems of management and marketing through which the organization operates" (Maguire et al., 1994). Alternatively, innovation has also been defined as the creative process through which additional economic value is extracted from knowledge whereby this additional value is obtained through the transformation of knowledge into new products, processes, or services (OECD, 1997). To fully understand the workings of the KBE, new economic concepts and measures are required which track phenomena beyond conventional market transactions. As suggested by the OECD, improved indicators for a KBE are needed for the following tasks: (i) measuring knowledge inputs; (ii) measuring knowledge stocks and flows; (iii) measuring knowledge outputs; (iv) measuring knowledge networks; and (v) measuring knowledge and learning " (OECD, 1997).

For KBE to be established there is also an issue of making sure that knowledge distribution channels are in place. This can be achieved through the establishment of formal and informal networks essential to economic performance and knowledge sharing as a public good. Another area that also needs attention is technological change as countries that do not move with these changes are left behind as far as development may be concerned. Technological change raises the relative marginal productivity of capital through the education and training of the labour force; investments in research and development; and the creation of new managerial structures and work organization. The UNECE Report of 2002 states that economic activities associated with the production and utilization of information and knowledge have become an engine of economic growth in the developed market economies, increasingly transforming all the other dimensions of development and the entire societal *modus Vivendi* and *modus operanti* of humanity.

This UNECE Report (ibid) further defines KBE as not just being the digital economy, which incorporates the production and use of computers and telecommunication equipment; and not quite the networked economy, which incorporates the telecommunication and networking growth during the last decades and its impact on human progress. It defines KBE as being a much complex and broader phenomenon and brings out the following dimensions of a KBE:

1. The KBE has a very powerful technological driving force – a rapid growth of information and telecommunication technologies (ICT);
2. Telecommunication and networking, stimulated by a rapid growth of ICTs, have penetrated all the spheres of human activity, forcing them to work into an absolutely new mode and creating new spheres. The information society has become a reality;
3. Knowledge, based on information and supported by cultural and spiritual values, has become an independent force and the most decisive factor of social, economic, technological and cultural transformation; and
4. The knowledge-based economy has allowed a quick integration of the enormous intellectual resources of these economies in transition into the European intellectual pool, thus further stimulating the development of the former countries.

Transformation into a KBE starts from the public sector and then replicates out to all the socio-economic sectors of a nation.

Explicitly put, it starts from the doorsteps of communities by first engulfing and adopting ICT usage which is the start-point of appropriate knowledge sharing. This view of ICT adoption is supported by PĂCEŞILĂ (2006) who ascertains that a KBE can't be conceived without technology, especially the advanced technology that allows knowledge transmission and appraisal of functional virtual markets. A knowledge economy in the public sector requires the utilization of all the available knowledge in order to improve transparency and provide for the services delivered to citizens, and for a better communication with the citizens/users/clients in order to improve knowing the level of their needs (PĂCEŞILĂ, 2006). Kriščiūnas and Daugėlienė (2006) further assert that the development of a knowledge economy is impossible without the implementation of ICT to the knowledge-based activity. Usually it is stated that a KBE is an economy that makes effective use

of knowledge for its economic and social development. This includes tapping foreign knowledge as well as adapting and creating knowledge for its specific needs (Dahlman, 2003). Kalim and Lodhi (2004) looks at the Swedish case of transformation towards a KBE and comes up with the following indicators determining country competitiveness in the realm of KBE: 1) renewal, development and innovation: the "power of innovation"; 2) knowledge capacity: the "power of exchange of knowledge" at a national and international level; 3) human capital and information technologies; and 4) investment in intellectual capital.

Dahlman et al. (2005) assert that knowledge is fuelling economic growth and social development in every region of the world and that ICTs provide the means for developing countries to accelerate their progress or even leapfrog into the current phase of development and to enable their integration into the global economy. For the case of developed countries, the situation is different. KBE allows further specialization, improvements in productivity, and the achievement of sustainable growth: knowledge capital is the only asset that can grow without limits; and new knowledge increases the efficient use of resources that are in finite supply. A practical case or KBE implementation can be that of Finland. Its economic transition has been from the resource-driven to knowledge- and then to innovation-driven development, thanks to the effective use of ICT. Diversification of both technology and exports was a prerequisite for improved performance. Finland's innovation system successfully converted R&D and educational capacity into industrial strengths. Finland's success shows that a strong knowledge economy can be built in a small and comparatively peripheral country. From Finland's case, it can be learnt that specialization in high-tech and R&D intensive production needs to be preceded by major structural changes in economic and social structures. It is important to note that a knowledge economy is an ensemble of elements that must be in balance. It is not necessarily the lack of technological infrastructure or skilled engineers that restrains economic growth. It might equally well be the lack of entrepreneurs or proper economic incentives and opportunities.

Especially noteworthy is the shift in the focus and content of industrial policies in the 1990s away from macroeconomic policies and industrial subsidies toward microeconomic "conditions-providing" policies. A specificity of the Finnish "model" has been the early application of a systems view of industrial policy. This systems view could be described as an acknowledgement of the importance of interdependencies among research organizations, universities, firms, and industries due to the increasing importance of knowledge as a competitive asset, especially in the case of small open economies with a well-developed welfare system. The systems view was concretized through an emphasis on responsive longer-term policies to improve the general framework conditions for firms and industries, especially in knowledge development and diffusion, innovation, and clustering of industrial activities. Dahlman et al. (2005) further notes that education is the key element of a knowledge-based, innovation-driven economy and that it affects both the supply of and demand for innovation. Zeman (2005) notes that the results (or outputs) of knowledge-based economy implementation are identified by the basic indicators of competitiveness: a) level and growth of labour productivity and GDP; b) employment - environmental sustainability; and c) social cohesion. Some of the most important attributes for a KBE are shown in Figure 1, (source: EFN Report: The Euro area and the Lisbon strategy, September 2004).

Besides an overall political, social, cultural and security environment that is conducive to the flourishing of a KBE, there are certain factors that can be identified as critical to its development and are indicative of the positioning as well as strengths and weaknesses of a country in that regard. These factors are key to African countries

in their specific context when in pursuit of transformation towards a KBE. These factors include the:

1. Quality of human resources: literacy; secondary school enrolment; tertiary educational enrolment; enrolment in science and technology-related subjects; science graduates; technical graduates; expenditure on education; thinking and innovation skills; a learning culture; lifelong learning facilities; English language skills; receptivity to change;

2. R&D: Public and private sector expenditure on R&D; personnel in R&D; scientists and engineers in R&D; patents filed;

3. Infostructure: newspapers; radios; television; telephone mainlines; mobile telephones; costs of international telephone calls; freedom/availability of information;

4. Infrastructure: investment in ICT infrastructure; electricity; personal computers; Internet hosts; Internet subscribers; Internet usage;

5. Economy: knowledge workers; knowledge-based industries; knowledge-based services; tacit and codified knowledge; knowledge embodied in work processes and products; e-commerce; high-technology exports; venture capital; openness to foreign knowledge workers; entrepreneurship; risk-taking culture.

In the Southern African region, Botswana is seen as the longest surviving democracy (Lekorwe et al., 2001). The bedrock of Botswana's democracy is embedded in the traditional Kgotla system. The Kgotla is a time tested forum where issues of public policy are discussed openly by the community (Lekorwe, 2001; also quoting from Holm & Molutsi, 1989). The institutional and legal frameworks are basically developed supporting almost all socio-economic frameworks. The growth in the diamonds trade has

Figure 1. Characteristics of a defined knowledge-based economy

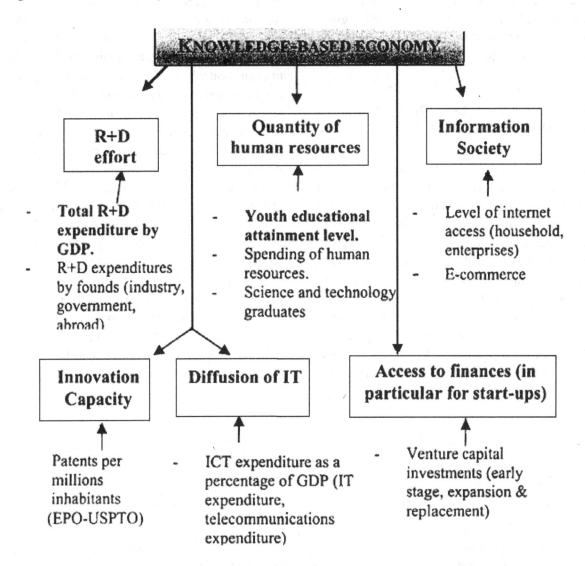

seen Botswana occupy a place as one of the most stable economies of Africa and boasts of having one of the fastest growing economies worldwide. However, all these developmental strands are thwarted by high unemployment rates and escalation of the HIV-AIDS virus, etc. From colonial times to the recent present, Botswana has largely been a resource-based economy. That is to say, its survival has always been dependent on producing natural resources for further processing by the developed world. One such important resource has been diamonds. Of late, Botswana has started moving towards a knowledge-based economy. In contemplating progression towards a full-fledged knowledge-based economy, Botswana needs to tackle several challenges. One such challenge is, of course, reducing its traditional overdependence on diamonds as a major contributor to the nation's GDP, and reducing the escalating spread of HIV-AIDS. It also needs to develop a solid human resource base educated to face the challenges of the knowledge age. The following section gives a detailed analysis of Botswana's vision towards turning into a KBE.

BOTSWANA'S CASE: RESOURCE TO KNOWLEDGE-BASED

Botswana has been among the fastest-growing economies in Africa over the past 40 years. Sound macroeconomic policies and good governance have parlayed the country's diamond resources in a remarkable transformation from one of the poorest countries in the world at Independence to a current upper middle-income status. At independence in 1966, Botswana was one of Africa's poorest countries. It had a weak human capacity (22 university graduates), few assets, an under-developed infrastructure (12 kilometers of paved road), and an abattoir as the only "industry." With

such statistics, there was no option but to strongly rely on resources (e.g. diamonds, cattle) as the economic mainstay. However, recently, there has been reduction in the demand for diamonds or even meat which have been the major exports from Botswana as a result of the world recession which hit the economy badly in 2007/08. Factors such as declining fertility rates, increased womens' participation in economic activities, access to better health, increased literacy, and escalating HIV-AIDS infection rates, may have had an effect on the growth rate of the population. This and numerous other factors have increased the need to diversify the economy and eventually move to one more knowledge-based. Figure 2 is a chart taken from KAM (2008) that shows how Botswana features against the different benchmarks that are used to assess the development of a country.

Botswana is currently ranked as a first-stage transition economy. The above chart has shown that Botswana has to do a lot if it wants to be at

Figure 2. KAM 2008 report

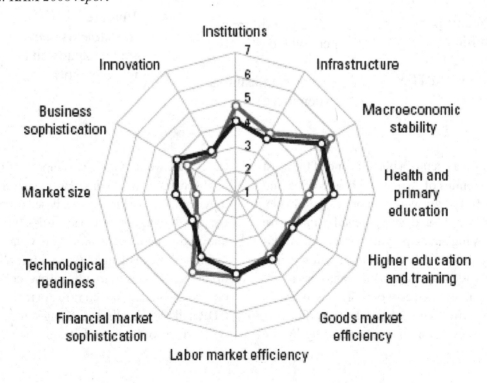

the competitive edge in this knowledge based age and justifies the government declaration that Botswana has to move towards positioning itself as a KBE.

Botswana is generally praised for its pursuit of sound economic policies, which have enabled it use its diamonds wisely. Its policy stance has been guided by Vision 2016, which sets a broad policy agenda for poverty reduction and macroeconomic stability. To make sure that the legal, institutional and the regulatory framework, together with an enabling environment for the maturation of a KBE, has required a great many initiatives to have been put in place to make sure that this vision is realized. On the policy front, some work has already been done, with the development of a Science and Technology (S&T) Policy (Botswana Ministry of Finance, 1998) and the setting up of the National Commission for Science and Technology (NCST), which plays the role of overall policy advisor to government on S&T matters. Other complementary institutions have been put in place. An example of these are the Botswana Research Science and Technology Investment Agency (BRSTIA), and the setting-up of a new Ministry of Communications, Science and Technology (MCST) in 2002, grouping together all communications, science and technology functions.

For a KBE, to be put in place, as mentioned above, there is need for strong research, efficient knowledge dissemination and knowledge sharing be put in place. In the case of Botswana, in parallel with the telecommunications regulation, other policies supportive of the reform process were put in place in 1996 and the early 2000s. An overarching science and technology (S&T) policy was adopted in 1998. The policy gives priority to strengthening telecommunications infrastructure and the use of ICTs, and attracting women to professions and careers in the field of science and technology.

Another strategy that has been seen in Botswana is the emphasis that on training the potential human resource for the country. Within

this framework, Botswana has put in place fiscal policies that specifically look at the advancement of education from the grassroots to the tertiary level (TKS, 2006). This has seen the establishment of the Tertiary Education Council (TEC) by Act of Parliament Cap 57:04 of 1999 to be responsible for "…promotion and coordination of tertiary education and for the determination and maintenance of standards of teaching, examination and research in tertiary institutions (Section 5(1)). The government of Botswana understands that for the country to transform towards a KBE, there is need to have a very well trained human resource base. This effort has been complimented by putting in place other policies in support of training a better human resource base. These include the College of Agriculture Act (1991), Botswana College of Distance and Open Learning Act (1998), Botswana Examinations Council Act (2002), the Vocational Training Act (1998), the Botswana International University of Science and Technology- BIUST Act (2005). Of the much talked about amongst these policies is the BIUST act of 2005. It is anticipated that the rationale for BIUST will echo with other emerging economies: economic growth and sustainable development; overcoming acute skill shortages including engineers and technologists; reducing the unreasonable costs of providing tertiary education for over 7000 students in 2007 studying internationally; addressing demand for skills and innovation for advanced industries including through technology transfer; internationalizing the economy and aspiring to be an international education hub; (Wilmoth, 2006).

Further, in making sure that Botswana remains abreast with its vision of coming up with competent human resource base for the purposes of KBE prioritization and strategizing, new education policies have been put in place. One of these so called 'vibrant' policies has been the putting in place of Human Resource Development Strategy, approved by Parliament on January 21st, 2009. This has been a follow-up on Tertiary Education Council (TEC) which was established by an act of parliament in 1999 specifically to standardize the quality of education in tertiary education institutions in Botswana. Also, the new tertiary education policy of April 2008 aims to change the landscape for the better of tertiary education in Botswana. This confirms that the institutional and regulatory framework towards production of competent human resource base has somewhat already been established in Botswana.

On another front, Botswana continues to show commitment in encapsulating ICT into its cultural norms. Widespread campaigns are evident in Botswana in encouraging the use of ICTs in almost all socio-economic setups. This encouragement of using ICTs in all socio-economic strata conforms to efficient knowledge sharing and management which is one of the pillars to establishing a KBE as efficient in service delivery, production systems, research knowledge sharing is facilitated. This commitment to putting in place efficient knowledge sharing paradigms and revamping ICT usage is further evidenced by the Botswana Telecommunication Company's (BTC) signatory status to three consortia that are intended to develop undersea optical fibre systems: the East Africa Submarine System (EASSY), to run alongside the eastern coast of Africa from Port Sudan through East African seaports down to Mtunzini in South Africa; the West Africa Festoon System

(WAFS), intended to run alongside the western coast of Africa from Nigeria through Gabon, DRC down to Angola, and possibly Namibia; and the Africa West Coast Cable (AWCC), proposed to run alongside the western coast of Africa from South Africa, Namibia through to the United Kingdom. Plans are also underway to establish an IT hub in Botswana. This is going to make sure that Botswana is seen as the most advanced country in as far as ICT usage is concerned. Once this subscription has transcended into tangible deployment of optical across all corners of the country, the cost to send data from one place to the next will be substantially reduced as throughput, data latency and transmission speed will be improved. As aforementioned, the institutional framework to pioneer the dream of transforming the country into a KBE has been set to some appreciable extent. Table 1 shows some of the regulatory agencies that have been put up in different socio-economic realms.

These different endeavors outlined here point out the commitment that Botswana has towards transforming itself as a knowledge-based economy. Looking at the different initiatives outlined above, it is evident that the institutional framework is quiet advanced. The only component that seems to be lacking and that no one pays much attention is the legal and regulatory framework. It is an-

Table 1. Summary of key S&T agencies and functions

Agency	Date Established	Major Function
National Commission for S&T (NCST)	May 2002	S&T research Policy advisory matters
Botswana Research, S&T Investment Agency (BRSTIA)	2006/07	Co-ordinate and monitor all government R&D funding (S&T research Purchasing matters)
Government owned National Research Centers	See different research institutes	Policy Advocacy matters
Botswana National Association of Scientists and Technologists -BNAST	-	Policy Advocacy matters
Tertiary Education Council (TEC)	March 1999	Higher education policy development, institutional guidelines and support

ticipated that a defined legal and regulatory framework with the local context flavor be put in place. This will help create trust and protect the weaker members of the society in the ICT environment.

FUTURE TRENDS

Looking at different platforms for a sound environment for KBE, the UNECE Report (2002) concludes that the strategy proposed for the improvement of the country's information and communication system should include the following benchmarks: a) the establishment of an independent regulatory body; b) the modification of license issued to incumbent telecom operators; and c) the development and adoption of standards in the quality of telecommunications services. For the case of Botswana, have these aspects been incorporated into the KBE transformation strategy? However, these benchmarks may be too hard to measure especially in the African context. It is thus imperative to understand that, in virtually all sectors, developing countries are still very far from the technological frontier, they still need to put priority on developing effective means of tapping the pre-existing and rapidly growing stock of global knowledge. Developing countries, like Botswana, need to put more weight than they do now on understanding, acquiring, adapting, diffusing, and using existing knowledge, including indigenous knowledge. This includes putting in place basic technological infrastructure such as norms and standards, metrology, testing, and quality control, as well as strong dissemination mechanisms and institutions such as technical information centers, productivity organizations, and agricultural and industrial extension agencies. Botswana has made considerable strides even when looked at using these guidelines and although has some work to do in liberalization of its financial markets, tackling the HIV-AIDS pandemic, addressing unemployment, reducing poverty amongst majority of its citizens, etc. it thus recommendable that a locally-drawn roadmap for transforming to a KBE be done.

To be able to eventually put in place a competent KBE agenda, there is need to consider the following principles:

1. There is need to promote more foreign-direct investment which will be consider of knowledge produced by local research and create more employment.

2. The quality of human resources will be the single most important factor. More and more citizens of Botswana need to be encouraged to go to school as education plays a crucial part in developing human capital and will play a critical role in shifting the economy towards a KBE. Lifelong learning should be ignored as it can provide the organizing principle which integrates economic development, social justice, cultural, political and scientific-technological literacy, national unity and cohesion as well as capacity-building for international competitiveness which is prerequisite to putting in place a KBE.

3. There is need to establish a National KBE Development Council which will be specifically responsible for coordinating all the efforts towards establishing a KBE.

4. The Private sector and the ordinary citizens should be involved in drawing the plans towards the establishment of a KBE.

5. There is need to have good public governance and low levels of corruption as these are essential to the knowledge economy.

6. There is need to put in place of an enabling environment by putting strong regulatory frameworks so that both the dynamism of the economy and social cohesion and welfare be maintained in the future.

7. Just as the case for Finland outline above, it is important to encompass two attitudes: an independent spirit of self-reliance and a

"can-do" mindset and a strong spirit of cohesiveness, high moral values, an emphasis on equality, and relatively equal distribution of national resources. These two characteristics can be preached to the ordinary citizens so that they buy-in to the idea of establishing a KBE and what should be done, thereof.

8. There is need to preach the willingness of the ordinary citizens to interact with the outside world in an open but strongly nationalistic way and for Botswana to have a flexible economy that is able to react to changing conditions (like putting in place proper diversification mechanisms to reduction in diamond demand which is the economic mainstay), and have in place a responsive education system.

9. Policies should be put in place to make sure that information is readily available to almost all socio-economic sectors and that people can have access to it at a reasonable cost.

10. There should be deliberate policies in place to make sure that the culture of innovation is encouraged throughout all the socio-economic setups.

If these principles and other attributes not mentioned here are observed and implemented, chances are high that the course for transformation from a resource to a knowledge-based economy by Botswana is likely to be reached.

CONCLUSION

This paper has surveyed the fundamental concepts on which this paradigm shift from a resource-based to knowledge-based economy is founded. The paper has looked at the major characteristics of a KBE and has contrasted it with the industrial and/or resource based economy. It brings out different initiatives that may be embarked on in transition from a resource to a KBE such as ICT development, nurturing of an appropriate human resource base, promoting a culture of innovation, investment in intellectual capital, etc. specifically, the paper has looked at the status of endeavors and initiatives done by Botswana towards shaping itself as a KBE, and also has emphasized the role of research and efficient knowledge management paradigms in shaping a country as a KBE. The paper also briefly looks at the Finland case of transforming to a KBE as a good example of how a small country can transform from a resource, to an industrial and then to a KBE. The lessons outlined in the Finland case in the course of discussion has helped this paper come up with specific recommendations on what Botswana should do if this vision of transforming to a KBE is to be realized.

From the surveys made and the initiatives discussed in this paper, it has been seen that Botswana has put in place start-up policies consolidating the transition of its economy from a resource to a knowledge-based one. It is thus suffice to say that the country is in tract to transforming to a KBE. The commitment towards this transformation is however left to the government and a few individuals which makes this vision very difficult to implement. It is thus important that strategic initiatives be put in place to sell this idea to the general population of Botswana so that amalgamated efforts can be devoted towards the same. The recommendations given in this paper may be strategic in realizing this KBE transformation dream for the case of Botswana. However, it is worth mentioning that future research works needs to be done on how certain stringent challenges such as reduction of HIV-AIDS infection rates, massive unemployment levels, overdependence on diamonds, etc. needs to be reduced or incorporated into KBE transformation policies so that this may not rob the country of its dream.

REFERENCES

Dahlman, C. J. (2003). Using knowledge for development: a general framework and preliminary assessment of China. In B. Grewal, L. Xue, P. Sheehan, & F. Sun (Eds.), *China's future in the knowledge economy: engaging the new world* (pp. 35-66). Prieiga per internet.

Dahlman, C. J., Routti, J., & Ylä-Anttila, P. (2005). *Finland as a knowledge economy: Elements of success and lessons learned*. Washington, DC: The International Bank for Reconstruction and Development.

Kalim, R., & Lodhi, S. (2004). *The Knowledge-Based Economy: trends and implications for Pakistan*. Retrieved May 15th, 2009 from www.pide. org.pk/.../The%20Knowledge%20Based%20 Economy.pdf

Kriščiūnas, K., & Daugėlienė, R. (2006). The assessment models of Knowledge-Based Economy penetration. *Engineering Decisions, 5*(50).

Lekorwe, M., Molomo, M., Molefe, W., & Moseki, k. (2001). *Public attitudes toward democracy, governance and economic development in Botswana* (Afrobarometer Paper No. 14).

Leung, K. C. (2004). *Statistics to measure the knowledge-based economy: The case of Hong Kong, China*. Paper presented at the 2004 Asia Pacific Technical Meeting of Information and Communication Technology (ICT) Statistic. Retrieved July 16th, 2009 from www.unescap. org/.../18.Statistics_to_measure_the_Knowledge-Based_Economy-Hong_Kong.pdf

Maguire, C., Kazlauskas, C., & Weir, A. D. (1994). *Information systems for innovative organizations*. London: Academic Press.

OECD. (1997). *The OECD Report on regulatory reform: Synthesis*. Paris: Organisation for Economic Co-operation and Development. Retrieved July 10th, 2009 from http://www.oecd.org/ dataoecd/17/25/2391768.pdf

Păceşilă, M. (2006). The impact of moving to Knowledge Based Economy in the public sector. *Management & Marketing Craiova, 1*, 113–118.

EFN Report. (2004, September). *The Euro area and the Lisbon strategy*.

Report, U. N. E. C. E. (2002). *Towards a Knowledge-Based Economy: ARMENIA – country readiness assessment report*. Retrieved May 30th, 2009 from http://www.unece.org/operact/enterp/ documents/coverpagarmenia.pdf

TKS- Towards a Knowledge Society. (2006). *A proposal for a tertiary education policy for Botswana* (Tech. Rep.). Retrieved July 27th, 2009 from http://www.tec.org.bw/tec_doc/ tec_rep_10_2006.pdf

Wilmoth, D. (2008). *Innovation in private higher education: the Botswana International University of Science and Technology*. Washington, DC: IFC international investment forum on private education.

Zeman, K. (2005). *Transformation towards Knowledge-Based Economy*. Paper presented at the Conference on Medium-Term Economic Assessment. Retrieved May 10th, 2009 from http://www.aeaf.minfin.bg/.../Karel_Zeman_paper_CMTEA2005.pdf

This work was previously published in The International Journal of Sociotechnology and Knowledge Development, Volume 2, Issue 2, edited by Elayne Coakes, pp. 53-62, copyright 2010 by IGI Publishing (an imprint of IGI Global).

Section 3

Chapter 9
A Framework for Analyzing Online Communities:
Sponsor and Member Value Proposition

M. Gordon Hunter
University of Lethbridge, Canada

Rosemary Stockdale
Swinburne University of Technology, Australia

ABSTRACT

This paper examines online communities and describes how they can be differentiated from other Internet supported group interactions. A definition of an online community is given and three generic types are identified. These types are defined by the community models based on the value proposition for the sponsors and members. The value proposition for members is strongly influenced by the model, as facilities and opportunities for interaction are structured by the site sponsors. Where online communities offer fulfillment of specific needs, people participate and become members. Additional benefits enhance the value of membership and encourage retention and greater interactivity. Significant benefits are gained from online communities for businesses, NGOs, other community organizations and individuals. Identifying the different types of communities and their characteristics is an important stage in developing greater understanding of how virtual communities can contribute to businesses, healthcare, community needs and a myriad of other contexts. Examples of the three generic types of online communities are included for further edification.

DOI: 10.4018/978-1-4666-0200-7.ch009

Copyright © 2012, IGI Global. Copying or distributing in print or electronic forms without written permission of IGI Global is prohibited.

INTRODUCTION

The term community has long been a difficult one to define. Researchers from fields such as sociology and anthropology have studied communities over many decades, seeking to determine the extent and structures of individuals' interactions with each other. Wilson and Peterson (2002, p. 455) highlight the transition from the study of communities as "reasonably complete and self-contained" entities in the 1940s through to a more flexible perception of them as "complex, spatially diverse" with asymmetrical, indirect connections. This more fluid concept of communities has been characterized by the notion that physical proximity is not a prerequisite for community building (Wilson & Peterson, 2002) and face-to-face communication is not a condition of community development. Developments in technology such as telegraphs, telephones and faster modes of transport have broken through any constraints of boundedness and support individuals' ability to remain part of a community unrestrained by geographic areas (Kollock & Smith, 1998). More recently, the debate on what constitutes a community has been broadened by the use of computer mediated communication to develop social networks that go beyond any geographical borders into the virtual world. Such developments have extended interest in the identification of community into the realm of Information Systems and raised further questions of what can actually be said to form a community in the online environment (Kollock & Smith, 1998; Wilson & Peterson, 2002).

Despite anecdotal evidence, fuelled by media stories, that use of the Internet reduces people's ability to interact socially there is growing recognition that communicating online can foster a new form of social contact (Butler, 2001). Rheingold (1993) asserts that the online space can replace socialization venues in the public space, such as clubs, cafes and pubs. His description of the WELL community shows how people used the available technology in the 1980s to form strong bonds with a wide group of virtual friends who supported each other through established stages of friendship including births, illnesses, marriages and death. With the advent of the Web and the explosion in Internet use there has been a vast expansion in the number of virtual gatherings of people with specific interests in a vast range of subjects. Commercial organizations have joined the trends towards creating communities and are seen to gain from being "part of the cultural fabric of an ongoing community" (Kozinets, Hemetsberger, & Schau, 2008, p. 352). Health communities have proliferated as people seek to find information and emotional support to cope with health issues (Leimeister et al., 2008); and local authorities, charities, governments and sports clubs all seek to extend their activities to communicate and inform in an online environment. There has been a plethora of research projects conducted regarding the use of the Internet to support the interactions of groups. This has led to further confusion over what is meant by a community and in disciplines such as anthropology, discussion as to whether a community can be created in the virtual environment (Wilson & Peterson, 2002). Within Information Systems, the concept has been more widely accepted and research has been extended to examine the influences that affect the ability of people and organizations to create 'community' within the virtual space (Ridings & Gefen, 2004). Nevertheless, there remains confusion as to how to identify communities and the meaning of the terminology that has evolved in this growing research area. The objective of this manuscript is not only to provide an overview description of the terms which have been employed; but to propose the use of a term from a perspective which incorporates aspects which facilitate participation in Internet supported group interactions. Thus, this manuscript presents a definition of "online community"; provides a differentiation from other Internet supported group interactions; and employs examples to further elucidate the proposed perspective in support of the definition.

The contribution made by this manuscript is the development of a consistent and appropriate definition of "online community" based upon a review of current research and the incorporation of a participation perspective. Also, a framework is proposed which could serve future research regarding the value proposition for sponsors and members. This investigation is situated within the purview of attempting to understand how member involvement may be enhanced through participation.

Clarity in this area will support the development and establishment of online communities that potentially provide many benefits to participants. An understanding of the aspects associated with member participation and ownership will assist many organizations to extract the full potential from online communities. This manuscript discusses definitions of "Online Communities" gleaned from many sources. Then further context is provided through the presentation of two frameworks for member participation in online communities. The literature review is organized by member roles and general purpose of online communities. Three generic types of online communities are identified and described in the following section along with examples. Some comments about future trends are included. Finally, conclusions are presented.

DEFINING ONLINE COMMUNITY

There has long been a range of meanings attached to the word 'community' (Hillery, 1963) and lack of a clear and consistent meaning persists in the online world. Community is coming to be seen as any interaction between people and the term is used freely in discussing any online communications. Additionally, there are many terms used to describe group interactions supported by the Internet. A list of generic terms in use include "learning communities", "thematic groups", and "collaborative knowledge networks", all of which create value by facilitating a space to enable groups to com-

municate in an environment of trust and innovative ideas. A key difference for group interactions and communities in the virtual world is the ability of members to be geographically dispersed. Other common terms that are employed in this context include the following:

- Virtual community (Hagel & Armstrong, 1997; Lee, Vogel, & Limayem, 2003) which integrates content and communication via computer mediated space.
- Virtual settlement (Jones, 1997) which includes virtual community, but adds concepts surrounding the idea of interactivity and sustained membership.
- Open Source communities were an early feature of group interaction on the Internet. They exist for the development of shared software. These communities are referred to as "open source" (Kidane & Gloor, 2007; Hemetsberger & Reinhardt, 2006).
- Community of Practice (Lin & Lin, 2006; Zhang & Watts, 2008) "...a group of people who share common concerns, problems, or passions for a domain, and who deepen their knowledge and expertise through interaction on an ongoing basis" (Lin & Lin, 2006, p. 1) The domain of this group relates to highly specialized and shared expertise (Wenger & Snyder, 2000) and may refer to a group within an organization or across organizational boundaries (Hara & Hew, 2007). The interaction does not necessarily incorporate the use of the Internet.

Rheingold (1993) sees communities as social aggregations that emerge when enough people form personal relationships through maintained discussion. His work has underpinned the ways in which others define a community in the virtual sphere. Preece (2000) uses Rheingold's (1993) view of a physical community and develops further meaning from Hillery's (1963) work on community within the physical environment. Hillery

(1963) includes the five components of interaction, space, activities, sentiment and institutions in his comparison of village or city communities with organizational entities such as prisons. Sentiment covers an awareness of community and the values related to it while institutions within the community include beliefs, socialization and recreation. The perspective of computer systems for online communities is added by Preece (2000), which reflects Jones' (1997) identification of a shared space or location. The idea of location in the physical sense was a facet of the work of Hillery (1963) who described communities as localized systems that are based around family and cooperation. In contrast Leimeister et al. (2008) see the need for a technical platform, but do not specify location or indeed a shared space. Social interaction is also included by Preece (2000) as an essential component of virtual community while Jones (1997) adds common obligations and responsibilities. Schubert and Ginsburg (2000) take a similar approach in their description of virtual communities as,

"... the union between individuals or organizations who share common values and interests using electronic media to communicate within a shared semantic space on a regular basis." (Schubert & Ginsberg, 2000, p. 30)

The inclusion of organizations in this description reflects the development of business related online communities, which has added further factors such as "expectations, mindset, shared semantics and beliefs of the participating parties" (Schubert & Ginsberg, 2000, p. 47) that are held to be necessary components in a business environment, but not essential to all online communities. There is consensus that community members must share a common interest (Leimeister et al., 2008; Stockdale & Borovicka, 2006; Schubert & Ginsburg, 2000; Preece, 2000) and a shared space.

While there is some overlap between these different terms, there are distinct differences in the range of activities and motivations that influence the behaviour and purpose of the varied memberships. To identify what we mean by online communities we have drawn up a definition from the work of many researchers including (Cheng & Vassileva, 2006; Jones, 1997; Preece, 2000; Rheingold, 1993).

In consideration of the above discussion, we therefore define an online community as:

A group of people that share a common interest and who communicate through a virtual space supported by computer mediated communications with some level of:

- Interactivity
- Variety of communicators
- Enjoyment
- Sustained membership
- Common values
- Socialization

What is Not an Online Community?

While a common definition is helpful to outline the scope of the subject of investigation, it is also important to note what does not fit within the adopted definition. Thus, the following terms are presented with a view to discussing how they do not fit within the proposed definition of an online community. All of the following terms are facilitated by some form of computer mediated communication.

A *static web* site simply presents information in a non-interactive manner and therefore cannot be said to represent an online community. *E-commerce* employs the Internet as a form of product and service distribution channel. This form of marketing does not meet the first three conditions of the above definition of an online community. Further, *E-business*, which incorporates E-commerce plus the provision of back-office support, also does not meet the necessary conditions for an online community. Additionally, there are a number of Internet services that for lack of on-going and sustained membership do not represent an online community. These types of services include examples such as *e-commerce book sellers* which incorporate *customer reviews*; *Customer Relationship Management systems* which incorporate the ability for customers to share experiences; and *life partner matching services*. Social networks, such as "*blogs*" come close to being considered online communities (Ma et al., 2006); for example www.fealty.net. However, as this example shows, they are primarily a one way presentation of information, rather like a public diary, without the components of sharing information, sustained membership and common values.

A more problematic application of the definition lies in *social networking sites* such as Facebook, MySpace or Twitter as they are commonly deemed to be communities. While many communities exist *within* these networks (for example a group of people in Facebook may have a common interest in a football team, a style of poetry, or a pop star) these sites are communication tools and not communities of themselves. They facilitate communication in much the same way as telegraphs and telephones, but cannot be deemed communities within the sense of the definition proffered above. So, the Facebook website provides the technology to facilitate the sharing of multiple common interests rather than a focused sharing of common interests surrounding a specific topic.

LITERATURE REVIEW

This section is divided into two aspects related to prior research into online communities. To begin research is reviewed which focuses on membership in socially constructed online communities. Then, online communities relating to business purposes are discussed. These two different aspects of online communities provide the context for the perspectives presented in the following section which analyzes online communities.

The following membership review is further categorized by the reasons members participate; the types of participation; the actions performed by members; and the needs of members which are addressed through their participation.

Members of online communities participated (Armstrong & Hagel, 1996) for the following reasons:

- **Transactional:** purchasing products or services
- **Interest-based:** exchange of information
- **Fantasy:** game playing
- **Relationship:** creation of an emotional bond

The Internet is an important source of online social interaction (Cummings et al., 2002). Individuals' intent to participate is based upon structural features such as a moderated site; and content features such as rate of posted comments and interactivity (Wise et al., 2006). Further, in their study of knowledge sharing in the legal profession Wasko and Faraj (2005) investigated why individuals contribute to online communities. They determined that individuals want to belong within their sphere of activity and were prepared to contribute to the community both to reciprocate for knowledge gained and because of their perceived enhancement of their personal reputation within the profession.

Four roles have been identified (Turner & Fisher, 2006) for those who are involved in online communities.

- First, "Questioners" are those individuals who actively participate. Questioners may post queries and comments; or they may be silent searchers. This latter term is also known as Lurker.

- Second, an "Answer Person" is one who is a highly active and influential advocate.
- Third, a "Community Manager" takes on the administrative duties facilitating the governing of the community. This term is also known as gatekeeper.
- Fourth, "Moguls" are highly esteemed technical and content experts capable of answering the most complex questions.

A sequential tiered series of actions performed by members of online communities (Hersberger et al., 2007) are described as follows:

Tier 1: Foundational building blocks

This tier forms the base of what constitutes a community. Four sets of building blocks are included. First, membership indicates acceptance by and identification with a group; which is initiated by participation in the group; involving the use of a common set of symbols; resulting in a sense of emotional and physical safety. Second, influence is reciprocal between the individual and the group. While group influence leads to conformity through the establishment and maintenance of norms, the level of an individual's influence on the group will lead to a feeling of belonging. Third, integration and fulfillment suggests that the more integrated an individual is within the group the higher will be their sense of fulfillment. Fourth, shared emotional connections involve the identification and participation in the history of the group, which is based on a perceived common purpose.

Tier 2: Social networks as information networks

This tier incorporates the concept of "tie strength". Strong ties exist in close relationships where new information is easily and frequently shared. Weak ties involve more informal social contacts.

Tier 3: Information exchange

This tier analyzes the evolution of virtual communities through models of information need, seeking, and exchange. The dynamic relationships within a group are dependent upon the reciprocal exchange of information.

Tier 4: Information sharing

This tier involves acquiring and sharing information which includes storing, recalling, associating, and disseminating information.

Members' needs (Stockdale, 2008) may be addressed by their participation in an online community. These needs are described as follows:

- **Functional:** This involves the need to search for information that is easy to access and reliably accurate.
- **Psychological:** This involves the need to address the desire for emotional support.
- **Social:** This involves the need to be a member of and be accepted by a group.
- **Hedonic:** This involves the need to enjoy interacting with other group members.

So, actions are taken (Stockdale, 2008) in response to addressing needs. As needs are successfully addressed membership will be sustained and a sense of community will be established. The end result will be a community in the traditional sense in that there will exist a group of individuals with a common purpose. But, the community will be "online" as it is facilitated through the use of computer technology and telecommunications. The above discussion of member participation has been employed in the development of the proposed framework described below.

Online communities have been established for many business purposes. For example, online communities exist for fiction writers (Porritt et al., 2006) while O'Sullivan (2007) reported on the use of hosted Internet forums for the promotion of arts organizations. The latter contends these forums add value through informing, involving, and providing an interface for members. He employs the term "brand communities" and defines it as, "...specialized non-geographically bound community, based on a structured set of social relationships among admirers of a brand" (O'Sullivan, 2007, p. 65). Businesses should develop a contingency model for conducting their own community building activities (Farquhar & Rowley, 2006). An interesting marketing technique (Mayzlin, 2006) called "promotional chat" is where firms disguise their promotions on the Internet as consumer recommendations. Because promoters and consumers are indistinguishable on the Internet, this form of marketing is possible. Fuller et al. (2006) investigated how members of online communities are involved in new product development. They determined that community based innovation provides a promising resource to a company's innovation process.

The above literature regarding online communities suggests they may be categorized by types which relate to sponsor and value proposition. Sponsor here is regarded as where the website resides and who are the main initiator and organizer of the online community. The term sponsor as used here may also be referred to as the "Community Manager" (Nonnecke et al., 2006). The value proposition relates to why a sponsor would initiate an online community; and consequently why a member would join, participate, and remain active over a sustained period of time.

ANALYSIS OF ONLINE COMMUNITIES

The previous discussion has outlined the actions taken by participating members of online communities and the needs that are addressed in response to these actions. In general, there are three types of online communities. Table 1 shows how the three types of online communities differ. It should be noted that the types of online communities outlined in the subsequent discussion will overlap to some extent. However, the main emphasis of each type has been categorized by the term presented in Table 1. Thus, their emphasis may be viewed as the orientation of the online community.

The remainder of this section presents a discussion of the various components of Table 1.

TYPES OF ONLINE COMMUNITIES - SPONSOR

The three types of online communities identified in Table 1 have been organized according to the sponsor of the sites. Sponsor models include business related, socially constructed or peer to peer communities, and volunteer oriented or community based. The motivations for creating the communities appear to vary in these models:

1. **Business related online communities** are established for the benefit of an enterprise. The purpose might be related to customer relationship management, branding, or simply gathering product or service feed-

Table 1. Types of online communities

Online Community	Sponsor Type	Value Proposition Sponsor	Value Proposition Member
Business Related	Business	Revenue	Product or Service
Socially Constructed	Individual or Group	Provide Knowledge	Obtain Knowledge
Volunteer Oriented	Organization	Revenue and Knowledge	Identify with Issue

back from customers. Lonely Planet (www. lonelyplanet.com) and other traveler/tourism sites enhance their brand and gather product (tourist information) in the form of contributions from members. Various open source sites (www.propellerheads. se) provide members with the opportunity to contribute to the further development of software resources thereby gaining product enhancement and feedback. A combination of branding, customer relationship management, product development ideas and feedback facilities can sometimes be found in one site as is the case with Lego (www. lego.com). In all cases the sponsor of the site is the business. An example is TradeMe.

TradeMe.co.nz: An Online Community within a Marketplace

TradeMe has established a strong community identity while operating as a commercial entity since its beginnings in 1999. The e-marketplace is similar to the eBay consumer-to-consumer model, offering an auction facility for the general public to list goods for sale. The founder, Sam Morgan, attributes his inclusion of community into his marketplace model to his familiarity with the community spirit that exists among traders gained from his background of visiting auction rooms and sales as a child (Ross & Holland, 2007). He replicated this sense of community from the beginnings of the early TradeMe site, recognizing that the 'Internet is a community' (Ross & Holland, 2007, p. 183). Morgan combined his experience of traders with his view of the Internet as a community to form a place where "New Zealanders wanted to hang out, grab a bargain and connect with other Kiwis" (Ross & Holland, 2007, p. 184). An interesting aspect of TradeMe's development has been its low-key approach to marketing. Although the reluctance to advertise began for financial reasons in the start-up period, the e-marketplace does not advertise and relies on word of mouth.

Morgan believes that the "brand was defined by the community" (Ross & Holland, 2007) and this perception remains with the current CEO who maintains that the quality of the e-marketplace encourages extensive blogging about the site by the general public that keeps the brand visible. He argues that once a successful community is established, it will succeed by the "dynamic of viral uptake" and "if you build a great site people won't be shy about blogging about it for you" (Kepes, 2008).

Morgan sold the company to Fairfax Media in 2006 for NZ$700 million. In the ten years of its existence TradeMe has expanded its range of services and facilities, which began with the idea of classified advertisements but soon moved into online auctions. There is a strong focus on community elements such as FindSomeone (dating), FlatMate and OldFriends. Profits were in excess of $40 million in 2006 and TradeMe accounts for nearly 70% of all Website traffic in New Zealand (MacManus, 2006).

The website offers both auction and classified advertisements although the former is by far the most popular. There are over a million items for sale in more than 25 categories from antiques to pottery, glass and toys. In addition there are property pages, cars and jobs pages. There are also business categories and a thriving livestock and equipment trade between farmers that one might normally associate with more conventional B2B marketplaces. Additional links to other services include finding a flat mate, a NZ news site, postings for lost pets and a travel site. The link to the community services displays newsletters, discussion forums and site statistics that indicate what sells and the best timing for setting auctions. There is even a webcam of the company offices.

TradeMe is very easy to use and sign-on requires a $10 deposit to set up an account that enables members to begin offering items for auction. There are multiple methods of payment and extensive instructions, fee scales and guidance on buying and selling. There are also TradeMe books (e.g., Saarinen, 2005) that break down the different processes into easy to understand language. Users of TradeMe vary from individuals to small and medium sized traders, farmers, car dealers and in the case of property all the real estate agents in New Zealand.

2. **Socially constructed online communities** may also be referred to as Peer to Peer. The online community is constructed by one or a number of persons to support a specific interest group for purely social, general information, or specific information related to, for instance health related issues such as BCANS, a breast cancer support group (www.bcans.ca). Socially constructed online communities may evolve beyond the individual and move to a business related model. For example, the long established 'news for nerds' community of Slashdot (www. slashdot) began as a socially constructed online community but has subsequently been bought by a business interest. An example of a socially constructed community is BCANS.

Breast Cancer Action Nova Scotia: A Peer to Peer Socially Constructed Online Community

Breast Cancer Action Nova Scotia is a survivor driven group that voices the unique concerns of people living with breast cancer. We are united in our desire to change the legacy of breast cancer through networking, support, education and research. (Statement was taken from the home page)

The site was created by women who had gone through the diagnosis and treatment for breast cancer and wished to share their experiences and gain support from other women. The origins of the group are in Nova Scotia and the community receives support from the Canadian Breast Cancer Foundation. There has been a steady development of facilities on the site and the revised site (2009) has a much more established feel than the earlier bcans.com site.

The BCANS site began in 1996 and was founded by Paula Leaman. Within 5 years the site was logging about 22,000 visits a month (Radin, 2006) and is continuing to grow. Radin (2006), who studied this web site from 1998 to 2001, reported that user sessions average 12–13 min in length. As this includes hasty and mistaken visits it means that many visitors are visiting for substantial periods of time.

At least two-thirds of participants are American, and another 20% or so are Canadian, but New Zealand and Australia are well represented. Visits in the first 2 weeks of May 2003 came also from Sweden, Belgium, the United Kingdom, the Netherlands, the Cayman Islands, Japan, the Philippines, Turkey, Finland, Germany, Brazil, Switzerland, Greece, Norway, Malaysia, Saudi Arabia, and France. Although there are still postings from overseas, the main focus of the site is Canadian based.

The early site carried a detailed history since its inception in the early 1990s as it evolved from a small group into a well established group with a vibrant membership and frequent postings. There were regular face to face meetings for local area members in Nova Scotia and a high level of trust evidenced by personal information and links to personal websites. Postings give evidence that reciprocity is widespread and support and advice offered where it is needed at any given time. There is a privacy policy. As well, there is strong evidence of self expression and encouragement to share spiritual support. Further, there is strong advocacy with evidence of actions taken listed.

There is a very strong sense of belonging - many indications of long term commitment to other members. Emotional support directed towards postings seeking help for new and established members. For example, recently there was a posting from the son of a member who has died. He posted a photograph of his new baby and received over a dozen responses from people who remembered his mother as a member from some years ago.

BCANS appears to be rapidly developing from a peer to peer site to a much more corporate looking site. They emphasize that their primary purpose is educational. The site is definitely more established and perhaps could be seen as more formalized and professional looking than previously, which is not surprising as it has grown so much and also as more people are gaining Web skills. The founder Paula Leaman left the group in 2007 after 10 years. Currently, there seems to be a group of volunteers that run both the site and the offices in Dartmouth.

The site has educational papers, lots of information about breast cancer, ongoing initiatives, a list of policies (including that they will not accept sponsorship from any commercial medical organization, such as pharmaceuticals). The site is now very well designed and appears to meet functional needs of users. The forums are still going strong and there are several. One is a discussion forum about cancer, one is more advocacy based (called the Soapbox) and another is for off-topic. There is a lively hedonic element evident in postings and activities. There continue to be many examples of shared episodes, writing books together, autobiographies, etc on the site. Although there are relatively few members there appear to be a lot of postings as membership (only registration) is not required for the forums.

It is difficult to track the movements (Radin, 2006) on this community as members/posters go silent and then start posting after a break. She states that,

... there is more continuity than is readily observable. Even the most active members sometimes take long breaks wherein their names are not visible in discussions for months, even years; however, they may continue to visit the site or to receive a daily digest of all posts via e-mail. (Radin, 2006, p. 596)

3.   **Volunteer oriented online communities** are more complex regarding sponsor. There are many different versions of sponsor models which impact upon the design and behaviour of the online community. There are two generic sponsor models as follows:*NGO/Charity*

This online community is constructed for an interest group mainly related to issues for the public good. This may include general health issues or aspects related to fundraising. In the case of OZMS (www.ozms.org) the focus of this Australian community is on peer support for people with multiple sclerosis. In contrast, CharityChannel (www.charitychannel.com) takes a broader focus and attracts members who are committed to any form of charity work.

Community Based Organization (CBO)

This online community is created by local teams or interest groups, such as sports clubs; legal aid; or citizen groups, with interests in political issues, gender matters, or ecological activities. There are a wide variety of communities in this group including Manchester United supporters (www.communitymanutd.com), environmentalists (www.greenpeace.com) and air traffic enthusiasts (www.vatsim.net). There are also examples of regional community newsletter sites moving towards the virtual community model (www.mysouthwest.com.au).

An example is Charity Channel.

CharityChannel. A community for people who work in charity organizations (Non profit professionals)

Charity Channel began as an email discussion forum back in 1992. It was founded by a charity worker who saw a need for people working within charity organizations to discuss issues pertinent to their work. It is an early example of an online community of practice. The site is also an example of an early peer to peer initiative that has undertaken a new form – almost could say it has been a victim of its own success. From its early origins it has developed into a community of over 100,000 participants and is available to nonprofit sector individuals and organizations although in 2003, a "small fee was implemented, based on the honor system. The fee covered the expenses incurred to keep this resource available to the nonprofit community." This was changed in 2008 when a registration system was introduced to formalize the community membership.

The site does accept advertising starting at US\$599 a month and gives a list of previous advertisers (many charities, universities, and education institutions).

Other features include:

- Articles contributed by the non-profit community
- Book reviews
- Live chat – community staff support desk
- FAQs (long and detailed with a facility to ask any question not already posted)
- Discussion forums (you have to register to get access to these so not sure how many there are)
- Weekly e-newsletter
- Radio channel
- Charity University (classes on for example how to get grants, how to be a board member etc). Cost roughly US\$100 a class, all online
- Consultants registry
- Career search

VALUE PROPOSITION

The influences of participation in online communities are visible in the value proposition for sponsors and for members. That is, the reason for the existence of the online community and why members would join and maintain their membership appears to be strongly influenced by the sponsor. Smith (2005) investigated the value proposition in online dating services; and Gopal et al (2005) developed a framework to analyze the value proposition in online options trading. In both cases the value proposition was related to the interpreted quality of the information exchanged amongst the participants. Further, Gu et al. (2007) investigated the value proposition in virtual investing-related communities. They suggest that the number of quality postings contribute to recognition of increased value as interpreted by the participants. They propose a statistical method to measure quality. The value propositions of revenue, personal motivation, and a combination of the two are discussed in the following paragraphs.

Value Proposition – Business Related Online Communities

The value proposition for sponsors of business related online communities is ultimately revenue. This may take the form of information that contributes to improved customer service, or may be related to a marketing strategy to enhance corporate or brand reputation. New product development may be based on information about customer preferences. Further, there may be an advantage obtained from gathering information from customers with specific expertise.

Members of business related online communities will buy-in to a product or service through using it or through the esteem associated with knowledge of the service. Members will become involved and remain so with the online community because of the reciprocal exchange of information regarding the product or service.

Value Proposition – Socially Constructed Online Communities

The value proposition for sponsors of socially constructed online communities is somewhat more complicated because of the more complex sponsor models. For example, the motivation for Peer to Peer may be self-esteem. The individual or group sponsors may gain fulfillment by being recognized as providing a knowledge repository, distributing information, and being thought leaders.

Members of socially constructed online communities will join and remain for various reasons. To begin a person may join because they are seeking information about a topic of interest, such as health information, or the activities of a sports club. Members will remain because they gain emotional support or fulfillment from the exchange of information with other members.

Value Proposition – Volunteer Oriented Online Communities

The value proposition for sponsors of volunteer oriented online communities may combine the revenue aspect of business related and the self-esteem issue for socially constructed online communities. Thus, the sponsors of NGO/Charity and CBOs may perform their duties as part of a formal position within these entities. However, in general, these individuals may work for these organizations because of a desire to associate their self-esteem with the mission of the entity.

Members of volunteer oriented online communities may become involved in the online community because it is part of their job or because they identify personally with the issue being addressed by the organization.

In general, while membership results in meeting the needs of individuals in all three types of online communities, there are also other benefits that may be gained. The advocacy role has been found in socially constructed online communities with a common interest that can be addressed by collective action. There may be a freeing of self expression in a relatively anonymous environment where no one has an obvious personal agenda. Finally, there may be a feeling of spirituality in the form of peace and self worth from contributing to a perceived noble cause.

FUTURE TRENDS

The origin of online communities is often said to lie in the Usenet groups of the pre-Web world of the Internet. The desire to communicate ideas, interests and experiences with others has been facilitated by the Internet. The Usenet groups have grown into more interactive communities. This has led to an increase in interest, types, and membership of online communities and what some see to be the exploitation of them by commercial interests. Thus, there are many opportunities for future research.

It is increasingly difficult to identify peer to peer communities as they compete with more professionally constructed communities that are better funded and managed. There has been a significant increase in the number of business sponsored communities with more evidence that firms are building on the techniques of targeted marketing to maximize the benefits of this form of customer interaction.

The potential of communities in the not-for-profit sector is as yet, not fully exploited. Local councils could make more use of the Internet to connect with their population to promote inclusive action. For example, they could promote events in sports clubs, schools, and community clubs while offering discussion boards for council actions, local businesses and the general population. Charities and other volunteer organizations are beginning to be more active in this area, but are not yet using the potential of these communities to the full, often because they have not identified their value propositions.

CONCLUSION

The purpose of this manuscript was to review the existing terms and frameworks employed for describing online communities in order to identify generic types and their characteristics. Within the definition of an online community given in this study, three groups of online communities are identified. These are defined by the sponsor models of the sites and based on the value proposition for the sponsors and members. These models strongly influence the profile of community members as people seek fulfillment of specific needs from their participation in a site. Continued membership requires not only that the value proposition for members offers fulfillment of needs, but also that further benefits can be gained.

The contribution from this manuscript is the framework which has been proposed. The framework presents a way of categorizing online communities based upon aspects related to sponsor involvement and member participation. This framework should serve to facilitate future research in this area.

There appear to be significant benefits to be gained from online communities for businesses, NGOs and other organizations; and individuals as sponsors and members. Examining the different types of communities and identifying their characteristics in this manuscript is an important stage in developing greater understanding of how virtual communities can contribute to businesses, healthcare, community needs and a myriad of other contexts.

REFERENCES

Armstrong, A., & Hagel, J. (1996). The Real Value of Online Communities. *Harvard Business Review, 7*(3), 134–141.

Butler, B. S. (2001). Membership Size, Communication Activity, and Sustainability: A Resource-Based Model of Online Social Structures. *Information Systems Research, 12*(4), 346–362. doi:10.1287/isre.12.4.346.9703

Cheng, R., & Vassileva, J. (2006). Design and Evaluation of an Adaptive Incentive Mechanism for Sustained Educational Online Communities. *User Modeling and User-Adapted Interaction, 16*(3-4), 321–348. doi:10.1007/s11257-006-9013-6

Cummings, J. M., Butler, B., & Kraut, R. (2002). The Quality of Online Social Relationships. *Communications of the ACM, 45*(7), 103–108. doi:10.1145/514236.514242

Farquhar, J., & Rowley, J. (2006). Relationships and Online Consumer Communities. *Business Process Management Journal, 12*(2), 162–177. doi:10.1108/14637150610657512

Fuller, J., Bartl, M., Ernst, H., & Muhlbacher, H. (2006). Community Based Innovation: How to Integrate Members of Virtual Communities into New Product Development. *Electronic Commerce Research, 6*, 57–73. doi:10.1007/s10660-006-5988-7

Gopal, R., Thompson, S., Tung, Y. A., & Whinston, A. B. (2005). Managing Risks in Multiple Online Auctions: An Options Approach. *Decision Sciences, 36*(3), 397–425. doi:10.1111/j.1540-5414.2005.00078.x

Gu, B., Konana, P., Rajagopalan, B., & Chen, H. M. (2007). Competition among Virtual Communities and User Valuation: The Case of Investing-Related Communities. *Information Systems Research, 18*(1), 68–85. doi:10.1287/isre.1070.0114

Hagel, J. I., & Armstrong, A. (1997). *Net Gain: Expanding Markets through Virtual Communities.* Boston: Harvard Business School Press.

Hara, N., & Hew, K. F. (2007). Knowledge-Sharing in an Online Community of Health-care Professionals. *Information Technology & People, 20*(3), 235–261. doi:10.1108/09593840710822859

Hemetsberger, A., & Reinhardt, C. (2006). Learning and Knowledge-building in Open-source Communities. *Management Learning, 37*(2), 187–214. doi:10.1177/1350507606063442

Hersberger, J. A., Murray, A. L., & Rioux, K. S. (2007). Examining Information Exchange and Virtual Communities: An Emergent Framework. *Online Information Review, 31*(2), 135–147. doi:10.1108/14684520710747194

Hillery, G. A. (1963). Villages, Cities and Total Institutions. *American Sociological Review, 28*(5), 778–791. doi:10.2307/2089915

Jones, Q. (1997). Virtual Communities, Virtual Settlements, and Cyber-archaeology: A Theoretical Outline. *Journal of Computer Mediated Communication, 3*(3). Retrieved September 7, 2009, from http://jcmc.indiana.edu/vol3/issue3/jones.html Kepes, B. (2008). If you build it will they come? *New Zealand Herald.* Retrieved November 19, 2008, from http://www.nzherald.co.nz/smallbusiness

Kidane, Y. H., & Gloor, P. A. (2007). Correlating Temporal Communication Patterns of the Eclipse Open Source Community with Performance and Creativity. *Computational & Mathematical Organization Theory, 13*(1), 17–27. doi:10.1007/s10588-006-9006-3

Kollock, P., & Smith, M. (1998). Communities in Cyberspace. In Smith, M., & Kollock, P. (Eds.), *Communities in Cyberspace* (pp. 3–24). London: Routledge.

Kozinets, R. V., Hemetsberger, A., & Schau, H. J. (2008). The Wisdom of Consumer Crowds: Collective Innovation in the Age of Networked Marketing. *Journal of Macromarketing, 28,* 339–354. doi:10.1177/0276146708325382

Lee, F. S. L., Vogel, D., & Limayem, M. (2003). Virtual Community Informatics: A Review and Research Agenda. *The Journal of Information Technology Theory and Applications, 5*(1), 47–61.

Leimeister, J. M., Schweizer, K., Leimeister, S., & Krcmar, H. (2008). Do Virtual Communities Matter for the Social Support of Patients? Antecedents and Effects of Virtual Relationships in Online Communities. *Information Technology & People, 21*(4), 350–374. doi:10.1108/09593840810919671

Lin, S. C., & Lin, F. R. (2006). An Ecosystem View on Online Communities of Practice. *International Journal of Communications Law & Policy,* 1-31.

Ma, W. W., Clark, T. H. K., & Li, P. (2006). Cognitive Style and Acceptance of Online Community Weblog Systems. *International Journal of Communications Law & Policy,* 1-12.

MacManus, R. (2006). *TradeMe: big fish in a small pond.* Retrieved September 7, 2009, from http://www.readwriteweb.com/archives/trademe_big_fish_small_pond.php

Mayzlin, D. (2006). Promotional Chat on the Internet. *Marketing Science, 25*(2), 155–163. doi:10.1287/mksc.1050.0137

Nonnecke, B., Andrews, D., & Preece, J. (2006). Non-public and Public Online Community Participation: Needs, Attitudes and Behavior. *Electronic Commerce Research, 6,* 7–20. doi:10.1007/s10660-006-5985-x

O'Sullivan, T. (2007). Sounding Boards: Performing Arts Organizations and the Internet Forum. *International Journal of Arts Management, 9*(3), 65–95.

Porritt, M., Burt, A., & Poling, A. (2006). Increasing Fiction Writers' Productivity through an Internet-Based Intervention. *Journal of Applied Behavior Analysis, 39*(3), 393–397. doi:10.1901/jaba.2006.134-05

Preece, J. (2000). *Online Communities. Designing Usability, Supporting Sociability*. New York: John Wiley and Sons.

Radin, P. (2006). To me, it's my life: Medical Communication, Trust and Activism in Cyberspace. *Social Science & Medicine, 62*, 591–601. doi:10.1016/j.socscimed.2005.06.022

Rheingold, H. (1993). *The Virtual Community: Homesteading on the Electronic Frontier*. Reading, MA: Addison-Wesley.

Ridings, C. M., & Gefen, D. (2004). Virtual Community Attraction: Why People Hang Out Online. *Journal of Computer-Mediated Communication, 10*(1).

Ross, E., & Holland, A. (2007). *50 Great E-Businesses and the Minds Behind Them:* Sydney, Australia: Random House.

Saarinen, J. (2005). *TradeMe, your ultimate guide to New Zealand's biggest online auction site*. Auckland, New Zealand: Penguin.

Schubert, P., & Ginsburg, M. (2000). Virtual Communities of Transaction: The Role of Personalization in Electronic Commerce. *Electronic Markets, 10*(1), 45–55. doi:10.1080/10196780050033971

Smith, A. D. (2005). Exploring Online Dating and Customer Relationship Management. *Online Information Review, 29*(1), 18–33. doi:10.1108/14684520510583927

Stockdale, R. (2008). Peer-to-Peer Online Communities for People with Chronic Diseases; A Conceptual Framework. *Journal of Systems and Information Technology, 10*(1), 39–55. doi:10.1108/13287260810876885

Stockdale, R., & Borovicka, M. (2006). Ghost Towns or Vibrant Villages? Constructing Business-Sponsored Online Communities. *International Journal of Communications Law & Policy*, 1-22.

Turner, T. C., & Fisher, K. E. (2006). Social Types in Technical Newsgroups: Implications for Information Flow. *International Journal of Communications Law & Policy*, 1-21.

Wasko, M. M., & Faraj, S. (2005). Why Should I share? Examining Social Capital and Knowledge Contribution in Electronic Networks of Practice. *Management Information Systems Quarterly*, 35–57.

Wenger, E. C., & Snyder, W. M. (2000). Communities of Practice: The Organizational Frontier. *Harvard Business Review, 78*(1), 139–144.

Wilson, S. M., & Peterson, L. C. (2002). The Anthropology of Online Communities. *Annual Review of Anthropology, 31*, 449–467. doi:10.1146/annurev.anthro.31.040402.085436

Wise, K., Hamman, B., & Thorson, K. (2006). Moderation, Response Rate, and Message Interactivity: Features of Online Communities and their Effects on Intent to Participate. *Journal of Computer-Mediated Communication, 12*(1). Retrieved from http://jcmc.indiana.edu/vol12/issue1/wise.html. doi:10.1111/j.1083-6101.2006.00313.x

Zhang, W., & Watts, S. A. (2008). Capitalizing on Content: Information Adoption in Two Online Communities. *Journal of the Association for Information Systems, 9*(2), 73–95.

This work was previously published in The International Journal of Sociotechnology and Knowledge Development, Volume 2, Issue 3, edited by Elayne Coakes, pp. 11-25, copyright 2010 by IGI Publishing (an imprint of IGI Global).

Chapter 10
Realising Virtual Reality:
A Reflection on the Continuing Evolution of New Media

Allan McLay
RMIT University, Australia

ABSTRACT

This paper addresses the continuing convergence and integration of digital electronic media, and in particular, virtual reality as an exemplar phenomenal media. The author explores and further develops the theme that each of such media entails a specific lexicon or language of use that continually evolves. For this media to be effective, however, it must be widely understood within its community of practice. In this paper, virtual reality is discussed as an exemplar new-media application as a means of virtual representation or reflection of events or behaviours in the real world from a socio-technical perspective.

The continuing development and Moore's Law style growth in micro-electronics and related digital technologies, has inexorably led to the development of specialised human-machine interface systems necessary for the integrated use of such technologies. It is largely this integration of underlying technology and interface systems with continually changing modes of use and user expectations that drives the continuing evolution of contemporary new-media. In turn, the continuing introduction of new new-media based applications continues to influence and in effect transform the way we communicate, work, make decisions, rest and play.

Given the endemic presence of media hype, marketing disinformation and occasional more outrageous predictions of over-excited techno-evangelists in the area of new technology and its

DOI: 10.4018/978-1-4666-0200-7.ch010

Copyright © 2012, IGI Global. Copying or distributing in print or electronic forms without written permission of IGI Global is prohibited.

application, it is sobering to reflect on Thomas Edison's observation, circa 1913: *It is possible to teach every branch of human knowledge with the motion picture. Our school system will be completely changed in ten years* (Attributed to Edison (1913) in Gould & Mason, 1985, p. 1.) Clearly, with the advantage of hindsight, a prediction about the role of motion film which failed to appreciate both the real potential and the limitations of film media.

Contemporary new-media is substantively based on the integration of multiple digital electronics and computer technologies. As such, it reflects a continuing convergence of what was previously considered disparate media with discontinuous applications. To a large extent this is no longer the case, as technologies and applications seemingly converge, or at least utilize common components and exhibit common characteristics and interdependencies. In turn, this raises many questions of process and practice in the use of such still evolving 'new media'. For example, Manovich (2001) referred to such convergence as a computer media revolution that is affecting all stages of contemporary communication and impacting on all types of communication media, whether text, images, sound, or graphics construction based. *How shall we begin to map out the effects of this fundamental shift?* (Manovich, 2001, p. 19-20) He subsequently developed his argument along the lines of cultural transcoding of new and meta-media. A form of differential aesthetic wherein both media and the multiple and often divergent social and organizational cultural contexts in which it operates and is operated on, are in a constant state of change and interaction (Manovich, 2001; Murphie & Potts, 2003; Charles, 2009). In the context of considering organizational culture as a system of shared meaning within a given organization (Robbins & Barnwell, 2006) the implication is that the parameters that influence and affect the collected/shared meanings, beliefs, assumptions, behaviours and practices within a contemporary organization, are subject not only to internal shared pressures and adjustments, but also are affected by the (initially) external influences for innovation and change resulting from perceived opportunities and threats associated with new inbound technology, such as in this case, new-media.

In effect, the traditional business construct of a value chain for contemporary new media hinges on new media's capacity to represent and add value to information in a form capable of translation, transformation, and distribution wherever and whenever digital processes and electronic network communication is accessible. Today, this implies virtually any time, anywhere on the globe (Lister et al., 2009). In large measure then, the technological aspects of new media can be seen as a continually evolving new form and set of technological artifacts, as a consequence of continuing and widespread digitalization and presumed technological convergence of networkable media and systems. Castells describes this mass diffusion of information and communications technology as being the key element in formulating a new social structure or 'networked society' (Castells, 1996). He further outlined a 'new economy' based on information and communications technology and exhibiting the three core characteristics of 'informational', 'global', and 'networked' (Castells (2000) cited in Flew, 2005). In a sociological sense this can interpreted in the case of new-media as a continuing growth in connectivity between: purpose (for the introduction of new-media); functionality (of new-media as an effective communicative medium); role (of new-media within a given communication context); place (both at a geographical level and 'logical' positioning within a given community of practice); relationships to contemporary cultural norms (whether within or between organizational contexts or at a broader societal context); and its potency (ostensibly resulting from both technology-technology and business-technology convergence (Andriole, 2005)) as an inherently transformative media. As such, it is essential that we explore the nature of

145

such potentially transformative media and determine just how, when and where we may utilize to best advantage its strengths whilst mitigating potential demerits (Woolgar, 2002).

However, the very notion of convergence is now itself a source of argument and re-thinking, from Manovich's 'cultural transcoding' (Manovich, 2001) to Jenkins' 'convergence culture' (Jenkins, 2006), Storsul and Stuedahl's 'ambivalence towards convergence' (Storsul & Stuedahl, 2007), and Knight and Weedon's 'shifting notions of convergence' (Knight & Weedon, 2009). The complexity and changing face of which, with regard to new-media and virtual reality (VR) related media in particular, is further compounded by the non-elemental character of new-media as a thriving hybrid of multiple (largely digital) technologies, sociological constructs (contexts, relationships, communicative behaviours and cultural norms) and (at least from a constructivist viewpoint) with an inherent capability to influence cognitive perceptions and related behaviours within or external to synthetic or virtual-world environments (Coyne, 1995). It is this *decoupling of space from place* (Shields, 2003, p. 42) to create virtual representations and constructions of real or imagined objects/subjects/environments and associated relationships, which most notably distinguish new-media VR applications from earlier communication media. Whilst new-media in its various forms, may be the current ontological unit of technological development resulting from intense digital technology convergence, its use to deploy conceptual virtual reality (the term in itself a classic oxymoron) as a working 'space' in which the media activates its users (or at least appears to, in a technologically deterministic sense) to scale the virtual mountains of innovation (or whatever virtual form or referent the virtual environment may take) reflects further McLuhan's much earlier observation about the context of new evolving media, that: *Today the environment itself becomes the artifact* (McLuhan (1964) cited in Heim, 1993, p. 66).

The actual term 'virtual reality' first appears in 1986 and is attributed to Jaron Lanier (early VR entrepreneur and founder of the ill-fated VR development company 'VPL Research') (Heim, 1998). Progressively, commercial VR products entered the marketplace. By year 2000, VR systems were available globally and had penetrated virtually all areas of industrial design, computer gaming/entertainment, defence strategy development and training, real-time military battlespace planning and management, medical research and training, nuclear research, and a growing array of real-time control systems and robotics. There would appear to be almost as many definitions of virtual reality as there are interested users of the technology and its associated systems. Each such user in turn bringing his or her own perceptions, interests and ownerships, to bear on their particular use and application of VR. These vary from the simplistic and pragmatic to the highly sophisticated and abstract. A wide array of integrated new-media technologies can be utilised to form virtual reality systems. These can vary from simple desk-top computers with broadband communications access to the internet enabling interactive applications such as Second Life to run on the office desk-top, through to highly sophisticated supercomputer-based systems supporting multiple overhead image projection onto surrounding screens with multi-directional surround sound, or semi-enclosed multi-wall projection environments called CAVEs used with stereo-vision shutter glasses and hand-held haptic control devices to provide interactive full surround/immersive three-dimensional imaging, or even hand-held 'touch' screen devices incorporating WiFi connection to either internet or local intranet applications.

The actual underlying technology bases of electronic and digital media have undergone constant, if at times rather erratic or spectacular, innovation and change and technological convergence. So also the communities of practice, the users of such technological innovation, have undergone continuing social and organizational cultural change with at times dramatic discontinuities. For example: the dot-com boom and bust of the late 1990s and early 2000s; the transition from analog to digital radio and television with its significant impact on user expectations of image and audio quality; the introduction of miniature MPEG players or iPods supporting 1000s of high fidelity quality audio files, videos and movies downloadable from the internet via secure broadband WiFi networks; and the introduction of high resolution computer graphics enabling special visual effects in video and movies integrated with and largely indistinguishable from actual photographic images.

Just as earlier analog or time dependent media have progressively converged with digital media to acquire a new form and extended functionality, so also did they acquire a new language that addresses concomitant changes and challenges in the field of mass-communication and associated user community cultural norms. For example, earlier communication media such as broadcast medium-wave radio was essentially constrained by geographic distribution and reception 'reach' and largely compliant with community based, or regionally specific interests and accepted patterns of behaviour, although the opportunity to institute focused information dissemination or 'propaganda' mode broadcasts was certainly not lost on some community groups (Shultze, 1988). Eventually, the introduction of short-wave radio bands, higher transmission power, increased receiver performance and low user entry costs, extended this reach well beyond local and even regional areas. By comparison, the new-media based communication technologies of today, such as the internet and world-wide-web, are virtually unconstrained by geographic reach (Lister et al., 2009) and certainly not by local or even regional cultural norms (despite attempts by some government's agencies to censor or constrain their populace's access to some content). They also reflect, in common with earlier electronic media, typical characteristics of successful innovation diffusion,

including: demonstrably improved performance over alternative media in a key area or multiple key areas of interest (for example, including but not limited to: global mass communications, speed of delivery, widespread access, potential for secure asynchronous and synchronous communication and interaction) with decreasing unit costs, multiple (competitive/non-monopolistic) providers of required technology and services, and increasing reliability, collectively resulting in widespread acceptance (Rogers, 2003). Such changes have also seen continuing departures from traditional forms of communication media use, as in the expanding use of online immersive virtual-world environments such as Second Life and the wide variety of semi-immersive virtual-world gaming systems (Boellstorff, 2008; Jenkins, 2006; Kreps, 2008; Manovich, 2001).

Increasingly, users of various forms of new media are being faced with frequent innovation and change in base technology, interface mechanisms and role and function of new media. Adjusting to such shifts and changes is increasingly not just a case of adapting to new base-technology or modified processes. Rather, developers and users alike are finding, exploring and indeed creating fundamental adaptations to role and function and congruent extension to the nature and characteristics of a given form of media and its potential influence and impact on its associated community of practice. Within and adapting in accord with these changes, the very 'language' and structure of new media is also evolving with time. A language that is being formed and reformed, both by convergent technologies and the convergence of similar, yet differing, communities of practice with in turn, changing needs and expectations and continuing adaptations in perceptions of social reality and context, behaviours and cultural norms (Flew, 2005).

In a similar vein of argument, Richard Caldine of the Centre for Staff Development at the University of Wollongong (circa 1994) extended many of his observations on imaging techniques and message structuring in educational television to the then growing areas of commonality between the then new media: Internet and early multi-media based systems. *An understanding of the language of television will assist those who in the future are faced with other screen-based media as the language of television forms the basis of the lexicon for multimedia* (Caldine, 1994, p. 3). This insight into the concept of a need to understand, or at least appreciate, the language of a particular media and their associated communities of practice, is of particular relevance, although many (including the author) would certainly challenge the inherent implications of attempting to use television as having an implicitly transferable media language.

One of the earliest documented evidences of the existence of such 'media language' dates to the broadcast on October 30th 1938 of a live-to-air radio play: H. G. Welles' War of the Worlds. Its graphic descriptions of an alien invasion produced wide-spread panic and mass hysteria. Listeners had taken the broadcast as reporting on an actual live event. It was, but it was a radio drama event. In 1938, most radio producers and listeners were yet to develop an understanding of the power and presence of radio media as a challenging and potentially gritty new aural art-form. Radio broadcasting was seen as a low-cost mass-communications media capable of distributing music, news, sports commentary, advertisements, and dissemination of information on issues of political and community interest through talks, interviews and religious programming (Gosling, 2004; Miller, 2000; Slouka, 1995). The advantages of being able to extend reach to large numbers of the populace distributed over vast areas, in real-time, at a time of one's choosing (at least for station owners, producers of programming and/or for those willing and able to pay for a favoured time-window) being a core driving influence on the acceptance and growth of broadcast radio media. This is highlighted for example in the wide-spread use of radio broadcasting for dissemination

of evangelical Christian religious programming from the earliest years of radio media in the USA (Schultze, 1988). This rapid uptake of a new media appears to have been largely driven by the simple principle of accessing the ever widening 'reach' and immediacy of radio broadcast media compared to the almost architectural limitations of the church pulpit, whilst retaining the rhetorical influence, impact and sense of immediacy in the mode of delivery. Here can be seen some of the earliest signs of ascendancy in the core-characteristics of: immediacy, presence and reach, in contemporary electronic media.

The introduction of public television in the late 1930's and early 1940's pushed the levels of power and presence of broadcast communications media even further, extending the language lexicon. During the same period lavish productions in colour movie film media began to expand globally, again exhibiting a further variation to media language, function, and status within society (Jenkins, 2006). Sixty years later, with the continuing growth in communications media and associated supporting technologies, has come a concomitant development in electronic media complexity, capability, applications, reach and pervasiveness, to the point of ubiquitousness. With this has also come a growth in perceptions of the language and functionalities of such media, although some would argue not necessarily in understandings.

Expanded functionalities in 'user' telecommunications media over the past two decades provide a particularly glaring example of media convergence and the potential for media language conflict: the fixed/wired telephone versus the mobile telephone with built in digital camera; iPod portable media player with Wi-Fi text messaging/email and internet access; mobile Global Positioning System (GPS) with built-in maps, location finding and travel directions. Each device with its own specific enhancements to communications, yet each also carrying inherent constraints and restrictions and collectively representing further convergence in both the telecommunications and information technology bases, and the characteristics of contemporary media and their associated communities of practice (Bell, 2007; Jenkins, 2006; Sobel Lojeski & Reilly, 2008).

Marshal McLuhan, creator of the aphoristic expressions: *the medium is the message* (McLuhan, 1964, p. 7); *radio: the tribal drum* (McLuhan, 1964, p. 297); and *the global village* (McLuhan & Fiore, 1968, title) was particularly concerned about electronic media, its impact on society and our understandings of communication. He categorized communication media as being either 'hot' or 'cold' based on the intensity of information involved, engagement of the user, and the required commitment and participation of the user, especially as this relates to the use of multiple senses (sensory perception) in order to effectively interpret message content (Flew, 2005; McLuhan, 1964).

McLuhan ascribes the status of 'hot' to photographic media, as photographic imaging is generally visually of high definition and as such well filled with data. The telephone and general auditory speech he describes as being 'cool' media because *so little is given and so much has to be filled in by the listener* (McLuhan, 1964, p. 22).

McLuhan's definition, established some 20 years prior to the introduction of multi-media and 30 years prior to the first effective large scale commercial virtual reality systems and technology (SGI Virtual Reality Center circa 1994) and the age of digital convergence (Yoffie, 1997) proves problematic when applied to virtual reality media. It would appear to classify virtual reality (VR) media as both hot and cool, depending on the design focus of the application:

- High in participation and immersive engagement by the user = cool
- High definition as in: *well filled with data* (McLuhan, 1964, p. 22) and extends (multiple) senses in high definition = hot).

Here can be seen the complexity of VR media and new media in general, with its capacity for concurrent intensive exposure to both high definition data and high level interaction through the immersive experience of tele-presence, exemplifying McLuhan's hot and cool media parameters in a unique form of duality.

McLuhan also proposed a tetrad of four laws or effects of media. These in turn highlight the complexities of endeavouring to uncover and understand the meanings and language of specific 'media'. He posed four questions to be asked of any medium: *What does it enhance or amplify in the culture? What does it obsolesce or push out of prominence? What does it retrieve from the past, from the previously obsolesced?* And here the tetrad projects into the future – *What does the medium reverse or flip into when it reaches the limits of its potential?* (McLuhan and McLuhan (1988) as cited in Levinson, 2001, p. 16).

For McLuhan, radio was an example of an enhancement to communications that extended oral forms of communication. In the terms of McLuhan's tetrad it enhanced or amplified oral communications. Similarly, it obsolesced the newspaper as a significant medium for written communication, retrieved something of the earlier prominence of oral communication, but with the further passage of time it in effect reversed into the medium of television with its more graphic use of combined sound and moving images (McLuhan and McLuhan (1988) as cited in Levinson, 2001, p. 16; Sui & Goodchild, 2003).

The following provides a further extrapolation of McLuhan's tetrad as applied to contemporary virtual reality media as an exemplar new media:

- Virtual reality amplifies sensory perception through stimulating the use of multiple senses (visual, auditory, tactile, and associated enhanced cognition factors)
- It obsolesces 2D and constrained 3D graphics-image based simulation by providing opportunity to access a whole-of-world

view (the Weltanschauung of systems thinking) through creation of multiple systems of systems in synthetic environments, or virtual worlds.

- It retrieves the artisan hands-on experiential mode of exploratory learning and skills development whilst reducing inherent risk and enhancing potential quality of outcomes.
- It reverses (potentially) into a closer understanding of the reality of the world around us and prepares the way for even more sophisticated visual media capable of providing connectivity for manipulating real world entities from within virtual world environments.

It is perhaps in this fourth characteristic that we see the most dramatic indicators of the future strategic potentialities for virtual reality technology and systems. However, the first three are clearly all implicit in contemporary virtual reality systems. Strategic positioning of such new media in contemporary organizations may well be seen as focusing on optimising the effects of these three characteristics.

In the first instance, amplifying sensory perception, there is widespread acceptance that the multi-sensory nature of new-media, particularly those capable of creating conditions of user immersion, does provide enhancement in perception and potentially in performance, although it is still difficult to find actual measures of the latter (Friedhoff & Peercy, 2000; Lister et al., 2009; Stair & Reynolds, 2006; Turban et al., 2002). Such measures should not be confused, as they often are, with measures of system performance, where virtual reality simulations can achieve design and testing results faster than traditional techniques (Stair & Reynolds, 2006). Whilst virtual reality new-media systems may well utilize multiple sensory stimulation, it is primarily the use of visualization that epitomizes virtual reality tools.

Historically, engineers have been long-time users of visualization tools and strategies, from pen and parchment, to pointing device and computer screen. All have played critical roles in the evolution of contemporary visualization aids as a means for developing virtual models of proposed and/or real-world structures. *Information visualization... was inspired by the idea of applying scientific visualization techniques to abstract information spaces. Information visualization focuses on the use of interactive techniques that can transform data, information, and knowledge into a form from which the human visual system can easily perceive its meaning* (Attributed to Robertson et al. (1993) in Chen, 2006, p. 156).

The impact on designers and project stakeholders alike of visualizing how a final product or structure might appear in the real world invokes a complex interaction of the perceptual, affective and cognitive domains of intellectual behaviour (Jones, 1996). *A good visualization is something that allows us to drill down and find more data about anything that seems important... in reality we are just as likely to see an interesting detail, zoom out to get an overview, find some related information in a lateral segue, and then zoom in again to get the details of the original object of interest* (Ware, 2004, p. 317). The use of immersive visualization may then further amplify sensory (albeit primarily visual) perception through direct engagement with virtual world objects and their affective relationships. In the context of using virtual worlds to support decision-making, a virtual world may or may not provide a direct visual correspondence with the real world. Rather, it must provide virtual representations of those parameters or characteristics that in the real world have or result in real and identifiable effects (Hunsinger, 2008). The actual construction of the virtual world may involve the use of shapes, colour, position, mobility, and other controllable or attributable characteristics. The core purpose being, to enable visualization of information, conditions, status, variables, in such a way that managers can effectively perceive, extract and interpret meaning from data so represented (Chen, 2006).

An example of the second characteristic, obsolescence, can be seen in a major project involving the progressive conversion of existing CAD graphics, used by some 200 parts and components suppliers for a large industrial manufacturer, to fully defined 3D objects importable into geographically distributed (global on-line) virtual reality environments. In time, even subtle design changes within the virtual world version of the product will result in virtual adjustments to the multiple component parts affected by the proposed change. Duly exported back to the suppliers, these adjustments may then result in appropriate re-engineering/design, re-tooling, and subsequent supply of new components much faster and potentially cheaper, than current techniques and procedures. This example of both the introduction of 3D visualization based new-media and the interaction between complex systems of systems, also demonstrates the continuing evolution and application of contemporary systems thinking as an holistic approach to the development of new ideas and their implementation. In this case, the introduction of a geographically distributed 3D virtual reality environment providing an effective alternative approach to the use of traditional 2D based visualization design tools, through introducing and integrating, in a systems context, contemporary new-media based tools for problem definition and resolution in an area of considerable design complexity (Maani & Cavana, 2000).

The third characteristic, retrieval, is more subtle in nature. In management terms, it is akin to the classic concept of 'management by walking around', enabling the manager to see, hear, feel what is actually happening in the organization in real-time. Its potential connectivity to Quality Management approaches is also particularly relevant. Another factor that potentially illustrates this third characteristic is the growing acknowledgement of Knowledge Management as a 21st

century motif for implementing effective executive decision support systems (Blecker, 2005). To be able to more effectively access the intellectual capital and corporate memory of the organization is a serious strategic challenge for many organizations. Connectivity between an organization's collective data and information collection and storage systems and a new media visualization tool such as VR, may well be a significant means of creating strategic advantage, through leveraging off the organization's unique knowledge, competence and skills base as strategic capabilities (Johnson et al., 2008). It is this very notion of connectivity that new forms of communications media very often address. Virtual reality research in particular, has facilitated new ways of thinking about the way we communicate complex messages and information, with a particular focus on the evolution of new (virtual) social structures that in turn facilitate acquisition of collective knowledge and shared meaning across both established and new communities of practice (Papargyris & Poulymenakou, 2008; Woolgar, 2002).

Using sophisticated visualization strategies such as virtual reality and associated technologies, to facilitate comprehension, understanding, and extract meaning embodied in the process of looking back at what was, reviewing the present for what is, and developing simulation and synthesis strategies to prepare for what might be, demands new approaches, new skills and new insights. These will certainly be among the key challenges facing company management, Quality systems professionals, production management staff and design technologists alike, in these early years of the 21st century (McLay, 2002). This focus on considering the impact of new-media on society through observing and evaluating its influence on and effective replacement of incumbent or old media, is strongly reflected in McLuhan's view that we may best understand a new media by using it in effect as a *rear-view-mirror* (McLuhan and Fiore (1968) as cited in Levinson, 2001, p. 173) at the very least during the transition era from the old to the new and progressively as it evolves, enhances and in turn is subsequently obsolesced and displaced (Jones, 2003; Theall, 1971).

McLuhan's idiomatic approach and aphoristic language may be difficult to follow with its implicit technological determinism style focus on media as a primary causal influence on society and contemporary culture. However, his insights into the place and role of electronic media in society is still of considerable significance when looking to the new-media of the 21st century, 40 years after McLuhan first published 'Understanding Media: The Extensions of Man' and enigmatically titled the first chapter: 'The Medium is the Message' (Levinson, 2001; McLuhan, 1964; Murphie & Potts, 2003).

The above analysis is of particular relevance to thinking about evolving technologies and new-media such as VR and the extent to which they influence or affect our lives and work environments (whether directly or indirectly) and our responses to and understandings of such media and its potential to 'add value' or enhance performance, or even simply to replace an outmoded mechanism. *For McLuhan, the 'grammar' of a medium structures human sensory responses to it, fundamentally altering perceptions of social reality* (Flew, 2005, p. 32). A key to the grammar of a media is an understanding of the structure and the manner of communication it supports. From earliest times the dominant forms of human communication have been synchronous, that is in real-time, at a defined point in time and between concomitant participants, as illustrated in oral communication and touch. The progressive development of alternative means of communication such as drawing, the written word, introduction of the printing press and eventually the development of electronic media, introduced asynchronous or time-displaced communication. The capacity to record and transport communications over space and time, both synchronous and asynchronous as with telephony, radio, television, the Internet and World-Wide-Web, has added further complexity

to the grammar, and by now multiple languages, uses, influences and impacts, of communication media. *With new-media, time does not necessarily adhere to the seemingly 'linear' constraints of either face-to-face conversation or early media... With electronic media, the boundaries of synchronous and asynchronous communication are being stretched and merged in new ways* (Jones, 2003, pp. 429-430); A form of incipient stretching of time, space and place in the introduction of new approaches to communication.

Similarly, new media such as virtual reality require an understanding of the media's particular capabilities, constraints and potentially transformative impacts on both its community of practice and surrounding social culture. This in turn is largely influenced through understandings of, and growing literacy in, the language of the media. *Like any media, the use or "reading" of VR has to be learned... That is, the user becomes literate with the medium... As a new medium, the "language" of VR is still in its infancy* (Sherman & Craig, 1995, p. 37). Curiously, although more than a decade later, this reference to infancy appears to still be the case, with some possible exceptions in some areas of immersive interactive VR computer gaming and the more recent development of online VR applications such as Second Life (Boellstorff, 2008; Kreps, 2008).

Soren Kolstrup, a media researcher with an interest in visual communications, has grappled with formulating understandings of the language of visual media (and in the context of this paper, new media such as VR) with an emphasis on the use of visual communications as being about: *Communicative pictures: the production of visual meaning, the transmission of visual meaning and the reception of visual meaning* (Kolstrup, 2003, p. 77). In order to perceive and understand such meanings in visual communications, Kolstrup (2003) argues for the development and application of an interactive visual grammar. The construction of such a grammar would then need to address fundamental issues such as the basis for constructing images and the subsequent basis for being able to understand and interpret meaning from such images. He proposed that such a grammar of visual language should address: theoretical and practical perspectives on all aspects of the construction of images; perspectives on the relationships between construction (of images) and their implied or intended meaning; and *insight into the fact that with a restricted number of elemental principles you can create a huge number of pictures...; insight into the ways picture construction and social use of the pictures are related, that is, the picture as part of a narrative, and argumentation, etc* (Kolstrup, 2003, p. 78).

Kolstup's grammar of visual language, and in particular his insightful reference to its use in relation to developing visualization as narrative and argumentation, is of particular interest and may well prove a powerful tool in developing a successful role for complex imagery (such as in 3-D virtual reality) in a broadened range of future applications outside of the film, television and print media. In the context of using new-media as a visualization tool, such a grammar may prove a necessity to enable widespread diffusion, use and effective extraction of meaning from complex three-dimensional images as representations of data. Current two-dimensional image constructions for such would include the ubiquitous bar-graph, pie-chart and vector diagram. Future applications and associated sociotechnical analyses for which complex multi-dimensional imagery may prove beneficial could include: identifying multi-dimensional contextual influences on an object or subject of enquiry; or futurist projections of a complex of influences or sensitivities affecting a community of practice. The use of 'image' as both representation of influencing factors and as an analysis tool to aid in the extraction and representation of 'meaning' through complex multi-dimensional visual communication, will in turn require a community of practice skilled in the use of such language and grammar (Kolstup, 2003). An example of diffusion of an earlier informal

version of a visual 'grammar' through a community of practice can be seen in the rapid evolution and diffusion of computer-gaming techniques, typically requiring rapid cognition processing and eye-hand coordination based on recognition of visual cues connected in turn to interpretation of cues implicit in the 'story-line' and constructed grammar of the game.

The role of language in the evolution of human culture has long been acknowledged, although the extrapolation to considering the language of communication media and its impact on culture has been less well understood. *Language in its widest sense... is the medium in which culture exists and through which it is transmitted...* (Dewey (1938) as cited in Betz, 2003, p. 413). By further extrapolation, the presence, role and use of new media is a growing reality in a world increasingly structured around the acquisition and distribution (usually through the medium of digital media) of information, its analysis, subsequent interpretation and communication of meanings to interested parties. Ken Pimental and Kevin Teixeira, early researchers in VR systems at Intel, argued at length for the use of VR in communicating ideas: *VR is more than a computer technology that places the user inside a 3-D world; it's the artificial world itself... a new kind of experience... a method of communicating ideas... VR might not only change the way we communicate, it might also change the way we think* (Pimental & Teixeira, 1993, pp. xv, p. 17). It is this potential for using new-media VR systems to help develop new ways of expressing and communicating complex and abstract ideas, that has attracted the attention of contemporary educators, strategic thinkers, and cognitive scientists alike (Boellstorff, 2008).

Certainly, the notion that the constructs of human language as a communications medium limits the possibilities of thought processes has long been an issue addressed by philosophers, linguists and anthropologists alike. As Mary Douglas then Professor of Social Anthropology at University College, London, explains so succinctly: *Language is not an independent variable, nor is thought controlled and formed by it. For both speech and thought are dependent parts of human communication. The control is not in the speech form but in the set of human relations which generate thought and speech* (Douglas, 1975, p. 176). It is this very notion of exploring relationships and ideas that new forms of communications media can help address. New-media and the use of virtual-world constructs (whether on-line or within closed environments such as virtual reality centres, CAVEs or desktop workstation systems) has opened new ways of thinking about the way we communicate complex messages and information, with a particular focus on the evolution of new (virtual) social structures (such as on-line communities) that in turn facilitate acquisition of collective knowledge and shared meaning across new communities of practice (Boellstorff, 2008; Papargyris & Poulymenakou, 2008).

The essential VR constructs of highly visual and multi-sensory stimulatory media presents strong attractions to educational researchers. New methods of representation of ideas and concepts are evolving along with concomitant restructuring of epistemological and ontological constructs of what it means to know or experience knowing in a virtual or synthetic world experience. This raises questions about the capacity of the user to perceive, let alone understand and duly interpret, meaning embedded in complex images and virtual environments (Desouza & Hensgen, 2004). In developing sophisticated imaging systems and technologies, we need to be cognizant of the inherent complexity of our visual perception processes and various mechanisms and constraints that impact on the user's ability to process visual information and extract meaning. Visual perception involves integrating elements of an image to establish meaning, whilst at the same time segregating and differentiating objects within our field of vision, separating them from their backgrounds to similarly extract meaning from their images (Danesi, 2002; Friedhoff & Peercy,

2000). A variety of cognition factors then affect our capacity to process and extract meaning from the images of the world that surrounds us. Applying our understanding of these factors to the mechanisms of immersive media can enable us to better understand and use the key parameters that can in turn enable effective perception and interpretation of implied (or otherwise) meaning in a simulated or virtual environment and to extrapolate or adapt such meanings, where relevant, to our understandings of the real world. *Reasoning determines what the mind does with sensory inputs, or perception. Mind assembles sensory data into conceptions, representations of objects – pictures, images, representations, ideas of things existing outside the mind, outside the self – external in the real world...* (Betz, 2003, p. 403). Whilst Betz was seeking to explore and explain something of the mind's capacity to comprehend and make rational determinations about the world around us, his subsequent imputation and use of Kantian styled argument implies a form of *a priori* reasoning in our comprehension and interpretation of images and sensory stimulation from our surrounding world (Papineau, 2004). Nothing could be further from the truth when dealing with rampant virtuality in some immersive synthetic world environments where nothing is necessarily what it seems and may well have no actual referent in the real world! (Hunsinger, 2008).

However, allowing that Betz (2003) was primarily concerned about elaborating on the mind's processes in constructing and interpreting images and sensory input from the real world, in turn, the connection to the way we relate to imaging and sensory stimulation in virtual worlds, and immersive visual media in particular, is all too apparent. Kantian or not, our real-world experience is the predicate for being able to comprehend and make sense of new images and forms, whether in terms of shape, colour, time-variance, or spatiality in a virtual world. In virtual reality environments these sensory parameters are primarily visual in nature, that is, sight remains the dominant stimulus, although certainly not the only one, even in a synthetic environment. Whilst visual immersion parameters may well be the most obvious, there are other factors that impact on our ability/capacity to perceive and relate to virtual objects, subject matter, or contextual relationships in synthetic environments. An example of how such factors are being identified and addressed can be seen in such projects as the development of a virtual reality-style Haptic Nanomanipulator as a means of touching and manipulating objects and particles too small, elusive, or time-dependent, to be observed or communicated within the normal or real world. This raises a range of issues in relation to the operator's ability to: *Communicate, perceive, act on, and understand inaccessible worlds: located too far away (e.g., a planet) dangerous (e.g., a toxic area) too large (e.g., a galaxy) too small (e.g., a nano-object) or evidently non-real (e.g. mathematical figures, numerical data, and computer fictitious worlds)* (Luciani, 2002).

There is also a further aspect to perception that goes beyond the above largely physiological exposition: the use of images and synthetic environments as representational mechanisms that provide insight and/or the means of exploration of ideas. In effect, a means of invoking a new way of thinking, whether about the old, the new, and the unknown (or at best, areas or issues with a high level of uncertainty). This implies taking new-media imaging and user sense stimulation to a new level of process. For example, as a means of exploring 'possibilities', searching for hidden associations or similarities between unlike parameters, explorations in design where new concepts can be created as imagined rather than as could not be constructed or easily realized in the real world. As such, a new means of communicating ideas, the explicit use of communications media as 'thinking tools'. Many authors have referred to new media in its various and convergent forms as being potentially new thinking tools, albeit with their own form of media language and potentially unique representational structures and

symbolisms, participatory culture, and as a form of communication through which new culture or cultural variance is constructed (Boellstorff, 2008; Flew, 2005; Pimental & Teixeira, 1993; Manovich, 2001). The evolution of VR as a means of implementing graphic illusion, of tele-presence, simulated experience in synthetic worlds, and virtual realism genuinely capable of fooling the senses, has meant a focus on critical aspects of simulated experience such as: immersion; interactivity; and a necessary leap of imagination! Indeed, in the light of the potentials of virtual world building, it appears there is an inherent risk that 17th Century philosopher Descartes' fundamental proposition *"Cogito ergo sum"* (I think therefore I am) (Descartes, 1642) may well be re-written by contemporary virtual world builders as being *'Cogito ergo virtualis'* (I think therefore I might be!).

These mind exercises provide us with both insights and challenges when developing new models of conceptualization and thinking practices. The very concept of using synthetic or virtual worlds, and virtual objects, constructs and models, and manipulating and using them as thinking tools (as distinct from use as highly structured and technologically focused design and development tools) potentially raises serious challenges for non technology-oriented future users, such as decision makers accustomed to working with established thinking, reporting, analysis processes, and rational decision-making practice premised on empirical observation and measurement, most likely in a commercially-oriented sense. *The bifurcation of nature between mind and matter, observer and observed, subject and object. It has become built into the whole of Western man's way of looking at things, including the whole of our science* (Williams and Magee (1999, Ch. 27) in Warburton, 1999, p. 254).

There has been much argument over the past 350 years since Descartes on possible relationships between observed and observer, the known and the knower, the material and non-material, and what it is to 'know' in an epistemological sense. In turn, modern philosophy has moved on to challenge these earlier viewpoints and to raise new positions. Yet, fundamental to the possibility of using such a technology (or set of technologies) as new-media VR, are these underlying questions and viewpoints dealing with the epistemological and ontological issues of enquiry relative to what is 'known' and the nature of 'being' (Cohen, 2000; Papineau, 2004). And, in the context of using virtual reality tools and systems, the possible positions of these questions and viewpoints within the construct of deliberately and with intent using illusion to: explore, express and communicate new ideas; construct virtual 'aesthetic' objects (Manovich, 2001) and relationships (possibly at times with no attributable or actual referent in the 'real' world); create, or at least induce, new communities of practice and engagement (as per Second Life) within (and in a related way external to) synthetic environments; and operating within and engaging in realizable experience within a synthetic or illusory virtual world rich with opportunities for creative imagination in ways that challenge and potentially extend our historic trajectory of knowledge and real-world experience (Hunsinger, 2008; Stuart, 2008). The perpetual movement, re-structuring and constant re-formation of knowledge (whether science based or otherwise) and our capacity to apply it to resolving new problems and old and exploring new opportunities, is a long-term driving force that will 'brook no delay' in the continuing enhancement of technology in its service. (Jonas, 1979) In turn, new technologies, as per the current amalgam instituted as new-media, is both a result of and a changing response to our growing and shifting knowledge base and a reflection of our capacity to extend knowledge through imaginative creativity.

There has been and continues to be, considerable debate among scholars on issues raised from the above and in considering the relationship(s) if any, between reality and perception. The whole argument of using technology to develop and present images or virtual representations derived from or representative of objects or events in the real world, as a valid process for furthering understandings of real objects or events, raises many issues, for example, in relation to the translation from a virtual construct premised on ideas, concepts and relationships expressed only in a synthetic environment, to a realizable construct or form or knowledge-based representation in the real-world. The very nature of the expression 'virtual reality' as an oxymoron (a conflict in terms or conjunction of contradictories (Oxford English Dictionary, 2005)) raises issues in itself. In the context of a synthetic or virtual world, the 'virtual' be it an expression of a particular style or representation of a surrounding condition or environment, or as a subject of interest or aesthetic object (Manovich, 2001) or representation of a process or set of data, may be of itself a reality in that particular context. It may be seen, 'virtually' touched, moved, adjusted, altered, admired, denigrated, or simply ignored and left alone. Almost exactly as it may have been perceived had it been in a 'real' world context. 'Almost', in that unlike conditions in the real world, changes, improvements, movements, positioning, or other forms of interaction, may entirely ignore the apparent influences of physics and the laws of natural science in the real world, and may well be completely reversed at the click of a button!

With regard to the construct of 'reality', ostensibly as per in the 'real' world, there is the potential to consider the existence of 'virtual' conditions that impact on our existence and everyday lives in very 'real' ways. The construct of 'organization' for example can relate to the way we plan and put things together for a particular purpose or to the 'existence' of an 'organization' meaning a company or firm or group of people working together for a common purpose (Oxford English Dictionary, 2005). The notion of organization is a virtual construct, albeit with a physical (real?) presence through its assemblage of people into a particular community or group of communities and very much a part of daily life in the real world. The use of 'technology', as per new-media, to induce an existence of a virtual reality outside of the constraints of the real world of our physical being, may then in itself be considered an innovative extension of existing virtualization strategies in our normal 'real' daily life. Whilst this paper primarily addresses issues in relation to the introduction of new-media virtual reality and whilst certainly supportive of innovative new-media tools and systems, it is strongly the author's position not to reflect a perspective that could be misconstrued as cybernetic determinism. In turn, it is the author's perspective that the whole conceptual area of developing and instituting technological innovation and change is subject to and/or invokes argument about power, process, purpose, actuality, (Jonas, 1979; Sui & Goodchild, 2003) and potentially as Heidegger might express it: *just a further manifestation of technological thinking* (attributed to Heidegger in Coyne, 1999, p. 141).

The very focus on developing highly effective illusion through VR technology and systems has also attracted its fair share of protagonists, those for whom the road to unreality is an unacceptable violation of our humanity by the technocratic dream-weavers of cyber-business and Silicon Valley. From critique to complaint, from critical analysis to the vagaries of the Luddites, from careful observation to wild allusion, all may be found throughout the literature on virtual reality.

The apparent difficulties of correlating the established position of scientific and philosophical thought and argument with the potential use of synthetic or virtual objects, processes, and relationships in virtual world incarnations, may well be the kind of 'Bold Idea' that Professor Sir Karl Popper valued as an important component of valuable science. Popper argued that our life experience and observations of the world around us may only be at best the outer layer of a many layered reality. It is thus the scientist's task *daringly to conjecture what these inner realities are like* (Popper (1974) in Warburton, 1999, p. 278) and then to go further, to explore and test such ideas, or in Popperian terms: bold scientific conjectures. Whilst Popper's life experience essentially preceded contemporary virtual reality systems and new-media technology, the veracity of his arguments remain and exhort us to actively explore 'layer by layer' our world and the many (and at times volatile) artifacts that science and technology have introduced into the complex of our experience.

Popper's construct of bold scientific conjectures, (Popper, 1974) the observations of contemporary philosopher Thomas Kuhn in his paper addressing anomaly, the emergence of scientific discoveries and the institution of paradigm change, (Kuhn, 1996) and Christensen's constructs of discontinuous and disruptive technological innovations, (Christensen, 1997) would appear to sit readily with the potential for advanced simulation and virtual reality technology and systems to institute, or at least be a pre-cursor of, paradigmatic change in the way we explore, examine, visualise, consider and make determinations about our world and its workings.

The potential for such change may be seen in the way we approach new information and knowledge-management technology, its application in the structures, processes and dynamics of contemporary commerce, its role in addressing the complexities of relationships in the world around us, and in the character and nature of personal and corporate competencies that we require in an increasingly information rich world (Johnson et al., 2008).

The continuing growth in complexity and dynamical capabilities of new media and the concomitant convergence of digital media (Yoffie, 1997; Pagani, 2003) will thus continue to challenge our concepts of the language and role of new media (Manovich, 2001) the applications for such new-media, particularly in the context of contemporary business – technology convergence (Andriole, 2005) and will see a growing diversity both within and between communities of practice associated with new-media virtual reality and new media *per se*. Communities of practice with interests as diverse as: interactive scientific visualization for data analysis; visualization as sketch-pad for multi-dimensional computer-aided design; visualization as immersive exploration and testing of new ideas, constructs and system level relationships; and creative visualization as dynamic virtual art form.

REFERENCES

Andriole, S. (2005). *The 2ⁿᵈ Digital Revolution*. Hershey, PA: IGI Global. doi:10.4018/978-1-59140-801-7

Bell, D. (2007). *Cyberculture Theorists: Manuel Castells and Donna Haraway*. London: Routledge.

Betz, F. (2003). *Managing Technological Innovation: Competitive Advantage from Change* (2nd ed.). New York: John Wiley & Sons.

Blecker, T. (2005). *Information and Management Systems for Product Customization*. Boston: Springer.

Boellstorff, T. (2008). *Coming of Age in Second Life: An Anthropologist Explores the Virtually Human*. Princeton, NJ: Princeton University Press.

Caldine, R. (1994). *An Introduction to Educational Television and Video*. Wollongong, Australia: University of Wollongong, Centre for Staff Development.

Castells, M. (1996). The Rise of the Network Society. In *The Information Age: Economy, Society and Culture* (*Vol. 1*). Malden, MA: Blackwell.

Castells, M. (2000). Materials for an Exploratory Theory of the Network Society. *The British Journal of Sociology*, *51*(1), 5–24. doi:10.1080/000713100358408

Charles, A. (2009). Book Review: Ambivalence Towards Convergence: Digitalization and the Media Age. In T. Storsul & D. Stuedahl (Eds.), *Convergence: The International Journal of Research into New Media Technologies*. Retrieved April 8, 2009, from http://con.sagepub.com/cgi/reprint/15/1/123.pdf

Chen, C. (2006). *Information Visualization: Beyond the Horizon* (2ⁿᵈ ed.). London: Springer Verlag. Christensen, C. (1997). *The Innovator's Dilemma: When New Technologies Cause Great Firms to Fail*. Boston: Harvard Business School Press.

Cohen, R. (2000). Ethics and Cybernetics: Levinasian Reflections. *Ethics and Information Technology*, *2*, 27–35. doi:10.1023/A:1010060128998

Coyne, R. (1995). *Designing Information Technology in the Postmodern Age: From Method to Metaphor*. Cambridge, MA: MIT Press.

Coyne, R. (1999). *Technoromanticism: Digital Narrative, Holism, and the Romance of the Real*. Cambridge, MA: The MIT Press.

Danesi, M. (2002). *Understanding Media Semiotics*. London: Arnold.

Descartes, R. (1642). Meditations. In N. Warburton (Ed.) (1999), *Philosophy: Basic Readings*. London: Routledge.

Desouza, K. C., & Hensgen, T. (2004). *Managing Information in Complex Organizations: Semiotics and Signals, Complexity and Chaos*. New York: M. E. Sharpe.

Dewey, J. (1938). Logic: The Theory of Enquiry, Henry Holt & Co. In F. Betz (Ed.) (2003), *Managing Technological Innovation: Competitive Advantage from Change* (2ⁿᵈ ed.). Hoboken, NJ: John Wiley & Sons.

Douglas, M. (1975). *Humans Speak, a critical essay in: Implicit Meanings - Essays in Anthropology*. London: Routledge & Kegan Paul.

Edison, T. (1913). *Attributed in Gould and Mason (1985). TAFE Board Telematics Program.* Melbourne, Australia: Office of the TAFE Board.

Flew, T. (2005). *New Media: An Introduction* (2nd ed.). South Melbourne, Australia: Oxford University Press.

Friedhoff, R. M., & Peercy, M. S. (2000). *Visual Computing*. New York: Scientific American Library.

Gosling, J. (2004). *The War of the Worlds Invasion: An Historical Perspective.* Retrieved April 19, 2004, from www.btinternet.com/~jd.gosling/wotw/radio.htm

Heim, M. (1993). *The Metaphysics of Virtual Reality*. New York: Oxford University Press.

Hunsinger, J. (2008). The Virtual and Virtuality: Toward Dialogues of Transdisciplinarity. In Panteli, N., & Chiasson, M. (Eds.), *Exploring Virtuality Within and Beyond Organizations: Social, Global and Local Dimensions*. New York: Palgrave Macmillan.

Jenkins, H. (2006). *Convergence Culture: Where Old and New Media Collide*. New York: New York University Press.

Johnson, G., Scholes, K., & Whittington, R. (2008). *Exploring Corporate Strategy* (8th ed.). Harlow, UK: Prentice Hall.

Jonas, H. (1979). Toward a Philosophy of Technology. In Kaplan, D. (Ed.), *Readings in the Philosophy of Technology*. Lanham, MD: Rowman & Littlefield.

Jones, C. V. (1996). *Visualization and Optimization*. Norwell, MA: Kluwer Academic Publishers.

Jones, S. (2003). *Encyclopedia of New Media*. Thousand Oaks, CA: Sage Publications.

Knight, J., & Weedon, A. (2009). Shifting Notions of Convergence. *Convergence: The International Journal of Research into New Media Technologies, 15*, 131-133. Retrieved April 8, 2009, from http://con.sagepub.com/cgi/reprint/15/2/131

Kolstrup, S. (2003). The Making of a Pedagogical Tool for Picture Analysis and Picture Construction. In Madsen, K. H. (Ed.), *Production Methods: Behind the Scenes of Virtual Inhabited 3D Worlds*. London: Springer Verlag. doi:10.1007/978-1-4471-0063-8_6

Kreps, D. (2008). Virtuality: Time, Space, Consciousness, and a Second Life. In Panteli, N., & Chiasson, M. (Eds.), *Exploring Virtuality Within and Beyond Organizations*. New York: Palgrave Macmillan.

Kuhn, T. (1996). *The Structure of Scientific Revolutions* (3rd ed.). Chicago: University of Chicago Press.

Levinson, P. (2001). *Digital McLuhan: A Guide to the Information Millennium*. London: Routledge.

Lister, M., Dovey, J., Giddings, S., Grant, I., & Kelly, K. (2009). *New Media: A Critical Introduction* (2nd ed.). Abingdon, UK: Routledge.

Luciani, A. (2002). *TNS Project Abstract. ICA Laboratory, Institut National Polytechnique de Grenoble*. Retrieved April 28, 2009, from http://usenet.jyxo.cz/cz.comp.grafika/0210/post-doc-vo-francuzsku.html

Maani, K., & Cavana, R. (2000). *Systems Thinking and Modelling: Understanding Change and Complexity*. Aukland, New Zealand: Pearson Education New Zealand.

Manovich, L. (2001). *The Language of New Media*. Cambridge, MA: MIT Press.

McLay, A. (2002). Applying Visualisation Technologies and Strategies for Effective Knowledge Management and Decision Analysis in Engineering and Technology-based Enterprises. In A. J. Subic, H. C. Tsang, C. Y. Tang, & G. Netherwood (Eds.), *Proceedings of the 3rd International Conference on Quality and Reliability*, Melbourne, Australia.

McLuhan, M. (1964). *Understanding Media: The Extensions of Man*. New York: McGraw-Hill.

McLuhan, M., & Fiore, Q. (1967). The Medium is the Message: An Inventory of Effects. In *Levinson, P. (2001), Digital McLuhan: A Guide to the Information Millennium*. London: Routledge.

McLuhan, M., & McLuhan, E. (1988). Laws of Media: The New Science. In *Levinson, P. (2001), Digital McLuhan: A Guide to the Information Millennium*. London: Routledge.

Miller, D. (2000) *Introduction to Collective Behavior and Collective Action*. Long Grove, IL: Waveland Publishing, Inc. Retrieved April 28, 2009, from http://jeff560.tripod.com/wotw.html

Murphie, A., & Potts, J. (2003). *Culture and Technology*. New York: Palgrave.

Orenstein, A. (1998). Epistemology Naturalised – Nature know thyself. In N. Warburton (Ed.) (1999), *Philosophy: Basic Readings*. London: Routledge.

Oxford University Press. (2005). *Oxford English Dictionary* (2nd ed.). Oxford, UK: Oxford University Press.

Pagani, M. (2003). *Multimedia and Interactive Digital TV: Managing the Opportunities Created by Digital Convergence*. Hershey, PA: IGI Global.

Papargyris, A., & Poulymenakou, A. (2008). Playing Together in Cyberspace: Collective Action and Shared Meaning Constitution in Virtual Worlds. In Panteli, N., & Chiasson, M. (Eds.), *Exploring Virtuality Within and Beyond Organizations*. Basingstoke, UK: Palgrave Macmillan.

Papineau, D. (Ed.). (2004). *Philosophy*. London: Duncan Baird.

Pimental, K., & Teixeira, K. (1993). *Virtual Reality: Through the New Looking Glass*. New York: McGraw-Hill.

Popper, K. (1974). The Problem of Demarcation. In N. Warburton (Ed.) (1999), *Philosophy: Basic Readings*. London: Routledge.

Robbins, S., & Barnwell, N. (2006). *Organization Theory: Concepts and Cases* (5th ed.). Upper Saddle River, NJ: Pearson.

Roberston, G., Card, S., & Mackinlay, J. (1993). Information Visualization Using 3D Interactive Animation. *Communications of the ACM, 36*(4), 57–71. doi:10.1145/255950.153577

Rogers, E. (2003). *Diffusion of Innovations* (5th ed.). New York: Free Press.

Schultze, Q. (1988). Evangelical Radio and the Rise of the Electronic Church 1921-1948. *Journal of Broadcasting & Electronic Media, 32*(3), 289. doi:10.1080/08838158809386703

Sherman, W. R., & Craig, A. B. (1995). Literacy in Virtual Reality: A New Medium. *ACM SIGGRAPH Computer Graphics, 29*(4), 37–42. doi:10.1145/216876.216887

Shields, R. (2003). *The Virtual*. London: Routledge.

Slouka, M. (1995). *War of the Worlds: Cyberspace and the High-Tech Assault on Reality*. London: Abacus.

Sobel Lojeski, K., & Reilly, R. R. (2008). *Uniting the Virtual Workforce*. Hoboken, NJ: John Wiley & Sons.

Stair, R., & Reynolds, G. (2006). *Principles of Information Systems: A Managerial Approach* (7th ed.). Boston: Thomson.

Storsul, T., & Stuedahl, D. (2007). *Ambivalence Towards Convergence: Digitalization and Media Change*. Göteborg, Sweden: Nordicom.

Stuart, S. (2008). From Agency to Apperception: Through Kinaesthesia to Cognition and Creation. *Ethics and Information Technology*, *10*(4), 255. doi:10.1007/s10676-008-9175-5

Sui, D., & Goodchild, M. (2003). A Tetradic Analysis of GIS and Society Using McLuhans Law of the Media. *The Canadian Geographer*, *47*(1), 5–17. doi:10.1111/1541-0064.02e08

Theall, D. F. (1971). *The Medium is the Rear View Mirror: Understanding McLuhan*. Montreal, Canada: McGill-Queen's University Press.

Turban, E., McLean, E., & Wetherbe, J. (2002). *Information Technology for Management: Transforming Business in the Digital Economy* (3rd ed.). New York: John Wiley & Sons.

Warburton, N. (Ed.). (1999). *Philosophy: Basic Readings*. London: Routledge.

Ware, C. (2004). *Information Visualization: Perception for Design* (2nd ed.). San Francisco, CA: Morgan Kaufmann Publishers.

Williams, B., & Magee, B. (1999). Descartes. In N. Warburton (Ed.) (1999), *Philosophy: Basic Readings*. London: Routledge.

Woolgar, S. (2002). *Virtual Society? Technology, Cyberbole, Reality*. Oxford, UK: Oxford University Press.

Yoffie, D. (1997). *Competing in the Age of Digital Convergence*. Boston: Harvard Business School Press.

This work was previously published in The International Journal of Sociotechnology and Knowledge Development, Volume 2, Issue 3, edited by Elayne Coakes, pp. 37-53, copyright 2010 by IGI Publishing (an imprint of IGI Global).

Chapter 11
Free, Open, Online
Help Forums:
Convenience, Connection, Control, Comfort, and Communication

Carla van de Sande
Arizona State University, USA

ABSTRACT

In contrast to course delivery, help seeking has not advanced with the technological capabilities and preferences of today's students. Help seeking in higher education remains primarily an individual, private, face-to-face activity. Open, online, help forums have the potential to transform help seeking into a public, social endeavor. These forums connect students with volunteer helpers who have the time, knowledge, and willingness to provide assistance with specific problems from coursework. Although many such forums currently exist and are a popular source of help seeking, they have remained largely off the radar of educational research. In this paper, a calculus help forum is examined for manifestations of convenience, connection, and control, which are commonly used to describe student expectations regarding information technology use. Results indicate that students can receive efficient, accessible, and self-regulated help. Two additional themes for student experience, comfort and communication, are proposed.

DOI: 10.4018/978-1-4666-0200-7.ch011

Copyright © 2012, IGI Global. Copying or distributing in print or electronic forms without written permission of IGI Global is prohibited.

INTRODUCTION

Many innovative efforts are underway to transform higher education to better serve the Net Generation (Larreamendy-Joerns & Leinhardt, 2006). The most dramatic change that has occurred in recent years is that students can now take courses online and are no longer required to physically visit campus to receive instructional materials, communicate with other students, and take assessments. In this way, online education addresses the prevailing need for education to be flexible, convenient, and compatible with other activities and commitments.

Socio-technical systems (cf., Coakes, 2002) are at the heart of this institutional shift from face-to-face to computer-mediated activities, linking the efficient and/or effective use of technology with the expectations of current students. For instance, students enrolled together in an online course make use of course forums or discussion boards to communicate with one another and to share and integrate knowledge. At the same time, the forums as a technical system influence the ways in which students communicate and collaborate with one another. These students, who interact in an ongoing basis and share common concerns and tasks, can be considered as an online community (Preece et al., 2004). Broader socio-technical communities in the context of higher education also exist, for instance when a large number of people (an extension of an academic department) have the opportunity to share information on study habits and discuss the content and exercises of lectures and seminars within an online knowledge sharing community, such as InPUD, (Jahnke, 2008).

However, when it comes to seeking problem-specific help on assignments, universities still provide students with many of the same options as existed previously. Students can visit their instructors during office hours or communicate with them via computer. For more anonymous help, most universities also staff help centers where students can receive face-to-face help on their course assignments during hours of operation. Although some progressive institutions offer computer-mediated access to their help centers (Schumann & Geiman, 2009), this model of help is still based on set, restricted hours of operation and one-on-one assistance. In this way, the provision of (anonymous) help in higher education appears to have become fossilized as a private, individual activity between a helper and a student that is generally conducted in face-to-face interaction. In particular, the role that social networks play in student expectations and experience has not been fully taken into account, especially given the body of research and controversy pointing to the use of socio-technical tools (such as Facebook) to facilitate students working together on assignments in study groups (Goodall, 2008; Selwyn, 2007; 2009).

What mode of assistance is more consistent with the way that students prefer to interact and learn with others? Just as students use the Internet routinely for finding information and communicating with others, they are also using the Internet as a resource for completing their assignments through participation in free, open, online help forums (van de Sande & Leinhardt, 2007b). Many such forums exist and allow students everywhere to communicate anonymously and asynchronously with volunteers around the world who have the time, willingness, and experience to help them. These forums cover a wide variety of subject areas at several levels, ranging from the language arts to the natural sciences in instruction that spans the elementary level to higher education. Mathematics is one of the more popular forum subject areas, with frequent and urgent requests for help in challenging and homework-intensive courses such as algebra and calculus. Students post queries (usually problem-specific questions from assignments) on these forums when they are seeking anonymous help constructing a solution to a problem or when they are seeking verification of a solution that has been constructed (either by themselves or in another resource such as a solution manual). In this way, students are currently redefining the way that they receive assistance and how they navigate help seeking. The purpose of this paper is to showcase some previously identified learning styles evident in open, online, help forums used by today's students, and to suggest additional constructs that may help describe the nature of activity in this emergent learning environment.

NET GENERATION LEARNING STYLES

Students born roughly between 1980 and 1994 have been dubbed 'digital natives' (Prensky, 2001) because they have grown up immersed in a technology-rich culture. These students live 'surrounded by and using computers, videogames, digital music players, video cams, cell phones, and other toys and tools of the digital age' (Prensky, 2001, p. 1). As a result of their upbringing and experiences with technology, these students are purported to have learning preferences or styles that differ from earlier generations (Barnes, Marateo, & Ferris, 2007; Prensky, 2001) and are unique to their cohort, also known as the 'Net Generation' or 'Net Geners' (Tapscott, 1999). The claim is that today's students '*think and process information fundamentally differently* from their predecessors' (Prensky, 2001, p. 1, emphasis in the original).

In terms of learning styles, Net Geners have been portrayed as frequent and sophisticated users of information technology (IT), who are active experiential learners, achievement-oriented, and proficient at multitasking (Dede, 2005; Frand, 2000; Oblinger & Oblinger, 2005). These students reportedly desire independence and autonomy, social interactivity, and structure in learning situations (Barnes et al., 2007). From the research characterizing student expectations for IT, three common, interrelated constructs have emerged: convenience, connection, and control (Caruso & Kvavik, 2005). *Convenience* describes the desire for ready and global accessibility to technology, services, and resources, and the press for immediacy, or a fast response time. *Connection* captures the desire of students to communicate with members of their communities anywhere and anytime, and the ability to work in teams. *Control* refers to the capability to multitask, customize resources, focus on grades and performance, manage the undergraduate experience, and designate the when and where of social interaction.

The central claims that have emerged from this body of research – namely that students today possess sophisticated IT knowledge and skills and, as a result, have particular learning preferences or styles that set them apart from earlier generations of students – are not universally accepted (cf., Bennett, Maton, & Kervin, 2008; Jones, Ramanau, Cross, & Healing, 2010). The homogeneity of IT proficiency by Net Geners has been called into question through the identification of a significant portion of young people who lack levels of access or technology skills: "It may be that there is as much variation *within* the digital native generation as *between* the generations" (Bennett et al., 2008, p. 779, emphasis in the original). The adoption of particular learning styles by a whole generation due to immersion in technology has also been challenged. Individual differences (e.g., cognitive skills) and situational factors (e.g., perception of task requirements) are claimed to outweigh similarities that may exist across multiple individuals.

The conclusions that have been reached, and critiqued, regarding the expectations and experiences of the Net Generation are often based on investigations targeting self-reported student activity and preferences. In order to gain insight into learning styles, researchers have asked students to describe how they learn, how they interact with others, and the role of IT in their lives (cf., Goodyear, Jones, Asensio, Hodgson, & Steeples, 2005). This body of research spans both small-scale qualitative studies (e.g., using case studies and interviews) and large-scale quantitative studies (e.g., using questionnaires and surveys). Our research program has adopted an alternative approach, akin to the analyses of transcripts to identify episodes of productive interaction (Mowrer, 1996). Instead of inquiring directly into the learning styles of young people, we observe an example of IT in widespread use and infer from analyses of activity what learning styles are evident. In particular, we are interested in exploring knowledge development in an un-regulated socio-technical learning environment, namely free, open, online homework help forums.

FREE, OPEN, ONLINE HOMEWORK HELP FORUMS

Open, online, help forums are found on websites and allow students to anonymously post course-related queries from a broad range of subject areas (such as mathematics, science, and business) that are then visible to others. These forums are 'open' in the sense that, unlike course forums or discussion boards, access is public and not restricted to any particular course or institution. Many of these sites are also free, making help available to anyone with Internet access. A casual web search for "free homework help" reveals that these forums are a popular resource for students around the world seeking help outside of the classroom. For instance, one such site (www.mathhelpforum.com) that offers help in arithmetic through higher mathematics had over 29,000 members and received an average of 152 queries daily in 2009. Other sites, that cover more subjects, boast 120,000 members and receive over 800 requests for help daily. Furthermore, these sites, although based in a particular country, take pride in participation

from students and helpers from around the globe (van de Sande, 2008b).

Open, online, homework help forums belong to a genre of technology-assisted education called 'networked learning.' Goodyear, Jones, Asensio, Hodgson, and Steeples (2005) offer the following definition, with an emphasis on human-human interaction:

Networked learning is learning in which information and communications technology (ICT) is used to promote connections: between one learner and other learners; between learners and tutors; between a learning community and its resources.

Significant efforts have been made to research and implement networked learning in higher education in order to modernize instruction (Bonk & King, 1998). Thus, asynchronous computer-mediated conferencing is becoming a standard instructional practice, with an expectation that students will engage in discussions of course content with their peers and instructors (De Smet, Van Keer, & Valcke, 2009).

Our interest is in networked learning that currently exists outside the aegis of higher education institutions. Open, online, homework help forums represent an unregulated learning network for help seeking. Participation in these forums is voluntary by both students and helpers (versus prescribed by course requirements or assigned) and, as such, forum activity provides a window into the specific and spontaneous questions students have relating to their coursework and the way in which these questions can be resolved. Students post queries on one of these forums when they have reached an impasse or wish to validate their work on some exercise from an assignment with the help of a more experienced other.

The extent of the learning network that a forum encompasses is determined, in part, by the structure of the forum. We have identified two commonly used forum structures (van de Sande

& Leinhardt, 2007b). Some forums have a pool of select, vetted helpers to whom incoming queries are assigned (Assigned Online Help or AOH). Forums with this structure support one-to-one, computer-mediated help seeking between students and others who have met certain qualifications (e.g., domain knowledge, communication skills, pedagogical approach). Other forums, however, do not restrict the group of helpers and allow any member to respond to a query or contribute to an ongoing thread (Spontaneous Online Help or SOH). SOH forums, in particular, have captured our attention because they provide a much more extensive help-seeking network with richer opportunities for collective knowledge development since more than one helper can be involved in any given exchange.

METHOD

General Methodology

This research employs a general methodology for observing activity in open, online, help forums that is nonintrusive and does not risk disrupting these natural online communities and potentially violating member trust. The process involves the selection of a target forum (e.g., calculus or intermediate/advanced algebra) which itself may be part of a larger forum (e.g., on a mathematics help site), the collection of archived exchanges on a specific instructional topic or problem type (e.g., the limit concept or investment word problems) over a prescribed time period or until a targeted quantity is reached, and a systematic indexing of these exchanges. In addition to recording the timing of contributions, each exchange is assigned a conversation code that tracks the number of participants, the sequencing of contributions, and the number of contributions in the thread. For example, a code of 1231 would be assigned to a thread with four postings containing contributions

from 3 different participants: a student [1] posted a problem and then two different tutors [2 and 3, respectively] responded, followed by a final contribution by the student [1]. Although these codes are unequivocally agnostic with respect to the quality of the contribution (e.g., mathematical accuracy and depth, and pedagogical sensitivity) and do not speak to any aspects of longitudinal forum participation by individuals, they allow one to catalogue and single out exchanges that involve multiple conversational turns, multiple participants, and multiple contributions by a single participant (in particular, by the student who initiated the thread). Each thread is also examined for the degree of resolution (closure) from the perspective of the student who initiated the thread: weak resolution describes unsupported expressions of appreciation, whereas strong resolution requires evidence of increased understanding concerning the task at hand.

In addition to these analyses performed on individual threads in the corpus, general and historical information on underlying forum practice is gathered from discussions in any existing community forum (where members submit suggestions and exchange ideas), from posted rules of engagement, and, when possible, from communications with the forum administrator (e.g., to specify the role of moderators and process for achieving status).

Choice of Forum and Topic

The popularity and availability of free, open, online help forums means that there is never a shortage of candidates for study. The *calculus* forum at www.freemathhelp.com (FMH) was selected for reporting here because calculus is a challenging and often intimidating mathematics course that many students are required to take for programs in the physical, biological, and many of the social sciences. In addition, calculus is a course that is typically taken by seniors in high school and freshman or sophomores at university. Therefore, at the time of the study, the students posting on the forum would presumably belong to the Net Generation. FMH was selected as a site because it has an extensive history (archives dating back to 2005), includes a search mechanism for locating exchanges that contain a keyword or phrase, and is active in terms of daily postings and membership. In addition, FMH was established in 2002 by Ted Wilcox, an enterprising high school junior at the time, and therefore himself a member of the Net Generation. At the time of data collection, FMH had attracted over 10,000 members and received over 85,000 total posts, contributing to more than 20,000 exchanges. Although there are larger, more popular forums, FMH had the additional feature of a member status policy based on amount of participation. Unlike some other free, open, online help forums (such as www.cramster.com and www.mathhelpforum.com), status in FMH is determined solely by the number of contributions to distinct threads rather than by a "reputation system" (Dellarocas, 2003) that allows community participants to rate the activities and contributions of others in the community. Because status-seeking can color social interactions in online communities (Lampel & Bhalla, 2007), it was decided that a forum with a policy in which status is dependent on number of contributions alone would be best suited for a broad exploration of the ways in which knowledge can be acquired and exchanged in this learning venue.

Having selected an open, online, help forum, the next step was to choose a subset of the threads for analysis.[1] The calculus forum of FMH contains requests for help spanning the wide range of curricular material that is commonly covered in single and multivariable calculus instruction, which is largely invariant in higher education. Most topics are present in the forum throughout any given time period because students may be taking any course during any quarter or semester anywhere in the world. Two instructional topics that are generally taught in an introductory single variable calculus course were chosen: *the limit* and *related rates*. These two topics reflect the diversity of the material that is characteristic of introductory calculus instruction (abstract and applied), are difficult for students to master (cf., Martin, 2000; Szydlik, 2000), and surface with fair regularity in the forum. One hundred threads on each topic dating back from April, 2008 were culled from the forum archives using the search tool. Thus, the time period covered is not exactly the same (approximately 14 months for limit and 21 months for related rates) but the number of exchanges analyzed was.

Population

FMH features member profiles that include self-reported information on occupation, location, and interests. Although the vast majority of students do not provide this information (presumably because of their peripheral participation), those helpers who participate in the FMH calculus forum and chose to reveal their occupations are advanced students, educators, professionals, and retired mathematics professors. In this sample participants came from twelve states in North America, Australia, Canada, New Zealand, and the Philippines. Of course, the anonymity of the environment opens wide the possibility for role-playing, so that members may be presenting an altered version of who they are and where they live in real or true self (McKenna, 2007).

As in many online groups (e.g., Ahuja & Galvin, 2003), FMH has members who post more frequently than others (core members) and those who temporarily drop by (peripheral members). This is true for both helpers and students in FMH. The sample contained 100 related rates exchanges initiated by 65 different students, with responses from 18 different helpers and 100 limit exchanges initiated by 67 different students, with responses from 23 different helpers. There was some overlap in participants (both students and helpers) across the two mathematical topics: 17% of these students posted queries on both limits and related rates, and 63% of the helpers provided assistance for both topics.

RESULTS

The 200 exchanges were examined for manifestations of the three themes capturing student expectations and experiences with IT: convenience, connection, and control. Timing was used as an indicator of convenience; connection was evidenced from the number of helpers per exchange together with qualitative analyses of what this brought to the discussion; control was manifest through displays of resolution from the perspective of the student. These analyses are followed by the presentation of an exchange in which all three themes emerge.

Convenience

Open, online, help forums foster convenient help seeking, both in terms of place and time. Because Internet access is the only prerequisite for participation, as mentioned previously, students and helpers from around the world are currently using the help forums. One mathematics help forum (www.mathhelpforum.com) used Google Analytics to produce a map pinpointing activity over a week-long period of time and was able to document participation from every inhabited continent (van de Sande, 2008b).

In terms of timing, because of the sense of urgency that accompanies many of the requests (i.e., an assignment due date is approaching or further progress on an assignment is impeded), convenience is characterized by being able to rely on a quick response time. There are two intervals of time that jointly contribute to the efficiency with which help is delivered. First, there is the length of time between when a student submits a request and that request becomes visible or accessible

to a helper, which we refer to as "administrative latency." For AOH forums, this interval depends on the timing of the assignment process and the procedures involved with matching requests with helpers. For SOH forums, this interval depends on the timing in which requests are published. Incoming requests can be subject to a screening process (e.g., for appropriateness), or, alternatively, may be published immediately (and possibly removed from the forum at a later time). For example, www.cyberpapy.com, an SOH help site based in France that covers various school subjects and is supported by a private foundation, screens incoming contributions for appropriateness, whereas FMH, administered by an individual, assigns moderator status to select members so that inappropriate posts can be removed following publication and posts can be split or moved. The calculus forum on FMH has five moderators, all core members, who perform these duties.

The second length of time that impacts forum efficiency is the time between when the request becomes accessible and when the request receives a response, or "response latency." Many AOH forums request that their helpers respond within a set amount of time. For example, www.mathnerds. com reports an average response time of 22 hours (van de Sande, 2007). SOH forums, on the other hand, do not specify an explicit goal for response latency, but depend on their helpers to efficiently field incoming requests and contribute to ongoing exchanges. The length of time between when a request is published and when it receives a first response depends on the size of the forum. Larger, more popular forums operate more efficiently. In this sample, the average response latency was 1 hour and 55 minutes for limit exchanges and 2 hours and 29 minutes for related rates exchanges, with median response latencies of 28 minutes and 42 minutes, respectively. This is consistent with the average response latency of roughly 1.5 hours for calculus requests over all topics in this forum (van de Sande & Leinhardt, 2007b).

Some SOH forums promote quick turnaround by allowing students to pay a small subscription fee that elevates the priority of their requests. For instance, on www.cramster.com, which follows a business model, the requests of paying student members are worth more karma points, which are accumulated by responding helpers towards prizes and public recognition. On this forum, the median response latency is roughly 30 minutes (van de Sande, 2009). The priority that is placed on maximizing convenience by minimizing response latency is dialogically evident in many SOH forums; helpers vie to be 'first on the scene' (even when forum status is not at stake) and make the speed with which they respond a subject of bantering: "Too fast for me, squito!"

Finally, only three queries in our sample of 200 did not receive any reply (two of which were self-answered by the student who posted the question), and this finding is consistent with other corpa from FMH (van de Sande, 2008a; van de Sande & Leinhardt, 2007a, 2008). The entry page to the forum displays recent threads, the number of views, and the number of replies, so this information is visible to students. The almost certain assurance of a reply sends out a message that a particular forum is a convenient means of receiving help and may be an important factor for encouraging and sustaining forum participation.

Connection

Online forums support connections between various members of an online community in the service of helping students. In SOH forums, students can connect with one or more helpers, and helpers can simultaneously connect with one another. As a gross quantitative characterization of "connectivity," one can look at numbers of helpers per thread. Figure 1 shows the percentage of exchanges in this sample in which various numbers of helpers participated. The pattern is roughly shared by topic, although exchanges on limit were somewhat more likely to attract multiple helpers. Overall, it is evident that multiple helpers often choose to contribute to an exchange (49%), which indicates that helpers are, at worst, operating cooperatively and, at best, collaboratively to respond to student questions. Admittedly, the nature of the question may bolster this percentage (trivial questions would require only a response from a single helper); but, the fact remains that, although involvement is optional in an SOH forum, multiple helpers often choose to chime in for questions of medium to high difficulty. Less surprising, given the relatively small ratio of helpers (core members) to students (peripheral members) (cf., Preece et al., 2004) and the closed-ended nature of the queries, is the result that three helpers is a natural upper boundary for the number of helpers who choose to take part in any given exchange.

Figure 1. Percentage of exchanges according to participating number of helpers

	0	 𝕏	 𝕏𝕏	 𝕏𝕏𝕏	 𝕏𝕏𝕏𝕏+
limit	1	41	38	17	3
related rates	2	58	26	13	1
across topics	1.5	49.5	32	15	2

The multilateral connections that FMH affords can serve a variety of purposes, including fostering authentic mathematical discourse, improving the accuracy of contributions through peer review (e.g., in "Wikipedia" fashion), and affording opportunities for the exchange of knowledge from more than a single perspective. Although difficult to establish a baseline for, and therefore quantify, each of these functions speaks to the way in which knowledge is acquired and exchanged in online, help forums.

First, knowledge is acquired and exchanged, both directly and perhaps vicariously, when helpers jointly work through the construction of a solution that is part of a student's curriculum, particularly when helpers engage in debates or discussions. This is noteworthy because, in other instructional settings, students are usually not privileged to experience mathematicians in action as they construct arguments and debate possible solution paths with one another. Rather than being granted access to the underlying process (that often includes false starts, questioning of assumptions, and reworking), students are presented with mathematics as a finished product. FMH affords the opportunity for students to witness mathematical discourse that is normally masked by the presentation of information in the classroom and in polished explanations. We hypothesize that students may profit through the exposure to inter-helper discourse in a manner similar to apprentices engaging in legitimate peripheral participation (Lave & Wenger, 1991). In addition, forum helpers themselves can benefit from these discussions as they have access to a support system of knowledgeable others and can unpack the mathematics of "routine" problems (van de Sande, 2008b).

Second, the accuracy of knowledge in FMH is collectively maintained. The folk saying 'many hands make light work' could be adapted to fit forum activity by making two small changes - 'many *eyes* make *right* work.' In what has been referred to as the "wikipedia-like" nature of SOH sites (van de Sande & Leinhardt, 2007b), one

sees FMH helpers (and occasionally students) reviewing the contributions of other helpers and either addressing errors directly or replacing them with accurate information. Accuracy is naturally a key issue here, since, unlike helpers in an AOH forum, SOH helpers are not vetted and also may be more prone to errors given the much larger volume of posts they handle in less time and on a regular basis. When helpers (and students) attend carefully to the contributions of others with the goal of constructively maintaining high standards for content and substance, the entire community benefits. In this sample of 200 exchanges, all errors were politely addressed and acknowledged, buffered by the use of emoticons. For example, in response to another helper's critique of her/his contribution, which was itself delivered without recrimination, one helper responded: "OK. My bad. We had to find a and b that made the limit 1. Sorry: oops: [Embarrassed]."

Finally, in SOH forums, knowledge reflecting alternative perspectives can emerge and become a topic of conversation. Helpers who have a different take on a problem may join in an exchange and share their insight with others in the forum community. According to the Good Samaritan hypothesis that addresses helper participation patterns in SOH forums (van de Sande & Leinhardt, 2008), the provision of assistance on the problem from one perspective can prompt fellow community members to contribute alternatives. That is, the action of others stimulates helper actions aimed at providing further assistance, in this case through the contribution of a novel way of thinking about the problem at hand that may prove helpful in the given situation. For example, in a related rates exchange from this sample in which the method being pursued by one helper was algebraically messy, a second helper entered the thread with an alternative approach, prefaced by "Let's try it this way." Following the presentation of the alternative solution method, which involved considerably less complicated mathematical expressions, the second helper elaborated on how this approach differed from the one on the table ("I think this is a little easier since we do not have to deal with radicals in our differentiation.") and pointed out how the two methods would have the same outcome ("…you should get the same result"). Furthermore, there is evidence that forum participation has heightened the awareness of some students regarding the mathematical practice of multiple solution paths. As expressed by one forum student in the sample, following an exchange with three helpers in which several perspectives on the problem emerged, "It seems like there are as many ways to solve it as there are people explaining it to me!" Students see knowledge being developed from multiple perspectives as a natural phenomenon in forum activity, rather than as an artificial characteristic of "school mathematics" – and, perhaps more importantly, even become excited by this phenomenon on occasion.

Control

The knowledge acquired on the forums is personalized and tailored to fit the individual needs of students. Students exercise control in the sense that they initiate discussions, can reflect on and question contributions from others, and are ultimately responsible for expressing the extent to which resolution has been achieved. In this way, students can use the forums to gain control over their understanding of the exercises they have trouble with. An examination of how students demonstrate the helpfulness of the knowledge they acquire through participation in FMH reveals how control is exhibited in forum activity.

Unlike some SOH forums (e.g., www.mathhelpforum.com), FMH does not have a specific mechanism (such as a 'thank you' button) for expressing thankfulness or appreciation. There are several ways that a participant can indicate that an issue has (or has not) been resolved. First of all, participants can be silent and opt not to further contribute to an exchange. Silence in computer-mediated exchanges may indicate acceptance or rejection of another's contributions and does not offer evidence for (or against) the achievement of resolution. Thus, in the forum discussions, if a student does not return to the exchange beyond the initial posting or following helper intervention, it is not clear whether the student feels that the issue has been settled or not. I refer to exchanges of this type as "*hangers*." On the other hand, when a student does acknowledge helpers' contributions, they can do so in either a *weak* or *strong* manner. For instance, an expression of appreciation, such as "Thank you!!!!" (regardless of the degree of enthusiasm) indicates a weak level of resolution on the part of the participant since this may simply be a residual of polite manners, representing a customary or even cultural response to receiving assistance. In contrast, the contribution of mathematical actions (e.g., the presentation of a solution to the problem) and assessments (e.g., reflections on differences in understanding) are stronger indications that the issue has been resolved to the satisfaction of the student. Finally, an exchange can evince *no resolution*, as when a student receives no response to a query or receives a refusal from forum helpers to provide further assistance.

Figure 2 shows the percentage of exchanges for each topic in which resolution could not be determined (hangers), in which resolution was evident and the strength of the expression (weak versus strong), and in which there was no resolution.

Although approximately 60% of the exchanges were "hangers" (with unspecified resolution), the majority of the remaining exchanges exhibited resolution from the student's perspective, in either a weak or strong manner. In addition, the number of exchanges exhibiting characteristics of strong resolution outnumbered those in which only weak resolution was evident by a factor of two. (This number may be conservative since, as one reviewer pointed out, weak resolution may occur if the student does not have time to describe fully how the help was helpful, which would then count as strong resolution.) Finally, there were

Figure 2. Percentage of exchanges for each topic by type of resolution

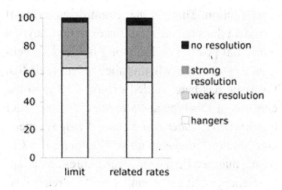

very few exchanges (3 on limit and 5 on related rates) for which the issue was *not* resolved and in which the outcome of the exchange from the student's perspective could be characterized as inconclusive or unhelpful. We can conclude that, despite the absence of a prompt for expressing resolution, students are demonstrating control over their understanding of subject material and knowledge acquisition (at least at the level of individual problems) through forum participation in this case.

An Example

We turn our attention now to an example of an exchange from the Freemathhelp forum in which the three themes characterizing student expectations for IT are evident. Figure 3 shows an exchange consisting of five posts that was initiated by jack and involved two other forum participants, pastel and squito.[2] Jack, a relatively new member of FMH, was seeking help constructing a solution to a limit exercise. In terms of knowledge development, this exchange shows how the forum provided jack with timely assistance (*convenience*) and how multiple helpers contributed to the joint construction of the solution from alternative perspectives (*connection*). Furthermore, it is evident how jack received personalized assistance and how he took initiative to both demonstrate and express how the

interaction was helpful in resolving the problem to his satisfaction (*control*).

- *The hardest part.* When jack posts the query[3] [2:29 pm] on limit, he indicates that the solution should not appeal to l'Hôpital's Rule and proposes substitution as an alternative strategy: "Again the hardest part is probably figuring out the "right" substitution, anything I tried didn't seem to lead anywhere..." The first helper, pastel, comes on the scene 39 minutes later [3:08 pm], showing how *convenient* the forum can be for students like jack. Pastel identifies the limit as an expression for cosine ("Since the majority of the proofs [use a form of this definition to show] that this limit is the cosine"); recommends a variable substitution ("and since they [the proofs] use the "x + h" form, you might want to substitute "a + y" for "x", so you have lim[y->0] [(sin(a + y)- sin(a)] / [y]"); provides a trigonometric identity for the expansion of the numerator ("sin(a + y) = sin(a)cos(y) + cos(a)sin(y) − sin(a)");[3] and, finally, suggests reorganizing the expression ("Split the limit into two pieces.") to support the application of two well-known trigonometric limits ("As y->0, you have the sin(y)/y going to 1, and the [cos(y) − 1]/y going to zero.").

- *Yay.* After receiving this detailed solution sketch (delivered with a friendly:wink: [Wink]), jack returns to the exchange [3:23 pm] and publishes the remaining steps of the solution: "So I get:

$$\lim_{y\to0}\frac{\sin a\cdot(\cos y-1)}{y}+\qquad."$$
$$\lim_{y\to0}\frac{\sin y\cdot\cos a}{y}=0+\lim_{y\to0}\cos a=\cos a$$

In addition to this correct implementation of pastel's suggestions, jack also indicates that the problem is resolved to his satisfaction

Figure 3. Exchange exemplifying themes of convenience, connection, and control

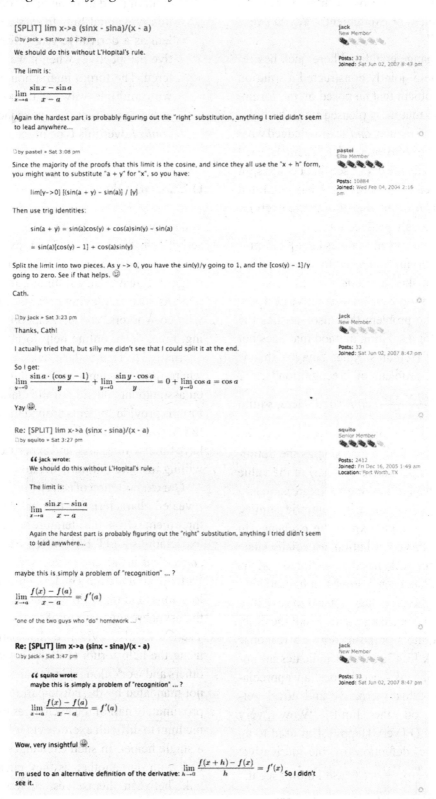

by concluding the post with an expression of happiness or excitement: "Yay:D [Very Happy]."

The exchange could end here; jack has received help, jointly constructed a solution to the problem that he posed on the forum, indicated that he is pleased with the help-seeking interaction, *and* acknowledged what piece of the help was helpful: "I actually tried that, but silly me didn't see that I could split it at the end." In short, jack has exhibited that he is now in *control* over the exercise that previously plagued him.

- *Maybe...* However, minutes later [3:27 pm] another forum helper, squito, enters the exchange, makes a *connection* to jack and pastel by proposing an alternative perspective on the problem that also satisfies the request for a solution method that does not rely on l'Hôpital's Rule: "maybe this is simply a problem of "recognition" ... ?
$$\lim_{x \to a} \frac{f(x) - f(a)}{x - a} = f'(a).$$" Here, squito is adopting an alternative perspective by framing the limit expression as the definition of the derivative of sin*(x)* at the value *x=a*, instead of framing the expression as a reorganization of trigonometric limits. Again, one might expect the exchange to end with this contribution, especially since the student, jack, has demonstrated that the problem has been resolved to his satisfaction and therefore has no need to revisit or re-enter the exchange. This is not the case.

- *Wow.* Squito's proposal draws a response from jack [3:47 pm] that indicates an understanding of - even more, an appreciation for - this alternative and novel perspective on the limit: "Wow, very insightful:D [Very Happy]. I'm used to an alternative definition of the derivative: $\lim_{h \to 0} \frac{f(x+h) - f(x)}{h} = f'(x)$ So I didn't see it."

Jack was apparently steeped in a particular form of the definition of the derivative, and this prevented him from seeing the problem as a derivative (e.g., from an alternative perspective) when it was first encountered. The forum interaction provided jack with multiple ways of thinking about the exercise and therefore gave jack even more *control* over this type of exercise.

DISCUSSION

Today's youth are accustomed to going online for activities that formerly required physical presence. Students routinely use the Internet for a wide range of recreational, vocational, and instructional pursuits such as playing games, communicating with co-workers, and participating in job training. Free, open, online help forums serve as an alternative to face-to-face help seeking, and are where many students are turning as they work on assignments outside of the classroom. These forums provide students around the world access to a network of more knowledgeable others who have time, willingness, and expertise that they are willing to share online with anonymous others.

Our examination of activity in one such forum revealed characteristics that are consistent with three themes from the literature describing student expectations for IT. FMH offers assistance that is *convenient*, in the sense of accessibility and timing. Participants hail from a wide range of geographical locations, and reply time is relatively fast, given the asynchronous nature of the communication. There was also evidence that participants are using the help forum to make *connections* with others and work alongside one another. Although not mandated by the participation structure, approximately half of the exchanges that addressed medium to difficult exercises involved more than a single helper. In such exchanges, helpers connect with one another as they engage in 'math talk' between themselves, review and correct one another's contributions, and add information from alternative perspectives (as in the example exchange). Finally, participation in the forum also allows students to exercise *control* over the way in which they acquire help and over troublesome exercises. They receive customized help and can pursue this activity until they feel that they have received adequate help on the exercise that is part of their coursework. The finding that students often went beyond simply saying *that* the forum had helped them and demonstrated *how* participation was helpful (despite such responses being unsolicited in this forum) indicates that students are exercising control of their understanding of the exercises in question.

Limitations

There are several key limitations of this study that will need to be addressed in future work. First, the methodology was restricted to analyses of archived transcripts. Additional insight into the ways in which students acquire and exchange knowledge in open, online, help forums calls for corroboration from interviews, surveys, and retrospective analyses (Riel & Harasim, 1994), as well as participative approaches, such as "netnography" (Kozinets, 2002).

Secondly, the methodology used does not support any conclusions regarding the effects of forum participation on student performance or attitudes towards subject matter *in the classroom*. It may be that students are using the help forums and that activity exhibits themes consistent with purported learning styles of the Net Generation, but this has little influence on the acquisition of domain knowledge more broadly. The goal of correlating the quality of online discussion contributions with emerging expertise in the classroom is recognized as a next step in understanding Web-based student experiences (Hara, Bonk, & Angeli, 2000).

Thirdly, this study centered on activity in a single open, online, homework help forum. The results cannot be generalized to activity in other forums. In fact, there is evidence that activity in

other SOH forums looks markedly different than that in FMH. On www.cramster.com (Cramster), for instance, convenience is maximized (by a much shorter reply time than FMH as discussed earlier), but connection and control are not as richly represented; on the calculus forum at Cramster, students rarely re-enter exchanges, contribute to the construction of solutions, or express in meaningful ways how the acquired information was helpful (van de Sande, 2009). Thus, the ways in which knowledge is acquired and exchanged can vary widely according to the forum in question, and future work is needed to uncover the reasons behind this variation.

Extensions

Despite its limitations, this study demonstrates the way in which open, online, help forums can be used to gain insight into student learning styles as they naturally occur (i.e., in the wild). The research reported here demonstrates how an open, online, help forum can promote *convenience* through accessibility and timing, *connection* through networking students and helpers, and *control* through student initiation. Two additional related constructs, namely *comfort* and *communication*, have emerged through examination of activity across many help forums and our understanding of student learning in other environments and contexts, and will need further investigation.

First, participating in an open, online, help forum, and perhaps even merely lurking (reading others' posts but contributing little, if at all), may bring *comfort* to many students. On entering a help forum site, one sees hundreds and hundreds of queries from fellow students, all aimed at seeking help on various course assignments and reflecting a lack of understanding or confidence. Seeing that one was not alone in having questions and not understanding course material – that many, many others are in the same boat, as it were – may serve as significant encouragement and motivation for students who otherwise would feel alone in their distress. In essence, the help forums may provide comfort as an online support community for confused students who are struggling with their coursework.

Further comfort for student participants might well come from the anonymity of the forums, together with the way students is positioned. Students may be more comfortable venturing "stupid" questions under the guise of a username than potentially risking ridicule from their peers or instructors. We know that many students refrain from asking questions in the classroom (Vander-Meij, 1988); the anonymity of open, online, help forums allows shy or intimidated students to ask their questions, those that arise during class and as they work on assignments outside of school.

On top of the anonymity that open forums provide, the way in which students are positioned in any given forum may also be critical to participation. Students no doubt derive comfort from having their questions taken seriously and being positioned as learners with legitimate difficulties. Students who post their questions on the forum are revealing their ignorance and making themselves vulnerable to others who are more knowledgeable in the given domain, even if this is done anonymously. Therefore, the tone that helpers take when responding to students and whether they position the students as competent learners is another indicator of comfort.

Second, participating in an open, online, help forum requires *communication* with (unknown) others around the mathematics or relevant subject area. Communicating mathematical text presents its own set of difficulties because of the specialized use of symbols, notation, and parsing structures. A mathematical expression can be completely different than intended, for instance, if parentheses are not used properly, and the correct way to use them when communicating mathematical text in a horizontal format (e.g., 1/x-1 vs. 1/(x-1)) is an issue for some students (van de Sande & Leinhardt, 2007b).

But beyond being able to "write math," students who use the help forums must be able to communicate their needs, and helpers must be able to communicate their responses. When posting a query, students must tackle issues such as appropriate language use, the amount of background information to reveal, and the way to express their (mis)understanding in order to get the needed help efficiently. When responding, helpers must tackle the same issues from their side of the fence. In the forums, the norms and maxims of face-to-face conversation (Grice, 1989) do not apply, but neither exactly do the norms of chat (casual online shorthand), which forums generally advise against. Somehow participants have to strike a balance between the formality of the material (school mathematics) and the informality of the encounters with others (who have different levels of expertise). Students and helpers who use the forums want to communicate with others constructively and efficiently. This much is clear. Navigating the appropriate communicative practices is what requires knowledge, and perhaps, practice.

REFERENCES

Ahuja, M. K., & Galvin, J. E. (2003). Socialization in virtual groups. *Journal of Management, 29*(2), 161–185. doi:10.1177/014920630302900203

Barnes, K., Marateo, R. C., & Ferris, S. P. (2007). Teaching and learning with the Net Generation *Innovate. Journal of Online Education, 3*(4).

Bennett, S., Maton, K., & Kervin, L. (2008). The 'digital natives' debate: A critical review of the evidence. *British Journal of Educational Technology, 39*(5), 775–786. doi:10.1111/j.1467-8535.2007.00793.x

Bonk, C. J., & King, K. S. (1998). *Electronic Collaborators: Learner Centered Technologies for Literacy, Apprenticeship, and Discourse.* Mahweh, NJ: Lawrence Erlbaum.

Caruso, J. B., & Kvavik, R. (2005). *ECAR study of students and information technology 2005: Convenience, connection, control, and learning.*

Coakes, E. (2002). Knowledge Management: A sociotechnical perspective. In Coakes, E., Willis, D., & Clarke, S. (Eds.), *Knowledge Management in the Sociotechnical World. The Graffiti Continues* (pp. 4–14). London: Springer.

De Smet, M., Van Keer, H., & Valcke, M. (2009). Cross-age peer tutors in asynchronous discussion groups: A study of the evolution in tutor support. *Instructional Science, 37*(1), 87–105. doi:10.1007/s11251-007-9037-2

Dede, C. (2005). Planning for Neomillennial Learning Styles: Implications for Investments in Technology and Faculty. In D. Oblinger & J. Oblinger (Eds.), *Educating the Net generation.* Boulder, CO: EDUCAUSE. Retrieved from http://www.educause.edu/educatingthenetgen/

Dellarocas, C. (2003). The digitization of word of mouth: Promises and challenges of online feedback mechanisms. *Management Science, 49*(10), 1407–1424. doi:10.1287/mnsc.49.10.1407.17308

Frand, J. (2000, September/October). The information-age mindset: Changes in students and implications for higher education. *EDUCAUSE Review, 25*, 14–24.

Goodall, B. (2008). Ryerson U. won't expel student over facebook study group. *The Chronicle of Higher Education.* Retrieved from http://chronicle.com/blogPost/Ryerson-U-Wont-Expel-Stud/3771/

Goodyear, P., Jones, C., Asensio, M., Hodgson, V., & Steeples, C. (2005). Networked Learning in Higher Education: Students' Expectations and Experiences. *Higher Education, 50*(3), 473–508. doi:10.1007/s10734-004-6364-y

Grice, H. P. (1989). *Studies in the way of words.* Cambridge, MA: Harvard University Press.

Hara, N., Bonk, C. J., & Angeli, C. (2000). Content analysis of online discussion in an applied educational psychology course. *Instructional Science, 28*, 115–152. doi:10.1023/A:1003764722829

Jahnke, I. (2008). Knowledge sharing through interactive social technologies: Development and change of social structures in Internet-based systems. In Bolisani, E. (Ed.), *Building the Knowledge Society on the Internet: Sharing and Echanging Knowledge in Networked Environments* (pp. 195–218). Hershey, PA: IGI Global.

Jones, C., Ramanau, R., Cross, S., & Healing, G. (2010). Net generation or digital natives: Is there a distinct new generation entering university? *Computers & Education, 54*, 722–732. doi:10.1016/j.compedu.2009.09.022

Kozinets, R. (2002). The field behind the screen: Using netnography for marketing research in online communities. *JMR, Journal of Marketing Research, 39*(11), 61–72. doi:10.1509/jmkr.39.1.61.18935

Lampel, J., & Bhalla, A. (2007). The role of status seeking in online communities: Giving the gift of experience. *Journal of Computer-Mediated Communication, 12*(2). doi:10.1111/j.1083-6101.2007.00332.x

Larreamendy-Joerns, J., & Leinhardt, G. (2006). Going the distance with online education. *Review of Educational Research, 76*(4), 567–605. doi:10.3102/00346543076004567

Lave, J., & Wenger, E. (1991). *Situated learning. Legitimate peripheral participation.* Cambridge, UK: University of Cambridge Press.

Martin, T. S. (2000). Calculus students' ability to solve geometric related-rates problems. *Mathematics Education Research Journal, 12*(2), 74–91.

McKenna, K. Y. A. (2007). Through the Internet looking glass: Expressing and validating the true self. In Joinson, A., McKenna, K., Postmes, T., & Reips, U.-D. (Eds.), *The Oxford Handbook of Internet Psychology* (pp. 205–221). New York: Oxford University Press.

Mowrer, D. E. (1996). A content analysis of student/instructor communication via computer conferencing. *Higher Education, 32*, 217–241. doi:10.1007/BF00138397

Oblinger, D., & Oblinger, J. (2005). Is it age or IT: first steps towards understanding the net generation. In D. Oblinger & J. Oblinger (Eds.), *Educating the Net generation.* Boulder, CO: EDUCAUSE. Retrieved from http://www.educause.edu/educatingthenetgen/

Preece, J., Abras, Ch., & Maloney-Krichmar, D. (2004). Designing and evaluating online communities: research speaks to emerging practice. *International Journal of Web Based Communities, 1*(1), 2–18.

Prensky, M. (2001). Digital Natives, Digital Immigrants. *Horizon, 9*(5), 1–6. doi:10.1108/10748120110424816

Riel, M., & Harasim, L. (1994). Research perspectives on network learning. *Machine-Mediated Learning, 4*, 91-113.

Schumann, S., & Geiman, R. M. (2009). *Experiences from an online mathematics center.* Paper presented at the American Mathematical Association of Two-Year Colleges (AMATYC).

Selwyn, N. (2007). *'Screw Blackboard...do it on Facebook!': an investigation of students' educational use of Facebook.* Paper presented at the Poke 1.0-Facebook social research symposium.

Selwyn, N. (2009). Faceworking: Exploring students' education-related use of Facebook. *Learning, Media and Technology, 34*(2), 157–174. doi:10.1080/17439880902923622

Szydlik, J. E. (2000). Mathematical beliefs and conceptual understanding of the limit of a function. *Journal for Research in Mathematics Education, 31*, 258–276. doi:10.2307/749807

Tapscott, D. (1999). Educating the Net Generation. *Educational Leadership, 56*(5), 6–11.

van de Sande, B., & van de Sande, C. (2009). *Open, online, physics homework forums: The wave of the future.* Paper presented at the American Association of Physics Teachers: Annual Winter Meeting.

van de Sande, C. (2007). *Help! Tutorettes on the calculus concept of limit.* Unpublished manuscript.

van de Sande, C. (2008a). *Drawing conclusions about diagram use in an online forum.* Paper presented at the Conference on Research in Undergraduate Mathematics Education (CRUME).

van de Sande, C. (2008b). *Open, online, calculus help forums: Learning about and from a public conversation.* Unpublished doctoral dissertation, University of Pittsburgh, PA.

van de Sande, C. (2009, June). *Does it help? Rating tutor responses in open, online help forums.* In C. Fulford & G. Siemens (Eds.), *Proceedings of ED-MEDIA 2009: World Conference on Educational Multimedia, Hypermedia, and Telecommunications* (pp. 4320-4326). Honolulu, HI: AACE.

van de Sande, C., & Leinhardt, G. (2007a). Help! Active student learning and error remediation in an online calculus e-help community. *Electronic Journal of e-Learning, 5*(3), 227-238.

van de Sande, C., & Leinhardt, G. (2007b). Online tutoring in the Calculus: Beyond the limit of the limit. *Éducation et Didactique, 1*(2), 115-154.

van de Sande, C., & Leinhardt, G. (2008, June) The Good Samaritan effect: A lens for understanding patterns of participation. In *Proceedings of the Eighth International conference for the Learning Sciences* (Vol. 2, pp. 240-247). Utrecht, The Netherlands: International Society of the Learning Sciences, Inc.

VanderMeij, H. (1988). Constraints on question asking in classrooms. *Journal of Educational Psychology, 80*, 401–405. doi:10.1037/0022-0663.80.3.401

ENDNOTES

[1] A portion of the work reported here was described in van de Sande (2008).

[2] The names of participants have been altered slightly to protect their identity but, at the same time, with an eye to capturing their persona.

[3] The original query contained two problems on limit that were "split" by the forum moderators into two separate threads.

[3] Pastel erroneously omits the second term of the numerator from the previous expression here. The equation should read "$\sin(a+y)-\sin(a) = \sin(a)\cos(y)-\cos(a)\sin(y)-\sin(a)$."

This work was previously published in The International Journal of Sociotechnology and Knowledge Development, Volume 2, Issue 4, edited by Elayne Coakes, pp. 1-17, copyright 2010 by IGI Publishing (an imprint of IGI Global).

Chapter 12
A Way Out of the Information Jungle:
A Longitudinal Study about a Socio–Technical Community and Informal Learning in Higher Education

Isa Jahnke
TU Dortmund University, Germany

ABSTRACT

The emergence of community-oriented Information and Communication Technology platforms, e.g., forum software or wikis, the penetration of media in society has increased. In academia, forms of communication and cooperation to share knowledge are changing under open Web 2.0 conditions. In this regard, teaching and learning scenarios are moving towards technology-enhanced lifelong learning communities. This contribution presents the results of a longitudinal study of a Socio-Technical Community (STC) launched in 2002. The STC, which supports the study organization as well as teaching and learning in higher education, has been evaluated from its founding to its sustainable development and transformation phase in 2009. The study shows results in three specific areas: The learners' satisfaction with the STC, the type and quality of use, and if the STC is a helpful support for students to progress through their studies more efficiently than without an STC. The central conclusion is that spaces for computer-mediated communication are important for students regarding informal learning about organizing their own studies. Informal learning with a socio-technical community is more effective than without due to its individualization of learning in large groups.

DOI: 10.4018/978-1-4666-0200-7.ch012

Copyright © 2012, IGI Global. Copying or distributing in print or electronic forms without written permission of IGI Global is prohibited.

INTRODUCTION

In the past decade, new community-oriented applications of Information and Communication Technology (ICT) have emerged, e.g., groupware systems or social software, Web 2.0 platforms (e.g., box.net; twitter). These applications have the potential to transform social systems (e.g., groups, companies, universities, non-profit organizations) into socio-technical networks, where socially and technically supported relationships are highly interwoven. In contrast to general web-based, online or virtual communities *in society* such as Wikipedia or Facebook, this paper is focused on socio-technical communities *in academia*, in particular higher education (HE). The challenge in creating such socio-technical systems – within organizations – is to design the interaction between social processes, educational elements and technical components. Whether this type of system really contributes to knowledge sharing and learning within organizations depends also on the culture and on the degree to which these socio-technical structures are adjusted to each other and how they are integrated. In other words, it depends on how efficiently and successfully the technical system interacts with the social system, and vice versa (Herrmann, Loser, & Jahnke, 2007).

When designing a socio-technical learning system in higher education, the overall research question is how to design (develop, introduce, evaluate) technology-enhanced learning successfully and what elements can be designed (general model). One answer is given by Jahnke, Terkowsky, Pleul, and Tekkaya (2010). A "successful design" depends on following three factors.

1.   First, the degree of structural coupling (degree of interdependency) of the three elements and its complex interconnections: Are the elements strong connected and formalized, or flexibly usable? How closely, loosely are the elements connected? The three elements are technical elements (e.g.,

learning management systems; social media, socio-technical community platform), social/organizational structures (e.g., forms of communication and participation, roles of instructor and students), and pedagogical/educational concepts (e.g., informal learning approaches, motivational systems).

2.   Second, the degree of quality: This degree shows how well the elements interact, for example, the greater the unity among these three elements, the better they share knowledge and co-construction of knowledge can take places, the better they learn.

3.   Third, "a successful design" depends on what the user's role is. Different target groups, people in different roles have different cognitive conceptions of success. Instructors, students, university managers, pedagogical experts, e-learning experts, define it in different ways. A good design includes different views, or at least, supports a common understanding (Herrmann et al., 2007). These three dimensions drive the design-based research process.

So, the implementation of Web 2.0 conditions in higher education depends on the design of a socio-technical system with educational elements (Wasson, 2007) – including motivational systems, different forms of participation, supporting me-centricity (Twenge, 2006), fostering active communication, and enabling a flow experience (to increase the motivation of learners to learn). In particular, an appropriate balance between informal and formal structures is needed (Jahnke & Koch, 2009). Prensky (2001) calls this new form of a networked generation of young people "digital natives", born in the Web 2.0 century, like native speakers, also known as the "internet generation" (Palfrey & Gasser, 2008).

In 2001, a project was started to initiate a socio-technical learning community to aid study organization, and to support teaching and learning in higher education. By applying the Design-Based

Research approach (Wang & Hannafin, 2005), a socio-technical community was designed to offer students opportunities to get in contact with different learners, to communicate and share knowledge about their studies. By conducting a long-term study (2002-2009), the development of the community was investigated regarding its social and technical changes over time (Jahnke, 2010). In this paper, we evaluate if this socio-technical community in higher education is an appropriate supporting structure for students in order to a) support informal learning and b) to find a way out of the "information jungle" (interview quote from a student at a German university in 2002).

In the following sections, a definition of a socio-technical community is provided, followed by the main and derived research questions. This is followed by a detailed description of the analyzed socio-technical community (STC). Subsequently, the evaluation method is elaborated upon. Finally, the empirical results are described; in particular the answer to the question if an STC supports learning processes in higher education.

SOCIO-TECHNICAL COMMUNITIES IN HIGHER EDUCATION (HE) AND INFORMAL LEARNING

Reshaping Teaching and Learning with Web 2.0

Current discussions in higher education focus on shifting the focus from the teacher teaching to the students learning (Barr & Tagg, 1995). This is a shift from teacher-centered teaching to student-centered learning concepts. Student-centered learning means reversing the traditional teacher-centered understanding of learning, putting students at the center of the learning process and letting them participate in the evaluation of their learning. The focus is shifted from the teacher, who possesses and communicates knowledge with a particular aim, to the students, who acquire the knowledge they need to solve a problem with the help of the teacher. Students gain a more active role and have to collaborate to learn.

It is important to note that a student-centered learning approach also means that students need to be better qualified in managing their own learning processes and therefore need more information about how their curriculum is structured. Administrative and organizational information as well as purely professional or subject-specific information must be presented. Such a learning approach refers to strategies which put the learner in control of constructing their own learning. This paradigm takes into consideration the pace, repetition, learning styles, motivation, self-regulation, and self-responsibility to learn.

With regard to this learning paradigm, Lave and Wenger (1991) have introduced their concept about "situated learning". It is a process of learning in a learning community of practice. This learning process can be characterized as a situated activity, for example students hear something new from the teacher, and immediately apply the new knowledge in their own context and experiences. The teacher's instructions and the student's learning processes are closely combined. The main aim is to foster a new balance between the teacher's instruction and the student's learning processes. Berger and Luckmann (1967) as well as Lave and Wenger (1991) argue that learning should not be viewed as simply the transmission of abstract and decontextualised knowledge from one individual to another, but a social process whereby knowledge is co-constructed. Therefore, such a learning approach should be situated in a specific context, and be embedded within particular social interactions.

Modern day learning systems are more flexible, adaptable to different existing levels of knowledge and learning strategies, but are usually controlled by the teacher as well. They often do not implement concepts that embed the whole learning process into the given curriculum neither they empower the students to manage their own learning nor they support informal learning processes. According to Collins and Halverson (2009), authors of the book "Rethinking Education in the Age of Technology", the net generation needs particularly online social networks with 'anytime, anywhere' access. One solution could be to introducing online or socio-technical communities. They would offer new possibilities to easily support students' learning (e.g. forums, wikis).

Socio-Technical Communities (STCs)

Communities of practice are generated through social relationships among individuals "who share a concern, a set of problems, or a passion about a topic, and who deepen their knowledge and expertise in this area by interacting on an ongoing basis" (Wenger, McDermott, & Snyder, 2002, p. 4). Since this definition does not focus on online groups, it is expanded by Preece, Abras, and Maloney-Krichmar (2004). They summarized that their observed online community evolved "according to how people interact with each other using software to support their interactions" (p. 16). Information systems researchers use the term 'online communities' to describe all social groups which have some kind of online presence. These differ in four areas:

- Group size (e.g., groups with 25 members or less to groups with 1,000 or more)
- Primary content (e.g., discussion boards about stock exchange, marathon training, or courses at universities)
- Lifespan (e.g., several years or only for organizing one off event)
- Presence (e.g., pure online communication, face-to-face communication or mixed)

In this contribution, an STC is defined with social relationships between people sharing an interest in topics or problems, fostered mainly by computer-mediated human interactions. Depending on the content, lifespan and group size, an STC

is an extended part of an existing institution. The difference to pure online communities is following: A socio-technical community (STC) delivers an interaction space for enabling communication between members and others *within an existing institution, organization, or company.* A STC is an extended part of an existing enterprise, and supports the specific focus of the enterprise, faculty or department (e.g., knowledge management at health care institutes; knowledge management at marketing companies; knowledge sharing about computer science studies). In contrast, online communities are often separate from any enterprises, and not included into a (non-)profit organization (e.g., Facebook, Twitter, or myspace.com – they have an internal structure but they are build for any needs people have).

Informal Learning and STCs

Flexible learning approaches support the learning progress of an individual by giving the learner different options for learning opportunities (what, how, when). This also means the learner have the freedom of access to learning content, location (virtual, physically), time and pace. "Flexibility means anticipating, and responding to the ever-changing needs and expectations of (…) learners" (Shurville, O'Grady, & Mayall, 2008).

Informal learning takes place when a learner needs to solve a problem or task outside an official course at school or university. Watkins and Marsick (1992) define informal learning[1] as to:

"(1) based on learning from experience; (2) embedded in the organizational context; (3) oriented to a focus on action; (4) governed by non-routine conditions; (5) concerned with tacit dimensions that must be made explicit; (6) delimited by the nature of the task, the way in which problems are framed, and the work capacity of the individual undertaking the task; and (7) enhanced by proactivity, critical reflectivity, and creativity".

Important factors for informal learning are the quality of the activity, reflection and creativity of the learner. Especially, supporting structures from the environment are essential (Watkins & Marsick, 1992). "Formal learning is related to a teacher and tutor, who give instructions and rules; informal learning is related to an inspiring environment and supporting structures" (translated by author, Dohmen, 2001, p. 19). Informal learning can supported by the individual itself, but also by the design of the learning environment, for example, Internet-enhanced communities. Actors in online communities often have similar problems, topics or share a passion to a domain with the goal to share their knowledge or/and to extend their expertise (Wenger et al., 2002). A well-orchestrated informal learning community with Web 2.0 conditions promotes open participation and also gives opportunities for communication – that means: when the users want to, and in particular *what* the learners want to discuss.

Following this approach, a socio-technical community at a university provides a new space for human communication. It enables new ways of communication and new connections among members within the university as well as outside the official organization. With introducing an informal online space, social complexity and information overload can be reduced – at least from the perspective of the members. For the members, it will be easier to get only such information they need at a specific time. It can be called "just-in-time-communication" (Jahnke, 2010).

The main research question is: Does an information and communication portal (a specific form of a learning environment at a university) support informal learning? If yes, to what extent? (RQ1) Derived questions are: Is a socio-technical community an appropriate communication space for learners to manage their own study organization? (RQ2). Does an STC organize the "jungle of information" for learners? (RQ3) Is the access to information with a socio-technical community better than without? (RQ4).

This has been empirically investigated in a longitudinal study from 2002 to 2009. The methods and results will be described in this paper.

METHOD, DATA ANALYSIS DESIGN

Background / Research Aim

The project on 'Organizational Development of the Computer Science Studies at Dortmund University (Jahnke, 2006) revealed many information deficiencies – from the students' perspective. The study analyzed the factors which have been an influence on the study organization (study planning and conduction) of students (Jahnke, Mattick, & Herrmann, 2005). The study show 8 factors that affects the study organization from the perspective of the students, for example, competency for self-organization, active participation at learning groups, role of the BA/MA in relation to the own life (how serious do students study?), beliefs and perceptions about the BA-study, availability of supporting structures giving orientation/help. Despite the fact that some students also have learning problems with the content of the courses, the study particularly illuminated lacks of information. Supporting structures had neither a sufficient quality nor were enough available. These critical factors affect the success or non-success of students if they get the computer science degree. In addition, the study also illustrated that there are many information sources but they are distribute among too many websites. In addition, information was also available in other sources like hardcopy brochures but just few people know where these brochures are. According to the students, many sources often have not a consistent structure, the information is not clear enough or the access to them is difficult. "You have to know where to find the right information; otherwise it's difficult at least for beginners" (ID-No 04, student, May 2001). For instance, the websites of the instructions and researchers were full with information students did not need for their own study planning (for instance research projects, marketing, publication for the scientific community and so forth). Information about courses, seminars, and lectures were not represented clearly. From the perspective of the students, it is an information overload. So, it is not a surprise when more than 75% of the students (n=384) wished to have a better structure about the content regarding study organization. In addition, the project also found out that there was a lack of feedback and assessments from study managers on students' progress. The project members concluded that students, who decide themselves when to attend lectures or seminars, had a lack of information about how to choose their lectures, in which semester to choose them, and how to plan and manage their studies. To solve this 'lack of information', the development of a socio-technical community called InPUD was introduced in 2002.

Within seven years, the InPUD-community was evaluated if it supports the students to progress through their studies more efficiently than before 2002..

Case Study: The InPUD-Community

Based on the project's results, an ICT system, called Informatics Portal University of Dortmund (InPUD), was implemented to solve the information deficiencies by supporting knowledge sharing between novice (new) and expert (senior) students, study advisors as well as faculty members (e.g., teachers, dean officers, administration officers). The InPUD-community can be described as a community system for computer science students at Dortmund University – launched in 2002.

The InPUD-community is a socio-technical community since it is part of an institute. InPUD is an extension of a department (Faculty of Computer Science), i.e., a supplement to the formal structure. According to Preece's four areas the InPUD-community is a) characterized by a large size, b) the InPUD-community shares knowledge

about study organization for getting the computer science degree, hints about 'how to study successfully', and study management at the university, and content of courses, lectures etc. c) it has an extended lifespan d) InPUD delivers a space for online communication.

The community is online available at http://in-pud.cs.uni-dortmund.de. The InPUD-community includes an overview of all classes and lectures that are offered during the course of a semester. The way that the information is structured is the same for each lecture or seminar. The information pertains to lectures, including any tutorials that are being held (and when), course materials, notices for examinations, lecturer contact information, and often a free discussion forum as well as news and search functions. Since universities offer a large variety of lectures, students have to create their own semester plan for lectures and choose which lectures to attend and when to attend them. Therefore, the information about the study management domain was combined with online discussion boards. The boards are embedded in an information website that includes facts about course guidance as well as graphical maps of how to study which course at which time (Figure 1 and Figure 2).

The discussion boards exist for both courses (e.g., to discuss exercises or content of lectures) and study organization, for example, 'where to register for examinations', 'where to find the university calendar and timetable', 'what do to when I have learning problems?' 'what classes are suited for semester 4?' etc. The decision about the topic on each discussion board mainly depends on what the students want to discuss. It ranges from discussions about course content, definitions or solutions for exercises to organizational issues, e.g., where and when is the next learning group, what could come up in the examination, or discussions about the quality of courses or the teacher's role. For the faculty, the last point could be a critical one, especially when the students criticize the teacher's instruction, but it can also be used

Figure 1. Screenshot InPUD portal

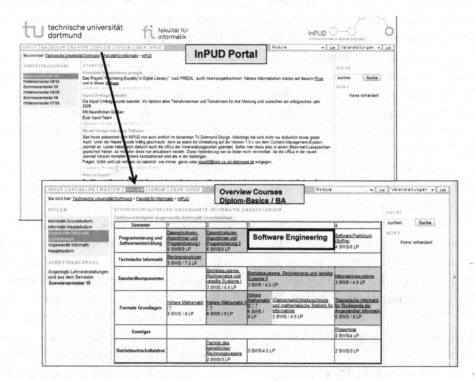

Figure 2. Screenshot InPUD portal with link to online boards

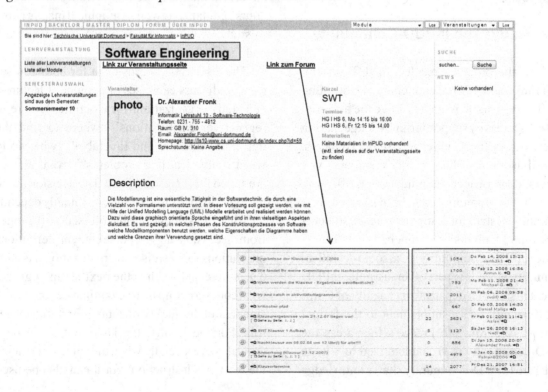

Figure 3. Screenshot InPUD discussions boards

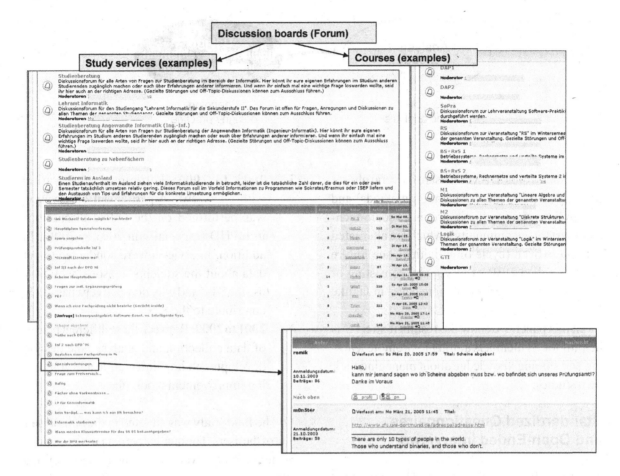

for a evaluation about courses and its quality. In 2008, there were more than 40 boards on-line, each with their own moderator (Figure 3).

Community members can share their knowledge under the condition of a minimum of formal regulations and limited university control. That means, every member can read any of the InPUD-content without login and without registration. But registration is required when answering or posing questions (with a free selectable username and email). This is different to learning management systems (LMS) which often require registration given by the technical administration desk when a user wants to read something.

Research Design and Data Analysis

From 2001 to 2008, a long-term field study was conducted with the design-based research (DBR) approach (Reeves, Herrington, & Oliver, 2005). According to Wang and Hannafin (2005) DBR is "a systematic but flexible methodology aimed to improve educational practices through iterative analysis, design, development, and implementation, based on collaboration among researchers and practitioners in real-world settings, and leading to contextually-sensitive design principles and theories" (p. 6).

Figure 4. DBR design in general

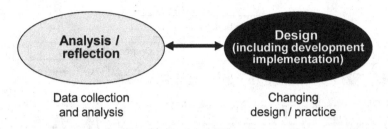

In other words, DBR consists of several phases of analysis (reflection, evaluation methods) and design (interventions for improving a socio-technical system or community), which are alternated and interwoven (cycle of activities), see Figure 4. The applied DBR of this study, consisting of nine phases, is described in more detail in Jahnke (2010, 2009).

In this paper, we show the results if an STC is helpful for its members aiming to promote learning and sharing knowledge about managing their own studies.

Standardized Questionnaires and Open-Ended Interviews

The data collection was conducted between 2002 and 2009. The data collection includes the following methods:

1. **2001 to 2002:** Open-ended interviews before the STC were launched. To find out the students' problems, 14 people were interviewed face-to-face (8 students and 6 professors/lecturers who were experienced study counselors) with an interview guide including open-ended questions in 2001 to 2002. The objective was to reveal the students' problems. One result was the lack of information and lack of feedback.
2. **2002 and 2009:** Standardized questionnaires *before* launching the STC and *seven years later*. This is then central data source for this paper.

3. **2003 to 2006:** Participant observation with interviews. A participant observation was performed on the online discussions in InPUD (especially in 2003 to 2006). In addition, interviews were conducted to get data about the students' reasons, why they use the STC and why they actively/passively contribute to the STC.
4. **2001 to 2009:** Between these different phases of data collection and analysis, the design, development, implementation and continuing improvements took place.

The field study was situated in the natural setting of the users. The qualitative data were recorded by audio. Notes were taken by an observer and later analysed using open coding (Bryman, 2008). The quantitative data was analyzed by using SPSS.

In this paper, we focus on the comparison between 2002 and 2009 answering if the STC supports informal learning. Therefore, the standardized questionnaires *before* launching the STC and *seven years later* will be used for the results (see b). The first standardized questionnaire was created in 2001/2002 which was sent out to a sample of the computer science students at the University of Dortmund (out of 430 questionnaires, 384 were returned). The sample represented approximately 20 percent of all computer science students enrolled on foundation courses. Between December 2008 and January 2009, a second quantitative survey including standardized and open-ended questions with 24 questions was conducted. The questionnaire was available for four weeks online and 345 questionnaires were returned. The study also considered user statistics (webpage requests 2002-2005 and online boards 2002-2009).

We evaluate if the InPUD-community is helpful as to: a) learners' satisfaction with the STC, b) type and quality of use, and c) if the STC is a good platform for students to communicate about their courses of study and problems in a more appropriate way than before its creation. The main hypothesis (H1) is: a socio-technical community like InPUD (STC) helps students to organize the own study better than without.

RESULTS

The pre-post evaluation in particular the post online survey was conducted in 2009. The sample amounts 345 from a total of 2,000 students enrolled at the Faculty of Computer Science. More than 84 percent of the respondents are male, and 15 percent are female. 45 percent are between 19 and 23 years old and 45 percent are between 24 to 28 years old. The others are older than 29 years, one respondent is younger than 19.

66 percent of the respondents are enrolled in the "old-fashioned" Diploma courses whereas almost 34 percent already enrolled at the Bachelor courses launched in 2007. Table 1 gives details about the respondents regarding their registration year at the InPUD-community, and how many respondents are in what semester enrolled at the

faculty. The data shows a constant distribution over time.

The sample consists of new and younger students as well as regular and older semesters. In addition, more than 33 percent use InPUD since its early years (2002-2004); 28 percent are users since 2005 or 2006 (phase of sustainable development), and 37 percent are users since 2007/2008 (transformation phase, e.g., Diplom changed to BA/MA).

Since InPUD's launch in September 2002, the number of users has increased steadily.

The number of webpage requests has grown consistently and the access rate usually peaks at the beginning of a new semester. In October 2002 there were only 171,408 requests. A year later, in October 2003, there were 292,155 requests and in October 2004 this had increased to 491,330 requests (see Figure 5). These requests have been continually increasing without marketing or any external advertising. In the end of 2009, more than 1,500 individuals had an account. This represents more than 75% of the 2,000 students enrolled at the faculty.

Since InPUD is open for everyone (e.g., people who want to study computer science in the future; teachers, instructors, administration officers), we do not know exactly how many community members are students. The account does not ask about the role, if the member is a student or not. But because of the titles and content of the sub boards, which are more interested

Table 1. Respondents' registration at InPUD Respondents regarding enrolled semester

Year	Percent (n=345)	Semester	Percent (n=345)
2002	4.5	1-2	16.1
2003	13.4	2-4	18.5
2004	15.7	5-6	15.5
2005	13.4	7-8	11.9
2006	14.9	9-10	14.3
2007	15.7	11 and more	23.8
2008	21.6		

Figure 5. Increase of participation over time (dark bars show beginning of a new semester)[2]

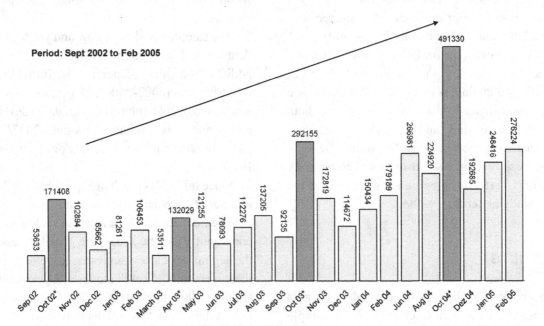

for students than for other people, we know that the vast majority of the community-members are students. In addition, we analyzed the number of the teachers, instructors, and study advisors since they are part of the community with their regular name. It ranges from 45 (in 2006) to not more than 100 teachers (in 2009).

Figure 6 reveals the number of new members in InPUD (grey bars, right) in relation to the new students per year enrolled at the computer science study (dark bars, left).

In the first year 2003 after launching the community, 130 new members did enroll at the community whereas 531 new students enrolled at the Faculty of Computer Science. In 2005, the phase of sustainable development, the faculty counted 237 new students and 232 did subscribe in InPUD. It can be that the number of new members in larger than the number of new students (cf., 2008 and 2009). This difference is possible since students from "older" semesters requested an account not in the semester when they enrolled at the faculty but later. Figure 6 illustrates only those users who did at least one contribution or more.

Users without contribution are not illustrated in this figure. The numbers of users without contribution over time is 511.

Figure 7 shows the number of contributions per individual in six posting categories over the entire period from 2002 to 2009. Over a time span of more than seven years, 1,545 members contributed actively. A core of about 191 individuals (12%), provided contributions regularly, ranging from 51 to 483 postings per individual.

The core members are especially the 'early adopters' and from today's viewpoint the 'elders'. These people have been active since InPUD's early years. However, some of the core members in InPUD are also new students (newbies) between the first and fourth semesters. The other active members made postings in the range from 1 to 9, 10 to 25, and 26-50. These members can be described as regulars, but can also include newbies.

The figure does not present the other 511 registered members who have not contribute (contribution is 0). According to Preece et al. (2004), there are various reasons for why they do not post (e.g., no motivation, no personal need,

Figure 6. New InPUD users per year (grey) in relation to new students per year (dark); figure shows only users with one contribution or more

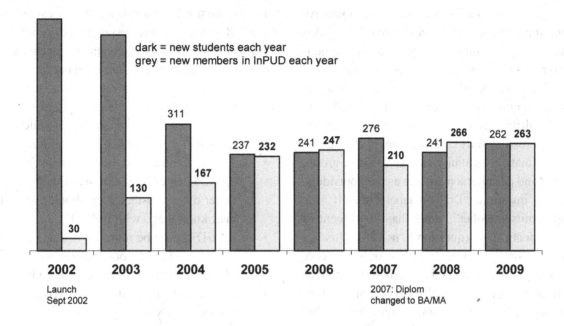

Figure 7. Absolute and relative frequency of users contributing in six posting categories

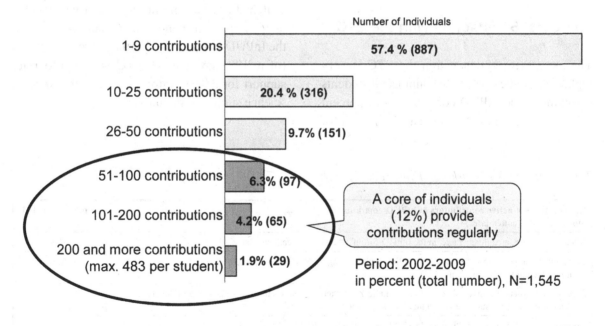

and curiosity without exposure). The online survey points out different reasons, why InPUD users have an account but do not actively contribute. An open question, where 113 answered, was coded afterwards. The most important factor for non-active contributing is that questions, community members have, are already online (32 percent, F1, Table 2). Following factors are named in detail:

The differences in the range of active contributions to reading only confirm Wenger et al. experiences that a community consists of a core group, active and peripheral members as well outsiders. On the question: "Do you label yourself as a community-member?" more than 70 percent of the students agree (question 6, n=188). This is a surprise since it means that not only the core members but also the active, regular and peripheral members rate themselves as part of the community. 62 percent of the respondents label themselves as regular members, 30 percent as newbies and 8 percent say they are experienced members (question 14).

Learners' Satisfaction with the STC

The users' satisfaction within the STC is very high. It has to be stressed that almost all students recommend the InPUD-community (94 percent of n=161, question 17). More than 92 percent (of

n=145) assess the InPUD-community with "very good". ("InPUD is great", "InPUD is great but I have some tips for improvements", question 16). Only 8 percent of the respondents do not like InPUD. The hints for improvements (open-ended question) were coded in five categories:

- Content (37 percent, e.g., "better linking", more information for specific modules),
- Design (33 percent, e.g., navigation),
- Teachers should use InPUD more than to-day (26 percent, e.g., "most of the teachers foster own websites, they should integrate their knowledge with InPUD"),
- InPUD should be more up to date (25 percent, e.g., better coordination with other official websites of the faculty), and
- Functions (9 percent, e.g., search function should be better, integrate RSS-feeds).

In addition, more than 75 percent disagree with the following statement: "If InPUD were switched off, I would not miss it" (question 10, n=191). In other words, the learners would miss the InPUD-community. Furthermore, 70 percent (of n=188) say that the STC is an appropriate support for getting information about computer science studies at the university.

Table 2. Reasons for lurking or just reading only

Reasons for non-active contributors at InPUD-community (open question, coded later)	In percent (n=113)
"Question, I have, are already there, in the InPUD-forum"; "answers already available" (F1)	31.8
Communication problems/weakness: "difficulties with language", "shy", "I'm afraid of asking sth.", "I do not want to ask stupid/dumb questions" (F2)	16.8
Forum as information source only (not for communication): "an account has the advantages to get information what happens in which sub boards"; "automatic notification via email" (F3)	15.9
No motivation: "no interests", "I'm too lazy", "I have no time" (F4)	15.4
Questions can be clarified on other ways: "Face-to-face is better"; different contact points available; no need for information online, "I see no necessity" (F5)	12.4
"No special topics available where I can say something" (F6)	8.0

Type and Quality of Use

The results of the written questionnaire shows that 97 percent of the respondents (of n=345) are known the InPUD-community very well. 92 percent of the students use the STC. The students use it to get news from the faculty (70 percent agreed to this) as well as from courses of the computer science department (88 percent of the respondents said 'yes').

The study also asked about the quality of the InPUD-community (see Table 3). More than two-thirds of the respondents say that the STC is helpful (92 percent), accessible (80 percent) and clearly structured (more than 66 percent agree). However, there are also some suggestions for improvements since information is not so easy to find (a mean of 2.4; scale 1 to 5, 1=strongly agree, 5=strongly disagree), and the information in InPUD is not complete [only 39 percent (strongly) agree, almost 40 percent say 'partially', 21 percent disagree].

Moreover, the question was for *what issues* the learners use the STC. The study wanted to know if InPUD helps to find answers regarding different questions that learners have (answers from 1 to 5, 1=strongly agree; 5= strongly disagree). In order to know how important a particular aspect is for the learners, the study also captured the degree of importance (1 to 5; 1=strongly important, 5= strongly irrelevant) and

also the degree of quality (measured by agreement). The higher the difference between *importance* and *agreement*, the more essential is the need for improvement. Table 4 shows for what issues the STC is valuable for the learners (based on individual ratings). The points (a) to (h) get the mean of 2.3 or better, whereas the points (i) to (l) just get a 3 (2.6).

The more interesting aspect is the difference between the means on the left and right in Table 4. The activity "when to attend what courses (a)" is important for the students (M=1.9); 79 percent say it is (very) important. And the respondents assess this activity with the mean of 2.2 (agreement); 67 percent (strongly) agree. We can conclude that the community is helpful to find solutions regarding when to attend what courses.

The STC is also helpful in finding solutions for the following item: "how to get in contact with other students (c)" (M=2.2; 65 percent say it is (very) important). The students assess this item with a high degree of importance and assign a 'good' (M=2.2; 68 percent (strongly) agree).

In contrast, InPUD should be improved in six areas since the importance is high but the agreement is rather low: "how to combine lectures, tutorials, practical courses, examinations (b)", "which person is responsible for what in the department (d)", "how and when to prepare for examinations (e), (f)", how important is a lecture

Table 3. Frequencies about InPUD's quality (percent; ø = mean)

The InPUD-community is...	Strongly agree (1)	Agree (2)	Partially (3)	Disagree (4)	Strongly Disagree (5)
...helpful for my studies. (n = 313, ø=1.42)	**69.3**	**23.0**	5.8	0.6	1.3
...accessible. (n = 308, ø= 1.60)	**57.5**	**29.9**	8.8	2.6	1.3
...clearly structured. (n = 308, ø= 2.16)	**26.3**	**41.6**	**24.7**	5.2	2.3
Information is easy to find. (n = 306, ø= 2.44)	16.3	**39.5**	**30.7**	10.8	2.6
...complete. (n = 298, ø= 2.80)	10.7	27.9	**38.9**	15.8	6.7

Table 4. "For what is InPUD valuable?" (means, 1=strongly agree/important; 5=strongly disagree/ irrelevant)

Important/ ir-relevant? (1-5)	In percent (1+2)	Question 5: "The InPUD-community helps me to find out ... (n=171)	In percent (1+2)	(Dis)Agree? (1-5)
1.9	79.1	... when to attend what courses". (a)	67.4	2.1
2.0	**73.6**	... how to combine lectures, tutorials, practical courses, examinations". (b)	**50.3**	**2.7**
2.2	65.5	... how to get in contact with other students (e.g., learning collabora-tively, solving exercises in teams)". (c)	68.0	2.2
2.2	**65.3**	... who is responsible for what in the faculty/department". (d)	**50.0**	**2.6**
2.2	**66.4**	... how to prepare for examinations". (e)	**33.5**	**3.1**
2.3	**64.7**	... when to prepare for examinations". (f)	**35.5**	**2.9**
2.3	**62.6**	... how important a lecture is for my studies". (g)	**39.5**	**2.9**
2.3	**69.8**	... when to expect some problems during my degree". (h)	**34.0**	**3.1**
2.6	50.0	... how many hours do I need to complete a course". (i)	30.2	3.0
2.6	53.1	... what skills/competencies are essential to successfully finish a degree in computer science". (k)	22.8	3.3
2.6	48.6	... what skills/competencies should I have learnt when I get my bachelor/master's degree". (l)	25.7	3.4

for my studies (g)", and "when to expect some problems during my degree (h)".

From the students' perspective, three items are not very important (M=2.6): Within the community, students do not expect to discuss or find solutions regarding to how many hours they might need to complete their studies (i), what skills/competencies could be essential to successfully finish a computer science degree (k), and what skills/competencies they should have learnt by the time they get the bachelor/master's degree (l). An explanation is that the students assume that each learner needs a varying amount of time to learn something (different types of learners). Moreover, they do not seem to focus on skills and competencies when they do their studies. It seems all they want is just a good grade. To conclude, a better awareness of learning outcomes as competence development (and why those competences) is required in higher education.

According to the different levels of activity, the members of the InPUD-community read and post ranging from very often to seldom (see Fig-ure 8). Almost 75 percent read (very) often per week (aggregation of "several times" and "once a week"). In contrast, 27 percent of the students write only once per month or less (39.6 percent, once per semester).

The reasons, why members the STC use, can be explained as follows (see Figure 9). More than 71 percent of the respondents write that they use the InPUD-community to ask subject-specific questions about courses. They do this often (once a week and more). The point is that a student can submit *individual* questions and discussion items.

Approximately two-thirds of the students use the STC as follows: sharing information about lectures and tutorials or other meetings, solving exercises online collaboratively, learning to handle different opinions and asking something about exercises. More than half of the members use InPUD for preparing for examinations, exchanging knowledge and information with others, helping others and asking organizational issues regarding study management and courses. Less than 40 percent use the STC for communicating

Figure 8. Frequency of reading and writing activities

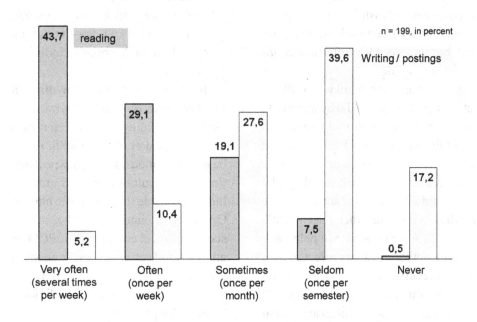

Figure 9. Frequency of different types of uses in the categories very often and often; (100 percent is per row. The answers "sometimes", "seldom" and "never" are not presented.)

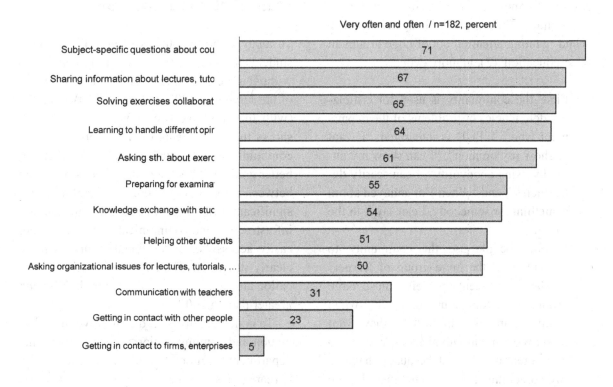

with teachers, getting in contact with other people or firms and enterprises (possible future employers). It does not mean that the students do not do such activities but they do it less often and probably outside the community.

An open question asked in detail why InPUD-members actively participate, and why they write contributions online for the community (question No. 9). Most of the answers are "I ask uncleared questions", and "I need answers or solutions". Some interviewees also mentioned that they like to help other students; "I help other students since I hope they will help me later, when I need help", "that's the sense of a community, we help each other", and "only active members affect active, vivid forums". Other interviewees did like the opportunity to get in contact with others at unusual time slots ("direct contact possibilities at unusual time in the night"), and stress the anonymity: "because of the anonymity, I can ask 'stupid' questions". During the data analysis of the open questions, two new reasons for active contribution were founded. These are 'criticizing deficiencies' (1) and 'gaining attention out of huge groups in higher education' (2), in more detail:

- First, the community is used for criticizing deficiencies or problems of the department where InPUD is integrated: "I want to show my opinion", "I can show my anger by using anonymity", I can scarify deficiencies", and "When I'm annoyed about something or somebody, I can say it in the forum".
- Second, people use the community to get out from the huge group of learners in classes. Students perceive those large groups as anonymous mass. So, when writing something in InPUD, they want to show their individual faces, and try to gain attention: "I post because I have to say something", and „Sometimes, I even want to say something". Some community members stressed especially the second

mentioned factor of awareness: "I think the professor will be aware of me when I'm active in InPUD. So, I'm not just a number for him but become an individual".

It is interesting that anonymity has a double function. Because of the anonymity, some students use the community to show their anger or to reveal aspects they do not agree with. In case it would be not anonymous, students expect negative sanctions or difficulties (e.g., bad grade) – although, highly probable this is not true but they expect it. On the other hand, some other members use the socio-technical community InPUD to gain more attention and getting out of the anonymity of large groups by saying something. By participating, some members expect their individual faces will be perceived by others.

Hypothesis: an STC Helps Students to Organize the Own Study Better Than Without

To analyze the hypothesis, if an STC supports students to organize their own study better than without a socio-technical community, the means of the surveys in 2002 (before InPUD) and 2009 (with InPUD) have been investigated. Table 5 shows the assessments of the information and communication structures that get a significantly better grade in 2009 than 2002. The comparison between the surveys in 2002 and 2009 indicates significant differences. In 2009, the information infrastructure and communication space is more easily accessible, better findable, and is more clearly structured. The opportunities for participation and communication are more helpful and greater than in 2002.

To conclude, the STC did improve the information and communication structure within the department. In more detail, the students ranked ten categories. The main result is that the students assess seven of ten categories as being significantly better in 2009 than in 2002 (see Table 6).

Table 5. Significant mean in 2002 and 2009

Items	2002 (before STC) n=391		2009 (with STC) n=292		Effect size		
The information and communication supply at the Department is…	M	SD	M	SD	F	Partial eta-squared	Sig. level
V1 easily accessible	**2.8**	1.01	**1.6**	0,85	143.47	.256	.000 **
V2 helpful	**2.9**	0.87	**1.3**	0,71	310.15	.426	.000 ***
V3 complete	**3.0**	0.86	**2.8**	1,04	6.48	.015	.002 *
V4 findable	**3.1**	1.04	**2.4**	0,98	33.93	.075	.000 *
V5 clear structured	**3.2**	0.91	**2.1**	0,96	126.74	.233	.000 *
Scale (from V1 to V5)	**3.0**	0.66	**2.0**	0.69	182.81	.289	.000 **

***very strong effect / ** strong effect / * effect M => 1=strongly agree, 5=strongly disagree

In particular, the knowledge sharing about "when to attend what courses", who is responsible for what in the department", "how to combine lectures, tutorials, practical courses, examinations", "how to get in contact with other students" is significantly better assessed in 2009 than seven years ago.

One explanation for InPUD's success is the individualization of learning. Despite huge classes (e.g., more than 800 students at a lecture, about 2,000 enrolled students), me-centricity and individualization of the learners are supported very well by a socio-technical community. It helps to initiate social relations through a technical system.

Table 6. Significant different means in 2002 and 2009

Items	2002 (before STC) n=346		2009 (with STC) n=124		Effect size	
Information & communication supply at the department helps to find answers for the following items...	M	SD	M	SD	Partial eta-squared	Sig. level
V6 when to attend what courses.	**2.5**	0.92	**2.1**	1.19	.044	.000 *
V7 when to prepare for examinations.	3.0	0.99	2.9	1.26	.013	n.s.
V8 who is responsible for what in the department.	**3.1**	0.96	**2.6**	1.10	.063	.000 *
V9 how important a lecture is for my studies	3.1	0.94	2.9	1.29	.011	n.s.
V10 how to combine lectures, tutorials, practical courses, examinations.	**3.2**	0.92	**2.7**	1.24	.026	.000 *
V11 how to prepare for examinations.	3.3	0.99	3.1	1.32	.042	n.s.
V12 how to get in contact with other students.	**3.4**	1.04	**2.2**	1.19	.014	.000 *
V13 how many hours do I need to complete the course.	**3.4**	0.89	**3.0**	1.24	.016	.006 *
V14 when to expect some problems during my degree	**3.6**	0.87	**3.1**	1.28	.003	.000 *
Scale (V6, V8, V10, V12, V13, V14)	**3.2**	0.58	**2.6**	0.79	.121	.000 *

* effect / n.s. = no significant difference 1=strongly agree, 5=strongly disagree

Students can ask and receive answers about what *they* want to discuss, when they want to.

Probably, a technology-enhanced community fails if the socio-technical designers would not have included rules for facilitation, contribution, and awareness about what topic is off-topic (what will be deleted when off-topic). In addition, during the research-based design process, the central roles of the target group[3] have been integrated into the process. With the significant differences in 2002 and 2009, the study also confirms this modified *role-grounded* design-based research procedure (Jahnke, 2010).

CONCLUSION

This contribution described a longitudinal study (over seven years) about the quality of a Socio-Technical Community (STC) in higher education (HE), and studied the effects of knowledge sharing and informal learning over time. The main research question was if such an STC at a university support informal learning in HE over time. The study differentiated specific issues supported by an STC.

It was illustrated that a socio-technical community is an appropriate communication space for learners to manage their own studies better than without STC (RQ2). Furthermore, information acquisition and knowledge sharing have been improved effectively. An STC organize the "jungle of information" for learners (RQ3), and the access to information with a socio-technical community is better than without (RQ4). The students assess the following four items significantly better than in 2002: The STC helps its members to find solutions regarding…

- When to attend what courses,
- How to combine several courses,
- Who is responsible for what in the department, and
- How to get in contact with other students.

Regarding these items, the community is helpful and has changed the information exchange positively – at least from the perspective of the students. Thus, InPUD is an appropriate supporting structure. By using the community, students can find a way out of the information jungle.

However, the aspect of "completeness" is not included. This aspect could not be improved over time. The community has more information but not any information a user needs. In addition, regarding the item „how and when to prepare for examinations", the community does not help qualitative better than before (without the InPUD-community).

The main research question was, if an information and communication portal (which is a specific form of a designed learning environment) at a university supports informal learning? If yes, to what extent? (RQ1) The main conclusion is that such a socio-technical community is an appropriate platform for participation and communication in higher education. Although it is embedded into formal university structures, students can use the community when they want and ask what they need. Students can communicate about their problems and *go through* their studies in a qualitatively better way than before the STC's launch. The results confirm the hypothesis that a socio-technical community promotes informal learning in higher education.

One explanation is that a socio-technical community delivers opportunities for the individualization of learning in huge groups. The open design (InPUD is without special login, just an email is needed; low/no control by the university), the double function of the portal (information *and* communication), and the optional participation by keeping private identity but public access, foster the success of the socio-technical community. Its members can obtain information, can ask questions and can give answers when they want, and when they need support (success factors in more detail in Jahnke & Herrmann, 2006). The evolved communication is individually customized to the members' needs, and enables the participants to engage at their own and the others learning progresses actively. Such a portal (combination of Web 1.0 and Web 2.0 conditions) provides a better information exchange than without such an infrastructure, and creates communication spaces for supporting flexible, informal learning.

In spite of these positive results, the study has its limitations. First, we have shown that there have been positive developments between 2002 and 2009 but we do not know exactly if InPUD is solely responsible for these changes or if other factors have played a role (for example, new generation of students, changes from old-fashioned German *Diplom* to BA/MA degrees). For example, the website of the department got a new university corporate design in 2007 but without improving its content. Because of these other aspects, it is not possible to say InPUD made the difference *only*. But there are many clues and empirical evidences suggesting InPUD plays a big role and has a great influence. From the survey in 2009 (more than 90 percent use InPUD) and contact to faculty's members, we know that the InPUD portal was and is the main website the students use. In addition, the forum is the central online space the department has, and the communication is better assessed than without the discussion boards. This is also underpinned by our qualitative interviews (in more detail see Jahnke, 2010). Thus, InPUD has definitely had a positive impact. So, the evaluation indicates many important trends and tendencies that the STC has affected. InPUD has had something to do with the institutional change of an improved information infrastructure and communication space at the investigated university.

Secondly, the written questionnaire in 2002 was not online in contrast to 2009. Question No 5 (see Table 4) was too complex for the online questionnaire. Although we did five pre-tests, nobody pointed that problem out. Because it had a too complex structure in its online version, more than 100 people (of 345 people) skipped the questionnaire after question 5 of 24. Of course,

we tested what kind of people fulfilled the online questionnaire. Fortunately, we did not find any hints that just a specific group of people answered after question 5. So we argue that the assumption cannot be confirmed that only people who like InPUD fulfilled all 24 questions. A further research should study the question 5. We will compare the question in two settings: online as well as offline (written questionnaire).

To summarize, according to the evaluation from 2002 to 2009 – before launching the community and seven years later – the study gives significant differences. The case study pointed out some effects of an implemented socio-technical community in higher education as to: First, an STC makes it easier for a community member to obtain the relevant information that s/he needs at a given time. It can reduce the social complexity and information overload from the official organization. Second, an STC can be an appropriate communication space for learners since it supports me-centricity and individualize learning in large groups. Such a designed socio-technical community is a valuable platform for learning in higher education, and in particular it supports informal learning.

ACKNOWLEDGMENT

I would like to thank Volker Mattick, Karsten Lettow and the Faculty of Computer Science at the TU Dortmund University, Germany.

REFERENCES

Barr, R. B., & Tagg, J. (1995). From teaching to learning. A new paradigm for undergraduate education. *Change*, *27*(6), 13–25.

Berger, P., & Luckmann, T. (1967). *The social construction of reality*. London: Penguin.

Bryman, A. (2008). *Social research methods* (3rd ed.). New York: Oxford University Press.

Collins, A., & Halverson, R. (2009). *Rethinking education in the age of technology: The digital revolution and schooling in America.* New York: Teachers College Press.

Dohmen, G. (2001). *Informal learning. An international review about an unattended form of human being for lifewide learning.* Bonn: BMBF. Retrieved January 15, 2010, from http://www.bmbf.de/pub/das_informelle_lernen.pdf

Herrmann, Th., Loser, K.-U., & Jahnke, I. (2007). Sociotechnical walkthrough: a means for knowledge integration. *The Learning Organization, 14*(5), 450–464.. doi:10.1108/09696470710762664

Jahnke, I. (2006). *Dynamics of social roles at knowledge management. Socio-technical requirements for communities in organizations.* Wiesbaden, Germany: DUV.

Jahnke, I. (2009). Socio-technical communities – from informal to formal? In Whitworth, B., & De Moor, A. (Eds.), *Handbook of Research on Socio-Technical Design and Social Networking Systems* (pp. 763–778). Hershey, PA: IGI Global. doi:10.4018/978-1-60566-264-0.ch050

Jahnke, I. (2010). Dynamics of social roles in a knowledge management community. *Computers in Human Behavior, 26*(4).. doi:10.1016/j.chb.2009.08.010

Jahnke, I., & Herrmann, Th. (2006). Success factors for cultivating socio-technical communities from the role perspective. In Heinecke, A. M., & Paul, H. (Eds.), *Mensch und Computer im Strukturwandel* (pp. 103–113). Munich, Germany: Oldenbourg.

Jahnke, I., & Koch, M. (2009). Web 2.0 goes academia: Does Web 2.0 make a difference? *International Journal Web Based Communities, 5*(4), 484–500. doi:10.1504/IJWBC.2009.028085

Jahnke, I., Mattick, V., & Herrmann, Th. (2005). Inpud: Knowledge management for organizing study progress. *Journal Hochschuldidaktik, 16*(1), 13–16.

Jahnke, I., Terkowsky, C., Pleul, Ch., & Tekkaya, E. (2010). Online learning with remote-configured experiments. In *Proccedings of DeLFI.* Duisburg, Essen: Deutsche E-Learning Fachtagung Informatik.

Lave, J., & Wenger, E. (1991). *Situated learning. Legitimate peripheral participation.* Cambridge, UK: Cambridge University Press.

Palfrey, J., & Gasser, U. (2008). *Born digital. Understanding the first generation of the digital natives.* Philadelphia: Basic Books.

Preece, J., Abras, Ch., & Maloney-Krichmar, D. (2004). Designing and evaluating online communities: Research speaks to emerging practice. *International Journal of Web based Communities, 1*(1), 2-18.

Prensky, M. (2001). Digital natives, digital immigrants. *The Horizon, 9*(5). Retrieved June 7, 2009, from http://www.marcprensky.com

Reeves, T. C., Herrington, J., & Oliver, R. (2005). Design research: A socially responsible approach to instructional technology research in higher education. *Journal of Computing in Higher Education, 16*(2), 97–116. doi:10.1007/BF02961476

Shurville, S., O'Grady, T. B., & Mayall, P. (2008). Educational and institutional flexibility of Australian educational software. *Campus-Wide Information Systems, 25*(2), 74–84.. doi:10.1108/10650740810866576

Twenge, J. (2006). *Generation Me. Why today's young Americans are more confident, assertive, entitled and more miserable than ever before.* New York: Free Press.

Wang, F., & Hannafin, M. J. (2005). Design-based research and technology-enhanced learning environments. *Educational Technology Research and Development*, 5(4), 5–23. doi:10.1007/BF02504682

Wasson, B. (2007). Design and use of collaborative network learning scenarios: The DoCTA experience. *Journal of Educational Technology & Society*, 10(4), 3–16.

Watkins, K., & Marsick, V. (1992). Towards a theory of informal and incidental learning in organisation. *International Journal of Lifelong Education*, 11(4), 287–300. doi:10.1080/0260137920110403

Wenger, E., McDermott, R., & Snyder, W. M. (2002). *Cultivating communities of practice: A guide to managing knowledge*. Boston: Harvard Business School Press.

ENDNOTES

[1] Discussion about appropriate or non-appropriate distinction of formal, non-formal, or informal learning should be done at other places (Dohmen, 2001).

[2] Because of technical problems with the InPUD server in 2005, we have only webpage request statistics until February 2005. Fortunately, the InPUD forum was not affected by these problems.

[3] The target group is the group for whom an STC will be build. One question is: what are central or important roles? As pointed in Jahnke (2006), central roles depend on the viewpoint of a role owner, and therefore, central roles are relative. A designer should ask: What problem is the target group faced with, and what socio-technical design can help to solve the problems?

This work was previously published in The International Journal of Sociotechnology and Knowledge Development, Volume 2, Issue 4, edited by Elayne Coakes, pp. 18-38, copyright 2010 by IGI Publishing (an imprint of IGI Global).

Chapter 13
The Diverging Effects of Social Network Sites on Receiving Job Information for Students and Professionals

Bart Rienties
Maastricht University, The Netherlands & University of Surrey, UK

Dirk Tempelaar
Maastricht University, The Netherlands

Miriam Pinckaers
TNT post BV, The Netherlands

Bas Giesbers
Maastricht University, The Netherlands

Linda Lichel
Maastricht University, The Netherlands

ABSTRACT

An increasing number of students, professionals, and job-recruiters are using Social Network Sites (SNSs) for sharing information. There has been limited research assessing the role of individuals seeking a job and receiving information about job openings in SNSs. In this regard, do students, non-managers, and managers benefit from job offers when they are a member of SNSs such as Facebook or LinkedIn? How can differences in receiving information about job openings be explained by the strength-of-weak-ties and structural holes theorems? Results of an online survey among 386 respondents indicate that users of SNSs with more contacts are more likely to receive information about job openings than others. Most information about job openings was transmitted via LinkedIn to professionals. Regression analyses indicate that LinkedIn professionals with more links are more likely to receive information about a job opening. In contrast, the structural holes theory is not supported in this setting. The authors argue that Higher education should actively encourage and train students to use LinkedIn to enhance their employability. Finally, new generation graduates' use of technology for different tasks and with different people than professionals is considered.

DOI: 10.4018/978-1-4666-0200-7.ch013

Copyright © 2012, IGI Global. Copying or distributing in print or electronic forms without written permission of IGI Global is prohibited.

INTRODUCTION

The Internet revolution has changed many aspects of our lives, including the way we search for information (Jones, Johnson-Yale, Millermaier, & Pérez, 2008), communicate with relatives and friends (Raacke & Bonds-Raacke, 2008; Ross et al., 2009; Walther, Van Der Heide, Kim, Westerman, & Tong, 2008), and find new jobs (DeKay, 2009; Eckhardt, Von Stetten, & Laumer, 2009; Joos, 2008; Kluemper & Rosen, 2009). The introduction of Social Network Sites (SNSs) such as Facebook, LinkedIn and Myspace have attracted millions of users who have integrated SNSs into their daily practices (Joos, 2008; Ross et al., 2009; Techcrunch.com, 2009; Walther et al., 2008). Boyd and Ellison (2008, p. 211) define social network sites as "web-based services that allow individuals to 1) construct a public or semi-public profile within a bounded system, 2) articulate a list of other users with whom they share a connection, and 3) view and transfer their list of connections and those made by others within the system".

The majority of SNSs primarily serve social purposes or tasks and aim to connect with friends, relatives and acquaintances. Within *private SNSs* such as Facebook users share substantial amounts of private information (e.g. pictures), communicate and collaborate with each other on a regular basis (Lewis, Kaufman, & Christakis, 2008; Subrahmanyam, Reich, Waechter, & Espinoza, 2008) and use game/utility applications. In contrast, *professional SNSs* such as LinkedIn are primarily used for business purposes and aim to: 1) connect experts; 2) share information about, and collaborate on, business cases and work fields; and 3) exchange job and function related information (DeKay, 2009; Valkenburg, 2008). With the availability of new technology as SNSs, the social environment of people has changed, which is in line with Mumford's (2000) view that technology can be considered as both an artefact and a process. In other words, both private and professional SNSs have significantly influenced the sociotechnical systems (STS) of organisations and humans.

An increasing number of students, graduates and professionals are becoming aware of the role of their public profile in SNSs in their everyday life (Kluemper & Rosen, 2009; Lewis, Kaufman, & Christakis, 2008; Ross et al., 2009). For example, organisations are actively looking for profiles in SNSs in order to check and verify a job applicant (Kluemper & Rosen, 2009; Valkenburg, 2008). In addition, organisations are actively recruiting new staff based upon public profiles of students and graduates in LinkedIn (DeKay, 2009; Kluemper & Rosen, 2009). In a similar way, research has highlighted that virtual world applications might be a vital source to recruit IT-professionals in times of talent shortage (Weitzel, Eckhardt, & Laumer, 2009). However, in times of *jobs* shortage and given the current difficulties that graduate students have in finding a job (Woolcock, 2009), the competition and the need to differentiate is increasing among graduates and job seekers. As a result, an increasing number of students, non-managers and managers are actively constructing public profiles in SNSs in order to increase their attractiveness and visibility for organisations; it becomes a part of their job search strategy.

Though there are more Web 2.0 services and SNSs available that may be used for sharing information about job openings, we will focus our attention on two currently widely used SNSs, namely Facebook and LinkedIn. In particular, Fountain (2005) argues that the use of personal contacts in an online setting could be useful to obtain information about a job opening. Although we acknowledge the importance of recruiters and (online) recruitment (e.g., Lee, 2007; Parry & Tyson, 2008; Weitzel et al., 2009; Yakubovich & Lup, 2006), our purpose of this study is to focus mainly on users in SNSs. Therefore, the purpose of this study is to examine the following questions: 1) How does the design of professional SNSs and private SNSs influence the behaviour of SNS users (i.e. students, non-managers and managers) in their sociotechnical system?; 2) Under which conditions do SNS users receive information and knowledge about new job openings?

In the following sections we define the informal and formal social roles in SNSs. The importance of receiving information of job openings in SNSs is then reviewed. Afterwards, two important mechanisms – strength of weak ties hypothesis and structural holes – are presented and respective hypotheses are developed. Then methodology part is introduced, followed by the results and an extensive discussion thereof.

Informal and Formal Social Roles in SNSs

Although an increasing number of students, graduates and professionals use SNSs in their daily lives, limited research[1] has been conducted in order to assess under which conditions SNS users receive job-related information. Most SNS research focuses on privacy issues and information disclosure (Dwyer, Hiltz, & Passerini, 2007; Lewis, Kaufman, & Christakis, 2008), impression management (Krämer & Winter, 2008; Walther et al., 2008) and personality characteristics (Gangadharbatla, 2008; Ross et al., 2009). Other research has focused on temporal patterns of SNS use; the relationship between a user's profile structure and his articulation of friendship; and the generation of social capital by online tools such as Facebook (Ellison, Steinfield, & Lampe, 2007).

Within sociotechnical systems (STS) research, several conceptual frameworks are available to understand the human aspects of knowledge sharing (Coakes, 2000; Coakes & Coakes, 2009). In order to understand successful implementation of technology into organisations, the sociotechnical model of Coakes (2000) distinguishes four components, namely people, tasks, structure and technology. Hermann et al. (2007, p. 452) elaborate this model by arguing that a "sociotechnical

system requires the integration of knowledge between the stakeholders". STS research reveals that social relationships or *social roles* are important to understand processes within organizations. In particular, the formal (explicit) and informal (implicit) social roles of people in sociotechnical systems have a strong influence on behavior. For example, Jahnke (2010, 2009) found in an online community for students at Dortmund University that online groups evolve from an online trust-based community with more *informal* roles to an online community where social mechanisms support *formal* knowledge management processes. Such groups resemble SNSs by giving members, for example students, the opportunity to stay in touch with contacts who share the same problems, search for the same information and establish a kind of social proximity (Jahnke, 2010).

Fountain (2005, p. 1255) argued that "new communication technology might be helping people to find jobs ... because it facilitates the personal communication between friends and acquaintances that often provide information about jobs". Of course we expect that the reasons why users who register for a professional social network site like LinkedIn differ from those who register to a private social network sites like Facebook. In addition, the social roles (Jahnke, 2010) or emergent roles (Strijbos & De Laat, 2010) that are formally and informally expected in Facebook and LinkedIn are different. For example, most profile information on LinkedIn form in essence an online Curriculum Vitae that can be shared with network relations, while in Facebook members are formally and informally expected to share and discuss their hobbies, interests or political beliefs with friends. Given the professional nature of LinkedIn, we expect that more job offers will be transferred in LinkedIn than in Facebook. At the same time, students are more likely to be member of Facebook than of LinkedIn, while the reverse holds for professionals (Jones et al., 2008; Lewis, Kaufman, Gonzalez, Wimmer, & Christakis, 2008; Valkenburg, 2008).

Social Network Sites and Job-Related Information

Fountain (2005) recognised that the growing importance of the Internet has influenced job searcher's strategies: "[i]ncreasingly, workers and employers are turning to the Internet, both as an information source in itself and as a way to access and transmit information that could also be found offline" (Fountain, 2005, p. 1237). Job search strategies are commonly categorized into formal and informal ones (Granovetter, 1974). *Formal job search strategies* are those that use employment agencies and advertisements such as help wanted signs. In addition, the Internet allows a job searcher to find and apply for more job openings using online vacancy databases like Monster.com than with traditional methods, such as browsing a newspaper's vacancy section.

Informal job search strategies include the use of personal contacts, such as relatives, friends and co-workers who act as referrals and provide inside information on job openings. The job searcher typically meets these personal contacts in a context unrelated to the search for information about job openings. This informal strategy saves on search costs compared to making use of formal channels, in this way contributing to job-finding (Boxman & Flap, 2001). In particular, Fountain (2005) argues that the use of personal contacts or ties in online settings can be useful for job searchers. Facing a large audience and employing functional platforms the use of SNSs may contribute to reducing the cost of transmitting information for both job searchers and recruiters. Moreover, SNSs may provide bridges for job searchers to valuable embedded resources and to distant parts of their social networks containing unique and valuable job information (Fountain, 2005). Available research on these SNSs suggests that most of these SNSs primarily support pre-existing social relationships (Ellison et al., 2007; Subrahmanyam et al., 2008). DiMaggio and colleagues (2001, p. 17) suggest

"that the Internet sustains the bonds of community by complementing, not replacing, other channels of interaction". Relationships in SNSs may be weak but typically there is some offline element among SNS relationships (Boyd & Ellison, 2008). In our article, the term job searcher refers to both passive job searchers, who have a job but might be interested in receiving information about job openings, as well as active job searchers who are actively seeking new employment.

Strength-of-Weak-Ties Hypothesis

The first mechanism that might explain why certain SNS users receive more information about job openings than others is the strength-of-weak-ties hypothesis. Granovetter (1974) found that the strength of a social relationship or tie affects job searchers by the amount and quality of information about job openings available to them. The strength of a tie can be defined as a combination of the amount of time spent together, the emotional intensity, the intimacy and the reciprocal services which characterize the tie (Granovetter, 1973). A tie is defined as weak when personal contacts see each other occasionally (Granovetter, 1974). Job searchers that use weak social ties, such as acquaintances or former colleagues, rather than strong social ties, such as close friends and family, are more effective in gathering and getting access to information on available jobs. The number of people who are potential recipients of job information is greater when weak ties are involved, which Granovetter (1973) calls the strength-of-weak-ties hypothesis. Such a weak tie can have a bridging function (Levin & Cross, 2004). A bridge is a line in a network which provides a unique path between different persons in different networks, through which important information like knowledge (Levin & Cross, 2004; Reagans & McEvily, 2003), new creative ideas (Perry-Smith, 2006), or a job opportunity (Granovetter, 1973) can be transmitted. Weak ties together with the interaction of a wide range of users might provide additional information and opportunities related to jobs. This expectation is expressed in the following hypothesis:

H1. SNS members who have received information about job openings via their SNS have a greater amount of weak ties in their SNS than SNS members who have not received information about job openings via their SNS.

Structural Holes

The second mechanism that might explain differences in receiving information about job openings is the degree to which users are in a structural hole position in their social network. Burt (1992) argues that individuals will gain more from social networks if they are able to position themselves on either side of a bridge that is in-between particular social networks. A bridge can be seen as a hole in the structure of the social networks and is therefore called structural hole. Thus, structural holes are those places in between networks where other relations or bridges are absent (Gargiulo & Benassi, 2000; Katz, Lazer, Arrow, & Contractor, 2004; Reagans & McEvily, 2003). Such a SNS user will be a broker between networks and will gain power in the sense that the broker is able to gain non-redundant information about job openings from multiple networks. According to Burt (2005, p. 11) "counts of relationships will never measure network value. The value of a relationship is not defined inside the relationship; it is defined by the social context around the relationship". These relationships form a social structure and this "social structure defines a kind of capital that can create for individuals or groups an advantage in pursuing their ends" (Burt, 2005, p. 5). Burt (1992) mentions three advantages of information benefits to a broker, namely: 1) access to less redundant and overlapping information; 2) early access to new information and; 3) the ability to

move ideas and information between groups. The degree to which a person is in a structural hole in his/her network and can act as a broker can according to Burt et al. (1998) be measured by the network entrepreneur personality index which will be described further in the method section. This brings us to our second hypotheses:

H2. SNS members who did receive information about job openings via their SNS have a higher network entrepreneur personality index than SNS members who have not received information about job openings via their SNS.

METHODS

Questionnaire Design

To the best of our knowledge, no research into the effects of SNSs on receiving information about job openings has been conducted before. In particular, no research has specifically compared how people share information about job openings in private and professional SNSs. Therefore, we developed our own measurement instrument in the format of a self-administered online questionnaire. Three steps were taken in order to create a reliable instrument. First of all, the measurement questions were drafted and transformed in questionnaire questions and alternative answer options were provided. The first draft version was distributed to three assessment experts and seven users of SNSs as recommended by Blumberg et al. (2005). Based upon their comments, the questionnaire was adjusted. Second, the measurement question sequence was arranged using so-called pre-determined routings and conditional jumps. By the use of special routing and conditional jumps, the respondents were guided through an adaptive questionnaire. This implies that the questions presented to each respondent are selected adaptively in order to minimize the number of answers needed and the chance of frustration associated with a long questionnaire.

For example, if a respondent indicated that (s) he is not member of a SNS, (s)he could fill in a maximum of 20 questions. When a respondent indicated to be a member of Facebook but did not receive any information about job openings, the respondent was provided with 23 questions, etc. Finally, the respondents received feedback about their network entrepreneur personality index (see below) and had a chance to win an I-Pod as an encouragement to fill in the questionnaire.

SNS Membership

Respondents had to indicate whether they were registered to a SNS. In the questionnaire, 2*2 possible SNSs sites were listed, namely Facebook and SNSs similar to Facebook such as Hyves or MySpace (Private SNSs), and LinkedIn and SNSs similar to LinkedIn such as Xing or Plaxo (Professional SNSs). Given that our research is focusing only on the two most frequently used private and professional SNSs, in the remainder of this article we will only use data gathered about Facebook and LinkedIn.

DEPENDENT VARIABLE: RECEIVING INFORMATION ABOUT JOB OPENINGS

The variable "receiving information about job openings" is measured by four measurement questions. First, for each SNS selected by the respondent, the question was posed whether the respondent received information about a job opening (e.g., "Did you ever receive information about a job opening via Facebook?"). Second, if a respondent indicated to have received information about a job opening, (s)he was asked from which of the four SNSs the respondent received most information about a job opening. Third, the frequency of receiving information about job openings was asked (once a year; more than once a year but less than once a month; once a month;

once a week; more than once a week). Fourth, the respondent had to indicate the total number (1-5) of contacts that offered information about a job opening.

INDEPENDENT VARIABLE 1: STRONG-AND-WEAK TIES

For each chosen SNS, respondents were asked two questions about the approximate number of contacts in their respective SNSs (e.g., 'How many contacts do you have in your LinkedIn account approximately?') and with how many of those contacts they thought to have a close relationship (i.e. 'With approximately how many of your LinkedIn contacts do you think you have a close relationship?; Please fill in an approximate number'). Tie strength was measured by the approximate number of contacts and with how many of those contacts respondents thought to have a close relationship, as was done by Tufeckci (2008). The number of weak ties was computed by subtracting the number of close ties from the total number of contacts.

INDEPENDENT VARIABLE 2: NETWORK ENTREPRENEUR PERSONALITY INDEX

Structural holes were measured by an instrument developed by Burt et al. (1998) called the network entrepreneur personality index. This instrument was derived from a study among 51 MBA-students who filled in a 252 statements long questionnaire developed by the Management Research Group (MRG), which was afterwards reduced to ten items. According to Burt (2005, p. 48), "[t]he items were selected because they best distinguished MBA students with closed networks from MBA students whose networks spanned structural holes". All ten bipolar items contain a positive and a negative personal quality[2]. The sum of the answers to the ten questions results in a score on the network entrepreneur personality index, which defines a probability of the respondent having an entrepreneurial network (i.e. including structural holes) or a propensity to brokerage. Respondents with a score under 5 points have a probability of less than 0.5 to have a contact network rich in structural holes. Those with a score of 5 and above have a propensity of 0.5 or more to own a contact network rich in structural holes. The study of Burt et al. (1998, p. 79) showed that "the average respondent made 3.9 positive choices. The scores ranged from 0 to 9, with a 2.1 standard deviation".

Research Subjects and Sampling Method

The web link to the questionnaire was transmitted electronically via several online services available on SNSs of the authors of this article. Contacts of the authors were requested to transmit the link of the questionnaire to their own contacts as well (i.e., snowball method). In addition, the questionnaire was posted on seven community websites, namely: 1) the LinkedIn community Maastricht University (7238 members); 2) LinkedIn Surfspace Network (375 members); 3) LinkedIn E-learning 2.0 (1455 members); 4) LinkedIn community Higher Education Research-network (80 members); 5) Facebook community Mondo Assicurativo (257 members); 6) Facebook community Corvinus University of Budapest (1,478 members); 7) Facebook community Universiteit Maastricht (698 members). The data collection could not be controlled in the sense of manipulation of variables, thus this study employs an ex post facto design (Blumberg et al., 2005). After filling in the questionnaire, all respondents received a thank-you email for their participation and a request to forward the questionnaire to others. All respondents were assured that the information given would be kept confidential.

In total 508 respondents started filling out the questionnaire, of which 409 respondents fully completed the questionnaire (80.4%). Those who were not a member of any SNS or only member of another SNS than Facebook or LinkedIn were removed, leading to 392 respondents of Facebook and/or LinkedIn from which we have complete records. Given the small number of unemployed (6) in our database, we removed them from our analysis. 81 of 386 respondents were students, 88 respondents worked as blue- or white collar worker in a non-management position (labelled as non-managers), while 217 respondents had a management or executive position or were self-employed (labelled as managers). 51.9% of students, 17% of non-managers and 22.1% of managers had a bachelor diploma as highest degree. 29.6% of students, 60.2% of non-managers and 50.7% of managers had a master degree as highest degree. Finally, 12.5% of non-managers and 25.3% of managers had a post-graduate degree such as PhD or MBA. The mean age in the sample was 34.09 years (SD = 10.03). The sample consists of 204 men (52% of the sample) and 182 women. Moreover, 61% have a Dutch nationality, followed by the American (9%), Belgian (8%) and German (6%) nationality and other nationalities (16%). Dutch SNS users are overrepresented, which is not surprising given that the social networks of the authors are mainly Dutch.

RESULTS

In our sample, 175 respondents are member of both Facebook and LinkedIn. 79 SNS users only have a Facebook account, while 138 respondents are exclusively registered to LinkedIn. 88% of the students, 75% of non-managers and 53% of managers in our sample are registered to Facebook, while 49% of the students, 82% of non-managers and 90% of the managers are registered to LinkedIn. In other words, (non)-managers are significantly more likely to be registered for LinkedIn, while students are significantly more likely to be registered for Facebook, as is illustrated in Table 1, describing the outcomes of an ANOVA analysis.

313 LinkedIn members maintain on average 104.37 contacts in their account (SD = 147.21) with on average around 27.28 close contacts (SD = 36.03). Managers have significantly more contacts and weak ties in LinkedIn than non-managers and students again using an ANOVA analysis. The 254 Facebook members have on average 139.64 (SD = 150.35) contacts, of whom 27.13 (SD = 42.66) are considered as close contacts. These results are in line with the findings of Lewis et al. (2008). Furthermore, students have significantly more contacts and weak ties in Facebook than non-managers and managers. No significant differences are found with respect to network entrepreneurial personality index when comparing managers, non-managers and students. Finally, of the 143 respondents who received information about a job opening by contacts, 17 respondents did so via their Facebook account and 126 respondents received information about a job opening via LinkedIn. In 88% of the cases of receiving information about job openings, it happened once a month or less. In total, 362 times information about a job opening was offered to 143 respondents, implying that most respondents received information about job openings by two

or more SNS contacts (M= 2.50, SD=1.34). In addition, 18 (22%) students received a job offer via SNS, while 29 (33%) of non-managers and 92 (42%) of managers received a job offer via a SNS, which signals a significant difference, resulting from an ANOVA analysis.

The results in Table 2 indicate that the average number of weak contacts of SNS members who received information about a job opening is significantly larger than the number of weak contacts for those who did not receive information about a job opening using an independent sample t-test. In addition, there is a significant difference in the number of weak contacts between LinkedIn members who received information about a job opening and those who did not. However, no significant difference is found for Facebook users. So we can infer that SNSs (in general) and LinkedIn members (in particular) who receive information about a job opening have more weak contacts in their online social network than those who did not receive job information. Furthermore, there is a significant difference between the network entrepreneur personality index for SNS members who received information about a job opening and those who did not. LinkedIn members and Facebook members who have received information about a job opening score significantly higher

Table 1. Descriptive statistics of SNS membership, network contacts and information about a job opening

	Students	Non-Manager	Manager	F
LinkedIn Membership (in %)	49.38	81.81	89.86	35.064**
Facebook Membership (in %)	87.65	75.00	52.53	20.287**
Contacts in LinkedIn	63.77	78.14	120.29	3.882*
Contacts in Facebook	184.07	120.72	122.45	4.360*
Weak contacts in LinkedIn	41.55	57.04	91.37	3.473*
Weak contacts in Facebook	149.35	94.50	99.55	3.975*
Close contacts in LinkedIn	22.23	21.10	29.23	1.839
Close contacts in Facebook	34.72	26.23	22.50	1.801
Network Entrepreneur Personality Index	5.75	5.52	5.62	0.570
Job information received (in %)	22.22	32.95	42.39	5.554**

on the network entrepreneur personality index than those who did not receive job information. Overall, we conclude that there are significant differences in the number of weak ties and network entrepreneur personality index scores for SNS and LinkedIn members who receive information about a job opening and those who did not, finding preliminary support for hypothesis 1-2.

When we distinguish students, non-managers and managers who received information about a job opening from those who did not in Table 3, the fact that the overall relationships carry over to LinkedIn, but not to Facebook, does not come at a surprise. As expected, there are strong differences in SNS characteristics between members of Facebook and LinkedIn with regard to using the SNS for exchange of information about a job opening. For students and professionals alike being member of LinkedIn is positively related to receiving job information, while being member of Facebook does not have any effect. For non-managers and managers having more contacts in LinkedIn is positively related to receiving job information. Furthermore, students and professionals with more weak ties in LinkedIn are significantly more likely to receive job opening information than students who have less weak

ties or who are not connected in LinkedIn. Finally, managers and non-managers who receive information about a job opening score significantly higher on the network entrepreneurial personality index than managers and non-managers who do not receive job information.

The correlation matrix in Table 4 indicates that there is a positive correlation between (total) received information about job openings and the number and type (close, weak) of connections within a SNS, when we analyze aggregate data, which is data of both SNSs together. The network entrepreneur personality index is positively correlated with receiving information about job openings but not correlated with the amount of received job opening information. Table 4 indicates that correlations of close contacts with receiving information about job openings are even stronger than correlations of weak contacts. This is a somewhat counterintuitive finding in the light of the strength-of-weak-ties hypothesis, but may be an artefact of the aggregation over both SNSs: LinkedIn members distinguish from Facebook members both in the share of weak and close contacts, and in the intensity of job information exchange. Therefore, a separate analysis for LinkedIn is called for.

Table 2. Weak ties and network entrepreneur personality index and receiving information about a job opening

	Job info received		No job info received		t-test	d-value
	M	SD	M	SD	difference	
Weak contacts[1]	143.75	133.33	107.05	156.66	2.347*	**0.25**
Weak contacts LinkedIn	108.96	118.92	52.45	135.61	3.840**	**0.47**
Weak contacts Facebook	104.23	124.24	116.26	135.62	-0.680	
Network Entrepreneur Personality Index score	5.95	1.28	5.44	1.44	3.505**	**0.37**
Personality Index score LinkedIn	6.11	1.23	5.47	1.35	2.908**	**0.50**
Personality Index score Facebook	5.83	1.30	5.43	1.48	2.087*	**0.26**

Independent sample T-test (2-sided) and Cohen d-value of Job offer received (n=143) vs. No Job information received (n=245)

[1] Maximum number of contacts of registered SNS

**Coefficient is significant at the 0.01 level (2-tailed).

*Coefficient is significant at the 0.05 level (2-tailed).

Table 3. Comparison of receivers of information about a job opening and non-receivers

	Students	Non-Manager	Manager
LinkedIn Membership (in %)	2.832**	2.578*	3.904**
Facebook Membership (in %)			
Contacts in LinkedIn		3.414**	3.061**
Contacts in Facebook			
Weak contacts in LinkedIn	2.683*	3.205**	2.304*
Weak contacts in Facebook			
Close contacts in LinkedIn	2.272*	2.285*	4.357**
Close contacts in Facebook			
Network Entrepreneur Personality Index		1.756†	2.681**

ANOVA F-value of job-info received vs no job-info received with students (N= 81), non-managers (n=88), and managers (n=217)
**Coefficient is significant at the 0.01 level (2-tailed).
*Coefficient is significant at the 0.05 level (2-tailed).
† Coefficient is significant at the 0.10 level (2-tailed).

Table 4. Correlations of information about job openings received, strong and weak ties and personality index

	M	SD	1	2	3	4	5
1. Job information received	0.37	0.48					
2. Total job info received	2.50	1.34	-0.14*				
3. Total contacts	154.23	166.64	0.26**	0.28**			
4. Weak contact	120.41	149.46	0.20**	0.25**	0.95**		
5. Close contacts	34.53	44.16	0.31**	0.29**	0.68**	0.50**	
6. Personality Index	5.63	1.40	0.18**	-0.07	0.08	0.06	0.09*

**Pearson correlation coefficient is significant at the 0.01 level (1-tailed).
*Pearson correlation coefficient is significant at the 0.05 level (1-tailed).

When conducting a regression analysis of LinkedIn members only with the amount of job-information received by a SNS-user as dependent variable, the independent variables close ties (b = 0.20) and weak ties (b = 0.18) predicts the amount of received information about job openings in a statistically significant manner. The structural holes hypothesis is rejected in our sample. Finally, when distinguishing between students, non-managers and managers, we find again that neither tie-strength nor network entrepreneurial personality index predicts the amount of received information about job openings for students. For non-managers, weak-ties (b = 0.44)

significantly predict receiving information about job openings, while close ties do not predict receiving information about job openings. In contrast, for managers it is primarily close ties (b = 0.27) and not weak ties that predict the amount of received information about job openings.

DISCUSSION

An increasing number of students, non-managers and managers are using SNSs like Facebook and LinkedIn to share and search for social, private and work-related information. In this research we addressed the question how the different sociotechnical designs of Facebook and LinkedIn influence knowledge sharing between people. Furthermore, this research tried to assess whether users of SNSs differ in receiving information about job openings and what the underlying conditions for receiving job information are for students, non-managers and managers. Despite the increasing popularity of SNSs, limited research has been done in order to assess the role of SNSs on receiving information about a job opening. We found that the type of SNS membership significantly influences whether or not to receive job information. As expected, most information about job openings is provided via the professional SNS of LinkedIn to managers. In contrast, being a member of a SNS like Facebook does not significantly contribute to receiving information about job openings. Probably the different purposes of the SNSs and the expected formal and informal social roles of members of the different SNSs are two reasons for this difference.

In line with sociotechnical theory, the actual use of technology (i.e., Facebook, LinkedIn) in our study depends on the interaction between people, tasks, processes and its environment. Facebook is primarily designed to keep in contact with friends and share private news, interests and comment on each other's daily live. LinkedIn is primarily designed for keeping in contact with social networks of business contacts and share new business or career opportunities. In addition, professionals are more likely to use LinkedIn, while Facebook is primarily used by students. This can be explained by the original reason of existence of Facebook, namely to interconnect university students (Boyd & Ellison, 2008). But this can also be explained by the fact that Facebook members want to meet personal and social needs: to keep in touch with old and current friends and to make new friends (Raacke & Bonds-Raacke, 2008). Given that more students primarily use Facebook (88%) rather than LinkedIn (49%), it may appear

that students should rather use LinkedIn if they want to receive information about a job opening. However, the social networks of professionals are probably more developed in terms of quality and diversity. Students who are member of LinkedIn are twice as likely as Facebook-members to receive information about job openings, but nonetheless the percentage of students receiving job information via a SNS is significantly lower than that for non-managers and managers. Since students are the professionals of the future, higher education institutions cannot start early enough by training and facilitating students in joining professional SNSs and building their online profile and (future) network. At the same time, organisations have to be aware that the young generation uses Facebook and LinkedIn in a different manner than their professionals within their organisation.

In this article, we also looked at the underlying mechanisms that may explain why some SNS users receive more information about job openings than others. In line with Granovetter (1974), we expected that SNS members with more weak SNS contacts will receive more information about job openings. From the results we can infer that LinkedIn members who receive job information have more weak ties in their online social network than those who do not receive job information. These outcomes are in line with the findings of Granovetter (1974), namely having more weak ties is the prime predictor of receiving job information, with having more strong ties playing no more than a secondary role. However, subsequent regression analysis indicates that having more weak ties does not per se lead to more information about job openings. An interesting finding is that the strength-of-weak-ties hypothesis seems to hold for non-managers, thus providing partial support for hypothesis 1. However, for managers it is mainly having more close ties that is relevant for receiving more job information, which contradicts hypothesis 1. A possible explanation of this unexpected difference may be that non-managers have a less well-developed social network than managers. In line with social capital theorem (Lin, Burt, & Cook, 2001), managers not only have significantly more links in LinkedIn than non-managers in our sample, but they also have more close links. A reasonable explanation may be that these close links of managers will also hold more powerful positions with more valuable resources in their social network than those of non-managers.

Although we expected that being a structural hole in a social network (Burt, 1992) is beneficial for receiving job information, we had to reject hypothesis 2. The results of this study indicate that SNS members who receive job information have a higher score on the network entrepreneur personality index than those who do not receive job information. However, subsequent regression analyses indicate that the network entrepreneur personality index does not adequately explain why some people receive job information while others do not. A possible explanation for this may be that the reduced 10-item measurement of network entrepreneur personality index of Burt et al. (1998) is suitable for distinguishing structural holes among MBA-managers, but not for more heterogeneous groups of SNS-users. The average scores among our 386 respondents on this personality measure are namely higher than those found by Burt et al. (1998), and have larger standard deviations.

Limitations and Further Research

Although this study was developed and designed with the highest care, there are several limitations. First, the sample of this research is obtained via nonprobability sampling. By first sending the questionnaire to other users of SNSs of the authors' social network as well as to several general network lists, we afterwards made use of the snowball method. The problem of a nonprobability sample is that it is arbitrary and subjective; each member does not have a known non-zero chance

of being included (Blumberg et al., 2005). This means there is a chance participants share the same demographic group or professional domain. This is for example reflected in the fact that the largest part of the sample is Dutch. However, despite the fact that via this sampling method only a snapshot of SNS-users was taken, it seems to resemble the typical user groups of SNSs (Lewis, Kaufman, Gonzalez et al., 2008). A second limitation is that we focussed only on LinkedIn and Facebook usage, while there are hundreds of SNSs, each with different purposes (Boyd & Ellison, 2008; Lewis, Kaufman, Gonzalez et al., 2008). However, Facebook and LinkedIn are currently the largest private and professional SNSs. We encourage other researchers to use our questionnaire to assess the design and the impact of local SNSs on receiving job information. Future research should specifically address the formal and informal social roles and the types of relationships between providers and receivers of job information. For example, what kind of roles do organisations expect graduates to perform in SNSs. Furthermore, the role of recruiters and recruitment strategies of companies and organisations need to be taken into account (Eckhardt et al., 2009; Kluemper & Rosen, 2009; Weitzel et al., 2009). Finally, it will be interesting to analyze the type of relations with the providers and receivers of job information.

While most recent research on SNS focussed on descriptive analyses of characteristics of SNSs and SNS users such as Facebook or MySpace, this study investigated the role of the social network on receiving job information via SNSs for students, non-managers and managers. Based on these findings, we can conclude that SNSs add value for particularly LinkedIn professionals who are actively or passively searching for jobs. Higher Educational Institutes should encourage their students and graduates to actively use LinkedIn. As job recruiters and firms are actively looking for excellent graduates in LinkedIn (Eckhardt et al., 2009; Kluemper & Rosen, 2009; Valkenburg,

2008), offering a short training programme for students how to increase the attractiveness of a LinkedIn profile for students may be a worthwhile investment. This training can for example be integrated in a professional development course for students or as a short online training course. Alternatively, Higher Educational Institutes can encourage their staff to actively use LinkedIn and stimulate their students to do the same. Overall, we conclude that value of SNS is mainly added through the number of close and weak tie contacts. However, we think that there is much more hidden in the phenomenon of social network sites.

ACKNOWLEDGMENT

We would like to thank the three anonymous reviewers for their elaborate and constructive feedback. Furthermore, we would like to thank the audience of EDINEB 2009 in Baltimore for their suggestions for improvement of our first draft.

REFERENCES

Blumberg, B., Cooper, D., & Schindler, P. (2005). *Business Research Methods* (9th ed.). New York: McGraw-Hill.

Boxman, E., & Flap, H. (2001). Getting Started: The influence of social capital on the start of the occupational career. In N. Lin, R. Burt, & S. K. Cook (Eds.), *Social Capital: Theory and Research* (4th ed., pp. 159-184). New Brunswick, NJ: Transaction publisher.

Boyd, D., & Ellison, N. (2008). Social Network Sites: Definition, History, and Scholarschip. *Journal of Computer-Mediated Communication, 13,* 210–230. doi:10.1111/j.1083-6101.2007.00393.x

Burt, R. S. (1992). *Structural Holes*. Cambridge, MA: Harvers University Press.

Burt, R. S. (2005). *Brokerage and Closure: An introduction to Social Capital* (1st ed.). New York: Oxford University Press.

Burt, R. S., Jannotta, J. E., & Mahoney, J. T. (1998). Personality correlates of structural holes. *Social Networks, 20*(1), 63–87. doi:10.1016/S0378-8733(97)00005-1

Coakes, E. (2000). Knowledge management: a sociotechnical perspective. In Coakes, E., Willis, D., & Lloyd-Jones, R. (Eds.), *The new SocioTech: graffiti on the long wall* (pp. 4–14). London: Springer Verlag.

Coakes, E., & Coakes, J. (2009). A Meta-Analysis of the Direction and State of Sociotechnical Research in a Range of Disciplines: For Practitioners and Academics. *International Journal of Sociotechnology and Knowledge Development, 1*(1), 1–52.

DeKay, S. (2009). Are Business-Oriented Social Networking Web Sites Useful Resources for Locating Passive Jobseekers? Results of a Recent Study. *Business Communication Quarterly, 72*(1), 101–105. doi:10.1177/1080569908330378

DiMaggio, P., Hargittai, E., Neuman, W., & Robinson, J. R. (2001). Social Implications of the Internet. *Annual Review of Sociology, 27,* 307–337. doi:10.1146/annurev.soc.27.1.307

Dwyer, C., Hiltz, S. R., & Passerini, K. (2007). *Trust and privacy concern within social networking sites: A comparison of Facebook and MySpace.* Paper presented at the AMCIS 2007, Keystone, CO.

Eckhardt, A., Von Stetten, A., & Laumer, S. (2009). Value contribution of it in recruiting: a multi-national causal analysis. In *Proceedings of the special interest group on management information system's 47th annual conference on Computer personnel research.*

Ellison, N. B., Steinfield, C., & Lampe, C. (2007). The benefits of Facebook 'friends:' Social capital and college students' use of online social network sites. *Journal of Computer-Mediated Communication*, *12*(4), 1143–1168. doi:10.1111/j.1083-6101.2007.00367.x

Fountain, C. (2005). Finding a Job in the Internet Age. *Social Forces*, *83*(3), 1235–1262. doi:10.1353/sof.2005.0030

Gangadharbatla, H. (2008). Facebook Me: Collective self-esteem, need to belong, and Internet self-efficacy as predictors of the iGeneration's attitudes toward social networking sites. *Journal of Interactive Advertising*, *18*(2).

Gargiulo, M., & Benassi, M. (2000). Trapped in Your Own Net? Network Cohesion, Structural Holes, and the Adaptations of Social Capital. *Organization Science*, *11*(2), 183–196. doi:10.1287/orsc.11.2.183.12514

Granovetter, M. S. (1973). The Strength of Weak Ties. *American Journal of Sociology*, *78*(6), 1360–1380. doi:10.1086/225469

Granovetter, M. S. (1974). *Getting a job: A study of Contacts and Careers* (1st ed.). Cambridge, MA: Harvard University Press.

Hermann, T., Loser, K. U., & Jahnke, I. (2007). The Socio-technical Walkthrough (STWT): a means for Knowledge integration. *The Learning Organization*, *14*(5), 450–464. doi:10.1108/09696470710762664

Jahnke, I. (2010). Dynamics of social roles in a knowledge management community. *Computers in Human Behavior*, *26*(4), 533–546. doi:10.1016/j.chb.2009.08.010

Jahnke, I., & Koch, M. (2009). Web 2.0 goes academia: does Web 2.0 make a difference? *International Journal of Web Based Communities*, *5*(4), 484–500. doi:10.1504/IJWBC.2009.028085

Jones, S., Johnson-Yale, C., Millermaier, S., & Pérez, F. S. (2008). Academic work, the Internet and U.S. college students. *The Internet and Higher Education*, *11*(3-4), 165–177. doi:10.1016/j.iheduc.2008.07.001

Joos, J. G. (2008). Social media: New frontiers in hiring and recruiting. *Employment Relations Today*, *35*(1), 51–59. doi:10.1002/ert.20188

Katz, N., Lazer, D., Arrow, H., & Contractor, N. (2004). Network Theory and Small Groups. *Small Group Research*, *35*(3), 307–332. doi:10.1177/1046496404264941

Kluemper, D. H., & Rosen, P. A. (2009). Future employment selection methods: evaluating social networking web sites. *Journal of Managerial Psychology*, *24*(6), 567–580. doi:10.1108/02683940910974134

Krämer, N. C., & Winter, S. (2008). Impression Management 2.0 The Relationship of Self-Esteem, Extraversion, Self-Efficacy, and Self-Presentation Within Social Networking Sites. *Journal of Media Psychology*, *20*(3), 96–106. doi:10.1027/1864-1105.20.3.106

Lee, I. (2007). An architecture for a next-generation holistic e-recruiting system. *Communications of the ACM*, *50*(7), 81–85. doi:10.1145/1272516.1272518

Levin, D. Z., & Cross, R. (2004). The Strength of Weak Ties You Can Trust: The Mediating Role of Trust in Effective Knowledge Transfer. *Management Science*, *50*(11), 1477–1490. doi:10.1287/mnsc.1030.0136

Lewis, K., Kaufman, J., & Christakis, N. (2008). The Taste for Privacy: An Analysis of College Student Privacy Settings in an Online Social Network. *Journal of Computer-Mediated Communication*, *14*(1), 79–100. doi:10.1111/j.1083-6101.2008.01432.x

Lewis, K., Kaufman, J., Gonzalez, M., Wimmer, A., & Christakis, N. (2008). Tastes, ties, and time: A new social network dataset using Facebook.com. *Social Networks, 30*(4), 330–342. doi:10.1016/j.socnet.2008.07.002

Lin, N., Burt, R. S., & Cook, K. S. (2001). *Social Capital: Theory and Research*. New Brunswick, NJ: Transaction Publisher.

Mumford, E. (2000). Technology and freedom: A socio-technical approach. In Coakes, E., Willis, D., & Lloyd-Jones, R. (Eds.), *The new SocioTech: graffiti on the long wall* (pp. 29–38). London: Springer Verlag.

Parry, E., & Tyson, S. (2008). An analysis of the use and success of online recruitment methods in the UK. *Human Resource Management Journal, 18*(3), 257–274. doi:10.1111/j.1748-8583.2008.00070.x

Perry-Smith, J. E. (2006). Social yet creative: the role of social relationships in facilitating individual creativity. *Academy of Management Journal, 49*(1), 85–101.

Raacke, J., & Bonds-Raacke, J. (2008). MySpace and Facebook: Applying the Uses and Gratifications Theory to Exploring Friend-Networking Sites. *Cyberpsychology & Behavior, 11*(2), 169–174. doi:10.1089/cpb.2007.0056

Reagans, R., & McEvily, B. (2003). Network Structure and Knowledge Transfer: The Effects of Cohesion and Range. *Administrative Science Quarterly, 48*(2), 240–267. doi:10.2307/3556658

Ross, C., Orr, E. S., Sisic, M., Arseneault, J. M., Simmering, M. G., & Orr, R. R. (2009). Personality and motivations associated with Facebook use. *Computers in Human Behavior, 25*(2), 578–586. doi:10.1016/j.chb.2008.12.024

Strijbos, J.-W., & De Laat, M. F. (2010). Developing the role concept for computer-supported collaborative learning: An explorative synthesis. *Computers in Human Behavior, 26*(4), 495–505. doi:10.1016/j.chb.2009.08.014

Subrahmanyam, K., Reich, S. M., Waechter, N., & Espinoza, G. (2008). Online and offline social networks: Use of social networking sites by emerging adults. *Journal of Applied Developmental Psychology, 29*(6), 420–433. doi:10.1016/j.appdev.2008.07.003

Techcrunch.com. (2009, July 6). Retrieved from http://www.techcrunch.com/2008/08/12/facebook-is-not-only-the-worlds-largest-social-network-it-is-also-the-fastest-growing/

Tufekci, Z. (2008). Grooming, gossip, facebook and myspace. *Information Communication and Society, 11*(4), 544–564. doi:10.1080/13691180801999050

Valkenburg, J. (2008). *Recruitment via LinkedIn: A practical guide for HR professionals, recruiters and employment market communication specialists*. The Hague, The Netherlands: Reed Business.

Walther, J., B., Van Der Heide, B., Kim, S.-Y., Westerman, D., & Tong, S. T. (2008). The Role of Friends' Appearance and Behavior on Evaluations of Individuals on Facebook: Are We Known by the Company We Keep? *Human Communication Research, 34*(1), 28–49. doi:10.1111/j.1468-2958.2007.00312.x

Weitzel, T., Eckhardt, A., & Laumer, S. (2009). A Framework for Recruiting IT Talent: Lessons from Siemens. *MIS Quarterly Executive, 8*(4), 175–189.

Woolcock, N. (2009, July 3). Fewer graduates securing jobs in the recession. *The Times*. Retrieved from http://www.timesonline.co.uk/tol/life_and_style/education/student/article6624351.ece

Yakubovich, V., & Lup, D. (2006). Stages of the Recruitment Process and the Referrer's Performance Effect. *Organization Science*, *17*(6), 710–723. doi:10.1287/orsc.1060.0214

ENDNOTES

1. The databases of Business Source Premier (EBSCO), Econlit, Reg. Business News, PsycARTICLES and Research Starters-Business were searched with simultaneous search keys 'social network', 'online' and 'job', which delivered a result list with 30 hits (only few of them being journal articles). These articles do not have the same topical focus as this article as they were addressing the emerging influence and importance of social network sites on recruitment processes or the use of SNSs by hiring managers. Five articles were pointing in the direction of an expected importance of SNSs for receiving information about a job opening.

2. For example, one question asked whether the respondent evaluated opportunities in terms of a) a chance to be in the position of authority, or b) long run implications. Respondents choosing a) over b) are associated with networks richer in structural holes than respondents choosing b) over a). As a result, they could gain 1 point (a positive choice) or no points (a negative choice).

This work was previously published in The International Journal of Sociotechnology and Knowledge Development, Volume 2, Issue 4, edited by Elayne Coakes, pp. 39-53, copyright 2010 by IGI Publishing (an imprint of IGI Global)

Section 4

Chapter 14
Performing Charlotte:
A Technique to Bridge Cultures in Participatory Design

Ann Light
Sheffield Hallam University, UK

Dorothea Kleine
University of London, UK

Royal Holloway
University of London, UK

Macarena Vivent
Universidad de La Frontera, Spain

ABSTRACT

This article describes the use of a performed persona as a device in cross-cultural design activities. The device serves to elicit knowledge and manage expectations in the context of participatory design workshops to explore the purpose and function of a tool for tracing the supply chain of ethical goods from producer to consumer. The use of the method with the staff of a wine producer in Chile is analyzed and the benefits and challenges identified in using the form live in workshops. The authors conclude that the device offers potential but also requires some confidence and skill to invoke.

INTRODUCTION

Let me introduce you to Charlotte... She is middle-aged, middle-class, from the middle of England, well educated by British standards and buys many *Fairtrade products. She is a mother of two and in fact it was her daughter who convinced her that ethical consumption is important. She is here to answer any questions you might have about the British market ...from her own perspective, of course!...*

DOI: 10.4018/978-1-4666-0200-7.ch014

Copyright © 2012, IGI Global. Copying or distributing in print or electronic forms without written permission of IGI Global is prohibited.

So began the first participatory design workshop session with Chilean wine producers in the meeting room at their bodega near Curicó in Chile, as part of the Fair Tracing (FT) project.

The rest of this article will explain how we came to be presenting consumer information to the winemakers of Chile, why we chose to present it in the shape of a performed persona and what effect it had on the work we were attempting to do together. To explain this, we will first introduce the wider FT project, before looking closely at the purposes of the workshop and how the persona served our ends. Finally we discuss hypothetical alternative approaches and look at the pros and cons of this kind of response in cross-cultural settings.

THE FAIR TRACING PROJECT (FT)

"Fair Tracing" (www.fairtracing.org) is a UK-led interdisciplinary project to research a bridging tool connecting producers with consumers in different global contexts. It aims to help bridge the divide between global North consumers and global South producers by using tracing technology to enhance trade. This includes, to some degree, bridging digital divides where some technologies are not available to producers. In particular, it is intended to give greater visibility to smaller producers in developing countries to help them make a presence in global markets. Indeed, the name of the tool acknowledges its conceptual link to the Fair Trade movement which supports producers in developing countries by guaranteeing them a minimum price for their produce and providing them with a social premium to invest in their businesses or communities. The tool is intended to increase and facilitate choice for both ethically minded traders and consumers who wish to understand and discuss the origin of their purchases. Of particular significance here is that small-scale producers in developing countries would be able to use a Fair Tracing (FT) tool to better understand the value

chains they operate in and distinguish their product offer by adding production information and communicating directly with consumers.

Material might include details of the economic and environmental costs of creation, the individual creator, their working environment and pay, through the steps of its transport to the point-of-sale to the consumer. Some aspects of this data transmission could be automated, while the creation of audio-visual and narrative material would be in the hands of the actors along the value chain and might include stories of corporate social responsibility, social or environmental impact and community.

The FT project was funded to research the building of such a bridging tool and to contribute understanding of its potential for implementation and use *in context*, beyond individual technological components[1], over a three year period till 2009. Part of the work engaged producers along representative value chains to explore their existing production and information gathering processes.

The wider FT project includes two producer case studies (see Kleine 2008, Chopra & Kundu 2008). Here we discuss a Chilean Fairtrade wine cooperative (validated by FLO, the Fairtrade Labelling Organizations International). In seeking producer groups for collaboration, we decided to build relations as full partnerships: bringing in producer representatives as informants to an investigation of feasibility and desirability and asking them to consult on ideas, partial prototypes[2] and potential uses. This involved setting up a collaboration agreement and including the partners in relevant parts of project discussions. It also involved commissioning a local academic researcher from a Chilean university who worked there on ICT and development projects, at the starting point of the chain to be the local link person. We looked closely at what we were asking of the producer partners in terms of time and energy and what the recompense might be, given that the tool was not going to materialize in the project's lifetime.

The team was also engaged in complementary consumer research: we surveyed and interviewed consumers (particularly those interested ethical shopping e.g., http://web4.cs.ucl.ac.uk/staff/C. Wallenta/fairtracingblog/?p=172), also conducting a literature review on the purchasing behavior of the British ethical shopper. Since the FT team represented part of the knowledge bridge in terms of connecting producers to users across cultures, this research was critical for shaping discussions about what the FT tool might become. Further, knowledge about Fairtrade wine consumers in Britain was valuable to producers, since data on wine consumers are expensive, data on Fairtrade consumers are limited and there is hardly any data on the cross-section. Information we gathered on consumers was made available to our producer partners in return for their time.

THE CHILEAN FIELD VISIT

The Chile project team made a first visit to the wine producer cooperative in late 2007. The design workshops took place during this visit. The agenda in visiting our partner producers on this trip included:

- To solicit their perspectives on the supply chain;
- To find out what media they use for record keeping, what software they use and their interest in the internet as a tool for marketing;
- To see the uses of the Fairtrade social fund and stimulate production of stories around local enterprise and social activities;
- To share any insights we had gained from conducting research with potential customers;
- To learn what the FT tool might offer.

Three researchers, social scientists skilled in different kinds of participatory practice, visited the wine producers: these were a Chilean sociologist with some spoken English and two British-based researchers; a bilingual geographer with a background in participatory action research and an HCI/social informatics specialist with experience in participatory design but limited capacity to understand Spanish.

Over two weeks, we interviewed key bodega personnel, several growers and their staff. We conducted interviews in their workspaces to glean incidental contextual information. Interviews lasted up to an hour and took place in Spanish, as most interviewees were either monolingual or felt more at ease in it. Subsequent design workshops were intended as a mechanism for collecting information and making sense of it with our partners at the bodega. The bodega employees, working between grape production and distribution and marketing, were ideally placed as collaborators with a wide understanding of the issues of production. We secured two sessions of nearly two hours when we could bring a majority of managers together (which included those responsible for logistics, oenology [creating the wine], IT, finance, quality assurance, the Fairtrade social programme and agricultural outreach). In a busy small business with staff stretched for time, this was a huge resource put at our disposal.

THE CONTEXT

The design workshops were a chance to consider the supply chain from grape to consumption and to reflect on the value of a tool which could link producers directly to consumers. Los Robles staff members know the bodega's production processes intimately, though at the time we visited the key position in marketing had been vacant for over half a year. We wanted the bodega staff to identify kinds of information they collect – or could collect with minimal overheads – to interest British people wanting to support Fairtrade and ethical production (the project's defined end point for the value chain). We considered that within the Chilean domestic market, the concept of "Fair Trade" was virtually unknown and environmental concerns were much less a priority. Thus, we wanted our producer partners to form judgments about tacit and recorded knowledge they collectively held at the bodega and whether this information would also interest a group of culturally-distinct consumers. In working with us, the team could learn more about the British market and consider consumer interests and thus be inspired to think of low-overhead relevant material. In listening to them, we would also benefit by hearing their perceptions of the value chain and learn of challenges in portraying it, including details of the politics along the chain.

We wanted to support our partner's thinking in design and marketing terms, drawing on our experience, while learning about everything from wine-making and local information flow, to the cultural context. But, in supporting their thinking, we wanted to avoid lecturing to them about the UK market and thus stifling ideas. Instead we wanted to stimulate discussion.

In addition, we wanted to work together to generate a sense of the functionality they would require in a tool that could connect up the value chain. Although this level of design thinking was quite abstract, it would be critical to ensuring that we kept the FT tool relevant to our producers' business needs. However, we had to accept we were largely without a common language and we were contending with the lively, informal style of these Chilean professionals, who knew each other well, were highly articulate, very committed to the business and thought nothing of all talking at once in animated Chilean Spanish.

THE TECHNIQUE

Working in new contexts, especially across cultures, often requires adaptation. Indeed, cross-cultural work can stimulate new methods of working, methods that are needed (Marsden 2007). We describe resulting developments in this spirit. Having recorded all our research engagements and captured video of the design workshops, we draw on our records here to analyze an emergent use of personas.

Before looking closely at what we did, we first introduce some background to working in a participatory way, with personas and with theatrical devices to show how other thinkers have influenced our work and raise some of the particular issues that affected working on a tool to bridge cultures and represent actors across the value chain.

The tool we discussed with the bodega staff had interesting parallels to our general work processes. Both bridged a cultural divide to produce greater understanding. To the bodega managers in the workshop, the FT team represented the consumer end, bringing with them localized knowledge of buying behavior in the UK. As facilitators, we also had a responsibility for keeping everyone in the discussions aware of consumer needs even as the producers articulated their own requirements and ideas for the tool. We had to recognize something of a paradox at a conceptual level: the partners' views of FT's activities would be highly determining – in that their thoughts would form the basis of everyone's understanding of the issues – but were also less informed by research into the behavior of the British consumer than the project team's. This gave the visiting team responsibility as the main owners of the research project to share insights from both ends of the bridge while nonetheless taking on board everything localized, situated and unique about the bodega's situation.

Robert Chambers describes a key moment in participatory action research as the step of "handing over the stick" to the group you work with (Chambers 1997). Chambers refers to the point where participants begin to use the stick to draw on the ground or write on the board and the researcher needs to step back. In designing a technology for bringing together consumers and multiple producers, many groups were entitled to share "the stick" to draw the system. However, because we were connecting these different groups, we needed to hand each group half the stick while stepping in for absent groups. The challenge was using a collaborative manner which sought to reduce power imbalances. As a business with a strong reliance on export, Los Robles needed the UK consumer, but the UK consumer might enjoy, but did not *need* Los Robles wine. The view of the consumer was therefore imperative to the producers. Our challenge was to manage this existing power asymmetry in a responsible and respectful way.

Issues of Cross-Cultural Work

We have drawn attention to the cultures that are being bridged in the work described here. On one side are *producers* in an emerging economy in Latin America where the spoken language is Spanish. On the other are *consumers* in Britain, one of the most industrialized countries in the world, where English is spoken and the generic history is one of lost empire, not freedom from colonization. We will not dwell on the attendant issues, such as different understandings of patriotism, the possibility of post-colonial power relations and the notions of identity and, thus, of appropriate representation that these factors contribute to, but allude to them as potentially significant sources of difference.

Communication is work that must be performed by individuals so that groups can engage in meaningful practices together. Doing this work 'across cultures' raises particular challenges. The potential for "miscomprehension" becomes greater across regional divides, differences in values, inconsistent priorities, etc. There is less common ground to depend on (Clark 1992), yet, until breaches become apparent, people may continue to assume that they understand each others' points of reference. The language barrier is in some ways less significant than the differences in cultural-historical experience. However, this too gives extra potential for mistaking meaning.

But cultures are not edifices with discernable boundaries. They dissipate and fragment if studied in context. Specific people can be viewed as intersections of many different influences (see also Irani et al 2008). To give an example, if we consider the IT manager at the Los Robles bodega, we see a youngish man with a new family and an interest in football. This makes him like billions of people round the world. He looked after several IT networks, computers and software packages that kept Los Robles functioning. Consequently, he had greater aspirations for the IT system at Los Robles than any other employee and felt the financial limitations and the indifference of others to the potential of software keenly. Yet, he was not given to using social media such as Facebook, taking more interest in the features of ICT that a systems administrator has need of. This made it easy for the HCI specialist to talk to him about certain aspects of the project – end-to-end thinking and back-end compatibility, for instance, and not others, such as Web2.0 interfaces. It was exactly the kind of conversation that one might have with a system administrator almost anywhere and raised similar issues. It was a professional conversation reflecting disciplinary concerns. In other words, if we look at the specific people we were dealing with, there were many points of intersection where perspectives overlapped and other points where they didn't, just as might be expected in any group. Part of our job was to find out where these intersections lay, both between individuals and between groups, and, further, to acknowledge how this interplayed with the existing nuances in the different disciplinary understandings among the incoming research team. We could then map out ways of working together that used our common ground as a bridge to understanding our differences better. This became a platform of shared inferences that allowed us to explore together how our ideas related to the British consumer.

Making it easier to work with our Chilean partners (and vice versa) was a shared experience of the professional world, interest in commerce and an appreciation for wine. Our partners were also at home with complex visual representations and a variety of types of IT interface. These well-educated professionals may have had more in common with us than they had with some of the workers in the vineyards around them.

Participatory Designing

The challenge of communicating has been discussed because it underpins collaboration, which is valuable, in turn, for offering a way to develop projects beyond the imposition of tools with no use or worth. We were keen to involve our partners in co-creating answers to our research questions to avoid delivering a solution to a group of people who didn't know they had a problem.

The solution-focussed approach suggests an absence of social as well as technological infrastructure and gives little credit to the values and perspectives of the supposed "beneficiaries". As Hickey & Mohan (2004) point out, in Development Studies, the failure of top-down, supply-driven – and one might add, often technocentric – development interventions gave rise to the movement developing participatory research and participatory practice. Predetermined and locally inappropriate technology was not taken up, and "recipients" of new technologies who had no say or stake in its creation had little interest in exploring its use.

It is also important to recognize that ideologies are embedded in new information and communication technologies. There are framing institutions with specific norms and expectations (Wajcman 2004), and the very systems are not neutral, but have cultural assumptions and political decisions written into them (Lessig 2006, and see Kleine 2007 and Light 2008 for a discussion in the FT context). If a system cannot be neutral, there needs to be a discourse with the users establishing their values and expectations and finding mechanisms of joint decision-making on the design of the system. Our initial work focused on creating a discourse on cultural frames of reference and social norms as well as practical local realities. We planned for an iterative design process with joint decision-making to take place over the following months.

But as mentioned earlier, we were not creating a local tool for use in one context (ie only by the bodega), as much participatory design work is conducted (Muller 2002). We were creating a bridge. This bridging singles the FT project out from many development projects. Not only are there deep epistemological and ontological issues involved in working across cultures, but we had to convey consumer information as an orientation for the producers. In other words, we were not interested in producers as an end point for the design but were engaging them in a design process for their consumers, with us. (Though the information provided by the emerging tool would then, in a further step, also be commercially relevant for producers.)

In general, we can contrast the development process for creating a generic tool with that for working in one context (e.g. Baecker & Greenberg 1995). It is possible to remain committed to a user-centred design process and produce either, but products that must work globally are developed by testing and customizing through a process of 'glocalisation' (see, for instance, a critique in Shen et al 2006) and, on the whole, only complex systems to be embedded into a small community of use are subject to full participatory design (PD). PD brings together user-experts on the ground with specialists who then design workable processes and tools together (Muller 2002), but much PD occurs only in academic contexts (see Dearden and Rizvi 2008, for an example of this within a development project). As a way of exploring the design space involved, the FT project decided to employ a PD approach as far as practicable. This would mean engaging closely with local people and seeing local conditions through their eyes. This raises certain new challenges, because PD was conceived to be used in well defined situations as Muller (2002) notes and our general wine value chain was amorphous in scope and in consistency. However, the tight band of staff at the Los Robles bodega was one well-defined unit with which to work collaboratively. That said, participation comes in many kinds and although we were keen to incorporate ideas from the producer about what we should research and why, we could only see the outcomes of our collaboration as informing the wider process rather than wholly defining it – because of the many bridges involved.

Nevertheless, as far as possible we embraced the participatory philosophy to be found in commentators like Chambers: seeking to move from top-down to bottom-up, from supply-push to demand-pull, from a focus on blue-prints to a focus on process. The goals were meant to be evolving and open, co-defined by the partners, who are actors in, not beneficiaries of development. Analytical assumptions involved holist, systemic thinking and methods were not standardized and universal, but diverse, local, and often spontaneously modified. Finally, the professional's interaction with local people is not instructing, but enabling and empowering (Korten 1984, Chambers 1997).

Using Personas

To facilitate the exchange of information and give the bodega staff speedy access to consumer thinking, we developed some personas to share with them.

Personas now have an august tradition of use in design. Cooper is credited with initiating the form (1999) and much has been written on them and the variety of contexts in which they are applied (Carroll 2000, Pruitt & Adlin 2006, Goodwin 2007). A quick definition would include that a persona is a composite of user research findings, operates in a scenario in certain ways determined by their characteristics and is used to personalize statistical data so that it speaks illustratively to designers and can be easily assimilated into the design process. Sometimes the development of personas is itself a collaborative process, sharing information among researchers, designers and clients. At other times, personas are handed over to others fully formed as part of narratives, or on small laminated cards, or in other forms such as cartoons, and so on. It is significant that they are communication devices so can be represented in many different ways.

Personas are not normally conceived as characters. Characters are not usually intended to be representative aggregations of characteristics, but instead strive for plausibility and depth. Nielsen (2005) criticized personas for being bland and stereotypical and proposed that they should be more like characters from fiction, but her workshop with Danish film scriptwriter and academic Mogens Rukov (workshop, Copenhagen, 2003) rather suggested the contrary and nicely illuminated the difference between characters designed to engage an audience and personas designed to inform a design process and not distract with incidental details. That said, successful personas do become like recognized people: the mark of a particularly successful deployment of personas may well involve everyone in the development process citing them, as, for instance: "Mary would like that." or "Dave would have a problem getting his fingers round those." The best personas work effectively as communication devices throughout development and also contain a good digest of data.

225

When we arrived in Chile, we already had three personas worked out for presenting our consumer research to the bodega staff. We intended to use this technique to convey an impression of who buys Fairtrade wine in the UK, what their priorities are and how ethical shoppers might use the FT tool. The Fairtrade Foundation/MORI weighted survey of over 2000 UK consumers showed that Fair Trade awareness is highest amongst the "AB1" group of well-educated and affluent consumers. Awareness is also highest among the 45-54 year olds (47 per cent). In line with other surveys on ethical consumption (Mintel 1999, 2001, 2004), women (42 per cent) are more likely than men (35 per cent) to be aware of the FLO mark. Nicholls & Opal summarize the survey data: "The idealized Fair Trade composite customer is a middle-aged, affluent and degree-educated woman" (2005:188).

Representative survey data was available for UK Fairtrade consumers generally, but not for UK Fairtrade wine consumers specifically. Our survey data was more focused though not representative. From these two sources, plus our accompanied shopping interviews, we were able to pull together the key attributes of Fair Trade shoppers for Chilean wine in the UK.

Our three personas, drawn from demographic traits, political motivations and purchasing patterns, could be summarized as follows:

Charlotte: Representing those people who vaguely feel it would be a good idea to buy Fair Trade and sometimes do, more so that they can talk about it than as part of a coherent alternative lifestyle;

Lucy: A young woman and committed ethical consumer who takes time to check where her purchases are coming from and will keep abreast of new developments, so that she can complete her wardrobe of organic cotton items as soon as items become available and order the latest recycled linen and rubber trainers online.

Ed: A man in his thirties, who is politically committed to buying ethically; something of an activist, he campaigns for better labeling, better

production practices and environmentally sensitive agriculture. He investigates the source of everything he buys and would not choose Chilean wine as his preference because of the distances involved, but might work out that it's more environmentally friendly than some other sources.

Of these, by far the most common type of consumer is Charlotte, or variants of her.

Using Performance

We intended to present our personas as quick descriptive sketches. However, the resulting personas felt insubstantial and dry in their textual incarnation. At this point too, they only existed in English. Having interviewed many of the Chilean staff before the first design workshop, we decided we might get more value out of the personas if they were dynamic and could respond to group needs. If we brought them to life, we could inject some fun, convey a memorable message and also use the technique to give direction to our design activities.

By engaging in an improvised presentation of a persona we were not doing something wholly new, but we were taking the concept into a new context. Both the playfulness and the performance have antecedents in designing. Role play and games that require the adoption of different parts have been used to good effect by design teams sharing insights (as Simarian 2003 reviews) and to convey different positions in complex issues. These are predicated on the idea that experiential engagement and performing roles give extra value to the process.

And performance is already recognized as useful in interaction design (Kantola et al. 2007; Light et al 2008; Macaulay et al. 2006) though not all of it involves working with characters and, where it does, many of the exchanges are scripted. In performance work, the technique of developing a character by subjecting them to improvised interviewing by a group is known as 'hot-seating'. It is this kind of activity that we were engaged in with our persona, although information extraction rather than character development motivated us. This use is more akin to that of Newell et al (2006) who have augmented scripted exchanges between actors with character 'hot-seating' as a way of helping designers learn about older people's behaviors and needs. We shared this emphasis on acting a role rather than merely animating a scenario. Where our use differs from Newell et al's, and thus might be educational here, is in providing running access to an interactive persona in a design workshop with stakeholders, and in a cross-cultural context and across two languages. We now go on to explore how the shape of our interactive persona was arrived at and how, in particular, the device distinguished itself from other uses by providing learning in both directions.

Evolving Our Performed Persona

In considering how to animate our personas, we decided that we should only present one, but that we should also include the other two in the principal persona's story. This was motivated by a desire to keep things simple, both in terms of presentation and in terms of the message being conveyed. A single source seemed an appropriate mechanism for working with a team unused to design workshops or listening to personas. However, our fear was that by collapsing our information into a solo voice, we were giving this voice too much authority – both as a representative of British consumption ideas and as a player in the room. We had to devise means of avoiding this.

Linking the personas as a family gave a back-story that would make a plausible pretext for any of them to talk about the others. Charlotte became mother to Lucy, and Ed became Lucy's boyfriend. Then it was only a question of deciding which persona should be primary and this was arrived at through a mixture of conviction and eventuality.

The European available to play the part of the persona was the monolingual researcher, who wasn't involved in facilitating because of the language barrier. So she adopted the middle-aged, relatively affluent and degree-educated, female shopper persona Charlotte (described above). We were lucky that apart from age (the researcher was slightly younger), the characteristics matched. Our middle-England persona was a good choice for the workshop because, not only was she characteristic of by far the most ubiquitous target user for the FT tool, but we could play her as an easily distracted, narrative-orientated person, able to contest a tendency in the staff to give too much technical detail for consumer needs. The rest of the personas became family to whom she could refer. So she presented her daughter as more committed to buying ethically than she was, and the daughter's hard-line boyfriend as mostly complaining about wine from South America appearing on her table because of food miles.

Charlotte was kept from becoming a caricature of Britishness, being articulate, but not necessarily linear in her thinking. She operated with certain mannerisms, like twiddling with her glasses, which made her seem human, plausible and non-intimidating. As with any performance, incidental behavior is impossible to avoid and so Charlotte became more of a character than a simple persona, through the process of being acted out. But this was part of the benefit of performance: the hope was that she would also be memorable for the bodega staff in just the way that other successful personas work to communicate by becoming reference points in decision making.

The Design Workshop

As noted above, we brought together in the first design workshop many of the bodega managers to help us understand their view of the wine value chain, the information they controlled as part of it, which parts of this information they could see being incorporated into a tool for representing the value chain and what kind of functionality that tool should offer. To do this, while representing the consumers (about which the producers knew relatively little but wanted – and, for the purposes of the exercise, needed – to know more) we had Charlotte present on hand for interventions.

The session opened with a 'chat' with Charlotte to orientate everyone and introduce the device. This was followed by a lengthy supply chain mapping process planned to elicit data from the staff (Figure 1). Charlotte spoke only in English, so the bilingual researcher translated. Playing her had the benefit of allowing the HCI researcher to be involved directly and help keep the session on track. Given the language challenge, Charlotte might not always understand what was transpiring in front of her. However, the co-creation of a supply chain diagram (with post-it notes to annotate it) gave clues as to what was going on, allowing Charlotte to interject. And when a question of the usefulness of data to a consumer arose, the bilingual researcher stopped the flow with "Shall we ask Charlotte?". She could then explain the dilemma to "Charlotte" and request a response, building up a pleasant tension. The suspense al-

lowed everyone to consider the question, as well as giving the research team a chance to brief the HCI specialist.

Charlotte used humor and character to give a verdict in such a way that it reflected on how much we knew of that aspect of consumer behavior, whether it applied to her or her fellow personas and what might interest her more instead. This way she could give a certainty measure for the information that the researchers had, as well as detail it from an informal perspective. So, if we knew that a certain approach had been tried and proved unsuccessful, Charlotte would speak firmly against it. But otherwise she took a more moderate line: for instance, when asked if she was interested in the temperature of the fermenting wine, she said: "*Well, yes... I suppose. I mean I want to know. But maybe even more important is what temperature to drink it at.*" In this way she steered technical discussions towards a more consumer friendly way of thinking. Thus the HCI researcher benefited

Figure 1. Bodega employees in Chile draw out the value chain and annotate it with new and existing information to use in marketing their wine to an international consumer audience from playing the role in being able to steer impressions and focus as well convey specific information.

To demonstrate that it was "Charlotte" speaking rather than our colleague, we used simple props (wine glass, spectacles) to identify the researcher in role as persona. This worked to mark the switch and also build character without the need for sophisticated role-play. Waving a glass of wine in one hand and reading glasses in the other, she could temper a suggestion playfully and avoid disheartening participants.

EVALUATING THE METHOD IN CONTEXT

We have run through the background to the method and given a taste of what ensued. We now look at how the use of a performed persona contributed to the communication task involved in working with the bodega staff and to the business of designing.

Benefits

There were several benefits to using this device. The first, as hinted, was the way guidance could be given quickly and playfully without damaging the standing of the enquirer. Protecting face is an issue in most social situations, can be a major part of social interaction in some cultures and may be even more pronounced where cultures meet. By asking the persona, like consulting the Oracle, staff with ownership of different types of data could compete to get their data into the design without losing face. Work hierarchies could be sidestepped. Because anyone's view could be challenged, Charlotte acted as a subtle leveler. At the same time, because Charlotte had distinct mannerisms and could ramble, she and her views were not above being smiled at. Indeed, the Charlotte tool allowed our otherwise impeccably polite Chilean partners to give looks and expressions of surprise and disbelief at the way British consumers thought. This manifested itself particularly, for example, on environmental

issues. So it proved an effective way of managing knowledge and expectations without placing one set of cultural attitudes over another.

It also shaped the sessions even better than anticipated. When everyone began talking at the same time, competition for attention replaced supportive conversation and ideas began to get lost. At these points, Charlotte stepped in loudly to ask a question in English and everyone went expectantly quiet. In this respect, it turned out to be beneficial that the persona spoke in a foreign language, because the translation process made time to think and added to the drama.

Third, it gave a taste of what a participatory user-centered design process could have involved if the worlds of producer and consumer had not been so far apart. We explained how we had gathered material for personas and created Charlotte and this gave the exercise some credibility (though not as a substitute for meeting consumer-users at the UK end). And it gave the HCI specialist (who till this point had found it difficult to intervene in the research process directly) a conspicuous role in activities. She was thereafter often hailed as "Charlotte" in the corridor and teased, which helped maintain amicable relations as we shadowed staff and questioned them. Some of her 'Holy Fool' status persisted and she could ask awkward questions naïvely (even in English) and get solicitous answers. In this way, it helped the team in their learning. Cooke (2004) makes the point that participatory action researchers should only work in languages that they understand as well as their own. Our experience in Chile showed that, in this case, working as a team with researchers of mixed language abilities could actually be used as a resource in order to subvert power dynamics which might exist between focus group participant and facilitator, local and "international" colleague, between more junior and more senior researcher. Our most senior researcher played Charlotte, and by letting participants to ask her questions, waiting for the translations and then answering in role, she set the tone for a relaxed, informal and democratic relationship between professionals. The aforementioned gentle teasing is indicative of the success of this.

Fourth, it shared the more general rationale that is used in animating personas, that doing so provides a stimulus that is more interesting than a pile of user research. In particular, where groups are working across cultures, a live and interactive means of passing over information has the major advantage that it can provide contextual information that would help convey the meaning of certain behaviors as static material cannot. In this way, unpremeditated angles can be addressed through informed improvisation. For instance, it was possible to show the difference in values between the Chileans and British ethical shoppers on the subject of patriotism and companies' investing in arms. Although tangential to Fair Trade wine, the subject came up in discussing beliefs and looking at ethical criteria for choosing products. Charlotte's first-person account helped avoid starting a long political discussion, while making everyone aware that significant differences exist.

Thus she helped with many aspects of communication that supported the primary purpose of getting everyone round the table. Specifically in designing, Charlotte gave a sense of who the tool was for, making the endeavor suddenly real in a way that both the composite nature of the persona and the overtly synthetic performance of it ought of have belied. Instead, her very human responses and her allusions to family conjured up a world to which the bodega employees had not much access, but now were engaging with. As well as being a device for transmitting information, she was also a means of generating empathy and commitment in the design team (McCarthy & Wright 2008).

As noted above, the tool had another subtlety to it in steering the design thinking. Charlotte offered a means of feeding in ideas that supported the researcher who did not speak Spanish, but it also allowed for communicating aspects that would

have been difficult even without the language barrier. Charlotte provided a means of raising subjects in a circumspect way that gave the local team more ownership of the ideas and therefore more control over the design. In particular, she opened up a space of multiple perspectives that contrasted slightly with the position of the visiting researchers and so produced an atmosphere where tentative suggestions could be hazarded and built upon in a participatory way. Her actor, the HCI researcher, was even capable of surprising herself as she listened to Charlotte's improvisations coming out of her mouth and saw aspects of the design space differently. So there was extra potential for reflection in the *visiting* team through this experiential engagement.

Challenges

Just as there were positives about the process, there were also factors that make it difficult to use a performed persona across cultures or limit its applicability.

Charlotte was a good tool in the contexts in which we used it not least because the Chilean bodega employees were a tight-knit group, of the same generation as the researchers, with a degree of self-assurance and a sense of fun. We had already established a relationship with everyone in the room by talking to them previously. So, preliminary, more formal social exchanges had been completed and proper form, including acting as "serious" professional researchers at these early meetings, had been observed. If it had been our first meeting with them, introducing Charlotte would probably have been an inappropriate way to start. Culturally sensitive issues of courtesy, status and mutual expectations needed considering. The group we worked with were educated and articulate, game to try out new techniques, prepared to trust us and willing to let go of social hierarchies long enough to make it a useful process, but not every group will be so disposed to play.

Working with a series of less connected individuals, or when the social backgrounds of researcher and group are even more divergent, would also prove more challenging with this kind of device, though, used well, it might provide some glue to unite them and build bridges.

Another contextual factor was the presence of someone in the research team who felt sufficiently confident at ad-libbing with persona data to play the role of Charlotte. Not every team will have someone who could plausibly take on a role. It requires the confidence to hold the floor and to keep up a consistent performance, beyond the facilitation skills that might be expected of a researcher in this territory. It also requires abandoning one's status as "authoritative researcher", accepting the playful aspect of the activity and being willing to see what happens.

And, beyond the individual, it required attentive team-working to carry it off. If the persona's home tongue is to be used – and good arguments beyond necessity emerged for doing so - another facet is how integral the interpreter is. Without anyone able to speak the local language, we would have been dependent on local translators and they would have to have been both competent in the language and sufficiently confident with the device to make it work. Although our team was interdisciplinary, we had worked together intensely for several days when we ran the first design workshop in this way. Attentive colleagues who could read the best moment for interruptions and input from Charlotte were very valuable. Without them, a more formal system of signals would have been necessary.

One issue across languages was, of course, ensuring interjections were timely and apt. The use of a visual exercise – constructing a supply chain together and thereby drawing out articulations of both the chain and the information that could be attached to it – gave our performer many clues as to what was going on. Also, she had a rudimentary grasp of the language so that she understood key

terms. Without this, it would have been harder to make comments, though perhaps even more useful to have a mechanism with which to stop the flow diplomatically and enquire after aspects of the work. In any case, some of the verbal clues about turn-taking and so on tend to be available across cultures and languages, and so someone without access to the language in use is not wholly unable to follow the rhythm of the discussion even if the meaning is obscure. Similarly, it is not clear how much of the performance might be lost in translation. However, the drama of it – the sudden alien voice, the gesturing at the image before them all, the bemused look on the face of the performers – is part of the communication that transmits across languages, and again much of it reaches across many cultures too.

A general weakness with introducing only one voice among multiple personas is that it gives undue prominence to what the speaker says. Our performance stressed the selectivity of the account by making Charlotte 'scatty' (to avoid the suggestion of authority) and by using references to other personas' behavior and thoughts. A richer way would have been to field a bigger cast, but that has cost implications. Another might be to explore playing the roles across the bodega staff, supported by role-playing material (in Spanish) but that would have distracted from the primary function of information elicitation, though offering other interesting learning and sharing opportunities. It would also demand far more of the individuals in the group and not everyone enjoys being involved in role play even if they find engaging with performers to be fun.

Another problem is the ephemerality of the dramatic form; no record exists unless, as here, a video is made. We can argue that the value of the interaction was in the moment – to help shape thinking in the workshop and for the suggestions that came out of it. But if vital learning has been captured, then an edited video – with subtitles – is a more communicative form than a document, especially across languages and cultures. That said, editing a video is time-consuming and an unedited session is not going to become a valuable resource. And in some cross-cultural contexts, taking video might distress participants or be harder to sustain over extended periods because of power limitations.

OUTCOMES

It is impossible to say what the sessions would have been like if we had used a different form of input for working with user data. We will never have those exact circumstances again to compare – indeed, we were lucky to get as much time as we did with our partners. However, in terms of effectiveness, we were able to work with the producer to identify a series of facts and stories together that, married up with further user research, should produce a successful basis for designing representational structures for the tool (Figure 2). We were able to prioritize the list we produced together and identify in rudimentary terms how each form of

data could be collected. And we heard a variety of perspectives on what function the tool should have and how this should be deployed.

The discussion was facilitated in what we considered to be a successful style and tone for the sessions. To give an example: as noted, we learnt during the workshop that the Chileans were not aware of the strong interest in environmental matters that we found many British Fairtrade consumers exhibited. Consequently, we spent time evaluating the cost of recording environmental data, how it might be managed, whether a statement about the environment would be useful in other contexts and what role it might play in the FT tool. This kind of commercially valuable dialogue had the bonus of paying producer partners back for their time, while providing cultural context in co-identifying information that could be useful in setting up the tool. Achieving that engagement suggests we found a balance in collaborating to evaluate the tool's viability, content and function. Charlotte was key to generating the shared knowledge, tone and discursive style enabling this. And, for some, the drama element was

Figure 2. Bodega employees' list of possible information types to share (squares mean facts, clouds mean narrative representation)

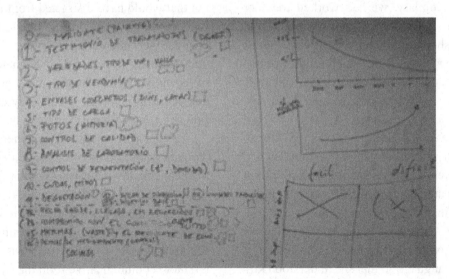

the most memorable of all the methods we used. On a return visit a year later, we found that participants reminisced about the workshop as "Ah yes, the one with Charlotte – how is she?"

DISCUSSION

We suggest here that performing a persona brings benefits that a paper version of the same persona could not. This suggestion is not based on a comparative study, but upon the way the device worked *in situ* when we used it with our Chilean partners. Not only did it convey information and do so with tact, but it allowed for an interaction with the information. This information may have come interpreted by a researcher but to all intents and purposes it worked as if it had come from a characteristic consumer, and so contrasted profoundly with what our first offering was to be: a written sketch. The device had the additional advantage of being transparent – it was clearly a researcher they had seen about for days who was playing Charlotte – and so did not seek to deceive. In acknowledging diversity of experience in the room through its flexibility and in encouraging a multiplicity of viewpoints, it became part of the weave of (contingent) designing behavior rather than just a communication device.

Perhaps a curious thing to note, but true nonetheless, was the effect performing Charlotte had on the HCI specialist. She found that she was responding to the perceptions and assumptions of the bodega staff, challenging her own expectations about what she thought by developing arguments in an embodied way. So occasionally Charlotte 'tricked' her actor into design thinking that went beyond what she might have engaged with if she had only had the one presence in the room. This was an entirely unforeseen eventuality and not core, but indicative of the change that embodiment brings to engaging with information.

We must still ask how far such a technique is applicable. Unusually, European researchers were working with producers in the global south to create a tool acceptable to the British market. In addition, the FT tool has to be embedded in both production and consumption worlds and broker between them. That too makes it unusual. We have yet to try the technique in other contexts where, like this one, shared cultural knowledge cannot be assumed. However, looking at the way that Charlotte was able to operate through this design workshop suggests that a variation would have potential in many situations. Its great benefit is that it can be altered on the fly according to the group's responses. But there are bound to be limits and if our partners had had less understanding of the world of research, it might not be clear the extent to which Charlotte was performing data. This brings interesting ethical questions of personification to bear.

In terms of our use of personas, Soegaard suggests that interaction design personas 'should be specifically made for the current design problem and thus not context-independent like "a generic marketing man" persona' (Soegaard, nd). Charlotte seems to walk the line between design and marketing in this respect. This is not because she is generic – she was custom designed as a potential user, based on consumer research. But her work was to mediate between cultures and so drew discussion of values, attitudes and interests rather more than specific interaction tasks. We were not engaging in specific interface design, with its details of use, at this point. We were looking at messages and functions and styling. So Charlotte remained context-independent in this respect, as does the tool in that it is intended to operate across products and across continents. The difference between our use and much persona use also asks for follow-up research to see if our experience can be replicated in more precise task-based contexts.

Meanwhile, the device was able to elicit individual responses from people round the table and reveal the diversity within the groups as well as between the visiting researchers and the bodega staff. This was useful in moving from stock responses to deepening the discussion and taking it into new territory. This is not a guaranteed path to insight and innovation but it is a necessary prerequisite. In this way it progressed the groups towards useful interaction design together and supported the form of the design activity as well as the conversation. We have also drawn attention to the empathetic response it elicited, which similarly is a prerequisite for good design.

In conclusion, there is increasing interest in cross cultural research and this article makes an argument that the use of improvisation and personas can provide an engaging way to think about different cultural values. Further, performing Charlotte not only has particular value in dealing with cross-cultural research, but also offers a device that can be used for co-constructing design in "development" contexts, thus helping to lessen the potential for imbalances in power in designing with people with different understandings and interests. However, we were trying this method out with a group of people for whom the device seemed a very good fit – indeed, this was one of the reasons which prompted us to try it. Clearly, in some contexts, the use of a dramatic form might be mystifying or disturbing in other ways and might prejudice outcomes for the worse.

When trying to design with people from different cultural backgrounds, there is bound to be a gap between understandings. We found the performed persona device of "Charlotte" a useful way to both identify these gaps and present a British consumer's point of view in a form that did not privilege it over the producer's view of the world. In line with Chambers' demands for action researchers, we were not presuming to instruct, but to enable an exchange of views amongst equals. Our method was locally appropriate, humorous, and we modified it spontaneously. Therefore in this article we do not advocate a specific persona

or performance method, we simply argue that a performed persona may be a useful tool to apply, in a locally appropriate and spontaneously modifiable way, in design situations involving participants from different cultures.

ACKNOWLEDGMENT

We are grateful for the support of the UK Engineering and Physical Sciences Research Council (Grant Number EP/E009018/1) and our friends at the Los Robles bodega, which, we are sad to report, was sold to a larger company during 2008. Many of the employees we spoke to are now working for other companies.

REFERENCES

Baecker, R. M., & Greenberg, S. (Eds.). (1995). *Readings in human-computer interaction: toward the year 2000* (2nd ed.). San Francisco, CA: Morgan Kaufmann.

Carroll, J. M. (2000). *Making Use - scenario-based design of human-computer interactions.* Cambridge, Massachusetts: The MIT Press.

Chambers, R. (1997). *Whose reality counts? Putting the first last,* Bourton-on-Dunsmore: ITDG Publishing.

Chopra, A., & Kundu, A. (2008). The Fair Tracing project: digital tracing technology and Indian coffee. *Contemporary South Asia, 16*(2), 217–230. doi:10.1080/09584930701733548

Clark, H. H. (1992). *Arenas of Language Use.* Chicago, IL: University of Chicago Press.

Cooke, B. (2004). Rules of thumb for participatory change events. In S. Hickey & M. Giles (Eds.), *Participation: from tyranny to transformation? Exploring new Approaches to Participation in Development* (pp. 42-57). London: Zed Books.

Cooper, A. (1999). *The Inmates Are Running the Asylum.* Indianapolis: SAMS.

Dearden, A., & Rizvi, H. (2008). Adapting Participatory and Agile Software Methods to Participatory Rural Development. In *PDC '08: Experiences and Challenges, Proceedings of the Participatory Design Conference* (pp. 221-225). Bloomington, Indiana: Indiana University Press.

Goodwin, K. (2007). *Perfecting Your Personas. User Interface.* Retrieved March 23, 2009, from http://www.uie.com/events/uiconf/2007/articles/perfecting_personas/

Hickey, S., & Mohan, G. (2004). Towards participation as transformation: critical themes and challenges. In S. Hickey & G. Mohan (Eds.), *Participation: from tyranny to transformation? Exploring new Approaches to Participation in Development* (pp. 3-25). London: Zed Books.

Irani, L., Dourish, P., Grinter, R., & Phillips, K. (2008). *Postcolonial Computing.* University of California Irvine.

Kantola, V., Tiitta, S., Mehto, K., & Kankainen, T. (2007). Using dramaturgical methods to gain more dynamic user understanding in user-centered design. In *Proceedings in Creativity and Cognition* (pp.173-182). Washington, DC: ACM.

Kleine, D. (2007). Striking a Balance. *Engineering and Technology, 2*(2), 30–33. doi:10.1049/et:20070202

Kleine, D. (2008). Negotiating partnerships, understanding power: doing action research on Chilean Fairtrade wine value chains. *The Geographical Journal, 174*(2), 109–123. doi:10.1111/j.1475-4959.2008.00280.x

Korten, D. C. (1984). *People-centred Development.* West Hartford, Connecticut: Kumarian Press.

Lessig, L. (2006). *Code: And Other Laws of Cyberspace, Version 2.0.* New York, NY: Basic Books.

Light, A. (2008, May). The Challenge of Representing a Sociotechnical System: Fair Tracing and the Value Chain. *Sociotechnical Aspects of Interaction Design.* London.

Light, A., Weaver, L., Healey, P. G., & Simpson, G. (2008). Adventures in the Not Quite Yet: using performance techniques to raise design awareness about digital networks. In *Proceedings. Design Research Society Conference*, Sheffield: *Design Research Society*

Macaulay, C., Jacucci, G., O'Neill, S., Kankaineen, T., & Simpson, M. (2006). The Emerging Roles of Performance within HCI and Interaction Design. *Interacting with Computers, 18*(5), 942–955. doi:10.1016/j.intcom.2006.07.001

Marsden, G. (2007). Social Impact plenary talk. In *Proceedings CHI 2007.* New York, NY: ACM.

Mintel (1999). *Green and Ethical Consumer Survey.* London: Mintel.

Mintel (2001). *Attitudes Towards Ethical Food Survey.* London: Mintel.

Mintel (2004). *Green and Ethical Consumer Survey.* London: Mintel.

Muller, M. J. (2002). Participatory Design: the third space in HCI. In J. Jacko & A. Sears (Eds.). *The Human-computer Interaction Handbook: Fundamentals, Evolving Technologies and Emerging Applications* (pp. 1051-1068). Hillsdale, NJ: Lawrence Erlbaum.

Newell, A. F., Morgan, M. E., Gregor, P., & Carmichael, A. (2006). Theatre as an intermediary between users and CHI designers. In *Proceedings CHI 2007* (pp. 111-116), New York, NY: ACM.

Nicholls, A., & Opal, C. (2004). *Fair Trade: market-driven ethical consumption.* London: Sage.

Nielsen, L. (2005). Then the picture comes in your mind of what you have seen on TV - A study of personas descriptions and use. In *The 5th Danish Human-Computer Interaction Research Symposium* (pp. 68-73), Copenhagen: CBS, Institut for Informatik.

Porter, M. E. (1985). *Competitive Advantage: Creating and Sustaining Superior Performance.* New York, NY: Free Press.

Pruitt, J., & Adlin, T. (2006). *The Persona Lifecycle: Keeping People in Mind Throughout Product Design.* San Francisco, CA: Morgan Kaufmann.

Shen, S. T., Woolley, M., & Prior, S. (2006). Towards culture-centred design. *Interacting with Computers, 18*(4), 820–852. doi:10.1016/j.intcom.2005.11.014

Simarian, K. T. (2003). Take it to the next stage: the roles of role playing in the design process. In *Proceedings CHI 2003* (pp. 1012-1013), New York, NY: ACM.

Soegaard, M. (2007). Personas. *Interaction Design Encyclopedia.* Retrieved March 23, 2009, from: http://www.interaction-design.org/encyclopedia/personas.html

Wajcman, J. (2004). *Technofeminism.* Oxford: Polity Press

Wright, P. C., & McCarthy, J. (2008). Empathy and experience in HCI. In *Proceedings CHI 2008* (pp. 637-646). New York, NY: ACM.

ENDNOTES

[1] So, for example, we knew that it would be possible to organize a tracking system using the assignment of numbers and chronology to each producer and production event from grape growing to wine drinking, but we did not know how far this process would be of use *in situ* along the value chain and for interested third parties.

[2] It was recognized that it would never be viable to build and test an end-to-end tool as part of the project: there would be too many variables to make it useful without more understanding of the issues. It might also be problematic from an ethical point of view to disrupt existing processes at producers' businesses by introducing a crude and potentially onerous back-end prototype.

This work was previously published in The International Journal of Sociotechnology and Knowledge Development, Volume 2, Issue 1, edited by Elayne Coakes, pp. 36-58, copyright 2010 by IGI Publishing (an imprint of IGI Global).

Chapter 15
Achieving Best Practice Manufacturing Involving Tacit Knowledge through the Cautious Use of Mixed-Mode Modelling

Miles G. Nicholls
RMIT University, Australia

Barbara J. Cargill
University of Melbourne, Australia

ABSTRACT

In the real world, 'optimal' solutions for many production process problems do not exist. In such circumstances, 'best practice' is the realistic outcome for which practitioners aim. The reasons for this stem from many causes, including that data associated with production processes are often corrupted and/or missing. These types of processes usually rely heavily on the subjective input of the process workers on the shop floor (tacit knowledge). This paper outlines how the use of mixed-mode modelling has been utilised to help solve these types of problems. The industry examples used in the paper incorporate the concept of Communities of Practice (CoPs) in the mixed-mode models that are developed as a means of capturing tacit knowledge and incorporating it into the solution process. Additionally, CoPs need to sit comfortably within the culture and values of the organisation and employee groups, and must be clearly owned and facilitated by the community of workers whose knowledge is to be shared. Finally, CoPs should be presented as opportunities to share, compare, and learn so that a 'craft' is not lost or diminished.

DOI: 10.4018/978-1-4666-0200-7.ch015

Copyright © 2012, IGI Global. Copying or distributing in print or electronic forms without written permission of IGI Global is prohibited.

1. INTRODUCTION TO THE TACIT KNOWLEDGE PROBLEM

In some industries, the manufacturing process itself is not able to be fully represented using a 'hard' model which contains known parameters together with a definitive mathematical model representing its operation. Some production processes that *appear* well defined and quantifiable are in *reality* at best 'guestimates', subject to complex sub-processes that determine their values. Often, these sub-processes are not fully understood despite the fact that they form a part of the 'known' production process. Under these circumstances, only models that approximate the process can be developed with the factory floor workers or production operators holding in a tacit form, a further understanding of the process that has not be made explicit. Often this is experience or simply intuition. Examples of production involving tacit knowledge (hereinafter referred to as '*the tacit knowledge problem*') are found in the aluminium smelting industry (see Nicholls & Cargill, 2008), float glass production and the refrigeration industry. The consequences of this tacit knowledge problem include greater product development costs and often considerable increases in product manufacture time for a job (make-span). This is particularly true in the refrigeration industry where product development (and in the case of the most extreme version of a customised product - the 'one-off') make-span times can be up to a year in some extreme cases.

Polyani (1966) is considered the authoritative source on tacit knowledge. Tacit knowledge is considered very important since it is regarded by many (Nonaka & Takeuchi, 1995; Collins, 2001) as "fundamental to all human knowing and knowledge (Gourlay, 2006, p. 60). Tacit knowledge is popularly treated as personal or private knowledge and acquired through an individual's experience. There is also considerable discussion surrounding whether tacit knowledge can be actually converted into explicit knowledge. Some have suggested that this is difficult to achieve (see Patel et al., 1999; Collins, 2001) while others, (Boiral, 2002; Gourlay, 2006) have adequately demonstrated that indeed tacit knowledge can be made explicit. However, the inability to articulate tacit knowledge in some situations is a real one and must be borne in mind (see Marchant & Robinson, 1999; Wagner et al., 1999; Zappavigna, 2006). An additional category of tacit knowledge exists, that of 'intrinsic knowledge'.

The capture, storage and interrogation of the tacit knowledge is the key to arriving at best practice under these circumstances (normally an iterative process) and this paper suggests how "Communities of Practice" (a people based 'soft' model) may be used to achieve the capture. The known aspects of the production processes can be represented by the usual 'hard' models (such as linear programming etc) which will depend on the soft models (say the Communities of Practice) to supply needed information. With this arrangement of hard and soft models, a soft heuristic solution algorithm (which integrates these) is required to arrive at a solution i.e., 'best practice'. This is the role of mixed-mode modelling, both as an approach to actually modelling the problem and also affecting its solution.

Section 2 explains the concept of mixed-mode modelling (essentially through a simple example) while Section 3 outlines its application to two industrial examples while also raising some of the difficulties associated with its use coupled with Communities of Practice. Section 4 discusses the difficulties in detail and suggests some ways of overcoming them.

2. MIXED-MODE MODELLING AND ITS USE

The term mixed-mode modelling covers a broad number of approaches encompassing "soft OR" and in this paper is used to describe the process of the bringing together of 'soft' and 'hard' sub-models which then, through an heuristic solution process (which is itself 'soft'), arrives at a 'best practice' solution to the problem at hand. Soft OR had its origins in the work by Checkland (1981) and Midgely (1992) and later further expanded in Checkland (1999) which revolved around the concept of systems thinking and essentially pursues thought processes rather than mathematical models. The term mixed-mode modelling can encompass (at least in a general context) the combining of a group of sub-model which are either all hard or all soft. However, in this paper the only examples of mixed-mode modelling that are considered are those that involve a mixture of hard and soft sub-models. This means that there is no deterministic/analytical solution algorithm that can be used to solve the problem. For a solution to be obtained, a solution heuristic is needed. The concept of mixed-mode modelling was initially proposed and explored by Lehaney (1996), Lehaney and Clarke (1997) and Mingers and Brocklesby (1996) and further extended and explored in Nicholls and Cargill (2001) (see also Nicholls, Clarke, and Lehaney, 2001 for a more general exposition of the topic).

The various models (hard and soft) in a mixed-mode modelling problem are independently 'solved' using hard or soft solution algorithms/heuristics as applicable, with the results passed on to the next appropriate sub-model which in turn is solved. This interdependence of sub-models is quite common in mixed-mode modelling. The end result may well be a number of possible solutions to the problem with the final 'best practice' solution being arrived at iteratively by panel consensus with judgement being applied by a management group. In mixed-mode modelling as dealt with in this paper, there is no overall analytical solution technique, no optimality and certainly no single correct answer. Additionally, the solution heuristic may well be set up so that the solution procedure is repeated at regular intervals as new and more accurate information and data is available. Figure 1 epitomises such an approach using a modified

example developed by Nicholls and Cargill (2001) and Nicholls (2009) (from which much of this illustrative example is drawn) where the Human Resources Management (HRM) and Production Planning and Scheduling (PPS) departments of a business are required to find best practice solutions to their own areas. Note here the PPS department requires direct input from the HRM department's solution. Following this, the business needs to arrive at overall best practice, which may require the alteration of the departmental solutions (a subjective iterative process).

In Figure 1, each of the operational areas of PPS, HRM and Management are subject to the environment (E) which would include such occurrences as the global financial crisis. Further, there are inputs to each of the areas as well, relating to aspects of their operations that might not be fully under their control. For example: in the PPS department, this might be costs of raw materials and their availability (I_1); in the HRM department it may be the Occupational Health and Safety Acts, Labour Laws etc (I_2); and in Management Assessment, it may well be shareholder's considerations (I_3). The demand for products and their prices are essentially the key input for the PPS department (although the prices and the range could be altered by Management). With this information, PPS set out to maximise profit using say linear programming (a hard model) utilising all the relevant information they have. However, one of the major inputs to their model will be the amount of labour available according to skill sets. This in part will be influenced heavily by the HRM department as one of their missions/objectives (in this example) is to oversee a reduction of y% of the company's permanent labour force. Additionally, there will also be environmental factors (E) at work. The required labour reduction will be occasioned by the use of (for example) natural attrition, voluntary redundancies or with a more severe impact on productivity, forced redundancies. The areas of labour reduction (e.g., cleaners, furnace maintenance

Figure 1. The mixed-mode modelling approach to attaining best practice solutions

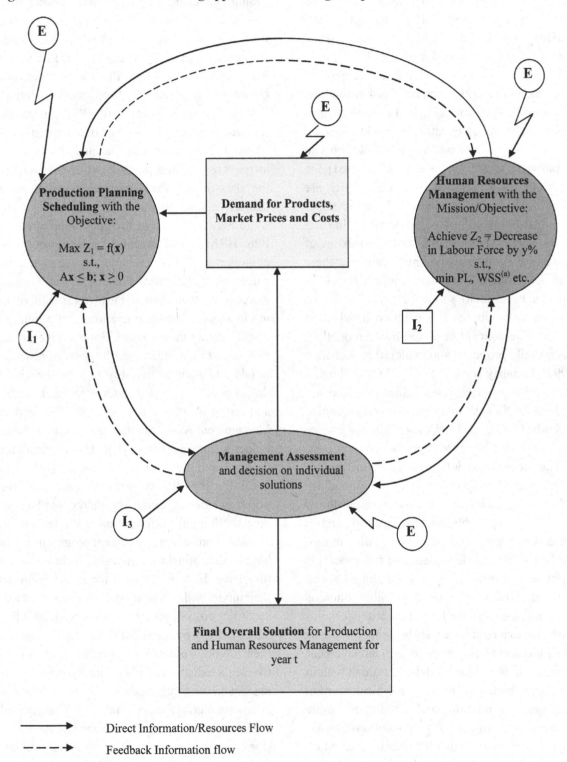

etc) would be determined in conjunction with the PPS department. The restrictions faced by HRM in achieving their objective could be that reductions in productivity should be below a specified amount, that industrial relations difficulties should also be below a specified level and that erosion of skill sets must not occur in excess of technically established limits. In this example, the HRM department will use a soft heuristic (possibly panel consensus or the expert panel approach) to arrive at their solution (See Nicholls and Cargill (2001) for more details) and then pass it on (i.e., the labour availability by area) to the PPS department as well as to management for consideration.

Management assessment (same as used in the HRM department) would then be used to determine whether the overall solution obtained was the best for the business. Has the right amount of 'social conscience' been incorporated into the strategies developed by the HRM department in order to achieve the required reduction in the labour? Best practice is then achieved by Management Assessment by passing onto the PPS and HRM departments, their assessments and then the process iterating until management judge best practice has been achieved. This process constitutes the soft solution heuristic for the model. In this instance, the soft model associated with the HRM department has triggered the need for mixed-mode modelling. However, in the real word, it can stem from a far more complex problem, the tacit knowledge problem (TKP) surrounding a process (or indeed unobservable data that is key to a sub-production process - see Nicholls & Cargill, 2008).

3. SOME EXAMPLES OF ACHIEVING BEST PRACTICE USING MIXED-MODE MODELLING

Having established the nature of the tacit knowledge problem and outlined the type of mixed-mode modelling to be used in this paper, two examples of the application of mixed-mode modelling

in circumstances that have the tacit knowledge problem (and in one case with missing key data also) are now examined. In both bases, the capture of tacit knowledge is achieved through the use of Communities of Practice (which is a sub model of the overall problem). A Communities of Practice approach (i.e., 'model') was chosen to achieve the capture of the tacit knowledge in the applications discussed in this paper due to its successful use in other applications. However, the use of this approach is not without the risk of failure if inappropriately or carelessly implemented. Discussion in the examples below will provide more detail with respect to the selection of Communities of Practice and the caution needed in its implementation. These examples also show the value of using mixed-mode modelling in production planning and make-span minimization involving knowledge management and knowledge engineering. The processes associated with the detailed tacit knowledge storage and interrogation will not be covered in detail in this paper. The difficulties associated with the use of Communities of Practice will also be raised.

3.1 The Aluminium Smelter Application

This application was first detailed by Nicholls and Hedditch (1993) and was based on the Portland Aluminium Smelter in Australia. Subsequently, the smelter was modelled using a mixed-mode modelling approach by Nicholls and Cargill (2008). The essence of this problem is that the 'real world' process of smelting aluminium has areas involving lack of full understanding of the production process as well as missing (or at best approximate) data.

The aluminium smelter is made up of four main Areas, the Anode Manufacturing Area, the Rodding Area, the Potrooms and the Ingot Mill (in the case of the specific smelter involved in the modelling – all were autonomous business entities). Anodes are carbon blocks (manufactured in

Figure 2. Production activity and process flow for the aluminum smelter

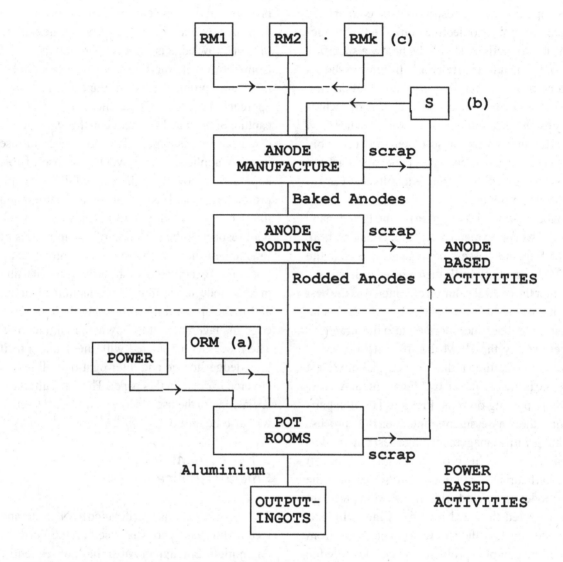

(a) Includes Alumina and **O**ther **R**equired raw **M**aterials
(b) Scrap (**S**) i.e., the residual of the anodes from the potrooms
(c) Raw Materials (**RM**) include Pitch and Coke

the Anode Area) which are placed in the reduction cells to allow the transmission of electrical current through mixture containing alumina. They are suspended in the pots by rods placed into the blocks in the Rodding Area. When the molten aluminium is siphoned off from the pots, it is taken to the Ingot Mill where it is placed in holding furnaces and then cast into ingots. The aluminium smelter production process is illustrated in Figure 2.

The behaviour in 'real time' of the reduction cells (referred to as 'pots' where the aluminium is actually produced) is not totally understood or predictable, as the actions of the operators tending the pots can significantly influence the pots' behaviour through use of their tacit knowledge or 'understanding'. This in turn affects the pots' output of aluminium. Additionally, in the smelting process, there are missing data (e.g., the exact production of aluminium over a given time in a reduction cell cannot be accurately measured).

Note: (a) Here *min PL* and *WSS* are levels of productivity loss and workforce skill sets that must not be not gone below and maintained respectively.

Further, the production efficiency (the 'current efficiency' [CE]) cannot be practically measured for all reduction cells (of which there might be in excess of 400 in the 'pot rooms') and can only be estimated over all cells over a monthly time period (meaning that its estimate is always lagging one month). This is not sufficiently accurate as the current efficiency is a critical parameter in the mathematical model of the smelter (see Nicholls & Cargill, 2008 for a detailed discussion of these problems).

Given the above difficulties, arriving at a best practice solution for the overall operation of the smelter, a mixed mode modelling approach is considered appropriate. This approach enables the capture of tacit knowledge and its subsequent incorporation into the mathematical model. This approach leads to a more accurate and meaningful 'solution' and also to a more stable operation of the reduction cells which in turn facilitates a more accurate estimate of the current efficiency and daily production. The basic mixed-mode model is illustrated in Figure 3 (adapted from Nicholls and Cargill, 2008, p21).

The hard model is the non-linear bi-level mathematical model of the smelter with the soft model being the capture and retention of the tacit knowledge using a Communities of Practice 'model'. The latter is the key to capturing the tacit knowledge, an approach that encourages the operators to learn from each other and impart their 'understanding' (i.e., tacit knowledge) to a repository within the smelter. As an ongoing mechanism, this approach enables a greater un-

derstanding to be obtained and, on an iterative basis, capture more knowledge over time. Tacit knowledge in the examples used in this paper can only be captured on an iterative basis.

3.1.1 Communities of Practice

Communities of Practice are not a new concept and have been have been discussed at length in the literature (see Wenger, 1998; Wenger, 2002; Wenger, 2003; Saint-Onge, 2003; Ackerman et al., 2003; Coakes & Clarke, 2006; Paquette, 2006). Communities of Practice in general have also been formally or informally in use in industry for some time (see Orr, 1996; Louis, 2006) and in a fledging manner were beginning to informally emerge at the Portland smelter. However, in the Portland application, tapping into this tacit knowledge and utilising it had not occurred (at least at the time the hard model was fully developed). The importance of the stable and efficient running of the reduction cells lies at the heart of 'best practice' in a smelter. Stable and reliable operation of the pots increases the CE which is important since a 1% improvement in CE could amount to millions in reduced costs. Hence, the opportunity to have the operators share their tacit knowledge and indeed by discussion produce 'generated' tacit knowledge is an important one (see Zappavigna, 2006 in particular for a discussion of tacit knowledge and Communities of Practice). The more informal the opportunities to share this knowledge the better, and indeed, encouragement might simply be the provision of a pleasant place to relax at meal times and talk. Communities of Interest (Fischer, 2001) are another alternative approach, but they are inherently more formal and as Fischer (2004) indicates, are essentially a "community of communities" (see also Brown & Duguid, 1991). Hence in this application, Communities of Interest are not applicable since there is only one Community of Practice in one area of the smelter under consideration. Additionally,

Figure 3. A mixed-mode modelling solution methodology for the smelter problem

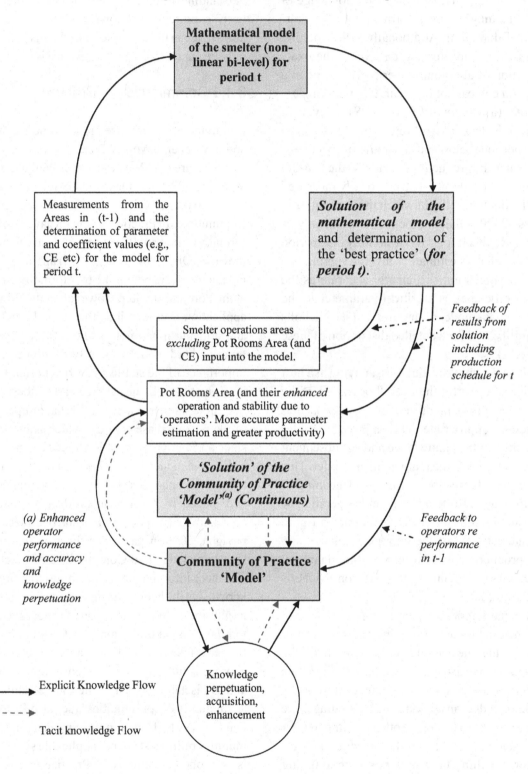

the context in which the Community of Practice is being considered requires a *very* informal structure (as issue discussed later in the paper). Hence, the provision of appropriate opportunities and encouragement for operators to exchange and share tacit knowledge constitutes the soft model, the Community of Practice. The deceptive simplicity of this will be discussed later in the paper.

It is not necessarily here assumed that the tacit knowledge that might potentially be gathered, built or group generated will be highly technical, 'scientific' or even totally accurate. The reality of a pot room workforce, and that of many other production groups in industry, is that the workers are of generally low educational level and are relatively simple, straightforward semi-skilled workers. They do not tend to assemble their tacit knowledge in highly systematic conceptual frameworks, nor analyse occurrences in great depth. Yet they instinctively know some things by virtue of long observation and trial and error experimentation. Drawing out such understanding, however basic, and then assisting the workers to construct some of this knowledge around key elements of an intellectual framework can actually generate robust knowledge that is then able to be 'captured' and passed on to others, becoming part of a knowledge repository. Left alone, the pot room workers may not generate that knowledge to such a level.

Equally, workers of the pot room floor, like most workers in production plants in any industry, are not the most senior staff within the organisation. There are real and influential power differentials between such workers and the 'management'. Workers frequently find that one of the key elements of power that they do in fact hold, when they clearly do *not* hold the power to plan, allocate resources, commit resources, or evaluate success overall, is the power of their pot room floor knowledge. Only *they* know how to make the pots behave in ways that will produce aluminium efficiently and safely. They may have

significant issues with sharing such knowledge, if it might mean that they lose the power of negotiation and the respect that this expertise brings into any production organisation's internal industrial dynamics.

By contrast, workers in more skilled production operations, such as in the following case example may be considerably more technically or even professionally trained and perhaps more senior in the organisation. They may have more real organisational power, and may have fewer issues with power differentials, or reluctance to disclose that which is known. Technician-level education and training (as a minimum) is likely to enable workers to assemble more of their intuitive and tacit learning around conceptual frameworks and theoretical constructs.

In either case, whether the tacit knowledge is derived from workers who are not highly educated or necessarily of superior intellect, or whether they are more technically aware, it is nonetheless knowledge. If the power differentials can be managed and a willingness to disclose what is known established, then the knowledge is of pivotal interest to the organisation if it can lead to production improvements. The only issues may be about how directly and formally such communities of practice can be conducted and with what incentives for collaboration.

3.2 The Commercial Refrigeration Manufacturing Application

Another industry that suffers from the tacit knowledge problem is that of commercial refrigeration design and manufacture. The time for manufacture of a working prototype from the time of receiving a customer's design specifications (or indeed from the manufacturer determining a new model themselves), can be up to one year. In order to remain internationally competitive (more critical in the current financial times) a minimum make-span is desired. This example stems from the work done by Nicholls and Eady (2008) and is the subject of ongoing doctoral research (Kanjanabootra, 2009). The key for the commercial refrigeration manufacturer at the moment, in Australia at least, is the ability to undertake speedy new product development in order to respond to the needs of industry, thereby maintaining a competitive edge (especially against off-shore competitors).

The design of the internal structure of a commercial refrigerator and its cooling unit is not an exact science that can be arrived at using a deterministic algorithm. In fact, the design of both of these components is undertaken using simulation packages (one to design the cooling space and the other to model the gas diffusion). Thus the first prototype of a new commercial refrigeration unit (i.e., product development or occasionally the 'once off' for a customer), will almost certainly not meet the legal and industry requirements or customer/prototype specifications and will require subsequent modification and testing. Figure 4 summarises this process and the phases of the make-span involved. In Figure 4, the first phase (Phase 1) is the initial simulation to design the case and cooling system using the design specifications. The second phase (Phase 2) is the testing and modification of this initial design in the refrigeration laboratory. Phase three (Phase 3) is the testing to determine if this design meets the marketing and costs requirements, followed by the fourth, which is effectively the 'tidy up'. The objective is therefore to minimise the number of iterations (M+N) associated with the building of the finally accepted new product.

At the heart of the tacit knowledge problem in the refrigeration design industry, are the refrigeration technicians and engineers who have built up over a number of years, bodies of tacit knowledge. Further, there is 'generated tacit knowledge' that occurs when groups of technicians/engineers get together to talk over design problems. The refrigeration industry also has another aspect to the tacit knowledge problem, that of the vastness

of the tacit knowledge and the consequent need to form a usable knowledge repository that can be readily accessed. Note, only the 'relevant' information for a design is needed, not *all* the information, therefore an 'intelligent' repository is required (determined perhaps using object oriented methodology). This is a problem currently being tackled by Kanjanabootra (2009). There are other forms of embedded tacit knowledge and explicit knowledge associated with this application but as their treatment and inclusion differs significantly from the approach being concentrated on in this paper, they will not be discussed.

The application of mixed-mode modelling in this application is illustrated in Figure 5, with the hard model being the simulation of the initial cabinet and cooling system, followed by the soft modelling of the tacit knowledge gathering and repository development to allow the access to the tacit knowledge in the production process and the incorporation of the tacit knowledge into the initial design. Access to the embedded knowledge (contained in existing products), tacit knowledge (what can be gathered – and when so harvested is ironically no longer tacit but 'new') together with explicit knowledge is required in Phase 1 and Phase 2 to supplement the use of the simulation modelling. The testing of the efficacy of the model developed is undertaken periodically to ensure that the production model developed is actually contributing to the minimization of the make-span.

The use of Communities of Practice as the sub-model for the capture and incorporation of tacit knowledge in the mixed-mode model developed to determine best practice in this instance has been implemented at a formal level with enthusiastic acceptance from those involved at the current stage of development. However, the extent of the knowledge, its complexity, its *relevance* and its storage and retrieval pose considerable problems.

Figure 4. *The refrigeration new product development process*

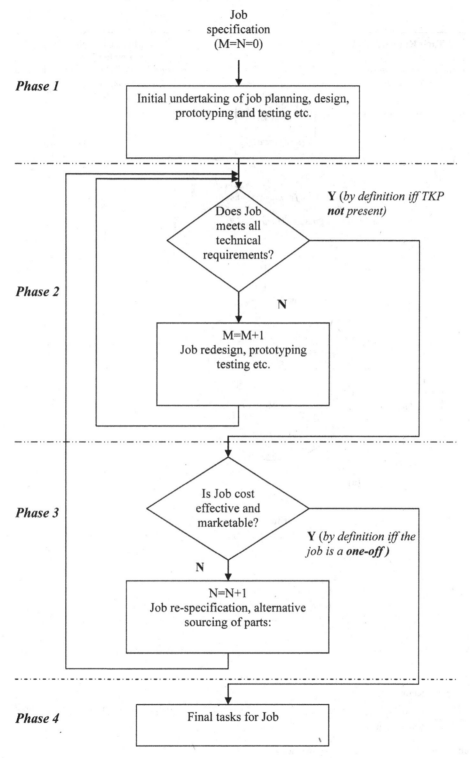

Figure 5. The mixed-mode modelling solution heuristic for new product development in commercial refrigeration

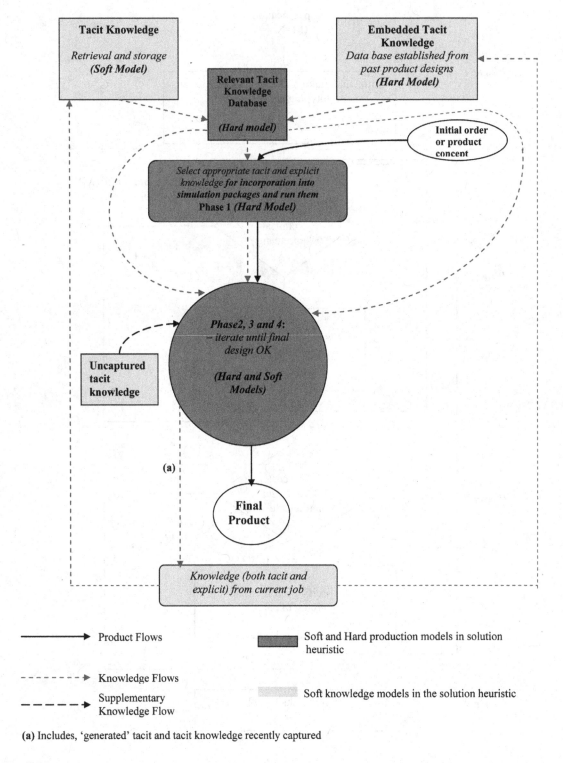

4. PROBLEMS ASSOCIATED WITH THE APPLICATION OF MIXED-MODE MODELLING

While the development of a mixed-mode model to arrive at best practice seems straightforward and logical enough, there are inherently problems associated with its implementation. The examples of mixed-mode modelling discussed in this paper all involve the tacit knowledge problem and use a Communities of Practice sub-model. Obtaining the tacit knowledge from the relevant people (the shop floor operators/engineers/refrigeration laboratory technicians who control the production processes) is a very delicate and critical task already mentioned. This section highlights these difficulties and suggests ways that may reduce the risks associated with the use of Communities of Practice.

Communities of Practice are essentially *informal* groups of people in a single organization (as in the case of 'commercial in confidence' operations of smelters and other manufacturing entities) or in more common knowledge areas, across organizations as well, becoming Communities of Interest. As Louis (2006), Davies, Duke, and Sure (2003) and Burk (2000) indicate, such Communities are founded on common knowledge or common work tasks where the coming together of people to share stories and discuss work practices (i.e., sharing explicit and tacit knowledge) gives support, knowledge and a sense of belonging to people. These interactions can occur in a real or a virtual sense depending on the nature of the organization and whether the Community exists beyond one work site.

It is worth noting that the name of 'Communities of Practice' was applied initially (see Orr, 1996; Louis, 2006) to a group of copy machine technicians who met in a social setting (around the water cooler). Here they shared common experiences and methods of doing their job that were not a part of the "technicians' manual". Membership of a particular Community of Practice or interest is not necessarily fixed but may vary considerably (as will its leadership). Given the case examples presented in this paper, the nature or classification that could be assigned to the Communities of Practice (see Vestal, 2003) is a hybrid of the 'best-practice' and 'knowledge stewarding' types. The aluminium smelting industry (especially) is ideally suited to the informal emergence of a Community of Practice and for their encouragement in a purposeful way by the organization. Anecdotally, the existence of at least one Community of Practice within the Portland smelter was noted (as found by Urpani, 1996) but it was at an embryonic state and very confined (effectively to a small group of process operators on one shift). The organisation had not stewarded any more systematic development of such communities for knowledge capture and enhancement. This would be required to systematise the exchange of knowledge as well as encourage the formalization and interchange of tacit knowledge. In some ways they can also take on the informal role of 'teacher'; and mentor for members of the Communities of Practice.

It should be noted that a critical value of any Communities Practice is the learning loop for the *perpetuation of knowledge* in the operators over time. Unless there is some process in place to bring the tacit knowledge into more explicit forms, there is a risk to the enterprise of knowledge loss over time. Each generation of skilled or semi-skilled workers with high levels of accumulated tacit knowledge needs to systematically pass this knowledge to the newcomer workers, or the organisation has failed to manage its knowledge base. Knowledge management is a source of competitive advantage and a key to a firm's longevity (see Saint-Onge, 2003; Lehaney, Clarke, Coakes, & Jack, 2004). A haphazard approach to the knowledge transfer from experienced hands to newcomers *may* be sufficient, but also leaves a large amount of knowledge preservation and transfer to chance. It might *not* happen in a comprehensive way. If there were to be a sudden and unexpected turnover of personnel, the knowledge base is deeply at risk, and so is the competitive advantage. A Community of Practice approach can therefore more consciously capture, preserve and perpetuate crucial knowledge of various processes which are otherwise difficult to codify into conventional training courses, even on-the-job ones.

Communities of Practice at their most effective have a fundamentally egalitarian, informal existence that is by definition not a mirror of the formal organisational reporting lines and structures (Saint-Onge, 2003; Ackerman, Pipek, & Wulf, 2003). They therefore need to disregard both organisational power and hierarchical politics and sit outside that sphere of influence, owned and clearly driven by the community of workers, and simultaneously be respected and acknowledged by the power and management group. Organisations more accustomed to patterns of conventional line authority that gives great power to managers may therefore have some difficulty with the existence of a collective activity which management does not own or drive or control. Yet this is the essence of the more open, egalitarian culture associated in modern management practice with the 'learning organisation' (see Senge, 1990). In encouraging Communities of Practice, it is therefore wise for management to firstly face the fact that they can neither control nor overly influence the Communities, but their support in terms of providing time, space and patronage/legitimacy to the activity is vital.

Whilst Communities of Practice do not sit in the conventional authority structure of the firm, they do need to reflect and sit comfortably with its organisational culture. Where there is, say, a strong history of antipathy between management and operatives, it would become very important that management be seen to be entirely unconnected with the desire for a Community of Practice to be established, since cynicism and some paranoia in the workers that management 'wants to get something extra, to exploit' would spell the death of the Community of Practice before it

ever formed. Where technical and professional expertise has tended to be seen as belonging to a group of unrealistic, somewhat irrelevant idealists who do not really know anything of value, then they must also be seen as quite separate from the process at least in the first instance. Respect cannot be forced in settings like this, and it is therefore wise to note local company conventions and traditions and to work with them in encouraging Communities of Practice.

Communities of Practice in Pot Rooms at the Smelter

There is little incentive for a strong Community of Practice to occur amongst the operators on the pot room floor other than through natural curiosity and a sense of being correct in their individual approaches to pot management. There is possibly even less incentive in this situation for a community of practice to evolve between the pot room operators and the professional engineering staff of the smelter, the cultural differences being somewhat more marked. However, Urpani (1996) uncovered the fact that in that same aluminium smelter, there was in fact some interaction between operators regarding their management of pots. Operators were actually astounded to find that generally, there were vast differences in the way each handled various situations. They had presumed that practice was 'standard'. This revelation (anecdotally) was seen as the catalyst for the subsequent greater degree of interaction between operators on this issue. However, there are excellent grounds for the smelter management to encourage the intermixing of the technicians and operators as well as the operators *per se* to expand their communities of practice activities. The technical analysis of pots is all too often confined to macro analysis of hundreds of pots as well as laboratory pots that are very small and operate under a very controlled and unrealistic environment.

In this smelter case, the existing culture presented a distant but mutually respectful relationship between senior management and the pot room operatives. Certainly the distance was generally sufficient that it would not be appropriate for management to direct that Communities of Practice be established, nor to be involved in them. The pot room workers (in the main) regarded the technical and professional employees with some degree of cynicism, seeing them as having 'no clue' about the real world at the furnace front. It would therefore not be appropriate for these professionals to be directly or immediately involved in Community of Practice discussions unless later invited willingly by the pot room workers at a point where some input from the white collar specialists might be welcomed.

In a context where a union is both powerful and has high potential to be obstructive, it would be unwise to proceed without their direct blessing, since there is a risk that any initiative which seems related to securing greater productivity or company advantage is just another form of potential exploitation. In this aluminium smelter example, union relationships with management were reasonably co-operative. Whilst the union was strong, there was no immediate history of extreme use/abuse of that power, and in the rural setting of the plant, it was always a concern of the union that employment remain high. Job loss would be a serious matter and whatever co-operation with management was needed to ensure the success of the smelter overall, would be given reasonable consideration. It would therefore be possible for a Community of Practice approach to be instituted and driven by local union leadership, and that would only have occurred if those leaders had been thoroughly educated and inspired to pick up this role. At least one of the strategies for establishing Communities of Practice is therefore to work closely with local union leaders to gain understanding of the nature and value of the Communities of Practice, and to then support the union's efforts in establishing the community

meetings by validating the necessary time, and providing simple facilitation in the form of some secretarial and organisational help *if requested*, and perhaps some refreshments or the like to enhance the experience of workers' meetings. The provision of a new tearoom for meeting purposes might be a simple enabler and encourager of community of interested practitioners' activity in production facilities such as this smelter. Even union-driven establishment of Communities of Practice relies upon workers continuing to feel that their participation is at all times voluntary, and that the sharing of knowledge remains something which is neither required nor carries any direct consequences if avoided and which is pleasurable and engaging for its own sake.

Further, the issue of potential productivity, if linked in any way in the minds of the operators with a possible shedding of jobs via greater efficiency from fewer people, is a matter that must be managed and addressed very early in the life of the 'communities' initiative. Operators will ask themselves whether their tacit knowledge, once identified and harvested, might not make it possible for management to do without the original holders of that know-how. If they do not raise it as a fear explicitly, they are highly likely to be thinking it nonetheless and such concern can undermine any and all efforts to create a culture where communities of interest could be fostered. Less educated workers in a rural setting will have few other employment options outside the smelter and job security is a compelling motive for preserving some form of *status quo*. What is needed is some explicit reassurance about employment stability where it is possible and a clear disconnection between Community of Practice knowledge gathering and transfer and job loss. If the motives of management are anything other than 'pure', the workers' defensive culture will preclude any genuine sharing of their tacit knowledge, so this is one of the most basic issues to elucidate.

Where a union is perhaps not best placed to be the driver of a Community of Practice initiative, shift supervisors and leading hands become the obvious point of ownership and leadership in the first instance. Virtually any and every processing or manufacturing plant will have persons designated as leading hands, or shift supervisors or suchlike, people who are clearly in amongst and of the workers. Again, this may require some dialogue to engage the interest and understanding of those leading hands, some awareness-raising generally to issues of knowledge loss/retention, some non-blaming direct discussion about the effectiveness of the training processes which are taking place on the plant floor.

In this case, pot room operatives were trained on-the-job in a highly informal manner with the significant exception of rigorous training for occupational safety reasons. Health and safety training was accepted as a given priority in such a highly dangerous environment, and so taken most seriously by all. All other training to do with the management of the processes in the pots was an unstructured process of mentoring, of anecdotal 'indoctrination' of new workers by 'old hands' who believed that they knew how the processes could be best managed for best outcome. This is an oral tradition of 'folk learning', and whilst it may be highly effective at best, it might also be highly inaccurate and inefficient at worst, or possibly very fragmentary, leaving significant gaps in new operatives' knowledge. In fact, many of the experienced operatives in the pot room held great pride in the knowledge that they had managed to accumulate over the years, and were quietly interested to demonstrate what they knew and compare with others' views when the opportunity came as described by Urpani (1996) and mentioned earlier in this paper.

A culture of pride in knowledge suggests that pot room workers would not respond overly well to suggestions that they form Communities of Practice in order to help the smelter become more profitable *per se*, not unless there was some bonus or financial benefit to be gained for themselves. Neither would they have wanted to engage simply because management or the professional specialists thought it a good idea and wished them to do so. They may well have resisted any effort to describe or see the Communities of Practice initiative as 'training' since they has long associated training with occupational health and safety training, which they respected and took seriously.

In linking the creation of a Community of Practice with the existing cultural values, it is therefore likely that the pot room workers would have been interested *if the initiative had been presented to them as a chance to demonstrate and compare their craft knowledge*, a subtle opportunity to allow gentle competition perhaps between shifts, or to allow older workers to share what they had intuitively learned over many years for the benefit of younger workers. Leading hands or shift supervisors are normally the best placed people to find the right level of challenge and flattery to engage their colleagues in this way. Once underway, it appears highly likely that the workers themselves would have had enough quiet interest in the exchange of knowledge to keep the process going. But for the undercurrent fear of job loss to remain at bay, the smelter managers would indeed have to have openly discussed and reassured operators about job security, and kept those promises.

Communities of Practice need to meet regularly in order to avoid becoming seen as 'flash in the pan' erratic events, but not necessarily every week. They may be steered by a shift supervisor to consider a particular topic at each meeting, but most properly should develop their own agenda of topics of interest to themselves. (e.g., "What do you do if the pots start doing X, and you can see the temperature rising by Y degrees? What's the best way you've found to stop process Z from escalating?"). The tacit knowledge is fragmentary, often poorly articulated and the process of surfacing it, sharing it, exploring its meaning and in some way structuring it for transfer or improvement of process is a slow and gradual process that plays out over time. It is also not a static body of knowledge, but rather one that is evolving continuously over extended periods of time. One or even several meetings will simply not achieve the knowledge body that is required to work towards the mixed mode modelling best practice approach outlined in this paper.

Communities of Practice in the Commercial Refrigeration Manufacturing Plant

Environments with generally more educated, skilled or professional workforces may be, on balance, more amenable to Communities of Practice if other issues raised above are also adequately managed. Operative-management power differentials may be less marked, and the desire for more formalised learning and training is culturally more compatible. Additionally, the refrigeration technicians and engineers described in the earlier example would be well aware of the competitive nature of the commercial refrigeration industry and possibly more aware that some competitive advantage for the firm would attach to quick turnaround times on production. This makes it easier to engage employees in a collaborative approach to surfacing the tacit knowledge. Issues of job security are also perhaps a little less fraught in a metropolitan setting where the location and the skills sets the workers hold both point to some alternative employment options and perhaps less anxiety about job loss if some efficiency is achieved.

Nonetheless, the Community of Practice approach to gathering and identifying tacit knowledge amongst the refrigeration workers would need to observe all the provisos mentioned above for the smelter to some extent. It would be equally important that the community activity is clearly owned by the technicians and professionals and that clear enabling and resourcing strategies were made by the management. Professional environments can also be deeply competitive cultures where each skilled technician or designer seeks to 'best' their colleagues, perhaps chasing performance related rewards, and unless that competitiveness can be quietened and harnessed to a more collaborative desire to share and improve the tacit knowledge contribution to best practice outcomes, then the community initiative can be futile. Semi-professional environments often regard knowledge management, development of a knowledge repository and collegial mentoring as a normal part of the individual's job description, and in this respect, the culture is often 'half-way there'. Performance management regimes in this kind of context may be best geared in part to collective goals of knowledge harvest and improved processes to which all in the group have contributed. At least some targets need to be collectively, team framed and achieved, and rewards less individually focused on certain tacit knowledge issues.

In the refrigeration industry case, the added problem is that there are literally enormous amounts of tacit (and generated tacit) knowledge available (the latter being that which is generated between the technicians/engineers in discussing product development problems) and held by the engineers and laboratory technicians that needs to be captured. Additionally, this tacit knowledge (and indeed explicit knowledge) is being continuously added to (especially given the level of intensive research and development that is going into to production of 'environmentally friendly' CO_2 refrigeration). In this context, one may well run the risk of overburdening the holders of the tacit knowledge with requests that they share it, thereby creating a degree of resentment given the already heavy workload being experienced.

In summary, Communities of Practice need to sit comfortably with the culture and values of the organisation, or part thereof, and of the employee groups within. They should be clearly owned and facilitated by the community of workers whose experience and knowledge is to be shared. Minimal leadership is best and may in fact become a rotating or shared function as agreed by the workers (in less

–educated and skilled situations). Communities of Practice are normally best presented to workers as opportunities to share, compare and learn for the benefit of all, especially newer workers, so that the 'craft' is not lost or diminished. They may be best presented to semi-professional employees as opportunities for continuous improvement of the processes and competitive advantage for the firm.

5. CONCLUSION

This paper has examined the use of a mixed-mode modelling approach as a methodology of facilitating best practice in manufacturing in situation that are faced with the tacit knowledge problem. In the development of the mixed-mode modelling in the cases used to illustrate the problem in the paper, one of the sub-models used was the Communities of Practice. This was used to facilitate the capture of tacit knowledge. The paper has raised some of the main problems associated with the use of these Communities of Practice and suggested some ways of overcoming them. It is hoped that the ideas contained in this paper will encourage others wishing to achieve best practice in similar situations, to do so using the approach outlined in this paper.

REFERENCES

Ackerman, M., Pipek, V., & Wulf, V. (Eds.). (2003). *Sharing expertise: Beyond knowledge management*. London: MIT Press.

Boiral, O. (2002). Tacit knowledge and environmental management. *Long Range Planning, 35*, 291–317. doi:10.1016/S0024-6301(02)00047-X

Brown, J. S., & Duguid, P. (1991). Organisational learning and communities-of-practice: Towards a unified view of working, learning and innovation. *Organization Science, 2*(1), 40–57. doi:10.1287/orsc.2.1.40

Burk, M. (2000). Communities of practice. *Public Roads, 63*(6). Retrieved April 14, 2009 from http://www.tfhrc.gov/pubrds/mayjune00/commprac.htm

Checkland, P. (1981). *Systems thinking, systems practice*. Chichester, UK: John Wiley and Sons.

Checkland, P. (1999). *Soft Systems Methodology: A 30-Year Perspective*. West Sussex, UK: John Wiley and Sons.

Coakes, E., & Clarke, S. (Eds.). (2006). *Encyclopedia of communities of practice and information and knowledge management*. Hershey, PA: IGI Global.

Collins, H. M. (2001). Tacit knowledge, trust and the Q of sapphire. *Social Studies of Science, 31*(1), 71–85. doi:10.1177/030631201031001004

Davies, J., Duke, A., & Sure, Y. (2003). OntoShare – a knowledge management environment for virtual communities of practice. In *Proceedings of the 2nd International Conference on Knowledge Capture* (pp. 20-27). New York: Association for Computing Machinery.

Fischer, G. (2001). Communities of interest: Learning through the interaction of multiple knowledge systems. In *Proceedings of the 24th Annual Information Systems Research Seminar, Ulvik, Norway* (pp. 1 -14). Retrieved April 20, 2009 from http://l3d.cs.colorado.edu/~gerhard/papers/iris24.pdf

Fischer, G. (2004). Social creativity: Turning barriers into opportunities for collaborative design. In F. de Cindio & D. Schuler (Eds.), *Proceedings of the Participatory Design Conference (PDC'04)*, University of Toronto, Canada (pp. 152-161).

Gourlay, S. (2006). Towards conceptual clarity for 'tacit knowledge': a review of empirical studies. *Knowledge Management Research and Practice, 4*, 60–69. doi:10.1057/palgrave.kmrp.8500082

Kanjanabootra, S. (2009). *Understanding how the adoption of Knowledge Engineering can improve business value through better product development and improvement processes.* Unpublished Doctoral thesis in progress, RMIT University, Melbourne, Australia.

Lehaney, B. (1996). Mixed-mode modelling. In Johnson, D., & O'Brien, F. (Eds.), *Operations Research Keynote Papers* (pp. 150–157). Birmingham, UK: Operational Research Society.

Lehaney, B., & Clarke, S. (1997). Soft systems methodology (and simulation) for mixed-mode modelling? In O'Brien, F., & Orman, A. (Eds.), *Operations Research Keynote Papers* (pp. 16–33). Birmingham, UK: Operational Research Society.

Lehaney, B., Clarke, S., Coakes, E., & Jack, G. (2004). *Beyond knowledge management.* Hershey, PA: IGI Global.

Louis, L. R. (2006). Technical issues facing work groups, Teams and knowledge networks. In Coakes, E., & Clarke, S. (Eds.), *Encyclopedia of communities of practice in information and knowledge management* (pp. 532–536). Hershey, PA: IGI Global.

Marchant, G., & Robinson, J. (1999). Is knowing the tax code all it takes to be a tax expert? On the development of legal expertise. In Sternberg, R., & Horvath, J. A. (Eds.), *Tacit knowledge in professional practice* (pp. 3–20). Mahwah, NJ: Laurence Erlbaum Associates.

Midgley, G. (1992). The sacred and the profane in critical systems thinking. *Systems Practice, 5,* 5–16. doi:10.1007/BF01060044

Mingers, J., & Brocklesby, J. (1996). Multi-methodology: Towards a framework for mixing methodologies. *Systemist, 18,* 101–131.

Nicholls, M. G. (2009). Mixed-mode modelling – What is it and how can it help? *Decision Line, 40*(3), 10–13.

Nicholls, M. G., & Cargill, B. J. (2001). The use of mixed-mode modelling for determining best practice for a business. In Nicholls, M. G., Clarke, S., & Lehaney, B. (Eds.), *Mixed-model modelling: mixing methodologies for organisational intervention: Applied Optimisation 58* (pp. 259–292). Boston: Kluwer Academic Publishers.

Nicholls, M. G., & Cargill, B. J. (2008). Determining best practice production in an aluminium smelter involving sub-processes based substantially on tacit knowledge – An application of communities of practice. *The Journal of the Operational Research Society, 59,* 13–24. doi:10.1057/palgrave.jors.2602320

Nicholls, M. G., Clarke, S., & Lehaney, B. (Eds.). (2001). *Mixed-mode modelling: Mixing methodologies for organisational intervention: Applied Optimisation 58.* Boston: Kluwer Academic Publishers.

Nicholls, M. G., & Eady, J. (2008). Overcoming the tacit knowledge problem in the commercial refrigeration industry using mixed-mode modelling. In M. A. Amouzegar (Ed.), *Proceedings of the 37th Annual Meeting of the Western Decision Sciences Institute* (pp. 555-558). San Diego, CA: Western Decision Sciences Institute.

Nicholls, M. G., & Hedditch, D. J. (1993). The development of an integrated model of an aluminium smelter. *The Journal of the Operational Research Society, 44,* 225–235.

Nonaka, I., & Takeuchi, H. (1995). *The knowledge creating company.* Oxford: Oxford University Press.

Orr, J. E. (1996). *Talking about machines: An ethnography of a modern job.* Ithaca, NY: Cornell University Press.

Paquette, S. (2006). Communities of practice as facilitators of knowledge exchange. In Coakes, E., & Clarke, S. (Eds.), *Encyclopedia of communities of practice and information and knowledge management* (pp. 68–73). Hershey, PA: IGI Global.

Patel, V. L., Arocha, J., & Kaufman, D. R. (1999). Expertise and tacit knowledge in medicine. In Sternberg, R. J., & Horvath, J. A. (Eds.), *Tacit knowledge in professional practice* (pp. 75–100). Mahwah, NJ: Laurence Erlbaum Associates.

Saint-Onge, H., & Wallace, D. (2003). *Leveraging communities of practice for strategic advantage*. Boston: Butterworth-Heinemann.

Senge, P. (1990). *The fifth discipline: The art and practice of the learning organization*. London: Century Business.

Urpani, D. (1996). *Knowledge acquisition from real world data*. Unpublished doctoral thesis, Swinburne University of Technology, Melbourne, Australia.

Vestal, W. (2003). Ten traits for successful communities of practice. *Knowledge Management Review, 56*, 6.

Wagner, R. K., Sujan, J., Sujan, M., Rashotte, C. A., & Sternberg, R. J. (1999). Tacit knowledge in sales. In Sternberg, R. J., & Horvath, J. A. (Eds.), *Tacit Knowledge in Professional Practice* (pp. 155–182). Mahwah, NJ: Laurence Erlbaum Associates.

Wenger, E. (1998). *Communities of Practice: Learning, meaning and identity*. Cambridge, UK: Cambridge University Press.

Wenger, E. (2002). *Cultivating communities of practice – a guide to managing knowledge*. Boston: Harvard Business School Press.

Wenger, E. (2003). Communities of practice and social learning systems. In Nicolini, D., Gherardi, S., & Yanow, D. (Eds.), *Knowing in organizations – A practice–based approach* (pp. 76–99). Armonk, NY: ME Sharpe Inc.

Zappavigna, M. S. (2006). Tacit knowledge in communities of practice. In Coakes, E., & Clarke, S. (Eds.), *Encyclopedia of communities of practice and information and knowledge mangement* (pp. 508–513). Hershey, PA: IGI Global.

This work was previously published in The International Journal of Sociotechnology and Knowledge Development, Volume 2, Issue 2, edited by Elayne Coakes, pp. 35-52, copyright 2010 by IGI Publishing (an imprint of IGI Global).

Compilation of References

Acharya, P., & Mahanty, B. (2008). Manpower shortage crisis in Indian information technology industry. *International Journal of Technology Management, 38*(3), 235–247. doi:10.1504/IJTM.2007.012712

Ackerman, M., Pipek, V., & Wulf, V. (Eds.). (2003). *Sharing expertise: Beyond knowledge management.* London: MIT Press.

Acuña, S. T., & Juristo, N. (2004). Assigning people to roles in software projects. *Software, Practice & Experience, 34*(7), 675–696. doi:10.1002/spe.586

Adaman, F., & Devine, P. (2002). A reconsideration of the theory of entrepreneurship: a participatory approach. *Review of Political Economy, 14*(3), 329–355. doi:10.1080/09538250220147877

Agarwal, R., & Ferratt, T. W. (2002). Enduring practices for managing IT professionals. *Communications of the ACM, 45*(9), 73–79. doi:10.1145/567498.567502

Ahuja, M. K., & Galvin, J. E. (2003). Socialization in virtual groups. *Journal of Management, 29*(2), 161–185. doi:10.1177/014920630302900203

Albert, S., Flournoy, D., & LeBrasseur, R. (2009). *Networked Communities: Strategies for Digital Collaboration.* Hershey, PA, USA: IGI Global.

Alegre, J., & Chiva, R. (2008). Assessing the impact of organizational learning capability on product innovation performance: An empirical test. *Technovation, 28*, 315–326. doi:10.1016/j.technovation.2007.09.003

Allee, V. (1997). 12 principles of knowledge management. *Training & Development, 51*, 71–75.

Allen, C. (Ed.). (2003). *HR-XML recommendation. Competencies (Measurable Characteristics). Recommendation.* Retrieved March 5, 2010, from http://www.hr-xml.org/

Amabile, T. M. (1988). A model of creativity and innovation in organisations. In Straw, B. M., & Cummings, L. L. (Eds.), *Research in Organisational Behaviour* (Vol. 10, pp. 123–167). Greenwich, CT: JAI Press.

Amit, R., Glosten, L., & Muller, E. (1993). Challenges to theory development in entrepreneurship research. *Journal of Management Studies, 30*(5), 815–834. doi:10.1111/j.1467-6486.1993.tb00327.x

Anderson, S., & Messick, S. (1974). Social competency in young children. *Developmental Psychology, 10*(2), 282–293. doi:10.1037/h0035988

Andriole, S. (2005). *The 2nd Digital Revolution.* Hershey, PA: IGI Global. doi:10.4018/978-1-59140-801-7

Archives of the ICF - Sudbury. (2006). [Intelligent Community Applications.]. *Top (Madrid), 21.*

Armstrong, A., & Hagel, J. (1996). The Real Value of Online Communities. *Harvard Business Review, 7*(3), 134–141.

Augoustinos, M., & Walker, I. (1995). *Social Cognition; an integrated introduction* (p.177). London: Sage.

Avison, D. E., Cuthbertson, C. H., & Powell, P. (1999). The paradox of information systems: Strategic value and low status. *The Journal of Strategic Information Systems, 8*(4), 419–445. doi:10.1016/S0963-8687(00)00026-3

Baccarini, D. (1996). The concept of project complexity - a review. *International Journal of Project Management, 14*(4), 201–204. doi:10.1016/0263-7863(95)00093-3

Baecker, R. M., & Greenberg, S. (Eds.). (1995). *Readings in human-computer interaction: toward the year 2000* (2nd ed.). San Francisco, CA: Morgan Kaufmann.

Bagby, J. W. (1957, May). A cross-cultural study of perceptual predominance in binocular rivalry. *J Abnorm Psychol.*, *54*(3), 331–334. doi:10.1037/h0046310

Balka, E. (2000). *New Brunswick: the call centre capital of North America.* Simon Fraser University. Retrieved August 25, 2008 from http://www.emergence.nu/events/budapest/balka.pdf

Barnes, K., Marateo, R. C., & Ferris, S. P. (2007). Teaching and learning with the Net Generation *Innovate. Journal of Online Education*, *3*(4).

Barr, R. B., & Tagg, J. (1995). From teaching to learning. A new paradigm for undergraduate education. *Change*, *27*(6), 13–25.

Bartlett, A. (1969). Sustainability 101: Arithmetic, Population, and Energy. In *Proceedings of the Energy Efficiency Policy Symposium*, Honolulu, Hawaii.

Bassellier, G., Reich, B. H., & Benbasat, I. (2001). IT Competence of Business Managers: A Definition and Research Model. *Journal of Management Information Systems*, *17*(4), 159–182.

Battré, D. (2008). Caching of intermediate results in DHT-based RDF stores. *International Journal of Metadata. Semantics and Ontologies*, *4*(3), 183–195.

Bechhofer, S., van Harmelen, F., Hendler, J., Horrocks, I., McGuinness, D. L., Patel-Schneider, P. F., & Stein, L. A. (2004). *OWLWeb Ontology Language Reference.* Retrieved from http://www.w3.org/TR/owl-ref/

Becker, W., & Dietz, J. (2004). R&D co-operation and innovation activities of firms-evidence for the German manufacturing industry. *Research Policy*, *33*, 209–223. doi:10.1016/j.respol.2003.07.003

Beer, S. (1979). *The Heart of Enterprise.* Chichester, UK: Wiley.

Belbin, R. M. (1982). *Management Teams: Why They Succeed or Fail.* New York: Halsted Press.

Bell, D. (2007). *Cyberculture Theorists: Manuel Castells and Donna Haraway.* London: Routledge.

Bennett, S., Maton, K., & Kervin, L. (2008). The 'digital natives' debate: A critical review of the evidence. *British Journal of Educational Technology*, *39*(5), 775–786. doi:10.1111/j.1467-8535.2007.00793.x

Berger, P., & Luckmann, T. (1967). *The social construction of reality.* London: Penguin.

Berkhout, F. (2006). Normative expectations in systems innovation. *Technology Analysis and Strategic Management*, *18*(3/4), 299–311. doi:10.1080/09537320600777010

Berners-Lee, T., Hendler, J., & Lassila, O. (2001). The Semantic Web. *Scientific American*, *284*(5), 34–43. doi:10.1038/scientificamerican0501-34

Bernstein, B., & Singh, P. J. (2006). An integrated innovation process model based on practices of Australian biotechnology firms. *Technovation*, *26*(5/6), 561–572. doi:10.1016/j.technovation.2004.11.006

Berry, F. (2007). Strategic planning as a tool for managing organizational change. *International Journal of Public Administration*, *30*, 331–346. doi:10.1080/01900690601117812

Bertrand, F., & Larrue, C. (2004). Integration of the Sustainable Development Evaluation Process in regional planning: Promises and problems in the case of France. *Journal of Environmental Assessment Policy and Management*, *6*(4), 443–463. doi:10.1142/S1464333204001821

Bessant, J., Lamming, R., Noke, H., & Phillips, W. (2005). Managing innovation beyond the steady state. *Technovation*, *25*(12), 1366–1376. doi:10.1016/j.technovation.2005.04.007

Betz, F. (2003). *Managing Technological Innovation: Competitive Advantage from Change* (2nd ed.). New York: John Wiley & Sons.

Blecker, T. (2005). *Information and Management Systems for Product Customization.* Boston: Springer.

Blumberg, B., Cooper, D., & Schindler, P. (2005). *Business Research Methods* (9th ed.). New York: McGraw-Hill.

Boellstorff, T. (2008). *Coming of Age in Second Life: An Anthropologist Explores the Virtually Human.* Princeton, NJ: Princeton University Press.

Boiral, O. (2002). Tacit knowledge and environmental management. *Long Range Planning, 35,* 291–317. doi:10.1016/S0024-6301(02)00047-X

Bonk, C. J., & King, K. S. (1998). *Electronic Collaborators: Learner Centered Technologies for Literacy, Apprenticeship, and Discourse.* Mahweh, NJ: Lawrence Erlbaum.

Bostrom, R. P., & Heinen, J. S. (1977). MIS Problems and Failures: A Socio-Technical Perspective. *Management Information Systems Quarterly,* 11–28. doi:10.2307/249019

Boxman, E., & Flap, H. (2001). Getting Started: The influence of social capital on the start of the occupational career. In N. Lin, R. Burt, & S. K. Cook (Eds.), *Social Capital: Theory and Research* (4th ed., pp. 159-184). New Brunswick, NJ: Transaction publisher.

Boyatzis, R. E. (1982). *The Competent Manager. A model for effective performance.* New York: John Wiley & Sons Ltd.

Boyd, D., & Ellison, N. (2008). Social Network Sites: Definition, History, and Scholarschip. *Journal of Computer-Mediated Communication, 13,* 210–230. doi:10.1111/j.1083-6101.2007.00393.x

Brandenburger, A., & Nalebuff, B. (1996). *Coopetition.* New York: Currency Doubleday.

Brooks, F. P. (1987, April). No Silver Bullet: Essence and Accidents of Software Engineering. *Computer Magazine.*

Brown, J. S., & Duguid, P. (1991). Organisational learning and communities-of-practice: Towards a unified view of working, learning and innovation. *Organization Science, 2*(1), 40–57. doi:10.1287/orsc.2.1.40

Bryman, A. (2008). *Social research methods* (3rd ed.). New York: Oxford University Press.

Buchanan, L., & O'Connell, A. (2006, January). A Brief History of Decision making. *Harvard Business Review,* 32–41.

Burch, G. St. J., Pavelis, C., Hemsley, D. R., & Corr, P. J. (2006). Schizotypy and creativity in visual artists. *The British Journal of Psychology, 97,* 177–190. doi:10.1348/000712605X60030

Burk, M. (2000). Communities of practice. *Public Roads, 63*(6). Retrieved April 14, 2009 from http://www.tfhrc.gov/pubrds/mayjune00/commprac.htm

Burt, R. S. (1992). *Structural Holes.* Cambridge, MA: Harvers University Press.

Burt, R. S. (2005). *Brokerage and Closure: An introduction to Social Capital* (1st ed.). New York: Oxford University Press.

Burt, R. S., Jannotta, J. E., & Mahoney, J. T. (1998). Personality correlates of structural holes. *Social Networks, 20*(1), 63–87. doi:10.1016/S0378-8733(97)00005-1

Busha, C. H., & Harter, S. P. (1980). *Research Methods in Librarianship – Techniques and Interpretation.* New York: Academic Press.

Butler, B. S. (2001). Membership Size, Communication Activity, and Sustainability: A Resource-Based Model of Online Social Structures. *Information Systems Research, 12*(4), 346–362. doi:10.1287/isre.12.4.346.9703

Byron, K. (2008). Differential effects of male and female managers' non-verbal emotional skills on employees' ratings. *Journal of Managerial Psychology, 23*(2), 118–134. doi:10.1108/02683940810850772

Caldine, R. (1994). *An Introduction to Educational Television and Video.* Wollongong, Australia: University of Wollongong, Centre for Staff Development.

Cam, C. N. (2004). A conceptual framework for socio-techno-centric approach to sustainable development. *International Journal of Technology, Management, and Sustainable Development, 3*(1), 59–66. doi:10.1386/ijtm.3.1.59/0

Cannon, J. (1994). Why IT Applications Succeed or Fail: The Interaction of Technical and Organizational Factors. *Industrial and Commercial Training Journal, 26*(1), 10–15. doi:10.1108/00197859410051226

Carroll, J. M. (2000). *Making Use - scenario-based design of human-computer interactions.* Cambridge, Massachusetts: The MIT Press.

Caruso, J. B., & Kvavik, R. (2005). *ECAR study of students and information technology 2005: Convenience, connection, control, and learning.*

Casado-Lumbreras, C., Colomo-Palacios, R., Gómez-Berbís, J. M., & García-Crespo, Á. (2009). Mentoring programmes: a study of the Spanish software industry. *International Journal of Learning and Intellectual Capital*, *6*(3), 293–302. doi:10.1504/IJLIC.2009.025046

Cassano-Piche, Vicente, K. J., & Jamieson, G. A. (2009). A test of Rasmussen's risk management framework in the food safety domain: BSE in the UK. *Theoretical Issues in Ergonomics Science*, *10*, 283–304. doi:10.1080/14639220802059232

Castells, M. (1996). The Rise of the Network Society. In *The Information Age: Economy, Society and Culture* (*Vol. 1*). Malden, MA: Blackwell.

Castells, M. (2000). Materials for an Exploratory Theory of the Network Society. *The British Journal of Sociology*, *51*(1), 5–24. doi:10.1080/000713100358408

Cavaleri, S., & Seivert, S. (2005). *Knowledge Leadership*. Burlington, MA: Elsevier.

Cayer, C. (1999). Innovation - a product of the learning organisation. In *Proceedings of the 4th International Conference on ISO 9000* (pp. 1-6).

Chambers, R. (1997). *Whose reality counts? Putting the first last*, Bourton-on-Dunsmore: ITDG Publishing.

Charles, A. (2009). Book Review: Ambivalence Towards Convergence: Digitalization and the Media Age. In T. Storsul & D. Stuedahl (Eds.), *Convergence: The International Journal of Research into New Media Technologies*. Retrieved April 8, 2009, from http://con.sagepub.com/cgi/reprint/15/1/123.pdf

Checkland, P. (1981). *Systems thinking, systems practice*. Chichester, UK: John Wiley and Sons.

Checkland, P. (1999). *Soft Systems Methodology: A 30-Year Perspective*. West Sussex, UK: John Wiley and Sons.

Chen, C. (2006). *Information Visualization: Beyond the Horizon* (2nd ed.). London: Springer Verlag. Christensen, C. (1997). *The Innovator's Dilemma: When New Technologies Cause Great Firms to Fail*. Boston: Harvard Business School Press.

Cheng, R., & Vassileva, J. (2006). Design and Evaluation of an Adaptive Incentive Mechanism for Sustained Educational Online Communities. *User Modeling and User-Adapted Interaction*, *16*(3-4), 321–348. doi:10.1007/s11257-006-9013-6

Choo, C. W., & Bontis, N. (Eds.). (2002). *The strategic management of intellectual capital and organizational knowledge*. New York: Oxford University Press.

Chopra, A., & Kundu, A. (2008). The Fair Tracing project: digital tracing technology and Indian coffee. *Contemporary South Asia*, *16*(2), 217–230. doi:10.1080/09584930701733548

Christiansen, D. (2008, February 25). Estimating Project Risk. *Information Technology Dark Side, a Corporate IT Survival Guide*. Retrieved from www.techdarkside.com

Chua, A., & Lam, W. (2005). Why KM projects fail: a multi-case analysis. *Journal of Knowledge Management*, *9*(3), 6–17. doi:10.1108/13673270510602737

Clark, H. H. (1992). *Arenas of Language Use*. Chicago, IL: University of Chicago Press.

Clegg, C. W. (2000). Socio-technical Principles for System Design. *Applied Ergonomics*, *31*, 463–477. doi:10.1016/S0003-6870(00)00009-0

Coakes, E. (2002). Knowledge Management: A socio-technical perspective. In Coakes, E., Willis, D., & Clarke, S. (Eds.), *Knowledge Management in the Sociotechnical World. The Graffiti Continues* (pp. 4–14). London: Springer.

Coakes, E. (2006). Storing and sharing knowledge: supporting the management of knowledge made explicit in transnational organizations. *The Learning Organization*, *13*(6), 579–593. doi:10.1108/09696470610705460

Coakes, E., & Clarke, S. (Eds.). (2005). *Encyclopedia of Communities of Practice in Information and Knowledge Management*. Hershey, PA: Idea Group Reference.

Coakes, E., & Coakes, J. (2009). A Meta-Analysis of the Direction and State of Sociotechnical Research in a Range of Disciplines: For Practitioners and Academics. *International Journal of Sociotechnology and Knowledge Development*, *1*(1), 1–52.

Coakes, E., & Ramirez, A. (2007). Solving Problems in Knowledge Sharing with Sociotechnical Approaches. *The Learning Organization, 14*(5).

Cohen, R. (2000). Ethics and Cybernetics: Levinasian Reflections. []. Dordrecht, The Netherlands: Elsevier.]. *Ethics and Information Technology, 2*, 27–35. doi:10.1023/A:1010060128998

Collazos, C. A., & García, R. (2007). Semantics-supported cooperative learning for enhanced awareness. *International Journal of Knowledge and Learning, 3*(4/5), 421–436. doi:10.1504/IJKL.2007.016703

Collin, A., & Holden, L. (1997). The nacional framework for vocational education and training. In Beardwell, I., & Holden, L. (Eds.), *Human Resource Management: A contemporany perspective* (pp. 345–377). London: Pitman.

Collins, J. (2001). *Good to Great*. London: Random House.

Collins, T. (2009). *What went wrong*. Retrieved from http://www.computerweekly.com/blogs/tony_collins/2009/05/what-went-wrong-with-234m-c-no.html

Collins, A., & Halverson, R. (2009). *Rethinking education in the age of technology: The digital revolution and schooling in America*. New York: Teachers College Press.

Collins, H. M. (2001). Tacit knowledge, trust and the Q of sapphire. *Social Studies of Science, 31*(1), 71–85. doi:10.1177/030631201031001004

Colomo-Palacios, R., García-Crespo, A., Gómez-Berbís, J. M., Casado-Lumbreras, C., & Soto-Acosta, P. (2010). SemCASS: technical competence assessment within software development teams enabled by semantics. *International Journal of Social and Humanistic Computing*.

Colomo-Palacios, R., Gómez-Berbís, J. M., García-Crespo, A., & Puebla Sánchez, I. (2008). Social Global Repository: using semantics and social web in software projects. *International Journal of Knowledge and Learning, 4*(5), 452–464. doi:10.1504/IJKL.2008.022063

Colomo-Palacios, R., Tovar-Caro, E., Garcia-Crespo, A., & Gomez-Berbis, M. J. (2010). Identifying Technical Competences of IT Professionals. The Case of Software Engineers. *International Journal of Human Capital and Information Technology Professionals, 1*(1), 31–43.

Cooke, B. (2004). Rules of thumb for participatory change events. In S. Hickey & M. Giles (Eds.), *Participation: from tyranny to transformation? Exploring new Approaches to Participation in Development* (pp. 42-57). London: Zed Books.

Cook, S. C., & Ferris, L. J. T. (2007). Re-evaluating systems engineering as a framework for tackling systems issues. *Systems Research and Behavioral Science, 24*(2), 169–181. doi:10.1002/sres.822

Cooper, A. (1999). *The Inmates Are Running the Asylum*. Indianapolis: SAMS.

Cormack, D., & New, G. (1997). *Why did I do that? Understanding and mastering your motives*. London: Hodder & Stoughton.

Cortright, J. (2001). New growth theory, technology and learning: A practitioner's guide. *U.S. Economic Development Administration, 4*, 35.

Costa, P. T., & McCrae, R. R. (1992). *Revised NEO Personality Inventory (NEO PI-R) and NEO Five-Factor Inventory (NEO-FFI) professional manual*. Odessa, FL: Psychological Assessment Resources.

Coyne, R. (1995). *Designing Information Technology in the Postmodern Age: From Method to Metaphor*. Cambridge, MA: MIT Press.

Coyne, R. (1999). *Technoromanticism: Digital Narrative, Holism, and the Romance of the Real*. Cambridge, MA: The MIT Press.

Cross, R., & Parker, A. (2004). *The Hidden Power of Social Networks*. Boston: Harvard Business School Press.

Cross, R., Prusak, L., & Parker, A. (2001). Knowing what we know: supporting knowledge creation and sharing in social networks. *Organizational Dynamics, 30*(2), 100–120. doi:10.1016/S0090-2616(01)00046-8

Cummings, J. M., Butler, B., & Kraut, R. (2002). The Quality of Online Social Relationships. *Communications of the ACM, 45*(7), 103–108. doi:10.1145/514236.514242

Cummings, T. G. (1978). Self-Regulating Work Groups: A Socio-Technical Synthesis. *Academy of Management Review, 3*(3), 625–634. doi:10.2307/257551

Curtis, B. (2002). Human Factors in Software Development. In Marciniak, J. J. (Ed.), *Encyclopedia of Software Engineering* (pp. 598–610). New York: Willey & Sons.

Dahlman, C. J. (2003). Using knowledge for development: a general framework and preliminary assessment of China. In B. Grewal, L. Xue, P. Sheehan, & F. Sun (Eds.), *China's future in the knowledge economy: engaging the new world* (pp. 35-66). Prieiga per internet.

Dahlman, C. J., Routti, J., & Ylä-Anttila, P. (2005). *Finland as a knowledge economy: Elements of success and lessons learned*. Washington, DC: The International Bank for Reconstruction and Development.

Daily Mail. (2008, April 15*). Two BA executives quit terminal 5 fiasco insurers refuse cover future luggage losses.* Retrieved from http://www.dailymail.co.uk/news/article-1015373/Two-BA-executives-quit-Terminal-5-fiasco-insurers-refuse-cover-future-luggage-losses.html

Danesi, M. (2002). *Understanding Media Semiotics*. London: Arnold.

Davenport, T. H., & Prusak, L. (1998). *Working Knowledge*. Boston, MA: Harvard Business School Press.

Davies, J., Duke, A., & Sure, Y. (2003). OntoShare – a knowledge management environment for virtual communities of practice. In *Proceedings of the 2nd International Conference on Knowledge Capture* (pp. 20-27). New York: Association for Computing Machinery.

Davies, J., Lytras, M. D., & Sheth, A. P. (2007). Semantic-Web-Based Knowledge Management. *IEEE Internet Computing, 11*(5), 14–16. doi:10.1109/MIC.2007.109

Davis, L. E., & Taylor, J. C. (1972). *Design of Jobs*. London: Penguin.

De Smet, M., Van Keer, H., & Valcke, M. (2009). Cross-age peer tutors in asynchronous discussion groups: A study of the evolution in tutor support. *Instructional Science, 37*(1), 87–105. doi:10.1007/s11251-007-9037-2

Dearborn, D. C., & Simon, H. A. (1958). Selective Perception: a Note on the Departmental Identifications of Executives. *Sociometry, 21*, 140–144. doi:10.2307/2785898

Dearden, A., & Rizvi, H. (2008). Adapting Participatory and Agile Software Methods to Participatory Rural Development. In *PDC'08: Experiences and Challenges, Proceedings of the Participatory Design Conference* (pp. 221-225). Bloomington, Indiana: Indiana University Press.

Dede, C. (2005). Planning for Neomillennial Learning Styles: Implications for Investments in Technology and Faculty. In D. Oblinger & J. Oblinger (Eds.), *Educating the Net generation*. Boulder, CO: EDUCAUSE. Retrieved from http://www.educause.edu/educatingthenetgen/

DeKay, S. (2009). Are Business-Oriented Social Networking Web Sites Useful Resources for Locating Passive Jobseekers? Results of a Recent Study. *Business Communication Quarterly, 72*(1), 101–105. doi:10.1177/1080569908330378

Dellarocas, C. (2003). The digitization of word of mouth: Promises and challenges of online feedback mechanisms. *Management Science, 49*(10), 1407–1424. doi:10.1287/mnsc.49.10.1407.17308

Dept of Finance and Personnel. Northern Ireland. (2009). *Successful Projects in Government*. Retrieved from http://spring.dfpni.gov.uk/annexa/project-management-sec1.htm

Descartes, R. (1642). Meditations. In N. Warburton (Ed.) (1999), *Philosophy: Basic Readings*. London: Routledge.

Desouza, K. C., & Hensgen, T. (2004). *Managing Information in Complex Organizations: Semiotics and Signals, Complexity and Chaos*. New York: M. E. Sharpe.

Dewberry, C., & Narendran, S. (2007, August). *The Development of the DASA: a Comprehensive Self-Report Measure of Decision-Making Ability and Style*. Presented at Twenty-first Research Conference on Subjective Probability, Utility and Decision-making, Warsaw, Poland.

Dewey, J. (1938). Logic: The Theory of Enquiry, Henry Holt & Co. In F. Betz (Ed.) (2003), *Managing Technological Innovation: Competitive Advantage from Change* (2nd ed.). Hoboken, NJ: John Wiley & Sons.

DiMaggio, P., Hargittai, E., Neuman, W., & Robinson, J. R. (2001). Social Implications of the Internet. *Annual Review of Sociology, 27*, 307–337. doi:10.1146/annurev.soc.27.1.307

Docker, T. (2008). *CITI*. Retrieved from www.citi.co.uk

Dodero, J. M., Sánchez-Alonso, S., & Frosch-Wilke, D. (2007). Generative Instructional Engineering of Competence Development Programmes. *Journal of Universal Computer Science, 13*(9), 1213–1233.

Dohmen, G. (2001). *Informal learning. An international review about an unattended form of human being for life-wide learning*. Bonn: BMBF. Retrieved January 15, 2010, from http://www.bmbf.de/pub/das_informelle_lernen.pdf

Douglas, M. (1975). *Humans Speak, a critical essay in: Implicit Meanings - Essays in Anthropology*. London: Routledge & Kegan Paul.

Draganidis, F., & Mentzas, G. (2006). Competency based management: a review of systems and approaches. *Information Management & Computer Security, 14*(1), 51–64. doi:10.1108/09685220610648373

Drazin, R., Glynn, M. A., & Kazanjian, K. (1999). Multilevel theorising about creativity in organisations. *Academy of Management Review, 24*(2), 286–307. doi:10.2307/259083

Dufour, Y., & Steane, P. (2007). Implementing knowledge management: a more robust model. *Journal of Knowledge Management, 11*(6), 68–80. doi:10.1108/13673270710832172

Duschinsky, P. (2009). *The Change Equation*. Cirencester, UK: Management Books 2000.

Dwivedi, Y. K., & Lal, B. (2007). Socio-economic determinants of broadband adoption. *Industrial Management and Data Systems Journal, 107*(5), 654–671. doi:10.1108/02635570710750417

Dwyer, C., Hiltz, S. R., & Passerini, K. (2007). *Trust and privacy concern within social networking sites: A comparison of Facebook and MySpace*. Paper presented at the AMCIS 2007, Keystone, CO.

Eckhardt, A., Von Stetten, A., & Laumer, S. (2009). Value contribution of it in recruiting: a multi-national causal analysis. In *Proceedings of the special interest group on management information system's 47th annual conference on Computer personnel research*.

Edison, T. (1913). *Attributed in Gould and Mason (1985). TAFE Board Telematics Program*. Melbourne, Australia: Office of the TAFE Board.

EFN Report. (2004, September). *The Euro area and the Lisbon strategy*.

Egan, G. (1973). *Face to face*. Monterey: Brooks/Cole.

Egan, G. (2002). *The skilled helper*. Pacific Grove: Brooks/Cole.

Eger, J. M. (2007). *Smart growth and the urban future. World Foundation for Smart Communities*. Retrieved November 5, 2007 from http://www.smartcommunities. org/library_cities.htm

Eijnatten, F. M. V., & Zwaan, A. V. D. (1998). The Dutch approach to organizational design: an alternative approach to business process reengineering. *Human Relations, 51*, 289–318. doi:10.1177/001872679805100305

Ellison, N. B., Steinfield, C., & Lampe, C. (2007). The benefits of Facebook 'friends:' Social capital and college students' use of online social network sites. *Journal of Computer-Mediated Communication, 12*(4), 1143–1168. doi:10.1111/j.1083-6101.2007.00367.x

Elvin, R. (2005). *Developing a risk estimation model from IT project failure (Tech. Rep.)* (Bronte-Stewart, M., Ed.). Paisley, UK: Paisley University.

Emery, M. (Ed.). (1993). *Participative Design for Participative Democracy*. Canberra, Australia: Australian National University.

Evangelista, R., & Sirilli, G. (1998). Innovation in the Service Sector: Results from the Italian Statistical Survey. *Technological Forecasting and Social Change, 58*, 251–269. doi:10.1016/S0040-1625(98)00025-0

Farquhar, J., & Rowley, J. (2006). Relationships and Online Consumer Communities. *Business Process Management Journal, 12*(2), 162–177. doi:10.1108/14637150610657512

Feldt, R., Torkar, R., Angelis, L., & Samuelsson, M. (2008). Towards individualized software engineering: empirical studies should collect psychometrics. In *Proceedings of the 2008 international workshop on Cooperative and human aspects of software engineering (CHASE '08)* (pp. 49-52).

Fensel, D. (2002). *Ontologies: A silver bullet for knowledge management and electronic commerce*. Berlin: Springer.

Fensel, D., van Harmelen, F., Horrocks, I., McGuinness, D. L., & Patel-Schneider, P. F. (2001). OIL: An ontology infrastructure for the semantic web. *IEEE Intelligent Systems, 16*(2), 38–45. doi:10.1109/5254.920598

Figler, R., & Hanlon, S. (2008). Management development and the unconscious from an analytical psychology framework. *Journal of Management Development, 27*(6), 613–630. doi:10.1108/02621710810877857

Fischer, G. (2001). Communities of interest: Learning through the interaction of multiple knowledge systems. In *Proceedings of the 24th Annual Information Systems Research Seminar,* Ulvik, Norway (pp. 1 -14). Retrieved April 20, 2009 from http://l3d.cs.colorado.edu/~gerhard/papers/iris24.pdf

Fischer, G. (2004). Social creativity: Turning barriers into opportunities for collaborative design. In F. de Cindio & D. Schuler (Eds.), *Proceedings of the Participatory Design Conference (PDC'04),* University of Toronto, Canada (pp. 152-161).

Fitzgerald, L. A. (2002). Chaos: the lens that transcends. *Journal of Organizational Change, 15*(4), 339–358. doi:10.1108/09534810210433665

Flew, T. (2005). *New Media: An Introduction* (2nd ed.). South Melbourne, Australia: Oxford University Press.

Flood, R. L., & Jackson, M. C. (1991a). *Creative Problem Solving*. Chichester, UK: Wiley.

Flood, R. L., & Jackson, M. C. (1991b). Total systems intervention: a practical face to critical systems thinking. *Systems Practice, 4,* 197–213. doi:10.1007/BF01059565

Flournoy, D. (2004). *The Broadband Millennium: Communication Technologies and Markets*. Chicago: International Engineering Consortium.

Ford, R. (2009, March 12). *The Times*. Retrieved from http://www.timesonline.co.uk/tol/news/politics/article5891179.ece

Fountain, C. (2005). Finding a Job in the Internet Age. *Social Forces, 83*(3), 1235–1262. doi:10.1353/sof.2005.0030

Frand, J. (2000, September/October). The information-age mindset: Changes in students and implications for higher education. *EDUCAUSE Review, 25,* 14–24.

Frey, T. (2006). *Watching the Income Tax System Implode*. Retrieved from www.futuristspeaker.com/2009/03/watching-the-income-tax-system-implode

Frey, T. (2009, March 27). The exponential nature of complexity - why the income tax system will collapse. *Impactlab*. Retrieved from www.impactlab.com/2009/03/27/watching-the-income-tax-system-implode

Friedhoff, R. M., & Peercy, M. S. (2000). *Visual Computing*. New York: Scientific American Library.

Friedman, T. L. (2006). *The World is Flat*. Farrar, Straus and Giroux, N.Y.

Friedman, T. (2000). *The Lexus and the olive branch*. New York: Anchor Books.

Fuller, J., Bartl, M., Ernst, H., & Muhlbacher, H. (2006). Community Based Innovation: How to Integrate Members of Virtual Communities into New Product Development. *Electronic Commerce Research, 6,* 57–73. doi:10.1007/s10660-006-5988-7

Furnham, A. (2005). *The psychology of behaviour at work: the individual in the organization*. Hove & New York: Psychology Press.

Gabriel, Y., & Griffiths, D. S. (2002). Emotion, learning and organizing. *The Learning Organization, 9*(5), 214–221. doi:10.1108/09696470210442169

Gangadharbatla, H. (2008). Facebook Me: Collective self-esteem, need to belong, and Internet self-efficacy as predictors of the iGeneration's attitudes toward social networking sites. *Journal of Interactive Advertising, 18*(2).

García-Crespo, A., Colomo-Palacios, R., Gomez-Berbís, J. M., & Tovar-Caro, E. (2009). IT Professionals' Competences: High School Students' Views. *Journal of Information Technology Education, 8*(1), 45–57.

Gargiulo, M., & Benassi, M. (2000). Trapped in Your Own Net? Network Cohesion, Structural Holes, and the Adaptations of Social Capital. *Organization Science, 11*(2), 183–196. doi:10.1287/orsc.11.2.183.12514

Gaunt, R. (1991). *Personal and group development for managers: an integrated approach through action learning*. Harlow: Longmans.

Gephart, R. P. (1993). The textual approach: risk and blame in disaster sense-making. *Academy of Management Journal, 36*(6), 1465–1514. doi:10.2307/256819

Gerwin, D., & Kolodny, H. (1992). *Management of Advanced Manufacturing Technology*. New York: Wiley.

Gilbert, C., Amalberti, R., Laroche, H., & Paries, J. (2007). Errors and Failures: Towards a New Safety Paradigm. *Journal of Risk Research, 10*(7), 959–975. doi:10.1080/13669870701504764

Gladwell, M. (2005) *Blink; the power of thinking without thinking*. London: Allen Lane.

Globerson, S., & Salvendy, G. (1984). A Socio-Technical Accounting Approach to the Evaluation of Job Performance. *International Journal of Operations & Production Management, 4*(3), 36–42. doi:10.1108/eb054718

Glynn, M. A. (1996). Innovative genius: a framework for relating individual and organisational intelligences to innovation. *Academy of Management Review, 21*(4), 1081–1111. doi:10.2307/259165

Goldberg, L. R. (1990). The structure of phenotypic personality traits. *The American Psychologist, 48*(1), 26–34. doi:10.1037/0003-066X.48.1.26

Gómez-Berbís, J. M., Colomo-Palacios, R., García Crespo, A., & Ruiz-Mezcua, B. (2008). ProLink: A Semantics-based Social Network for Software Project. *International Journal of Information Technology and Management, 7*(4), 392–404. doi:10.1504/IJITM.2008.018656

Goodall, B. (2008). Ryerson U. won't expel student over facebook study group. *The Chronicle of Higher Education.* Retrieved from http://chronicle.com/blogPost/Ryerson-U-Wont-Expel-Stud/3771/

Goodwin, K. (2007). *Perfecting Your Personas. User Interface.* Retrieved March 23, 2009, from http://www.uie.com/events/uiconf/2007/articles/perfecting_personas/

Goodyear, P., Jones, C., Asensio, M., Hodgson, V., & Steeples, C. (2005). Networked Learning in Higher Education: Students' Expectations and Experiences. *Higher Education, 50*(3), 473–508. doi:10.1007/s10734-004-6364-y

Gopal, R., Thompson, S., Tung, Y. A., & Whinston, A. B. (2005). Managing Risks in Multiple Online Auctions: An Options Approach. *Decision Sciences, 36*(3), 397–425. doi:10.1111/j.1540-5414.2005.00078.x

Gosling, J. (2004). *The War of the Worlds Invasion: An Historical Perspective.* Retrieved April 19, 2004, from www.btinternet.com/~jd.gosling/wotw/radio.htm

Gourlay, S. (2006). Towards conceptual clarity for 'tacit knowledge': a review of empirical studies. *Knowledge Management Research and Practice, 4*, 60–69. doi:10.1057/palgrave.kmrp.8500082

Granovetter, M. S. (1973). The Strength of Weak Ties. *American Journal of Sociology, 78*(6), 1360–1380. doi:10.1086/225469

Granovetter, M. S. (1974). *Getting a job: A study of Contacts and Careers* (1st ed.). Cambridge, MA: Harvard University Press.

Gray, P., & Hovav, A. (2008). From Hindsight to Foresight: Applying Futures Research Techniques in Information Systems. *Communications of AIS*, (22), 211-234.

Gregoriades, A., & Sutcliffe, A. G. (2006). Automated assistance for human factors analysis in complex systems. *Ergonomics, 49*(12/13), 1265–1287. doi:10.1080/00140130600612721

Grice, H. P. (1989). *Studies in the way of words*. Cambridge, MA: Harvard University Press.

Gruber, T. R. (1993). A translation approach to portable ontology specifications. *Knowledge Acquisition, 5*(2), 199–220. doi:10.1006/knac.1993.1008

Gruber, T. R. (2008). Collective knowledge systems: Where the social web meets the semantic web. *Web Semantics: Science. Services and Agents on the World Wide Web, 6*(1), 4–13.

Gu, B., Konana, P., Rajagopalan, B., & Chen, H. M. (2007). Competition among Virtual Communities and User Valuation: The Case of Investing-Related Communities. *Information Systems Research, 18*(1), 68–85. doi:10.1287/isre.1070.0114

Guzman, G. A. C., & Wilson, J. (2005). The "soft" dimension of organizational knowledge transfer. *Journal of Knowledge Management, 9*(2), 59–74. doi:10.1108/13673270510590227

Hackman, J., & Oldham, G. (1980). *Work redesign*. Reading: M. A: Addison-Wesley.

Hackman, R., & Oldham, G. R. (1976). Motivation Through the Design of Work: Test of a Theory. *Organizational Behavior and Human Performance, 16*, 250–279. doi:10.1016/0030-5073(76)90016-7

Haga, W. J., Graen, G., & Dansereau, F. Jr. (1974). Professionalism and role making in a service organisation: a longitudinal investigation. *American Sociological Review, 39*, 122–133. doi:10.2307/2094281

Hagel, J. I., & Armstrong, A. (1997). *Net Gain: Expanding Markets through Virtual Communities*. Boston: Harvard Business School Press.

Hanseth, O., Jacucci, E., Grisot, M., & Aanestad, M. (2006). Reflexive Standardization: Side Effects and Complexity in Standard Making. *Management Information Systems Quarterly, 30*, 563–581.

Hara, N., Bonk, C. J., & Angeli, C. (2000). Content analysis of online discussion in an applied educational psychology course. *Instructional Science, 28*, 115–152. doi:10.1023/A:1003764722829

Hara, N., & Hew, K. F. (2007). Knowledge-Sharing in an Online Community of Health-care Professionals. *Information Technology & People, 20*(3), 235–261. doi:10.1108/09593840710822859

Hargadon, A. (2003). *How Breakthroughs Happen*. Boston: Harvard Business School Press.

Hargreaves, D. H. (1967). *Social Relations in a Secondary School*. London: Routledge and Kegan Paul.

Heim, M. (1993). *The Metaphysics of Virtual Reality*. New York: Oxford University Press.

Heiskanen, T. (2004). A knowledge-building community for public sector professionals. *Journal of Workplace Learning: Employee Counselling Today, 16*(7), 370–384.

Hemetsberger, A., & Reinhardt, C. (2006). Learning and Knowledge-building in Open-source Communities. *Management Learning, 37*(2), 187–214. doi:10.1177/1350507606063442

Hermann, K. (2007). Post mass production paradigm (PMPP) trajectories. *Journal of Manufacturing Technology Management, 18*(8), 1022–1037. doi:10.1108/17410380710828316

Hermann, T., Loser, K. U., & Jahnke, I. (2007). The Sociotechnical Walkthrough (STWT): a means for Knowledge integration. *The Learning Organization, 14*(5), 450–464. doi:10.1108/09696470710762664

Herrmann, T., Hoffmann, M., Loser, K.-U., & Kunau, G. (2004). A modelling method for the development of groupware applications as socio-technical systems. *Behaviour & Information Technology, 23*(2), 119–135. doi:10.1080/01449290310001644840

Herrmann, T., & Loser, K.-U. (1999). Vagueness in models of socio-technical systems. *Behaviour & Information Technology, 18*(5), 313–323. doi:10.1080/014492999118904

Hersberger, J. A., Murray, A. L., & Rioux, K. S. (2007). Examining Information Exchange and Virtual Communities: An Emergent Framework. *Online Information Review, 31*(2), 135–147. doi:10.1108/14684520710747194

Hickey, S., & Mohan, G. (2004). Towards participation as transformation: critical themes and challenges. In S. Hickey & G. Mohan (Eds.), *Participation: from tyranny to transformation? Exploring new Approaches to Participation in Development* (pp. 3-25). London: Zed Books.

Hillery, G. A. (1963). Villages, Cities and Total Institutions. *American Sociological Review, 28*(5), 778–791. doi:10.2307/2089915

Holland, J. L. (1985). *Making Vocational Choices: A Theory of Vocational Choices and Work Environments* (2nd ed.). Englewood Cliffs, NJ: Prentice Hall.

Howell, J. M. (2005). The right stuff: identifying and developing effective champions of innovation. *The Academy of Management Executive, 19*(2), 108–119.

Howell, J. M., & Higgins, C. A. (1990). Champions of Technological Innovation. *Administrative Science Quarterly, 35*, 315–341. doi:10.2307/2393393

Huang, C. Y., & Lo, J. H. (2006). Optimal resource allocation for cost and reliability of modular software systems in the testing phase. *Journal of Systems and Software, 79*(5), 653–664. doi:10.1016/j.jss.2005.06.039

Hunsinger, J. (2008). The Virtual and Virtuality: Toward Dialogues of Transdisciplinarity. In Panteli, N., & Chiasson, M. (Eds.), *Exploring Virtuality Within and Beyond Organizations: Social, Global and Local Dimensions.* New York: Palgrave Macmillan.

ICF – Fredericton. (2008). *Top 7 Intelligent Community Award.* Retrieved August 25, 2008 from http://www.intelligentcommunity.org/index. php?src=gendocs&ref=Top7_2008_Fredericton_NB_Canada&category=Community

ICF – Gangnam-Gu. (2008). *Top 7 Intelligent Community Award.* Retrieved August 25, 2008 from http://www.intelligentcommunity.org/index. php?src=gendocs&ref=Top7_2008_Gangnam_Korea&category=Community

ICF - Manchester. (2006). *Top 7 Intelligent Community Award.* Retrieved August 25, 2008 from http://www.intelligentcommunity.org/index. php?src=gendocs&ref=Top7_2006_Manchester_UK&category=Community

ICF - Northeast Ohio. (2008). *Top 7 Intelligent Community Award.* Retrieved August 25, 2008 from http://www.intelligentcommunity.org/index. php?src=gendocs&ref=Top7_2008_Northeast_Ohio_USA&category=Community

ICF - Sunderland. (2007). *Top 7 Intelligent Communities of the Year.* Retrieved August 25, 2008 from http://www.intelligentcommunity.org/index. php?src=gendocs&ref=Top7_2007_Sunderland_UK&category=Community

ICF - Taipei. (2006). *Top 7 Intelligent Community Award.* Retrieved August 25, 2008 from http://www.intelligentcommunity.org/index.php?src=gendocs&ref=Top7_2006_Taipei_Taiwan&category=Community

ICF - Tianjin. (2006). *Top 7 Intelligent Community Award.* Retrieved August 25, 2008 from http://www.intelligentcommunity.org/index.php?src=gendocs&ref=Top7_2006_Tianjin_China&category=Community

Irani, L., Dourish, P., Grinter, R., & Phillips, K. (2008). *Postcolonial Computing.* University of California Irvine.

ISO. (1999). *International Standard 113407, Human Centred Design.* International Standards Organisation.

Ives, B., & Olsen, M. H. (1984). User involvement and MIS success: A review of research. *Management Science, 30*(5), 586–603. doi:10.1287/mnsc.30.5.586

Jahnke, I. (2006). *Dynamics of social roles at knowledge management. Socio-technical requirements for communities in organizations.* Wiesbaden, Germany: DUV.

Jahnke, I. (2008). Knowledge sharing through interactive social technologies: Development and change of social structures in Internet-based systems. In Bolisani, E. (Ed.), *Building the Knowledge Society on the Internet: Sharing and Echanging Knowledge in Networked Environments* (pp. 195–218). Hershey, PA: IGI Global.

Jahnke, I. (2009). Socio-technical communities – from informal to formal? In Whitworth, B., & De Moor, A. (Eds.), *Handbook of Research on Socio-Technical Design and Social Networking Systems* (pp. 763–778). Hershey, PA: IGI Global. doi:10.4018/978-1-60566-264-0.ch050

Jahnke, I. (2010). Dynamics of social roles in a knowledge management community. *Computers in Human Behavior, 26*(4), 533–546. doi:10.1016/j.chb.2009.08.010

Jahnke, I., & Herrmann, Th. (2006). Success factors for cultivating socio-technical communities from the role perspective. In Heinecke, A. M., & Paul, H. (Eds.), *Mensch und Computer im Strukturwandel* (pp. 103–113). Munich, Germany: Oldenbourg.

Jahnke, I., & Koch, M. (2009). Web 2.0 goes academia: Does Web 2.0 make a difference? *International Journal Web Based Communities, 5*(4), 484–500. doi:10.1504/IJWBC.2009.028085

Jahnke, I., Mattick, V., & Herrmann, Th. (2005). Inpud: Knowledge management for organizing study progress. *Journal Hochschuldidaktik, 16*(1), 13–16.

Jahnke, I., Terkowsky, C., Pleul, Ch., & Tekkaya, E. (2010). Online learning with remote-configured experiments. In *Proccedings of DeLFI*. Duisburg, Essen: Deutsche E-Learning Fachtagung Informatik.

Jenkins, H. (2006). *Convergence Culture: Where Old and New Media Collide*. New York: New York University Press.

Johnson, G., Scholes, K., & Whittington, R. (2008). *Exploring Corporate Strategy* (8th ed.). Harlow, UK: Prentice Hall.

Johnson, M. W. (1999, September/October). A feasibility test for corporate vision. *Strategic Change*, *8*(6), 335–348. doi:10.1002/(SICI)1099-1697(199909/10)8:6<335::AID-JSC442>3.0.CO;2-7

Jonas, H. (1979). Toward a Philosophy of Technology. In Kaplan, D. (Ed.), *Readings in the Philosophy of Technology*. Lanham, MD: Rowman & Littlefield.

Jones, Q. (1997). Virtual Communities, Virtual Settlements, and Cyber-archaeology: A Theoretical Outline. *Journal of Computer Mediated Communication*, *3*(3). Retrieved September 7, 2009, from http://jcmc.indiana.edu/vol3/issue3/jones.html

Jones, C. V. (1996). *Visualization and Optimization*. Norwell, MA: Kluwer Academic Publishers.

Jones, C., Ramanau, R., Cross, S., & Healing, G. (2010). Net generation or digital natives: Is there a distinct new generation entering university? *Computers & Education*, *54*, 722–732. doi:10.1016/j.compedu.2009.09.022

Jones, S. (2003). *Encyclopedia of New Media*. Thousand Oaks, CA: Sage Publications.

Jones, S., Johnson-Yale, C., Millermaier, S., & Pérez, F. S. (2008). Academic work, the Internet and U.S. college students. *The Internet and Higher Education*, *11*(3-4), 165–177. doi:10.1016/j.iheduc.2008.07.001

Joos, J. G. (2008). Social media: New frontiers in hiring and recruiting. *Employment Relations Today*, *35*(1), 51–59. doi:10.1002/ert.20188

Kafai, Y. B., & Resnick, M. (1996). *Constructionism in practice: designing, thinking, and learning in a digital world*. Mahwah, NJ: Lawrence Erlbaum Associates.

Kahn, R. L., Wolfe, D. M., Quinn, R. P., Snoek, D. J., & Rosenthal, R. A. (1964). *Organizational Stress: Studies in Role Conflict and Ambiguity*. Chichester: Wiley.

Kalim, R., & Lodhi, S. (2004). *The Knowledge-Based Economy: trends and implications for Pakistan*. Retrieved May 15th, 2009 from www.pide.org.pk/.../The%20Knowledge%20Based%20Economy.pdf

Kanjanabootra, S. (2009). *Understanding how the adoption of Knowledge Engineering can improve business value through better product development and improvement processes*. Unpublished Doctoral thesis in progress, RMIT University, Melbourne, Australia.

Kansal, V. (2006). Enterprise Resource Planning Implementation: A Case Study. *Journal of American Academy of Business*, *9*(1), 165–170.

Kantola, V., Tiitta, S., Mehto, K., & Kankainen, T. (2007). Using dramaturgical methods to gain more dynamic user understanding in user-centered design. In *Proceedings in Creativity and Cognition* (pp.173-182). Washington, DC: ACM.

Karaszewski, R. (2008). The influence of KM on global corporations' competitiveness. *Journal of Knowledge Management*, *12*(3), 63–70. doi:10.1108/13673270810875868

Katz, N., Lazer, D., Arrow, H., & Contractor, N. (2004). Network Theory and Small Groups. *Small Group Research*, *35*(3), 307–332. doi:10.1177/1046496404264941

Kepes, B. (2008). If you build it will they come? *New Zealand Herald*. Retrieved November 19, 2008, from http://www.nzherald.co.nz/smallbusiness

Kidane, Y. H., & Gloor, P. A. (2007). Correlating Temporal Communication Patterns of the Eclipse Open Source Community with Performance and Creativity. *Computational & Mathematical Organization Theory*, *13*(1), 17–27. doi:10.1007/s10588-006-9006-3

King, L. (2009). ERP and e-commerce systems creating £600,000 bill. *CIO Magazine*. Retrieved from http://www.cio.co.uk/news/3202489/erp-and-e-commerce-systems-creating-600000-bill/?otc=44

Kleine, D. (2007). Striking a Balance. *Engineering and Technology*, *2*(2), 30–33. doi:10.1049/et:20070202

Kleine, D. (2008). Negotiating partnerships, understanding power: doing action research on Chilean Fairtrade wine value chains. *The Geographical Journal, 174*(2), 109–123. doi:10.1111/j.1475-4959.2008.00280.x

Klein, L. (2005). *Working Across the Gap: The Practice of Social Science in Organisations*. London: H. Karnac.

Kline, S. J., & Rosenberg, N. (1986). An overview of innovation. In Landau, R., & Rosenberg, N. (Eds.), *The Positive Sum Strategy*. Washington, DC: National Academy Press.

Klopp, M., & Hartmann, M. (1999). *Das Fledermausprinzip – Strategische Früherkennung für Unternehmen*. Stuttgart, Germany: Logis.

Kluemper, D. H., & Rosen, P. A. (2009). Future employment selection methods: evaluating social networking web sites. *Journal of Managerial Psychology, 24*(6), 567–580. doi:10.1108/02683940910974134

Knight, J., & Weedon, A. (2009). Shifting Notions of Convergence. *Convergence: The International Journal of Research into New Media Technologies, 15*, 131-133. Retrieved April 8, 2009, from http://con.sagepub.com/cgi/reprint/15/2/131

Know Inc. (2006). *KnetMap*. Retrieved from http://www.knowinc.com

Kogut, B. (1988). Joint Ventures: Theoretical and Empirical Perspectives. *Strategic Management Journal, 9*, 312–332. doi:10.1002/smj.4250090403

Kollock, P., & Smith, M. (1998). Communities in Cyberspace. In Smith, M., & Kollock, P. (Eds.), *Communities in Cyberspace* (pp. 3–24). London: Routledge.

Kolstrup, S. (2003). The Making of a Pedagogical Tool for Picture Analysis and Picture Construction. In Madsen, K. H. (Ed.), *Production Methods: Behind the Scenes of Virtual Inhabited 3D Worlds*. London: Springer Verlag. doi:10.1007/978-1-4471-0063-8_6

Kontoghiorghes, C., Awbre, S. M., & Feurig, P. L. (2005). Examining the relationship between learning organization characteristics and change adaptation, innovation, and organizational performance. *Human Resource Development Quarterly, 16*(2), 183–211. doi:10.1002/hrdq.1133

Korten, D. C. (1984). *People-centred Development*. West Hartford, Connecticut: Kumarian Press.

Koudal, P., & Coleman, G. C. (2005). Coordinating operations to enhance innovation in the global corporation. *Strategy and Leadership, 33*(4), 20–32. doi:10.1108/10878570510608013

Kouzes, J. M., & Posner, B. Z. (1995). *The leadership challenge* (2nd ed.). San Francisco: Jossey-Bass.

Kozinets, R. (2002). The field behind the screen: Using netnography for marketing research in online communities. *JMR, Journal of Marketing Research, 39*(11), 61–72. doi:10.1509/jmkr.39.1.61.18935

Kozinets, R. V., Hemetsberger, A., & Schau, H. J. (2008). The Wisdom of Consumer Crowds: Collective Innovation in the Age of Networked Marketing. *Journal of Macromarketing, 28*, 339–354. doi:10.1177/0276146708325382

Krämer, N. C., & Winter, S. (2008). Impression Management 2.0 The Relationship of Self-Esteem, Extraversion, Self-Efficacy, and Self-Presentation Within Social Networking Sites. *Journal of Media Psychology, 20*(3), 96–106. doi:10.1027/1864-1105.20.3.106

Kreps, D. (2008). Virtuality: Time, Space, Consciousness, and a Second Life. In Panteli, N., & Chiasson, M. (Eds.), *Exploring Virtuality Within and Beyond Organizations*. New York: Palgrave Macmillan.

Kriščiūnas, K., & Daugėlienė, R. (2006). The assessment models of Knowledge-Based Economy penetration. *Engineering Decisions, 5*(50).

Kroes, P., Franssen, M., Poel, I., & van de,., & Ottens, M. (2006). Treating socio-technical systems as engineering systems: some conceptual problems. *Systems Research and Behavioral Science, 23*(6), 803–814. doi:10.1002/sres.703

Kuhn, T. (1996). *The Structure of Scientific Revolutions* (3rd ed.). Chicago: University of Chicago Press.

Kuipers, B. S., & De Witte, M. C. (2005). Teamwork: a case study on development and performance. *International Journal of Human Resource Management, 16*(2), 185–201. doi:10.1080/0958519042000311390

Lampel, J., & Bhalla, A. (2007). The role of status seeking in online communities: Giving the gift of experience. *Journal of Computer-Mediated Communication, 12*(2). doi:10.1111/j.1083-6101.2007.00332.x

Lanzenberger, M., Sampson, J., Rester, M., Naudet, Y., & Latour, T. (2008). Visual ontology alignment for knowledge sharing and reuse. *Journal of Knowledge Management, 12*(6), 102–120. doi:10.1108/13673270810913658

Larreamendy-Joerns, J., & Leinhardt, G. (2006). Going the distance with online education. *Review of Educational Research, 76*(4), 567–605. doi:10.3102/00346543076004567

Latham, G. P., & Kinne, S. B. (1974). Improving job performance through training in goal setting. *The Journal of Applied Psychology, 59*, 187–191. doi:10.1037/h0036530

Lave, J., & Wenger, E. (1991). *Situated learning. Legitimate peripheral participation.* Cambridge, UK: University of Cambridge Press.

Lee, F. S. L., Vogel, D., & Limayem, M. (2003). Virtual Community Informatics: A Review and Research Agenda. *The Journal of Information Technology Theory and Applications, 5*(1), 47–61.

Lee, I. (2007). An architecture for a next-generation holistic e-recruiting system. *Communications of the ACM, 50*(7), 81–85. doi:10.1145/1272516.1272518

Lehaney, B. (1996). Mixed-mode modelling. In Johnson, D., & O'Brien, F. (Eds.), *Operations Research Keynote Papers* (pp. 150–157). Birmingham, UK: Operational Research Society.

Lehaney, B., & Clarke, S. (1997). Soft systems methodology (and simulation) for mixed-mode modelling? In O'Brien, F., & Orman, A. (Eds.), *Operations Research Keynote Papers* (pp. 16–33). Birmingham, UK: Operational Research Society. ·

Lehaney, B., Clarke, S., Coakes, E., & Jack, G. (2004). *Beyond knowledge management.* Hershey, PA: IGI Global.

Leimeister, J. M., Schweizer, K., Leimeister, S., & Krcmar, H. (2008). Do Virtual Communities Matter for the Social Support of Patients? Antecedents and Effects of Virtual Relationships in Online Communities. *Information Technology & People, 21*(4), 350–374. doi:10.1108/09593840810919671

Lekorwe, M., Molomo, M., Molefe, W., & Moseki, k. (2001). *Public attitudes toward democracy, governance and economic development in Botswana* (Afrobarometer Paper No. 14).

Lennard, H. L., & Bernstein, A. (1966). Expectations and behaviour in therapy. In B.J. Biddle & E. J. Thomas (Eds.), *Role Theory* (pp. 179-185). New York: Wiley.

Leonard-Barton, D., & Sensiper, S. (1998). The role of tacit knowledge in group innovation. *California Management Review, 40*(3), 112–132.

Lesser, E. L., & Storck, J. (2001). Communities of practice and organisational performance. *Knowledge Management, 40*(4). Retrieved from http://www.research.ibm.com/journal/sj/404/lesser.html

Lessig, L. (2006). *Code: And Other Laws of Cyberspace, Version 2.0.* New York, NY: Basic Books.

Leung, K. C. (2004). *Statistics to measure the knowledge-based economy: The case of Hong Kong, China.* Paper presented at the 2004 Asia Pacific Technical Meeting of Information and Communication Technology (ICT) Statistic. Retrieved July 16th, 2009 from www.unescap.org/.../18.Statistics_to_measure_the_Knowledge-Based_Economy-Hong_Kong.pdf

Levin, D. Z., & Cross, R. (2004). The Strength of Weak Ties You Can Trust: The Mediating Role of Trust in Effective Knowledge Transfer. *Management Science, 50*(11), 1477–1490. doi:10.1287/mnsc.1030.0136

Levinson, P. (2001). *Digital McLuhan: A Guide to the Information Millennium.* London: Routledge.

Lewis, K., Kaufman, J., & Christakis, N. (2008). The Taste for Privacy: An Analysis of College Student Privacy Settings in an Online Social Network. *Journal of Computer-Mediated Communication, 14*(1), 79–100. doi:10.1111/j.1083-6101.2008.01432.x

Lewis, K., Kaufman, J., Gonzalez, M., Wimmer, A., & Christakis, N. (2008). Tastes, ties, and time: A new social network dataset using Facebook.com. *Social Networks, 30*(4), 330–342. doi:10.1016/j.socnet.2008.07.002

Liebowitz, J. (2009). My Top 10 Lessons on Lessons Learned Systems. *International Journal of Sociotechnology and Knowledge Development, 1*(1), 53–57.

Light, A. (2008, May). The Challenge of Representing a Sociotechnical System: Fair Tracing and the Value Chain. *Sociotechnical Aspects of Interaction Design*. London.

Light, A., Weaver, L., Healey, P. G., & Simpson, G. (2008). Adventures in the Not Quite Yet: using performance techniques to raise design awareness about digital networks. In *Proceedings. Design Research Society Conference*, Sheffield: *Design Research Society*

Lin, S. C., & Lin, F. R. (2006). An Ecosystem View on Online Communities of Practice. *International Journal of Communications Law & Policy*, 1-31.

Lin, N., Burt, R. S., & Cook, K. S. (2001). *Social Capital: Theory and Research*. New Brunswick, NJ: Transaction Publisher.

Lister, M., Dovey, J., Giddings, S., Grant, I., & Kelly, K. (2009). *New Media: A Critical Introduction* (2nd ed.). Abingdon, UK: Routledge.

Liu, L., Yu, E., & Mylopoulos, J. (2003). Security and privacy requirements analysis within a social setting. In *Proceedings of the IEEE Joint International Conference on Requirements Engineering*, Los Alamitos, CA (pp. 151-161). Washington, DC: IEEE Computer Society Press.

Locke, E. A., & Latham, G. P. (1990). Work motivation: The high performance cycle. In U. Kleinbeck, H_H. Quast, H. Thierry, & H. Hacker (Eds.), *Work Motivation*. Hillsdale, NJ: Lawrence Erlbaum.

Louis, L. R. (2006). Technical issues facing work groups, Teams and knowledge networks. In Coakes, E., & Clarke, S. (Eds.), *Encyclopedia of communities of practice in information and knowledge management* (pp. 532–536). Hershey, PA: IGI Global.

Lucas, H. C. (1975). *Toward Creative Systems Design*. New York: Columbia University Press.

Lucas, L. M. (2005). The impact of trust and reputation on the transfer of best practices. *Journal of Knowledge Management*, 9(4), 87–101. doi:10.1108/13673270510610350

Luciani, A. (2002). *TNS Project Abstract. ICA Laboratory, Institut National Polytechnique de Grenoble*. Retrieved April 28, 2009, from http://usenet.jyxo.cz/cz.comp.grafika/0210/post-doc-vo-francuzsku.html

Lyons, T. F. (1971). Role Clarity, need for clarity, satisfaction, tension, and withdrawal. *Organizational Behavior and Human Performance*, 6, 99–110. doi:10.1016/0030-5073(71)90007-9

Lyytinen, K., & Newman, M. (2008). Explaining information systems change: a punctuated socio-technical change model. *European Journal of Information Systems*, 17(6), 589–613. doi:10.1057/ejis.2008.50

Ma, W. W., Clark, T. H. K., & Li, P. (2006). Cognitive Style and Acceptance of Online Community Weblog Systems. *International Journal of Communications Law & Policy*, 1-12.

Maani, K., & Cavana, R. (2000). *Systems Thinking and Modelling: Understanding Change and Complexity*. Aukland, New Zealand: Pearson Education New Zealand.

Macaulay, C., Jacucci, G., O'Neill, S., Kankaineen, T., & Simpson, M. (2006). The Emerging Roles of Performance within HCI and Interaction Design. *Interacting with Computers*, 18(5), 942–955. doi:10.1016/j.intcom.2006.07.001

MacManus, R. (2006). *TradeMe: big fish in a small pond*. Retrieved September 7, 2009, from http://www.readwriteweb.com/archives/trademe_big_fish_small_pond.php

Macris, A., Papadimitriou, E., & Vassilacopoulos, G. (2008). An ontology-based competency model for workflow activity assignment policies. *Journal of Knowledge Management*, 12(6), 72–88. doi:10.1108/13673270810913630

Maguire, C., Kazlauskas, C., & Weir, A. D. (1994). *Information systems for innovative organizations*. London: Academic Press.

Mahesh, V. (1993). *Thresholds of Motivation*. New Delhi: Tata McGraw-Hill.

Majchrzak, A., & Borys, B. (2001). Generating testable socio-technical systems theory. *Journal of Engineering and Technology Management*, 18(3/4), 219–241. doi:10.1016/S0923-4748(01)00035-2

Malhotra, Y. (2004). Why knowledge management systems fail? Enablers and constraints of knowledge management in human enterprises. In M.E.D. Koenig & T.K. Srikantaiah (Eds), *Knowledge management lessons learned: what works and what doesn't* (pp. 87-112). Medford, NJ: Information Today.

Manovich, L. (2001). *The Language of New Media.* Cambridge, MA: MIT Press.

Manz, C. C., & Stewart, G. L. (1997). Attaining Flexible Stability by Integrating Total Quality Management and Socio-technical Systems Theory. *Organization Science, 8*(1), 59–70. doi:10.1287/orsc.8.1.59

Marchant, G., & Robinson, J. (1999). Is knowing the tax code all it takes to be a tax expert? On the development of legal expertise. In Sternberg, R., & Horvath, J. A. (Eds.), *Tacit knowledge in professional practice* (pp. 3–20). Mahwah, NJ: Laurence Erlbaum Associates.

March, J. C., & March, J. G. (1977). Almost random careers: the Wisconsin School Superintendency 1940-1972. *Administrative Science Quarterly, 22*, 377–409. doi:10.2307/2392180

March, J. C., & March, J. G. (1978). Performing sampling in social matches. *Administrative Science Quarterly, 23*, 434–453. doi:10.2307/2392419

Marples, D. L. (1968). Roles in a Manufacturing Organization. *Journal of Management Studies, 5*(2), 183–204. doi:10.1111/j.1467-6486.1968.tb00828.x

Marqués, D. P., & Simón, F. J. G. (2006). The effect of knowledge management practices on firm performance. *Journal of Knowledge Management, 10*(3), 143–156. doi:10.1108/13673270610670911

Marsden, G. (2007). Social Impact plenary talk. In *Proceedings CHI 2007.* New York, NY: ACM.

Martin, T. S. (2000). Calculus students' ability to solve geometric related-rates problems. *Mathematics Education Research Journal, 12*(2), 74–91.

Maslow, A. (1943). Theory of human motivation. *Psychological Review, 50*, 370–396. doi:10.1037/h0054346

Maturana, H., & Varela, F. (1987). *The tree of knowledge: Biological roots of human understanding.* Boston: New Science Library.

Mayzlin, D. (2006). Promotional Chat on the Internet. *Marketing Science, 25*(2), 155–163. doi:10.1287/mksc.1050.0137

McClelland, D. C. (1987). *Human Motivation.* New York: Cambridge University Press.

McClelland, D. C. (1973). Testing for competence rather than for 'intelligence'. *The American Psychologist, 28*, 1–14. doi:10.1037/h0034092

McCrae, R. R., & Costa, P. T. (2006). *Personality in Adulthood.* New York: Guildford.

McFadzean, E., O'Loughlin, A., & Shaw, E. (2005). Corporate entrepreneurship and innovation part 1: the missing link. *European Journal of Innovation Management, 8*(3), 350–372. doi:10.1108/14601060510610207

McGuire, M., Rubin, B., Agranoff, R., & Richards, C. (1994). Building development capacity in nonmetropolitan communities. *Public Administration Review, 54*(5), 426–433. doi:10.2307/976427

McKenna, K. Y. A. (2007). Through the Internet looking glass: Expressing and validating the true self. In Joinson, A., McKenna, K., Postmes, T., & Reips, U.-D. (Eds.), *The Oxford Handbook of Internet Psychology* (pp. 205–221). New York: Oxford University Press.

McLay, A. (2002). Applying Visualisation Technologies and Strategies for Effective Knowledge Management and Decision Analysis in Engineering and Technology-based Enterprises. In A. J. Subic, H. C. Tsang, C. Y. Tang, & G. Netherwood (Eds.), *Proceedings of the 3rd International Conference on Quality and Reliability,* Melbourne, Australia.

McLuhan, M. (1964). *Understanding Media: The Extensions of Man.* New York: McGraw-Hill.

McLuhan, M., & Fiore, Q. (1967). The Medium is the Message: An Inventory of Effects. In *Levinson, P. (2001), Digital McLuhan: A Guide to the Information Millennium.* London: Routledge.

McLuhan, M., & McLuhan, E. (1988). Laws of Media: The New Science. In *Levinson, P. (2001), Digital McLuhan: A Guide to the Information Millennium.* London: Routledge.

Menzel, H. C., Aaltio, I., & Ulijn, J. M. (2007). On the way to creativity: Engineers as intrapreneurs in organizations. *Technovation, 27*(12), 732–743. doi:10.1016/j.technovation.2007.05.004

Metcalfe, R. (1998, March 2). *Asian tour provides useful insight on Silicon Valley's worldwide Internet edge.* IDG. net, www.infoworld.com.

Michaels, E., Handfield-Jones, H., & Axelrod, B. (2001). *The War for Talent*. Boston: Harvard Business Press.

Midgley, G. (1992). The sacred and the profane in critical systems thinking. *Systems Practice, 5*, 5–16. doi:10.1007/BF01060044

Miller, D. (1990). *The Icarus Paradox: how exceptional companies bring about their downfall*. New York: Harper Business.

Miller, D. (2000) *Introduction to Collective Behavior and Collective Action*. Long Grove, IL: Waveland Publishing, Inc. Retrieved April 28, 2009, from http://jeff560.tripod.com/wotw.html

Mingers, J., & Brocklesby, J. (1996). Multimethodology: Towards a framework for mixing methodologies. *Systemist, 18*, 101–131.

Mintel (1999). *Green and Ethical Consumer Survey*. London: Mintel.

Mintel (2001). *Attitudes Towards Ethical Food Survey*. London: Mintel.

Mintel (2004). *Green and Ethical Consumer Survey*. London: Mintel.

Mirijamdotter, A., Somerville, M. M., & Holst, M. (2006). An Interactive and Iterative Evaluation Approach for Creating Collaborative Learning Environments. *Electronic Journal of Information Systems Evaluation, 9*(2), 83–92.

Mithas, S., & Krishnan, M. S. (2008). Human Capital and Institutional Effects in the Compensation of Information Technology Professionals in the United States. *Management Science, 54*(3), 415–428. doi:10.1287/mnsc.1070.0778

Mitleton-Kelly, E. (1998, April 12). *Organisations as complex evolving systems*. Paper presented at the OACES Conference, Warwick.

Mkandawire, T. (2001). Social policy in a development context. *United Nations Research Institute for Social Development*. Retrieved August 25, 2008 from http://www.unrisd.org/unrisd/website/document.nsf/0/C83739F8E9A9AA0980256B5E003C5225?OpenDocument

Mocan, A., Facca, F. M., Loutas, N., Peristeras, V., Goudos, S. K., & Tarabanis, K. A. (2009). Solving Semantic Interoperability Conflicts in Cross-Border E-Government Services. *International Journal on Semantic Web and Information Systems, 5*(1), 1–47.

Morello, D., Kyte, A., & Gomolski, B. (2007). *The quest for talent: You ain't seen nothing yet*. Retrieved March 4, 2010, from http://www.gartner.com/DisplayDocument?ref=g_search&id=569115&subref=advsearch

Morse, G. (2006). Frontiers: Decisions and Desire. *Harvard Business Review*, 42–51.

Moss Kanter, R. M. (1983). *The Change Masters*. New York: Simon and Schuster.

Moss Kanter, R. M. (1988). When a thousand flowers bloom: structural, collective, and social conditions for innovation in organisations. *Research in Organizational Behavior, 10*, 169–211.

Mowrer, D. E. (1996). A content analysis of student/instructor communication via computer conferencing. *Higher Education, 32*, 217–241. doi:10.1007/BF00138397

Muller, M. J. (2002). Participatory Design: the third space in HCI. In J. Jacko & A. Sears (Eds.). *The Human-computer Interaction Handbook: Fundamentals, Evolving Technologies and Emerging Applications* (pp. 1051-1068). Hillsdale, NJ: Lawrence Erlbaum.

Muller, A., Valikangas, L., & Merlyn, P. (2005). Metrics for innovation: guidelines for developing a customized suite of innovation metrics. *Strategy and Leadership, 33*(1), 37–45. doi:10.1108/10878570510572590

Mumford, E. (2000). Technology and freedom: A socio-technical approach. In Coakes, E., Willis, D., & Lloyd-Jones, R. (Eds.), *The new SocioTech: graffiti on the long wall* (pp. 29–38). London: Springer Verlag.

Mumford, E. (2006). The story of socio-technical design: reflections on its successes, failures and potential. *Information Systems Journal, 16*(4), 317–342. doi:10.1111/j.1365-2575.2006.00221.x

Murphie, A., & Potts, J. (2003). *Culture and Technology*. New York: Palgrave.

Musick, E. (2006). *The 1992 London Ambulance Service Computer Aided Dispatch System Failure*. Retrieved from http://erichmusick.com/writings/06/las_failure.html

Naeve, A., Sicilia, M. A., & Lytras, M. D. (2008). Learning processes and processing learning: from organizational needs to learning designs. *Journal of Knowledge Management, 12*(6), 5–14. doi:10.1108/13673270810913586

National Audit Office report. (2009, March 12). *The National Offender Management Information System*. London: The Stationery Office. Retrieved from http://www.nowpublic.com/environment/correlation-between-population-growth-and-emissions-growth-chart

Newell, A. F., Morgan, M. E., Gregor, P., & Carmichael, A. (2006). Theatre as an intermediary between users and CHI designers. In *Proceedings CHI 2007* (pp. 111-116), New York, NY: ACM.

Nicholls, A., & Opal, C. (2004). *Fair Trade: market-driven ethical consumption*. London: Sage.

Nicholls, M. G., & Eady, J. (2008). Overcoming the tacit knowledge problem in the commercial refrigeration industry using mixed-mode modelling. In M. A. Amouzegar (Ed.), *Proceedings of the 37th Annual Meeting of the Western Decision Sciences Institute* (pp. 555-558). San Diego, CA: Western Decision Sciences Institute.

Nicholls, M. G. (2009). Mixed-mode modelling – What is it and how can it help? *Decision Line, 40*(3), 10–13.

Nicholls, M. G., & Cargill, B. J. (2001). The use of mixed-mode modelling for determining best practice for a business. In Nicholls, M. G., Clarke, S., & Lehaney, B. (Eds.), *Mixed-model modelling: mixing methodologies for organisational intervention: Applied Optimisation 58* (pp. 259–292). Boston: Kluwer Academic Publishers.

Nicholls, M. G., & Cargill, B. J. (2008). Determining best practice production in an aluminium smelter involving sub-processes based substantially on tacit knowledge – An application of communities of practice. *The Journal of the Operational Research Society, 59*, 13–24. doi:10.1057/palgrave.jors.2602320

Nicholls, M. G., Clarke, S., & Lehaney, B. (Eds.). (2001). *Mixed-mode modelling: Mixing methodologies for organisational intervention: Applied Optimisation 58*. Boston: Kluwer Academic Publishers.

Nicholls, M. G., & Hedditch, D. J. (1993). The development of an integrated model of an aluminium smelter. *The Journal of the Operational Research Society, 44*, 225–235.

Nielsen, L. (2005). Then the picture comes in your mind of what you have seen on TV - A study of personas descriptions and use. In *The 5th Danish Human-Computer Interaction Research Symposium* (pp. 68-73), Copenhagen: CBS, Institut for Informatik.

Nonaka, I., & Takeuchi, H. (1995). *The knowledge-creating company*. New York: Oxford University Press.

Nonaka, I., & Konno, N. (1998). The concept of 'BA' – building a foundation for knowledge Creation. *California Management Review, 40*(3), 40–54.

Nonaka, I., & Reinmoller, P. (2000). Dynamic Business Systems for Knowledge Creation and Utilization. In Despres, C., & Chauvel, D. (Eds.), *Knowledge Horizons: The Present and the Promise of Knowledge Management* (pp. 89–112). Oxford, UK: Butterworth-Heinemann.

Nonaka, I., & Takeuchi, H. (1995). *The knowledge creating company*. Oxford: Oxford University Press.

Nonnecke, B., Andrews, D., & Preece, J. (2006). Non-public and Public Online Community Participation: Needs, Attitudes and Behavior. *Electronic Commerce Research, 6*, 7–20. doi:10.1007/s10660-006-5985-x

Nosek, J. T. (2004). Group cognition as a basis for supporting group knowledge creation and sharing. *Journal of Knowledge Management, 8*(4), 54–64. doi:10.1108/13673270410556361

O'Sullivan, T. (2007). Sounding Boards: Performing Arts Organizations and the Internet Forum. *International Journal of Arts Management, 9*(3), 65–95.

Oblinger, D., & Oblinger, J. (2005). Is it age or IT: first steps towards understanding the net generation. In D. Oblinger & J. Oblinger (Eds.), *Educating the Net generation*. Boulder, CO: EDUCAUSE. Retrieved from http://www.educause.edu/educatingthenetgen/

OECD. (1997). *The OECD Report on regulatory reform: Synthesis*. Paris: Organisation for Economic Co-operation and Development. Retrieved July 10th, 2009 from http://www.oecd.org/dataoecd/17/25/2391768.pdf

Olphert, W., & Damodaran, L. (2007). Citizen Participation and engagement in the Design of e-Government Services: The Missing Link in Effective ICT Design and Delivery. *Journal of the Association for Information Systems*, *8*(9), 491–507.

Orenstein, A. (1998). Epistemology Naturalised – Nature know thyself. In N. Warburton (Ed.) (1999), *Philosophy: Basic Readings*. London: Routledge.

Orr, J. E. (1996). *Talking about machines: An ethnography of a modern job*. Ithaca, NY: Cornell University Press.

Oxford University Press. (2005). *Oxford English Dictionary* (2nd ed.). Oxford, UK: Oxford University Press.

Păceşilă, M. (2006). The impact of moving to Knowledge Based Economy in the public sector. *Management & Marketing Craiova*, *1*, 113–118.

Pagani, M. (2003). *Multimedia and Interactive Digital TV: Managing the Opportunities Created by Digital Convergence*. Hershey, PA: IGI Global.

Palfrey, J., & Gasser, U. (2008). *Born digital. Understanding the first generation of the digital natives*. Philadelphia: Basic Books.

Palmquist, M. (2005). Retrieved from http://www.colo-state.edu/Depts/WritingCenter/references/research/content/page2.htm

Papargyris, A., & Poulymenakou, A. (2008). Playing Together in Cyberspace: Collective Action and Shared Meaning Constitution in Virtual Worlds. In Panteli, N., & Chiasson, M. (Eds.), *Exploring Virtuality Within and Beyond Organizations*. Basingstoke, UK: Palgrave Macmillan.

Papineau, D. (Ed.). (2004). *Philosophy*. London: Duncan Baird.

Paquette, S. (2006). Communities of practice as facilitators of knowledge exchange. In Coakes, E., & Clarke, S. (Eds.), *Encyclopedia of communities of practice and information and knowledge management* (pp. 68–73). Hershey, PA: IGI Global.

Parry, E., & Tyson, S. (2008). An analysis of the use and success of online recruitment methods in the UK. *Human Resource Management Journal*, *18*(3), 257–274. doi:10.1111/j.1748-8583.2008.00070.x

Pascale, R., Millemann, M., & Gioja, L. (1997). Changing the way we change (Harvard Business School survey). *Harvard Business Review*, *75*(6), 127–139.

Patel, V. L., Arocha, J., & Kaufman, D. R. (1999). Expertise and tacit knowledge in medicine. In Sternberg, R. J., & Horvath, J. A. (Eds.), *Tacit knowledge in professional practice* (pp. 75–100). Mahwah, NJ: Laurence Erlbaum Associates.

Pava, C. (1983). *Managing New Office Technology: An Organizational Strategy*. New York: Free Press.

Pava, C. (1986). Redesigning Socio-technical Systems Design: Concepts and Methods for the 1990s. *The Journal of Applied Behavioral Science*, *22*(2), 201–222. doi:10.1177/002188638602200303

Perry-Smith, J. E. (2006). Social yet creative: the role of social relationships in facilitating individual creativity. *Academy of Management Journal*, *49*(1), 85–101.

Peters, T. J., & Waterman, R. H., Jr. (1982). *In Search of Excellence: Lessons from Americas Best Run Companies*. New York: Warrner Books.

Piattelli, P. (1994). *Inevitable Illusions: how mistakes of reason rule our minds*. New York: Wiley.

Pimental, K., & Teixeira, K. (1993). *Virtual Reality: Through the New Looking Glass*. New York: McGraw-Hill.

Pinchot, G. (1985). *Intrapreneuring: Why you Don't Have to Leave the Corporation to Become and Entrepreneur*. New York: Harper and Row.

Popper, K. (1974). The Problem of Demarcation. In N. Warburton (Ed.) (1999), *Philosophy: Basic Readings*. London: Routledge.

Porra, J., & Hirschheim, R. (2007). A Lifetime of Theory and Action on the Ethical Use of Computers: A Dialogue with Enid Mumford. *Journal of the Association for Information Systems*, *8*(9), 467–478.

Porritt, M., Burt, A., & Poling, A. (2006). Increasing Fiction Writers' Productivity through an Internet-Based Intervention. *Journal of Applied Behavior Analysis*, *39*(3), 393–397. doi:10.1901/jaba.2006.134-05

Porter, M. E. (1985). *Competitive Advantage: Creating and Sustaining Superior Performance.* New York, NY: Free Press.

Porter, M. E. (2008). The Five Competitive Forces that Shape Strategy. *Harvard Business Review*, 79–93.

Preda, A. (2006). Socio-Technical Agency in Financial Markets: The Case of the Stock Ticker. *Social Studies of Science*, 35(5), 753–782. doi:10.1177/0306312706059543

Preece, J., Abras, Ch., & Maloney-Krichmar, D. (2004). Designing and evaluating online communities: Research speaks to emerging practice. *International Journal of Web based Communities*, 1(1), 2-18.

Preece, J. (2000). *Online Communities. Designing Usability, Supporting Sociability.* New York: John Wiley and Sons.

Prensky, M. (2001). Digital natives, digital immigrants. *The Horizon*, 9(5). Retrieved June 7, 2009, from http://www.marcprensky.com

PricewaterhouseCoopers Survey. (2007, March 8). Leadership flaws add to IT project failures. *Computing magazine*. Retrieved from http://www.computing.co.uk/computing/news/2184964/leadership-flaws-add-project

Pruitt, J., & Adlin, T. (2006). *The Persona Lifecycle: Keeping People in Mind Throughout Product Design.* San Francisco, CA: Morgan Kaufmann.

PublicService.com. (2009, March 12). *Offender IT is a 'spectacular failure.* Retrieved from http://www.public-service.co.uk/news_story.asp?id=8869

Putnam, L. L., & Mumby, D. K. (1993). Organizations, emotion and the myth of rationality. In S. Fineman (Ed.), *Emotion In Organizations* (pp. 36-57). London: Sage Publications.

Pyöriä, P. (2007). Informal organizational culture: the foundation of knowledge workers' performance. *Journal of Knowledge Management*, 11(3), 16–30. doi:10.1108/13673270710752081

Raacke, J., & Bonds-Raacke, J. (2008). MySpace and Facebook: Applying the Uses and Gratifications Theory to Exploring Friend-Networking Sites. *Cyberpsychology & Behavior*, 11(2), 169–174. doi:10.1089/cpb.2007.0056

Radin, P. (2006). To me, it's my life: Medical Communication, Trust and Activism in Cyberspace. *Social Science & Medicine*, 62, 591–601. doi:10.1016/j.socscimed.2005.06.022

Rasmussen, J. (1997). Risk Management in a Dynamic Society: A Modelling Problem. *Safety Science*, 27, 183–213. doi:10.1016/S0925-7535(97)00052-0

Reagans, R., & McEvily, B. (2003). Network Structure and Knowledge Transfer: The Effects of Cohesion and Range. *Administrative Science Quarterly*, 48(2), 240–267. doi:10.2307/3556658

Reeves, T. C., Herrington, J., & Oliver, R. (2005). Design research: A socially responsible approach to instructional technology research in higher education. *Journal of Computing in Higher Education*, 16(2), 97–116. doi:10.1007/BF02961476

Report, U. N. E. C. E. (2002). *Towards a Knowledge-Based Economy: ARMENIA – country readiness assessment report.* Retrieved May 30th, 2009 from http://www.unece.org/operact/enterp/documents/coverpagarmenia.pdf

Resnick, L. B., Levine, J. M., & Teasley, S. D. (Eds.). (1993). *Perspectives on socially shared cognition.* Washington, DC: American Psychological Association.

Revans, R. W. (1982). *The origins and growth of action learning.* London: Chartwell-Bratt.

Rheingold, H. (1993). *The Virtual Community: Homesteading on the Electronic Frontier.* Reading, MA: Addison-Wesley.

Ridings, C. M., & Gefen, D. (2004). Virtual Community Attraction: Why People Hang Out Online. *Journal of Computer-Mediated Communication*, 10(1).

Riel, M., & Harasim, L. (1994). Research perspectives on network learning. *Machine-Mediated Learning*, 4, 91-113.

Robbins, S., & Barnwell, N. (2006). *Organization Theory: Concepts and Cases* (5th ed.). Upper Saddle River, NJ: Pearson.

Roberston, G., Card, S., & Mackinlay, J. (1993). Information Visualization Using 3D Interactive Animation. *Communications of the ACM*, 36(4), 57–71. doi:10.1145/255950.153577

Rogers, E. (2003). *Diffusion of Innovations* (5th ed.). New York: Free Press.

Romer, P. (1992). *Two strategies for economic development: Using ideas and producing ideas.* Retrieve reference info.

Romer, P. (1993). Implementing a national technology strategy with self-organizing industry investment boards. *Brookings Papers on Economic Activity: Microeconomics, 2*, 345. doi:10.2307/2534742

Romer, P. (1994). The origins of endogenous growth. *The Journal of Economic Perspectives, 8*(1), 3–22. doi:10.1257/jep.8.1.3

Rosenfeld, R., & Servo, J. C. (1991). Facilitating change in large organisations. In Henry, J., & Walker, D. (Eds.), *Managing Innovation.* London: Sage.

Ross, C., Orr, E. S., Sisic, M., Arseneault, J. M., Simmering, M. G., & Orr, R. R. (2009). Personality and motivations associated with Facebook use. *Computers in Human Behavior, 25*(2), 578–586. doi:10.1016/j.chb.2008.12.024

Ross, E., & Holland, A. (2007). *50 Great E-Businesses and the Minds Behind Them.* Sydney, Australia: Random House.

Rothwell, R. (1994). Towards the fifth-generation innovation process. *International Marketing Review, 11*(1), 7–31. doi:10.1108/02651339410057491

Rourke, S. (2008). *Shedding light on a sustainable future.* Intelligent Community Forum. Retrieved on August 31, 2008 at http://www.intelligentcommunity.org/.

Ruano-Mayoral, M., Colomo-Palacios, R., García-Crespo, A., & Gómez-Berbís, J. M. (2010). Software Project Managers under the Team Software Process: A Study of Competences Based on Literature. *International Journal of Information Technology Project Management, 1*(1), 42–53.

Ruano-Mayoral, M., Colomo-Palacios, R., Gómez-Berbís, J. M., & García-Crespo, A. (2007). A Mobile Framework for Competence Evaluation: Innovation Assessment Using Mobile Information Systems. *Journal of Technology Management & Innovation, 2*(3), 49–57.

Saarinen, J. (2005). *TradeMe, your ultimate guide to New Zealand's biggest online auction site.* Auckland, New Zealand: Penguin.

Saint-Onge, H., & Wallace, D. (2003). *Leveraging communities of practice for strategic advantage.* Boston: Butterworth-Heinemann.

Sarbin, T. R., & Williams, J. D. (1953). *Contributions to Role Taking Theory.* Working Paper. University of California. Berkeley.

Schambach, T. (1994). *Maintaining professional competence: an evaluation of factors affecting professional obsolescence of information technology professionals.* Unpublished doctoral dissertation, University of South Florida, FL.

Schein, E. H. (1992). *Organizational culture and leadership* (2nd ed.). San Francisco: Jossey-Bass.

Scheir, P., Lindstaedt, S. N., & Ghidini, C. (2008). A Network Model Approach to Retrieval in the Semantic Web. *International Journal on Semantic Web and Information Systems, 4*(4), 56–84.

Scherer, K., & Tran, V. (2003). Effects of emotion on the process of organizational learning. In M. Dierkes, A. Antal, J. Child, & I. Nonaka (Eds.), *Handbook of Organizational Learning and Knowledge* (pp. 369-92). Oxford: Oxford University Press.

Schubert, P., & Ginsburg, M. (2000). Virtual Communities of Transaction: The Role of Personalization in Electronic Commerce. *Electronic Markets, 10*(1), 45–55. doi:10.1080/10196780050033971

Schultze, Q. (1988). Evangelical Radio and the Rise of the Electronic Church 1921-1948. *Journal of Broadcasting & Electronic Media, 32*(3), 289. doi:10.1080/08838158809386703

Schumann, S., & Geiman, R. M. (2009). *Experiences from an online mathematics center.* Paper presented at the American Mathematical Association of Two-Year Colleges (AMATYC).

Schwaninger, M. (2006). Theories of viability: a comparison. *Systems Research and Behavioral Science, 23*(3), 337–347. doi:10.1002/sres.731

Selwyn, N. (2007). *'Screw Blackboard...do it on Facebook!': an investigation of students' educational use of Facebook*. Paper presented at the Poke 1.0-Facebook social research symposium.

Selwyn, N. (2009). Faceworking: Exploring students' education-related use of Facebook. *Learning, Media and Technology, 34*(2), 157–174. doi:10.1080/17439880902923622

Senge, P. (1990). *The fifth discipline: The art and practice of the learning organization*. London: Century Business.

Senge, P. M. (2004). Learn to Innovate. *Executive Excellence, 21*(6), 3–4.

Shah, A. (2005, July 2). The Scale of the Debt Crisis. *Global Issues*. Retrieved from http://www.globalissues.org/article/30/the-scale-of-the-debt-crisis

Shaw, E., O'Loughlin, A., & McFadzean, E. (2005). Corporate entrepreneurship and innovation part 2: a role- and process-based approach. *European Journal of Innovation Management, 8*(4), 393–408. doi:10.1108/14601060510627786

Shenkel, A., Teigland, R., & Borgatti, S. P. (2001). *Theorizing structural properties of communities of practice: a social network approach*. Paper presented at Academy of Management annual conference.

Shen, S. T., Woolley, M., & Prior, S. (2006). Towards culture-centred design. *Interacting with Computers, 18*(4), 820–852. doi:10.1016/j.intcom.2005.11.014

Sherman, W. R., & Craig, A. B. (1995). Literacy in Virtual Reality: A New Medium. *ACM SIGGRAPH Computer Graphics, 29*(4), 37–42. doi:10.1145/216876.216887

Shields, R. (2003). *The Virtual*. London: Routledge.

Shurville, S., O'Grady, T. B., & Mayall, P. (2008). Educational and institutional flexibility of Australian educational software. *Campus-Wide Information Systems, 25*(2), 74–84.. doi:10.1108/10650740810866576

Simarian, K. T. (2003). Take it to the next stage: the roles of role playing in the design process. In *Proceedings CHI 2003* (pp. 1012-1013), New York, NY: ACM.

Slouka, M. (1995). *War of the Worlds: Cyberspace and the High-Tech Assault on Reality*. London: Abacus.

Smith, P. A. C., & McLaughlin, M. (2003). Succeeding with knowledge management: getting the people-factors right. In *Proceedings of the 6th World Congress On Intellectual Capital & Innovation*. Hamilton, Canada: McMaster University.

Smith, A. D. (2005). Exploring Online Dating and Customer Relationship Management. *Online Information Review, 29*(1), 18–33. doi:10.1108/14684520510583927

Smith, B. (2003). Ontology. An Introduction. In Floridi, L. (Ed.), *Blackwell Guide to the Philosophy of Computing and Information* (pp. 155–166). Oxford, UK: Blackwell.

Smith, M. E. (2003). Changing an organisation's culture: correlates of success and failure. *Leadership and Organization Development Journal, 24*(5), 249–261. doi:10.1108/01437730310485752

Smith, P. (2010). Affective Factors for Successful Knowledge Management. *International Journal of Sociotechnology and Knowledge Development, 2*(1), 1–11.

Smith, P. A. C. (2005a). Knowledge sharing and strategic capital: the importance and identification of opinion leaders. *The Learning Organization, 12*(6), 563–574. doi:10.1108/09696470510626766

Smith, P. A. C. (2005b). Organisational change elements of establishing, facilitating, and supporting CoPs. In Coakes, E., & Clarke, C. (Eds.), *Encyclopedia of Communities of Practice in Information and Knowledge Management* (pp. 400–406). Hershey, PA: Idea Group Reference.

Smith, P. A. C. (2005c). Collective learning within CoPs. In Coakes, E., & Clarke, C. (Eds.), *Encyclopedia of Communities of Practice in Information and Knowledge Management* (pp. 30–31). Hershey, PA: Idea Group Reference.

Smith, P. A. C., & Saint-Onge, H. (1996). The evolutionary organization: avoiding a Titanic fate. *The Learning Organization, 3*(4), 4–21. doi:10.1108/09696479610148109

Smith, P. A. C., & Sharma, M. (2002a). Developing personal responsibility and leadership traits in all your employees, part 1: shaping and harmonizing the high-performance drivers. *Management Decision, 40*(8), 764–774. doi:10.1108/00251740210441018

Smith, P. A. C., & Sharma, M. (2002b). Rationalizing the promotion of non-rational behaviors in organizations. *The Learning Organization, 9*(5), 197–201. doi:10.1108/09696470210442132

Soane, E., Dewberry, C., & Narendran, S. (2009). The role of perceived costs and perceived benefits in the relationship between personality and risk related choices. *The Journal of Risk.*

Sobel Lojeski, K., & Reilly, R. R. (2008). *Uniting the Virtual Workforce.* Hoboken, NJ: John Wiley & Sons.

Soegaard, M. (2007). Personas. *Interaction Design Encyclopedia.* Retrieved March 23, 2009, from: http://www.interaction-design.org/encyclopedia/personas.html

Sommerville, I., & Rodden, T. (1996). Human social and organizational influences on the software process. In Fuggetta, A., & Wolf, A. (Eds.), *Software Process (Trends in Software 4)* (pp. 89–110). New York: John Wiley & Sons.

Soros, G. (1998). *The Crisis of Global Capitalism.* London: Little, Brown and Company.

Stacey, R. D. (2001). *Complex Responsive Processes in Organizations: Learning and Knowledge Creation.* London: Routledge.

Stahl, B. C. (2007). ETHICS, Morality and Critique: An Essay on Enid Mumford's Socio-Technical Approach. *Journal of the Association for Information Systems, 8*(9), 479–490.

Stair, R., & Reynolds, G. (2006). *Principles of Information Systems: A Managerial Approach* (7th ed.). Boston: Thomson.

Standish Group International, Inc. (2009, June 11). *Extreme Chaos, 2004-2009* (T. Wieberneit quote). http://blog.ciber.com/article.cfm?articleid=2009111592458

Stockdale, R., & Borovicka, M. (2006). Ghost Towns or Vibrant Villages? Constructing Business-Sponsored Online Communities. *International Journal of Communications Law & Policy,* 1-22.

Stockdale, R. (2008). Peer-to-Peer Online Communities for People with Chronic Diseases; A Conceptual Framework. *Journal of Systems and Information Technology, 10*(1), 39–55. doi:10.1108/13287260810876885

Storsul, T., & Stuedahl, D. (2007). *Ambivalence Towards Convergence: Digitalization and Media Change.* Göteborg, Sweden: Nordicom.

Stoyeck, R. (2009). *The Magic of Compounding.* Retrieved from www.stocksatbottom.com

Strijbos, J.-W., & De Laat, M. F. (2010). Developing the role concept for computer-supported collaborative learning: An explorative synthesis. *Computers in Human Behavior, 26*(4), 495–505. doi:10.1016/j.chb.2009.08.014

Stuart, S. (2008). From Agency to Apperception: Through Kinaesthesia to Cognition and Creation. *Ethics and Information Technology, 10*(4), 255. doi:10.1007/s10676-008-9175-5

Subrahmanyam, K., Reich, S. M., Waechter, N., & Espinoza, G. (2008). Online and offline social networks: Use of social networking sites by emerging adults. *Journal of Applied Developmental Psychology, 29*(6), 420–433. doi:10.1016/j.appdev.2008.07.003

Sui, D., & Goodchild, M. (2003). A Tetradic Analysis of GIS and Society Using McLuhans Law of the Media. *The Canadian Geographer, 47*(1), 5–17. doi:10.1111/1541-0064.02e08

Sullivan, P. (1998). *Profiting from intellectual capital: Extracting value from innovation.* New York: John Wiley and Sons.

Surowiecki, J. (2006). *The Wisdom of Crowds: Why the Many are Smarter Than the Few.* London: Abacus.

Szydlik, J. E. (2000). Mathematical beliefs and conceptual understanding of the limit of a function. *Journal for Research in Mathematics Education, 31,* 258–276. doi:10.2307/749807

Tapscott, D., & Willians, A. D. (2008). *Wikinomics.* New York: Penguin Group.

Tapscott, D. (1999). Educating the Net Generation. *Educational Leadership, 56*(5), 6–11.

Techcrunch.com. (2009, July 6). Retrieved from http://www.techcrunch.com/2008/08/12/facebook-is-not-only-the-worlds-largest-social-network-it-is-also-the-fastest-growing/

Teece, D. J. (1998). Capturing value from knowledge assets: the new economy, markets for know-how and intangible assets. *California Management Review*, *40*(3), 55–79.

Theall, D. F. (1971). *The Medium is the Rear View Mirror: Understanding McLuhan*. Montreal, Canada: McGill-Queen's University Press.

Thornbery, N. (2001). Corporate entrepreneurship: antidote or oxymoron. *European Management Journal*, *19*(5), 526–533. doi:10.1016/S0263-2373(01)00066-4

Tidd, J. (2001). Innovation management in context: environment, organization and performance. *International Journal of Management Reviews*, *3*, 169–183. doi:10.1111/1468-2370.00062

TKS- Towards a Knowledge Society. (2006). *A proposal for a tertiary education policy for Botswana* (Tech. Rep.). Retrieved July 27th, 2009 from http://www.tec.org.bw/tec_doc/tec_rep_10_2006.pdf

Trigo, A., Varajao, J., & Barroso, J. (2009). A practitioner's roadmap to learning the available tools for Information System Function management. *International Journal of Teaching and Case Studies*, *2*(1), 29–40. doi:10.1504/IJTCS.2009.026297

Trigo, A., Varajão, J., Soto-Acosta, P., Barroso, J., Molina-Castillo, F. J., & Gonzalvez-Gallego, N. (2010). IT Professionals: An Iberian Snapshot. *International Journal of Human Capital and Information Technology Professionals*, *1*(1), 61–75.

Trist, E., & Murray, H. (1993). *The Social Engagement of Social Sciences* (*Vol. 2*). Philadelphia: University of Pennsylvania.

Tufekci, Z. (2008). Grooming, gossip, facebook and myspace. *Information Communication and Society*, *11*(4), 544–564. doi:10.1080/13691180801999050

Turban, E., McLean, E., & Wetherbe, J. (2002). *Information Technology for Management: Transforming Business in the Digital Economy* (3rd ed.). New York: John Wiley & Sons.

Turley, R. T., & Bieman, J. M. (1995). Competencies of exceptional and nonexceptional software engineers. *Journal of Systems and Software*, *28*(1), 19–38. doi:10.1016/0164-1212(94)00078-2

Turner, T. C., & Fisher, K. E. (2006). Social Types in Technical Newsgroups: Implications for Information Flow. *International Journal of Communications Law & Policy*, 1-21.

Tushman, M. L., & Nadler, D. (1986). Organizing for innovation. *California Management Review*, *28*(3), 74–92.

Tversky, A., & Kahneman, D. (1974). Judgements under uncertainty: heuristics and biases. *Science*, *185*, 1124–1131. doi:10.1126/science.185.4157.1124

Twenge, J. (2006). *Generation Me. Why today's young Americans are more confident, assertive, entitled and more miserable than ever before*. New York: Free Press.

Ulbo de Sitter, L., Friso den Hertog, J., & Dankbaar, D. (1997). From complex organizations with simple jobs to simple organizations with complex jobs. *Human Relations*, *50*(5), 497–534. doi:10.1177/001872679705000503

Ulich, E., Schupbach, H., Schilling, A., & Kuark, J. (1990). Concepts and procedures of work psychology for the analysis, evaluation and design of advanced manufacturing systems: a case study. *International Journal of Industrial Ergonomics*, (5): 47–57. doi:10.1016/0169-8141(90)90027-Y

Urpani, D. (1996). *Knowledge acquisition from real world data*. Unpublished doctoral thesis, Swinburne University of Technology, Melbourne, Australia.

Valkenburg, J. (2008). *Recruitment via LinkedIn: A practical guide for HR professionals, recruiters and employment market communication specialists*. The Hague, The Netherlands: Reed Business.

van de Sande, B., & van de Sande, C. (2009). *Open, online, physics homework forums: The wave of the future*. Paper presented at the American Association of Physics Teachers: Annual Winter Meeting.

van de Sande, C. (2007). *Help! Tutorettes on the calculus concept of limit*. Unpublished manuscript.

van de Sande, C. (2008a). *Drawing conclusions about diagram use in an online forum*. Paper presented at the Conference on Research in Undergraduate Mathematics Education (CRUME).

van de Sande, C. (2008b). *Open, online, calculus help forums: Learning about and from a public conversation.* Unpublished doctoral dissertation, University of Pittsburgh, PA.

van de Sande, C. (2009, June). *Does it help? Rating tutor responses in open, online help forums.* In C. Fulford & G. Siemens (Eds.), *Proceedings of ED-MEDIA 2009: World Conference on Educational Multimedia, Hypermedia, and Telecommunications* (pp. 4320-4326). Honolulu, HI: AACE.

van de Sande, C., & Leinhardt, G. (2007a). Help! Active student learning and error remediation in an online calculus e-help community. *Electronic Journal of e-Learning, 5*(3), 227-238.

van de Sande, C., & Leinhardt, G. (2007b). Online tutoring in the Calculus: Beyond the limit of the limit. *Éducation et Didactique, 1*(2), 115-154.

van de Sande, C., & Leinhardt, G. (2008, June) The Good Samaritan effect: A lens for understanding patterns of participation. In *Proceedings of the Eighth International conference for the Learning Sciences* (Vol. 2, pp. 240-247). Utrecht, The Netherlands: International Society of the Learning Sciences, Inc.

Van de Ven, A. H. C. (1986). Central problems in the management of innovation. *Management Science, 32,* 590–607. doi:10.1287/mnsc.32.5.590

van Merkerk, R., & Robinson, D. (2006). Characterizing the emergence of a technological field: Expectations, agendas and networks in Lab-on-a-chip technologies. *Technology Analysis and Strategic Management, 18*(3/4), 411–428. doi:10.1080/09537320600777184

Vanac, M. (2007). JumpStart ranks 9th in early stage investments. *Cleveland.com.* Business Section. Retrieved October 20, 2008 from http://blog.cleveland.com/business/2007/06/jumpstart_ranks_9th_in_early_s.html

VanderMeij, H. (1988). Constraints on question asking in classrooms. *Journal of Educational Psychology, 80,* 401–405. doi:10.1037/0022-0663.80.3.401

Verbong, G., & Geels, F. (2007). The ongoing energy transition: Lessons from a socio-technical, multi-level analysis of the Dutch electricity system (1960–2004). *Energy Policy, 35*(2), 1025–1037. doi:10.1016/j.enpol.2006.02.010

Vestal, W. (2003). Ten traits for successful communities of practice. *Knowledge Management Review, 56,* 6.

Von Bertalanffy, L. (1950). The Theory of Open Systems in Physics and Biology. *Science,* (3): 23–29. doi:10.1126/science.111.2872.23

Von Förster, H. (1981). *Observing Systems: Selected Papers of Heinz von Förster.* Seaside, CA: Intersystems Publications.

Von Glasersfeld, E. (1996). *Radikaler Konstruktivismus.* Frankfurt, Germany: Suhrkamp.

Vossen, G., Lytras, M. D., & Koudas, N. (2007). Editorial: Revisiting the (Machine) Semantic Web: The Missing Layers for the Human Semantic Web. *IEEE Transactions on Knowledge and Data Engineering, 19*(2), 145–148. doi:10.1109/TKDE.2007.30

Wagner, R. K., Sujan, J., Sujan, M., Rashotte, C. A., & Sternberg, R. J. (1999). Tacit knowledge in sales. In Sternberg, R. J., & Horvath, J. A. (Eds.), *Tacit Knowledge in Professional Practice* (pp. 155–182). Mahwah, NJ: Laurence Erlbaum Associates.

Wailgum, T. (2009). *Famous ERP Disasters Dustups and Disappointments.* Retrieved from http://www.cio.com/article/486284/10_Famous_ERP_Disasters_Dustups_and_Disappointments

Wajcman, J. (2004). *Technofeminism.* Oxford: Polity Press

Walther, J., B., Van Der Heide, B., Kim, S.-Y., Westerman, D., & Tong, S. T. (2008). The Role of Friends' Appearance and Behavior on Evaluations of Individuals on Facebook: Are We Known by the Company We Keep? *Human Communication Research, 34*(1), 28–49. doi:10.1111/j.1468-2958.2007.00312.x

Walz, D. B., Elam, J. J., & Curtis, B. (1993). Inside a Software Design Team: Knowledge Acquisition, Sharing, and Integration. *Communications of the ACM, 36*(10), 63–77. doi:10.1145/163430.163447

Wang, F., & Hannafin, M. J. (2005). Design-based research and technology-enhanced learning environments. *Educational Technology Research and Development, 5*(4), 5–23. doi:10.1007/BF02504682

Warburton, N. (Ed.). (1999). *Philosophy: Basic Readings*. London: Routledge.

Ware, C. (2004). *Information Visualization: Perception for Design* (2nd ed.). San Francisco, CA: Morgan Kaufmann Publishers.

Warren, P. (2006). Knowledge Management and the Semantic Web: From Scenario to Technology. *IEEE Intelligent Systems, 21*(1), 53–59. doi:10.1109/MIS.2006.12

Wasko, M. M., & Faraj, S. (2005). Why Should I share? Examining Social Capital and Knowledge Contribution in Electronic Networks of Practice. *Management Information Systems Quarterly*, 35–57.

Wasson, B. (2007). Design and use of collaborative network learning scenarios: The DoCTA experience. *Journal of Educational Technology & Society, 10*(4), 3–16.

Waters, E., & Sroufe, L. (1983). Social Competence as a Developmental Construct. *Developmental Review, 3*, 79–97. doi:10.1016/0273-2297(83)90010-2

Watkins, K., & Marsick, V. (1992). Towards a theory of informal and incidental learning in organisation. *International Journal of Lifelong Education, 11*(4), 287–300. doi:10.1080/0260137920110403

Weick, K. E. (1979). *The social psychology of organizing*. Reading, MA: Addison-Wesley.

Weitzel, T., Eckhardt, A., & Laumer, S. (2009). A Framework for Recruiting IT Talent: Lessons from Siemens. *MIS Quarterly Executive, 8*(4), 175–189.

Wells, L. A., & Bogumil, W. A. (2001). Immigration and the global IT work force. *Communications of the ACM, 44*(7), 34–38. doi:10.1145/379300.379307

Wenger, E. (1998). *Communities of Practice: Learning, meaning and identity*. Cambridge, UK: Cambridge University Press.

Wenger, E. (2002). *Cultivating communities of practice – a guide to managing knowledge*. Boston: Harvard Business School Press.

Wenger, E. (2003). Communities of practice and social learning systems. In Nicolini, D., Gherardi, S., & Yanow, D. (Eds.), *Knowing in organizations – A practice–based approach* (pp. 76–99). Armonk, NY: ME Sharpe Inc.

Wenger, E. C., & Snyder, W. M. (2000). Communities of Practice: The Organizational Frontier. *Harvard Business Review, 78*(1), 139–144.

Wenger, E., McDermott, R., & Snyder, W. M. (2002). *Cultivating communities of practice: A guide to managing knowledge*. Boston: Harvard Business School Press.

West, M. A., & Farr, J. (1990). *Innovation and Creativity at Work*. Chichester, UK: Wiley.

Whitworth, B. (2009). The Social Requirements of Technical Systems. In B. Whitworth (Ed.), *Handbook of Research on Socio-Technical Design and Social Networking Systems*. Information Science reference. http://www.igi-global.com/reference/details.asp?ID=33019.

Wiig, K. M. (2000). Knowledge management: an emerging discipline rooted in a long history. In C. Despres & D. Chauvel (Eds.), *Knowledge horizons*. Boston, MA: Butterworth-Heinemann (pp,3-26).

Wikipedia. (2009a) *Population Growth*. Retrieved from http://en.wikipedia.org/wiki/File:Population_curve.svg

Williams, B., & Magee, B. (1999). Descartes. In N. Warburton (Ed.) (1999), *Philosophy: Basic Readings*. London: Routledge.

Wilmoth, D. (2008). *Innovation in private higher education: the Botswana International University of Science and Technology*. Washington, DC: IFC international investment forum on private education.

Wilson, S. M., & Peterson, L. C. (2002). The Anthropology of Online Communities. *Annual Review of Anthropology, 31*, 449–467. doi:10.1146/annurev.anthro.31.040402.085436

Wise, K., Hamman, B., & Thorson, K. (2006). Moderation, Response Rate, and Message Interactivity: Features of Online Communities and their Effects on Intent to Participate. *Journal of Computer-Mediated Communication, 12*(1). Retrieved from http://jcmc.indiana.edu/vol12/issue1/wise.html. doi:10.1111/j.1083-6101.2006.00313.x

Woolcock, N. (2009, July 3). Fewer graduates securing jobs in the recession. *The Times*. Retrieved from http://www.timesonline.co.uk/tol/life_and_style/education/student/article6624351.ece

Woolgar, S. (2002). *Virtual Society? Technology, Cyberbole, Reality*. Oxford, UK: Oxford University Press.

Wright, P. C., & McCarthy, J. (2008). Empathy and experience in HCI. In *Proceedings CHI 2008* (pp. 637-646). New York, NY: ACM.

Yakubovich, V., & Lup, D. (2006). Stages of the Recruitment Process and the Referrer's Performance Effect. *Organization Science, 17*(6), 710–723. doi:10.1287/orsc.1060.0214

Yoffie, D. (1997). *Competing in the Age of Digital Convergence*. Boston: Harvard Business School Press.

Yu, E. (1994). *Modelling strategic relationships for process reengineering* (Tech. Rep. No. DKBS-TR-94-6). Toronto, Canada: University of Toronto.

Zahra, S. A. (1995). Corporate entrepreneurship and financial performance: the case of management leveraged buyouts. *Journal of Business Venturing, 10*(3), 225–247. doi:10.1016/0883-9026(94)00024-O

Zappavigna, M. S. (2006). Tacit knowledge in communities of practice. In Coakes, E., & Clarke, S. (Eds.), *Encyclopedia of communities of practice and information and knowledge mangement* (pp. 508–513). Hershey, PA: IGI Global.

Zeman, K. (2005). *Transformation towards Knowledge-Based Economy*. Paper presented at the Conference on Medium-Term Economic Assessment. Retrieved May 10th, 2009 from http://www.aeaf.minfin.bg/.../Karel_Zeman_paper_CMTEA2005.pdf

Zhang, W., & Watts, S. A. (2008). Capitalizing on Content: Information Adoption in Two Online Communities. *Journal of the Association for Information Systems, 9*(2), 73–95.

About the Contributors

Elayne Coakes is a senior lecturer in business information management. She has a BA (Pub Admin) from Sheffield Polytechnic, a MSc (information systems), and a PhD (information systems) from Brunel University. Her current research relates to knowledge sharing in organizations. She is an internationally acknowledged expert on sociotechnical thinking and knowledge management. She was a visiting professor in Seville University (Spain), under the government grant scheme for distinguished, international scholars, a visiting research fellow in Queens University (Canada), and a keynote speaker at Manchester University (UK) at the Tribute day for Enid Mumford. As the Vice-Chair of the BCS Sociotechnical Special Group she is active in promoting information systems and has edited three books of international contributions in this field. Since then she has co-authored *Beyond Knowledge Management* and the *Encyclopedia of Communities of Practice in Information and Knowledge Management*. Additionally, she has published more than sixty book chapters, peer reviewed journal articles, and conference papers.

* * *

Sylvie Albert, Doctorate in Business Administration, Certified Economic Developer and Human Resource Manager, is Assistant-Professor of Strategy in the Faculty of Management at Laurentian University since 2004, and President of the management consulting firm Planned Approach Inc. since 1997. This is her second book dealing with online communities. Dr. Albert is a researcher and evaluator for selection of the Top 7 International Intelligent Community Awards, a member of the Council of Ontario Universities, and a former Director of two Ontario (Canada) provincial boards on community development dealing with telecommunication innovation. Dr. Albert has acted as Project Manager and advisor on many telecommunication networks across Canada and has been called upon to assist government in drawing policy and planning for regional telecommunication project development and evaluation. She was also a Municipal Director of Economic Development (1992-1997), and a Human Resource Consultant (1986-1992).

Barbara Cargill is Dean of International Programs at Trinity College, The University of Melbourne, where she leads a successful pre-university bridging program for international students. Formerly a Professorial Fellow in the Faculty of Business & Enterprise at Swinburne University of Technology, she held roles as Head of School, Dean, and acting DVC through a ten year leadership period. Barbara has had previous careers as a counsellor, organisational psychologist, and a consultant in organisational change and management development prior to twenty-four years in academia. She holds a Bachelor of Arts, Master of Education, and Doctor of Business Administration. Her current research interests are in leadership of entrepreneurship within universities, strategic change and mixed-mode modelling.

Ricardo Colomo-Palacios is an Associate Professor at the Computer Science Department of the Universidad Carlos III de Madrid. His research interests include applied research in Information Systems, Software Project Management, People in Software Projects and Social and Semantic Web. He received his PhD in Computer Science from the Universidad Politécnica of Madrid (2005). He also holds a MBA from the Instituto de Empresa (2002). He has been working as software engineer, project manager and software engineering consultant in several companies including Spanish IT leader INDRA. He is also an Editorial Board Member and Associate Editor for several international journals and conferences and Editor in Chief of International Journal of Human Capital and Information Technology Professionals.

Peter Duschinsky is a change management consultant with over 30 years of experience of bringing best practice and new ways of working into the UK business and public sectors. After a career in British Telecom, Peter moved into best practice programme management to run a national best practice experience-sharing group and was for 8 years a director of BuyIT, the UK's national e-business experience-sharing and best practice organization, where in 2000 he established the e-procurement Best Practice Group, with 40+ senior level members from industry, trade & professional institutions and government. In 2003, Peter left BuyIT to set up The Imaginist Company in order to focus on helping smaller companies survive and thrive in e-business and became an acknowledged expert in the complex public sector customer-supporter relationship with smaller companies. He led a National e-procurement Project for local government, where his work helped to form current government policy towards small and medium sized suppliers. This work led to his developing a new capability/complexity assessment methodology: INPACT (Integrated Process and Culture Transformation) to help his clients improve the level of success from their modernization and change projects. He has set out the principles of his approach in his new book, The Change Equation, available on Amazon. Peter is working with Elayne Coakes at the Westminster Business School to refine and calibrate his methodology. He is based in London.

Don M. Flournoy, Ph.D., is a Professor of Telecommunications in the School of Telecommunications, Ohio University, Athens. His research interests lie in the application of information and communication technologies (ICTs) to the solution of human problems. He is the author of seven books, including The Broadband Millennium: Communication Technologies and Markets, Chicago: International Engineering Consortium, 2004, and hundreds of scholarly articles and papers. From 1990-2007, Dr. Flournoy was Director of the Ohio University Institute for Telecommunications Studies. He is the founding Editor, Online Journal of Space Communication (www.spacejournal.org), and serves as Education VP on the board of the Society of Satellite Professionals International (www.sspi.org), the professional development association of the satellite and space industry. Prof. Flournoy holds an undergraduate degree from Southern Methodist University (1959), and graduate degrees from the University of London-UK (1961) and the University of Texas (1965). He was Assistant Dean, Case Institute of Technology, Cleveland (1965-1969); Associate Dean, State University of New York/Buffalo (1969-71); Dean of the University College at Ohio University (1971-81).

Angel García-Crespo is the Head of the SofLab Group at the Computer Science Department in the Universidad Carlos III de Madrid and the Head of the Institute for promotion of Innovation Pedro Juan de Lastanosa. He holds a PhD in Industrial Engineering from the Universidad Politécnica de Madrid (Award from the Instituto J.A. Artigas to the best thesis) and received an Executive MBA from the Instituto de Empresa. Professor García-Crespo has led and actively contributed to large European Projects of the FP V and VI, and also in many business cooperations. He is the author of more than a hundred publications in conferences, journals and books, both Spanish and international.

Bas Giesbers obtained a Master degree in educational and developmental psychology at Tilburg University, the Netherlands. He gained experience as an educational technologist and teacher in distance education and is currently working as project leader e-learning at the department of Educational Research and Development of the Maastricht University School of Business and Economics. The projects he is involved in mainly concern remedial teaching; i.e. the development and implementation of pedagogical approaches that allow prospective international bachelor and master students as well as professionals to deal with deficiencies in their knowledge and skills. In this context, Bas conducts research on the support of collaborative (e-)learning by means of ICT in general and web-videoconference in particular.

M. Gordon Hunter is a Professor Information Systems in the Faculty of Management, University of Lethbridge, Alberta, Canada. He has also been appointed Visiting Professor, London South Bank University. He has held visiting positions at universities in Australia, England, Germany, Monaco, New Zealand, Poland, Turkey, and USA. In 2009 Gordon was a Fellow at the University of Applied Sciences, Munich, Germany. During 2005 Gordon was an Erskine Fellow at the University of Canterbury, Christchurch, New Zealand. Gordon's research approach takes a qualitative perspective employing Personal Construct Theory and Narrative Inquiry to conduct in depth interviews. He applies qualitative techniques in interdisciplinary research such as Multi-Generation Small Business, Healthcare, and cross-cultural investigations. His current research interests in the information systems (IS) area include the effective management of IS with emphasis on the personnel component; the role of Chief Information Officers; and the use of IS by small business.

Isa Jahnke, Assistant Professor, got the Diploma degree of social science in 1998, PhD in 2005 and is Assistant Professor since 2008. She worked three years at a business consultancy. From 2001-2004, she was at the Dortmund University at the Department of Computer Science, then 2005-2008 at the University of Bochum (Information and Technology Management), and now at the Center for Research on Higher Education and Faculty Development (HDZ) at the TU Dortmund University, Germany. Her research focuses on teaching and learning processes using digital media. In more detail, she studies socio-technical learning communities for designing higher education. Isa Jahnke has written more than 50 papers. Currently, she is project leader for "DaVINCI – creativity-fostered learning cultures at universities" (funded by Federal Ministry of Education and Research, Germany) and member of the European project PeTEX "Platform for eLearning and telemetric experimentation".

Martin Johnson is the director of the Thalidomide Trust. He has gained degrees in Divinity, Management, and Behavioural Science. He has published a number of management and medical papers. Recent work has involved uncovering the history of the drug Thalidomide, as a by-product of developing a European support network for thalidomiders. He served for 21 years in the Royal Air Force, first as a pilot on Vulcan and Canberra aircraft, and later in administrative roles and as a NATO intelligence specialist. His career after leaving the RAF included working as a Financial and Management Adviser, mainly with small companies, and then as a Hospice CEO. After 6 years in this role, during which he oversaw the expansion of adult care and the development of a children's hospice, he was appointed to the Thalidomide Trust in 2000. Since then, the Thalidomide Trust has developed a Volunteer Visitor Service, and an innovative approach to supporting the health needs of the beneficiaries. The period has also seen the overturning of inappropriate taxation of Trust payments to beneficiaries, and a major new settlement with Diageo plc.

Linda Lichel studied at Maastricht University School of Business and Economics (International Business) and during her Bachelor educations she gained international experience at EDHEC in France. She obtained her Masters degree in Strategic Marketing in August 2008. Her final master thesis dealt is titled: "Product Harm Crises: The Impact of Post-Crisis Advertising Appeals on Consumer Attitude." After graduating she started her PhD at the department of Marketing & Supply Chain Management at Maastricht University. Her research focus lies on consumer behavior in Online Social Networks.

Marcos Ruano Mayoral is a consultant at EGEOIT, Spain. Formerly he was a Research Assistant of the Computer Science Department at Universidad Carlos III de Madrid. He holds a BSc in Computer Systems from Universidad de Valladolid and a MSc in Computer Science from Universidad Carlos III de Madrid. He has been involved in several research projects as information management engineer and software consultant.

Allan McLay. Post-graduate Program Director and Senior Lecturer: Engineering Management and Quality Management. School of Aerospace, Mechanical and Manufacturing Engineering, RMIT University, Melbourne, Australia. Experienced academic in the tertiary-education sector in Australia, UK and Thailand. Extensive consulting and advisory services to State and Federal Government agencies covering issues in: technology management; innovation & change management; advanced information and communications technologies; cleaner production; educational program development. Active involvement in the development and implementation of innovation and change in many areas of university life and the education system nationally, with a particular focus on the introduction and use of telematic media in the delivery and management of educational programs and services. Current research interests include: the development of a proposed 'taxonomy' for identifying essential characteristics in organizations interested in the application of advanced visualization systems, particularly as related to the management of engineering and technology-based environments; the development of strategic management systems and associated planning frameworks with a socio-technical orientation and their implementation in engineering and technology-based organizations; developing and testing strategies for collaborative learning in mixed populations of local and international postgraduate students.

Miles G. Nicholls is a Professor of Business Modelling and Deputy Head Research in the Graduate School of Business at RMIT University in Melbourne, Australia. Miles received his MEc and PhD from Monash University where he specialised in econometrics and operations research. He has spent the last fifteen years managing research as well as researching in his areas of interest - mixed-mode modelling and production and process modelling. Miles has published in excess of eighty refereed papers in journals and conferences and published in journals such as the Journal of the Operational Research Society, European Journal of Operational Research, Operations Research, Journal of Global Optimization, and the Journal of Heuristics.

Miriam Pinckaers obtained a Master's degree with honour in International Business at Maastricht University, the Netherlands. She wrote her master thesis on "The added value of online social networks for jobseekers". The results of this thesis where presented at the 16th EDiNEB conference for Advances in Business Education and Training in Baltimore, USA. Miriam currently works as a management trainee at TNT N.V.; a company offering mail and express services globally. In her current role she is employed as a Human Resources and Operations Advisor. Here she is involved in projects concerning change management, employee motivation, education & development and absenteeism policy.

Bart Rienties, PhD, is lecturer higher education academic practices and initiatives at University of Surrey and affiliated assistant professor of effective use of E-learning at Maastricht University. As economist and educational psychologist he conducts mini-disciplinary research on work-based and collaborative learning environments and focuses on the role of social interaction in learning.

Pedro Soto-Acosta is a Professor of Management at the University of Murcia (Spain). He holds a PhD in Management Information Systems (MISs) and a Master's degree in Technology Management from the University of Murcia. He received his BA in Accounting and Finance from the Manchester Metropolitan University (UK) and his BA in Business Administration from the University of Murcia. He attended Postgraduate Courses at Harvard University (USA). His work has been published in journals such as the European Journal of Information Systems, the International Journal of Information Management, the Information Systems Management, and the Journal of Enterprise Information Management, among others.

Rosemary Stockdale is an Associate Professor in the Faculty of ICT at Swinburne University of Technology in Melbourne, Australia. She has worked in universities in New Zealand, Austria, Western Australia and Scotland, teaching and researching in Information Systems. Her research interests include uses of information systems in the health sector and the development and uses of online communities. Dr Stockdale has published in a range of Information Systems journals including *Information and Organization* and the *European Journal of Operational Research* and is an associate editor of the *Journal of Systems and Information Technology.*

Dirk Tempelaar, PhD, is senior lecturer in the Department of Quantitative Economics of the Maastricht University School of Business and Economics. His main teaching is in the areas of statistics and research methods, and the design of problem-based learning programs in these topics. The preparation of prospective bachelor and master students by offering on line summer courses in math and statistics is a second major focus. His research interest is in understanding student learning in self-regulated learning contexts, and investigating students' learning patterns in blended learning environments.

Carla van de Sande is an Assistant Professor of Mathematics Education at Arizona State Univeristy, having completed her doctoral work in Cognitive Studies at the University of Pittsburgh in 2008. Her research focuses on help seeking, in particular how high school and university students get help for completing their mathematics course assignments. She studies help seeking both in traditional face-to-face contexts (help centers) and in emergent online environments (forums). This research, which targets formal learning in informal settings, extends our understanding of student learning beyond the walls of the classroom and should help us to better support autonomous, self-regulated learners.

Index